C000049914

# Children in need
local authority support for children and families

The authors are barristers in the public law team of Doughty Street Chambers in London (www.doughtystreet.co.uk) who specialise in cases involving children 'in need', amongst other areas. Between them, they have acted in the vast majority of the key cases under Part III of the Children Act 1989, including *R (Howard League for Penal Reform) v SSHD and DoH* (which established that the Act's protections continue to apply to children in custody); *R (J) v Caerphilly CBC* (duty to assess and the role of personal advisers); *R (S) v Sutton LBC* (the leading case on local authority duties to homeless children leaving custody); *R (G) v Nottingham CC and Nottingham University Hospitals NHS Trust* (removal of newborn from a young mother; duties of the local authority to mother and child); *R (O) v Barking and Dagenham LBC* (primacy of leaving care provisions over asylum support provisions); *R (A) v Croydon LBC* (age assessments); and *R (G) v Southwark LBC* (local authority duties to homeless teenagers).

The purpose of the Legal Action Group is to promote equal access to justice for all members of society who are socially, economically or otherwise disadvantaged. To this end, it seeks to improve law and practice, the administration of justice and legal services.

# Children in need

local authority support for children and families

Ian Wise QC, Steve Broach, Caoilfhionn
Gallagher, Alison Pickup, Ben Silverstone
and Azeem Suterwalla

 Legal Action Group
2011

This edition published in Great Britain 2011
by LAG Education and Service Trust Limited
242 Pentonville Road, London N1 9UN
www.lag.org.uk

While every effort has been made to ensure that the details in this text are
correct, readers must be aware that the law changes and that the accuracy
of the material cannot be guaranteed and the author and the publisher
accept no responsibility for any losses or damage sustained.

British Library Cataloguing in Publication Data
a CIP catalogue record for this book is available from the British Library.

Crown copyright material is produced with the permission of the
Controller of HMSO and the Queen's Printer for Scotland.

 This book has been produced using Forest Stewardship
Council (FSC) certified paper. The wood used to produce
FSC certified products with a 'Mixed Sources' label comes
from FSC certified well-managed forests, controlled sources
and/or recycled material.

ISBN  978 1 903307 85 4

Typeset by Regent Typesetting, London
Printed in Great Britain by Hobbs the Printers, Totton, Hampshire

# Foreword

by Lord Justice Munby

Ian Wise and his colleagues at Doughty Street have written an invaluable handbook and guide to an intricate area of law that is of vital importance to some of the most vulnerable and disadvantaged people in our society. They, and the Legal Action Group, are to be thanked and congratulated.

*Children in Need* describes itself as comprehensive and accessible. It is both. The authors display an enviable mastery of the mass of statutes, statutory instruments, guidance and cases through which they guide us so expertly. Equally important, they write with a clarity which makes a technical subject accessible not merely to lawyers but also to all the others who will, I hope, make this book their first point of reference.

*Children in Need* is not just a theoretical text. It is a handbook for the real world. The authors have much practical experience of handling cases of the kind they discuss. In particular, they bring to bear their practical experience of litigation in the Administrative Court, providing illuminating suggestions and advice for those less familiar with the forensic realities.

Claimants and local authorities alike will, I am sure, find much of value and assistance in *Children in Need*, to the great benefit of children in need and their families.

James Munby
6 April 2011

# Authors

**Ian Wise QC** is the head of the public law team at Doughty Street Chambers in London. He has been involved in a number of the most high profile public law cases in recent years including the leading cases in relation to age assessment (*R (A) v Croydon LBC*) and duties to homeless teenagers (*R (G) v Southwark LBC*), both won in the House of Lords/Supreme Court. Ian's practice covers a wide range of public law areas and he specialises in healthcare, local government (including community care and education) and children's law. Ian was lead author for chapter 1, 'Introduction' and general editor.

**Steve Broach** is a public lawyer focusing on the rights of children and disabled or otherwise vulnerable adults in cases concerning health, education, social care and related issues. Steve has a particular commitment to the rights of disabled children and is co-author of *Disabled children: a legal handbook* (LAG, 2010). Before coming to the Bar, Steve worked in a number of senior voluntary sector roles, including campaign manager for Every Disabled Child Matters. Steve is currently chair of AbleChildAfrica, a charity working for disabled children across Africa. Steve was lead author for chapter 4, 'Services to children "in need"' and co-ordinated the production of the book.

**Caoilfhionn Gallagher** is a public law specialist, and has particular expertise in prison law and community care for children and vulnerable adults. She regularly acts for homeless and vulnerable children in prison and the community, and works closely with Kids Company for children whose lives are at risk through gang violence. She is a co-author of *Blackstone's Guide to the Human Rights Act* (OUP, 5th edn, 2009) and is rated as a leading junior by both Chambers and Partners and the Legal 500. Caoilfhionn was lead author for chapter 5, 'Duties and powers to accommodate children' and chapter 7, 'Leaving care'.

**Alison Pickup** is a public law practitioner with a wide-ranging claimant practice, including immigration and asylum, prison law, social welfare, and EU law. She also acts in civil claims for damages against public authorities, particularly unlawful detention and discrimination claims. In 2010, she was shortlisted for the LAPG Young Legal Aid Barrister of the Year award. She is recommended in the Legal 500 for immigration. Alison was lead author for chapter 6, 'Services for migrant children and their families'.

**Ben Silverstone** specialises in the fields of public and human rights law whose work focuses on the rights of individuals in the community care, social welfare and education contexts. Ben wrote the chapter on welfare benefits in *Disabled children: a legal handbook* (LAG, 2010). Prior to joining Doughty Street Chambers, Ben worked at Bail for Immigration Detainees, the United Nations High Commissioner for Refugees and Amnesty International. He was also a visiting fellow in constitutional and administrative law at City University, London. Ben was lead author for chapter 2, 'Legal fundamentals'.

**Azeem Suterwalla** specialises in public law and human rights law across a range of subject areas, notably community care, children, education, immigration, asylum support and prison law. Azeem has worked on litigation at all levels up to the House of Lords/Supreme Court and European Court of Human Rights. He is rated as a leading junior in Chambers and Partners. Before coming to the bar Azeem worked for two years for the United Nations in the Middle East, as a policy analyst in Gaza City. Azeem was also the judicial assistant to the former Master of the Rolls, Lord Justice Clarke, in the Court of Appeal between October and December 2005. Azeem was lead author for chapter 3, 'Age disputes: child or not?'.

# Acknowledgments

The authors are grateful to all our colleagues in chambers and the many solicitors with whom we work to bring cases promoting and protecting the rights of children 'in need'.

We are also grateful to our publisher, Legal Action Group (LAG), and in particular our editor, Esther Pilger, with whom it is always a great pleasure to work. We hope this book will make a contribution to the extensive list of excellent practitioner texts that LAG publishes which provide such assistance to those acting for and advising vulnerable people.

The authors thank Luke Clements and Janet Read for their kind permission to reproduce elements of *Disabled children: a legal handbook* (Broach, Clements and Read, LAG, 2010) in original or amended form.

We also thank a number of students at BPP Law School who provided valuable support with case research; Sri Carmichael, Sophie Conway, Serena Fasso, Janet Lucitt, Richard McLean, Karl Masi and Manisha Patel. Karl Masi and Manisha Patel also researched the background facts in relation to numbers and circumstances of children 'in need' that are cited in the introduction.

Despite the assistance we have had, all mistakes remain our own and we would be grateful for any comments or corrections via Steve Broach at s.broach@doughtystreet.co.uk.

This book is dedicated to everyone working on the frontline to protect the rights and interests of children 'in need' and their families.

The law is stated as at 1 March 2011 although where it has been possible to include further developments we have endeavoured to do so.

Ian Wise QC
Steve Broach
Caoilfhionn Gallagher
Alison Pickup
Ben Silverstone
Azeem Suterwalla

Doughty Street Chambers
April 2011   ix

# Contents

**APPENDICES**

# Legal entitlements

This book sets out the detailed legal scheme designed to protect the rights and interests of children 'in need' and their families. As set out in chapter 2, the law is found in many sources – international conventions, Acts of Parliament, regulations, statutory guidance and so on. Many of these sources of law overlap and there remains significant confusion about what public bodies *must* do to support children 'in need' (duties) and what they *may* do (powers), an issue discussed in detail in chapter 2: see paras 2.30–2.35.

Distinguishing between powers and duties is essential because it is only when a public body has a duty to act that it can be meaningfully said that a child has a 'right' to some benefit or service. To help focus minds, we provide below a list of some of the key 'entitlements' to which children, young people and/or their families may benefit.

This summary is only a very general guide, and readers should consult the relevant chapter for necessary background information in relation to each entitlement. It should also be borne in mind that even if a public body only has a power, not a duty, to confer a particular benefit on a child or their family so that no entitlement to the benefit arises, that power still has to be exercised rationally, reasonably and fairly: see para 2.34.

## Children 'in need' are entitled to ...

- *Participate* in any decision taken about their lives: see paras 2.25 and 4.28.
- Have decisions taken about them with their *best interests* considered first as a primary consideration: see para 2.27.
- Respect for their rights to *family and private life*, which may entail the provision of services to achieve the realisation of these rights: see paras 2.14–2.19.
- An independent *determination of their age* by the court if their claimed age is disputed by the state: see chapter 3.

- An *initial assessment* to determine what additional needs for services and support they may have: see para 4.27.
- A *core assessment*, if they may need support from a number of different agencies: see para 4.27.
- *Services to meet their assessed needs*, where the conditions in one of the specific statutory duties are met or where intervention is required to secure their well-being: see paras 4.39 and 4.46–4.53.
- a *care plan* following an assessment, which should be a 'realistic plan of action (including services to be provided)': see para 4.86.
- *Suitable accommodation*, if their parent or parents are prevented (for whatever reason) from providing them with suitable accommodation or care: see paras 5.9–5.36.
- *Support as a 'looked after' child if* they are accommodated for more than 24 hours: see paras 5.76–5.113.
- A *personal adviser and pathway plan after* the age of 16 if they are 'leaving care': see chapter 7.
- *Legal aid* to challenge any failure to realise these entitlements: see para 2.69.

## Families are entitled to ...

- Assessments of their children to include consideration of *family circumstances and parenting capacity*, with services provided as necessary: see para 4.29.
- *Accommodation*, if the family's immigration status means that they are ineligible for Housing Act accommodation and it is necessary to provide accommodation to prevent a breach of one or more family member's convention rights: see chapter 6.
- Assessments and services under the *Carers Acts*. This is outside the scope of the book but is covered in chapter 8 of *Disabled children: a legal handbook* (LAG, 2010).

# Table of cases

References in the right-hand column are to paragraph numbers.

# Table of statutes

References in the right-hand column are to paragraph numbers.

# Table of statutory instruments

References in the right-hand column are to paragraph numbers.

# Table of international treaties, conventions and directives

References in the right-hand column are to paragraph numbers.

# Table of guidance

References in the right-hand column are to paragraph numbers.

**WELSH GUIDANCE**

**LOCAL AUTHORITY CIRCULARS**

# Abbreviations

| | |
|---|---|
| ACA 2002 | Adoption and Children Act 2002 |
| ADD | Attention deficit disorder |
| ADHD | Attention deficit hyperactivity disorder |
| ADSS | Association of Directors of Social Services |
| ARE | Appeal rights exhausted |
| BCIA 2009 | Borders, Citizenship and Immigration Act 2009 |
| CA 1989 | Children Act 1989 |
| CA 2004 | Children Act 2004 |
| CAF | Common Assessment Framework |
| CCA 1980 | Child Care Act 1980 |
| CL Regs 2010 | Care Leavers (England) Regulations 2010 |
| CLCA 2000 | Children (Leaving Care) Act 2000 |
| CLCE Regs 2001 | Children (Leaving Care) (England) Regulations 2001 |
| CPPCR Regs 2010 | Care Planning, Placement and Case Review (England) Regulations 2010 |
| CPR | Civil Procedure Rules |
| CRAE | Children's Rights Alliance for England |
| CRD | Case Resolution Directorate |
| CSA Regs 1991 | Children (Secure Accommodation) Regulations 1991 |
| CSDPA 1970 | Chronically Sick and Disabled Persons Act 1970 |
| CYPA 2008 | Children and Young Persons Act 2008 |
| CYPP | Children and Young People's Plan |
| DCSF | Department for Children, Schools and Families |
| DfE | Department for Education |
| DfES | Department for Education and Skills |
| DHSS | Department of Health and Social Security |
| DoH | Department of Health |
| DTO | Detention and training order |
| ECA 1972 | European Communities Act 1972 |
| ECHR | European Convention on Human Rights |
| ECtHR | European Court of Human Rights |
| EEA | European Economic Area |
| EU | European Union |
| HA 1996 | Housing Act 1996 |
| HDC | Home detention curfew |
| HPU | Homeless Persons Unit |
| HRA 1998 | Human Rights Act 1998 |
| IA 1971 | Immigration Act 1971 |
| IA 1988 | Immigration Act 1988 |

| | |
|---|---|
| IAA 1999 | Immigration and Asylum Act 1999 |
| IPP | Indefinite detention for public protection |
| IRO | Independent reviewing officer |
| LASSA 1970 | Local Authority Social Services Act 1970 |
| LC Guidance | Leaving Care Guidance |
| LGO | Local government ombudsman |
| LSC | Legal Services Commission |
| LSCB | Local Safeguarding Children Board |
| NAA 1948 | National Assistance Act 1948 |
| NASS | National Asylum Support Service (now abolished) |
| NCAS | National Care Advisory Service |
| NIAA 2002 | Nationality, Immigration and Asylum Act 2002 |
| NRPF | No recourse to public funds |
| OCD | Obsessive-compulsive disorder |
| OS | Official Solicitor |
| PSIC | Person subject to immigration control |
| PSO | Public services ombudsman |
| RAS | Resource Allocation System |
| RPE Regs 2006 | Children Act 1989 Representation Procedure (England) Regulations 2006 |
| RPW Regs 2005 | Children Act 1989 Representation Procedure (Wales) Regulations 2005 |
| SSHD | Secretary of State for the Home Department |
| STC | Secure Training Centre |
| TCEA 2007 | Tribunal, Courts and Enforcement Act 2007 |
| TFEU | Treaty on the Functioning of the European Union |
| UASC | Unaccompanied asylum-seeking child |
| UKBA | UK Border Agency |
| UNCRC | United Nations Convention on the Rights of the Child |
| WWS Regs 2002 | Withholding and Withdrawal of Support (Travel Assistance and Temporary Accommodation) Regulations 2002 |
| YJB | Youth Justice Board |
| YOI | Young Offender Institution |
| YOT | Youth Offending Team |

# CHAPTER 1

# Introduction

> ### Key points
> - The purpose of this book is to explain the statutory obligations of local authorities towards vulnerable children and their families.
> - The law in this area has developed from a duty to support children in order to keep them out of care or the criminal justice system, to a duty to safeguard and promote welfare of children and provide services to those 'in need'.
> - Children are in need of support from local authorities not due to any fault on their part, but due to their circumstances.
> - There are 375,900 children accepted to be 'in need' by local authorities in England, although the number of children actually or potentially in need of support is likely to be in the region of one million.
> - Proper assessment is the key to understanding the needs of vulnerable children, so attempts to undermine the assessment duty should be resisted.
> - There is a specific duty in certain circumstances to meet the assessed needs of children 'in need'.
> - Resources are irrelevant where children's services have a duty to meet the needs of a child.
> - Areas of particular concern – such as disabled children, unaccompanied asylum-seeking children, homeless teenagers and children leaving custody – are dealt with in greater detail in subsequent chapters.
> - The fundamental legal obligations are straightforward; the needs of vulnerable children should be met to ensure proper respect for the dignity of the child.

## Purpose of the book

1.1   Local authority support for children[1] and families is generally regarded as a 'good thing', unsurprisingly attracting overwhelming public and political support. In the main, local authorities have been left to get on with providing support as best they can, and when problems have been identified relatively minor changes to the basic scheme found in Part III of the Children Act (CA) 1989 have been made. The requirements under CA 1989 Part III for local authorities

---

1   Under CA 1989, a 'child' is any person under the age of 18: section 105(1).

to provide support to children and families have attracted far less attention than the (often coercive) powers and duties found in other parts of the CA 1989. Apart from a few exceptions, it is only relatively recently that the courts have had to consider the duties and powers of local authorities in relation to vulnerable children. Over the last few years there have, however, been numerous cases before the higher courts which have examined these obligations. As a result, the fundamental legal duties of local authorities towards children 'in need'[2] are becoming clear.

1.2    In this book we attempt to piece together the jigsaw of statutory provisions and case-law so that it can be better understood by those who work with vulnerable children. It is our hope that it will help to ensure that the needs of vulnerable children are more effectively met by those who owe these children and their families legal obligations. Our intention is that this book will be accessible to non-lawyers, such as families of children 'in need' and social workers, as well as legal advisers.

## Development of the statutory scheme

1.3    Before considering the operation of the current scheme requiring support for children 'in need' it is important to consider how it took its shape. Before the passing of CA 1989, child care law was 'widely criticised as confusing, unnecessarily complex and in places unjust'.[3] Section 1 of the Child Care Act (CCA) 1980 placed a duty on every local authority 'to make available such advice, guidance and assistance as may promote the welfare of children by diminishing the need to receive children into or keep them in care ... or to bring children before a juvenile court'. CCA 1980 was repealed by CA 1989. CA 1989 s17 provided a very different focus to its predecessor. It requires local authorities to '(a) safeguard and promote the welfare of children within their area who are in need; and (b) so far as is consistent with that duty, to promote the upbringing of such children by their families, by providing a range and level of services appropriate to those children's needs'.[4] However, it also provided a clear recognition that parents and others with 'parental responsibility'[5] have the primary

2  Within the meaning of CA 1989 s17(10); see chapter 4 at paras 4.10–4.13.
3  *R (G) v Barnet LBC* [2003] UKHL 57, [2004] 2 AC 208 per Lord Nicholls at [17].
4  CA 1989 s17(1).
5  CA 1989 s3(1).

duty to secure children's well-being and that the principal role of a local authority is to support parents and families.

1.4       The purpose of CCA 1980 s1 was to prevent children being taken into care or coming before the juvenile court. By contrast, the purpose of CA 1989 s17 was to safeguard and promote the welfare of vulnerable children, if possible within the family. At the same time, the 1989 Act introduced the concept of a child 'in need' which under section 17(10) and (11) was defined in very wide terms, including every child with any significant level of disability. The CA 1989 therefore represented a sea change in the way in which local authorities were to engage with children. Its intention was to 'ensure that in all cases the children concerned should receive the standard of care and protection and professional review appropriate to their needs'.[6]

1.5       The genesis of CA 1989 Part III was the concern expressed by the Short Committee in 1985 about the inadequacy of the role of local authorities in carrying out preventative work with children.[7] This led to a review of child care law by the Department of Health and Social Security (DHSS) which reported in 1985. Among the findings of this review was that child care law was too complex and was at times contradictory. Shortly after the DHSS review was published, the Law Commission began an investigation into 'Child law, guardianship and custody', which concentrated on the private law aspects of child law.[8] Also during this period there were three high-profile inquiries into the tragic deaths of children which revealed shortcomings in social services support: Jasmine Beckford (1985), Kimberley Carlile[9] (1986) and Tyra Henry (1988). Further criticism of the UK child care system was made at this time by the European Court of Human Rights in relation to the failure to ensure that the interests of parents were represented in childcare proceedings.[10] Throughout this period international concern was growing about the rights of children, and in November 1989 the General Assembly adopted the United Nations Convention on the Rights of the Child (UNCRC) which was ratified by the UK in December 1991, just two months after CA 1989 came into force. All these factors came together to influence the development of CA 1989, which was described by Lord Mackay in introducing the bill in the House of Lords as 'the most comprehensive

---

6   *R (G) v Barnet LBC* [2003] UKHL 57, [2004] 2 AC 208 per Lord Nicholls at [18].

7   The Short Committee was named after Renee Short MP who chaired the House of Commons Health Committee.

8   Law Comm No 172.

9   The facts of which were chillingly similar to those of the recent Baby P case (2007).

10   *W v UK* (1987) 10 EHRR 29.

and far reaching reform which has come before Parliament in living memory'.[11]

1.6     Attitudes to vulnerable children had changed during the 1980s, hence the contrast between the language of CCA 1980 s1 and CA 1989 s17. Although there have been some important changes since 1989, the basic structure of CA 1989 has remained in place. The most notable changes were amendments by the Children (Leaving Care) (England) Act 2000 (discussed in detail in chapter 7) which, in recognition of the disadvantages faced by children who had been 'looked after'[12] by local authorities, placed additional duties on children's services until a young person becomes at least 21. A further important development occurred subsequent to the report into the death of Victoria Climbié in 2003[13] with Children Act (CA) 2004, which introduced children's services departments, amalgamating the child care sections of social services and education departments of local authorities to ensure that services for children were integrated. CA 2004 ss10 and 11 also placed on a statutory footing the five 'well-being' criteria,[14] which are to inform all aspects of decision-making concerning children, and required partner organisations to co-operate with children's services authorities to safeguard and promote the well-being of all children (not just children within the statutory definition of 'in need').

1.7     The law also now recognises the evolving societal concept of childhood which places increasing emphasis on the wishes and feelings of the individual child and stresses the developmental needs of children.[15] The UNCRC provides a right for children to be able to express their feelings and have them taken into account,[16] a right given statutory force in the context of the provision of accommodation for children under CA 1989 s20(6) and generally under CA 1989 s17(4A).[17] This right to have the wishes and feelings of the child taken into account is consistent with the right to respect for the

---

11  Hansard, HL vol 502 col 488.

12  See chapter 5 at paras 5.76–5.98 for the definition of 'looked after' status.

13  CM 5730, January 2003.

14  Being physical and mental health and emotional well-being, protection from harm and neglect, education, training and recreation, the contribution made by them to society and social and economic well-being: CA 2004 s10(2).

15  Although a recent report by the Children's Society found that 'excessive individualism is causing a range of problems for children'; *The good childhood* The Children's Society, 2009.

16  UNCRC article 12 (right to participation).

17  Inserted by CA 2004 s53(1).

child's private life found in article 8 of the European Convention on Human Rights (ECHR).[18] Recent statutory guidance states that 'children should feel that they are active participants and engaged in the process when adults are trying to solve problems and make decisions about them'.[19]

1.8    It is contended that the basic structure and principles underpinning the obligations of local authorities towards vulnerable children are sound. Deficiencies in CA 1989, not least the lack of ongoing obligations to 'looked after' children leaving care, have largely been rectified by subsequent legislation. Problems in the delivery of services for children 'in need' have to a very significant extent arisen because of a lack of understanding of these obligations, underpinned by perceived scarcity of resources. Lack of compliance with the obligations towards children and families has been compounded by a prevailing attitude among the legal community (from the judiciary downwards) that this law is 'soft law'. It is not; the duties owed by local authorities are clear and enforceable and it is no exaggeration to suggest that downgrading these duties to mere discretionary powers undermines the rule of law.

## Not the child's fault!

1.9    Children are in need of support from local authorities not because of any fault on their part, but due to their circumstances; for example, they may not have the parental support necessary to ensure that they can develop and thrive, or they may be disabled. The statutory definition of a child 'in need' found in CA 1989 s17(10) is deliberately wide and the threshold for children to access support to meet their needs is necessarily low. The role of social services – whose functions with regard to children are now performed by dedicated children's services departments of local authorities – in relation to supporting children in need was a crucial part of CA 1989. CA 1989 introduced the concept of parental responsibility[20] and recognised

---

18   The procedural rights owed under article 8 ECHR apply to children as well as adults and even apply to babies whose interests are protected by article 8, see *CF v Secretary of State for the Home Department* [2004] EWHC 111 (Fam), [2004] 2 FLR 517 at [158]. See also *ZH (Tanzania) v Secretary of State for the Home Department* [2011] UKSC 4, [2011] 2 WLR 128.

19   HM Government, *The Children Act 1989 guidance and regulations, volume 2: care planning, placement and case review*, March 2010 at para 1.10.

20   CA 1989 ss2–4.

that the needs of some children are such that parents need support in order to secure a reasonable standard of health and development for the child, and with respect to disabled children to have the opportunity of leading as 'normal' a life as possible.[21] Whilst recognising that children's needs are generally best met within the family, CA 1989 also of course recognised that some parents are either unwilling or unable to look after their children. For these children a duty is placed on local authorities to look after them, whether through a formal care order or by providing accommodation and services for them. The circumstances in which a child can come to be 'in need' are too numerous to list. The essential point is that it does not matter how the child comes to be in need of support, what matters is that if a child is, for whatever reason, in need of support, such support as is needed should be provided.

1.10   This basic scheme is not controversial. It attracts widespread support not just because it is a necessary feature of the welfare state but because it goes to the core values of civilised society. There may be debate about the best and most effective ways of meeting the needs of vulnerable children, but in the absence of any effective alternative there is no disputing the central role of local authorities in ensuring that the needs of such children are recognised and met.

1.11   The real challenge is not one of principle, but of understanding and implementation. The authors would contend that given the importance of the CA 1989 Part III scheme it is astonishing that it is so badly understood. This is all the more so given the potential consequences of local authorities not meeting their duties towards children 'in need'. To take perhaps the highest-profile recent example, the London Boroughs of Ealing, Brent and Haringey all failed to identify and meet the needs of Victoria Climbié before she died in February 2000. It is important to recall that it was not lack of resources that prevented them from taking effective action; the inquiry into her death found that all three of these local authorities had underspent the sums allocated to them for providing services for children.[22]

1.12   Victoria Climbié's death was an extreme, although sadly not unique, example of the consequences of local authorities failing to identify and meet the needs of vulnerable children in their area. The authors have dealt with scores of less extreme cases where local

---

21   CA 1989 Sch 2 para 6.
22   House of Commons Health Committee: The Victoria Climbié Inquiry Report: HC 570, June 2003, para 42, p13.

authorities have failed to meet their duties towards children in need in their area, or have actively sought to avoid these duties. *R (G) v Southwark LBC*[23] (discussed in detail in chapter 5) was one of many such cases. In all these cases, whether the child 'in need' is a disabled child or a homeless teenager, the consequences of the relevant local authority not taking appropriate action can be profound and enduring. This is why the CA 1989 Part III scheme must be both promoted (in the sense of raising awareness of the duties and obligations it imposes) and protected (in the sense of challenging any attempts to downgrade these duties to powers).

## How many children 'in need' are there?

1.13   Although it is clear that there are a considerable number of children 'in need' in England, the precise number is difficult to determine. Official figures record that 375,900 such children are recognised by local authorities.[24] However, given that there are some 770,000 disabled children under the age of 16 in the UK,[25] the vast majority of whom are in England, and disabled children are but one category of children 'in need', the official figure is likely to considerably underestimate the actual number of children 'in need'.

1.14   The needs of 39 per cent of children assessed as being 'in need' arise from abuse or neglect, with a further 16 per cent of such children having needs arising from 'family dysfunction'.[26] The relatively recent figures show that only 6 per cent of disabled children receive regular support.[27] This suggests that local authority involvement is largely in the form of crisis management rather than as a result of a systematic assessment and understanding of the needs of children in their area as required by CA 1989 Sch 2 para 1.[28]

---

23  [2009] UKHL 26, [2009] 1 WLR 1367.
24  Statistics taken from the Department for Education (DfE), Statistical Release, 30 November 2010. OSR28/2010 *Children in need in England, including their characteristics and further information on children who were the subject of a child protection plan (children in need census – final) year ending 31 March 2010*, www.education.gov.uk/rsgateway/DB/STR/d000970.
25  *Every disabled child matters*, www.ncb.org.uk/cdc.
26  See fn 24 above.
27  Commission for Social Care Inspection (2005), Social Services Performance Assessment Framework Indicators, CSCI/ONS.
28  See chapter 4 at paras 4.24–4.35 regarding the duty to assess children who are or who may be 'in need'.

1.15    It is self-evident that if there is a general lack of understanding of the powers and duties of local authorities towards children 'in need' there will be an under-recording of the numbers of such children. We would suggest that it is reasonable to assume from the above that there may be up to one million children who are actually or potentially 'in need' of local authority support in England – around 9 to 10 per cent of the 11 million children in England.

1.16    There are in the region of 64,000 children in England who are 'looked after' by local authorities.[29] These children are either the subject of a care order or are accommodated under CA 1989 s20. As explained in chapter 5, it is probable that there are considerably more children who should be supported under CA 1989 s20 than are currently receiving such support. This is particularly so for 16- and 17-year-olds who meet the criteria for support under CA 1989 s20(1) and for whom there is a mandatory duty placed on children's services to provide accommodation and support under that section. Reluctance to support homeless 16- and 17-year-olds is at least in part based on the historical model of children's homes where support ceased at 16, but is also to a considerable degree influenced by a desire on the part of children's services managers to avoid the ongoing obligations they would have to children accommodated under CA 1989 s20 under the leaving care provisions, which are discussed at chapter 7.[30]

1.17    In summary, although we know that there were 375,900 children identified by children's services departments in England as being in need of their services in 2010, the likelihood is that there are at least 100,000 more children in need who have not been identified, and perhaps as many as 500,000 more children, most of whom will be disabled, whose needs have not been assessed but who potentially meet the statutory definition of a child 'in need' and hence are eligible for support from their local authority.

---

29  DfE, *Children looked after by local authorities in England (including adoption and care leavers) – year ending 31 March 2010*, www.education.gov.uk/rsgateway/DB/SFR/s000960.

30  Statistics revealed by a Freedom of Information request from 'Inside Housing' show that in 2007–2010, 82 per cent of 16- and 17-year-olds seeking accommodation from local authorities did not have their needs assessed, and despite the judgment of the Supreme Court in *R (G) v Southwark LBC* (see chapter 5) in 2009 the overwhelming majority of such children are dealt with by housing departments rather than children's services: Inside Housing, 'Who cares?', 7 January 2011, www.insidehousing.co.uk/analysis/in-depth/who-cares?/6513139.article.

## Support

1.18    Apart from the relatively small number of children 'in need' who are the subject of care proceedings, these children do not have any independent support unless and until they are assessed and deemed eligible for local authority services. Given that a child in need of support could not be expected to know what children's services should be doing for him or her,[31] it is all the more important that children's services departments have systems in place to identify children who are or may be 'in need'. Too often children who need such support are only identified as a result of acute events such as abuse or exclusion from school. Support for children 'in need' must not be merely a fire-fighting service, no matter how important it is to make sure that any blazes which do erupt in a child's life are quickly dampened down. Rather, such support should safeguard and promote the welfare of the child, and where possible *prevent* traumatic events rather than merely react to them.

1.19    In the absence of a proactive approach from children's services, it is still more vital that those involved with children are aware of the obligations that children's services have towards children in need of support. Having identified a potential need for support, it is then crucial that there is a rigorous assessment of the child. Proper assessment is the key to understanding the needs of every child who is actually or potentially 'in need'.

1.20    As explained in chapter 4, although there is no explicit duty to assess children who are or may be in need of services, the House of Lords said in *R (G) v Barnet LBC and others* that a duty to assess was implicit in the CA 1989.[32] The legal duty to assess is, however, made unequivocal by the *Framework for the assessment of children in need and their families*[33] ('the Assessment Framework'), guidance issued under statute which in effect established a duty to assess the needs of all children who may be in need of services.

1.21    Despite proper assessment being central to any understanding of the needs of a particular child, the assessment duty has been criticised as involving unnecessary bureaucracy which distracts social workers

---

31    *R (M) v Hammersmith & Fulham LBC* [2006] EWCA Civ 917, (2006) 9 CCLR 418 at [73].

32    *R (G) v Barnet LBC* [2003] UKHL 57, [2004] 2 AC 208, (2003) 6 CCLR 500.

33    Department of Health, Department for Education and Employment and Home Office, *Framework for the assessment of children in need and their families* (policy guidance), TSO, 2000.

from their core functions of supporting children.[34] It is, however, important to recognise that the completion of an assessment is not an end in itself, a trend encouraged by the requirement placed by central government on children's services to collate statistics of completed assessments. Proper assessment is instead essential to getting to grips with the needs of vulnerable children. Given the complexity of the lives of many children in need of support, assessment frequently needs to be multi-disciplinary and engage a range a professionals – in effect a 'core assessment' (see chapter 4 at para 4.27). This is a time-consuming and laborious task, the importance of which should be emphasised and welcomed rather than undermined.

1.22    It is nevertheless recognised that repetitious assessments of children can be unhelpful. We are firmly of the view that a 'core assessment' completed as required by the Assessment Framework ought to provide all the necessary information required to understand the needs of a particular child and inform decisions about the support necessary to meet those needs.

1.23    The Assessment Framework requires that at the conclusion of the assessment a 'realistic plan of action' be drawn up which sets out how the child's needs are to be met. This should make clear who is going to do what, where and when for the child. Without this, the assessment process is pointless.

1.24    What next? Curiously, in contradistinction to disabled adults[35] there is no overt statutory duty on children's services authorities to meet the assessed needs of children in need of services, although such a duty is effectively established by the Assessment Framework: see para 4.39. It may of course be unreasonable or irrational to fail to meet such assessed needs and it may breach the positive obligations of the authority under article 8 ECHR not to do so. It may also be a breach of Chronically Sick and Disabled Persons Act 1970 s2 to refuse to provide services found to be necessary to meet the needs of a disabled child.[36] The circumstances where a duty may arise to meet the assessed needs of a child 'in need' are discussed in detail in chapter 4. In our experience it is, however, rare for a children's services authority simply to refuse to meet the assessed needs of a child

---

34  See, for example, *The Munro review of child protection: part one, a systems analysis* Professor Eileen Munro, 2010, DFE–00548–2010 at para 2.22, p33.

35  Under the Chronically Sick and Disabled Persons Act 1970, National Assistance Act 1948 s29 and the statutory guidance published by the Department of Health in 2010; *Prioritising need in the context of putting people first*, which replaced the well-known Fair Access to Care Services guidance.

36  See *R v Kirklees MBC ex p Daykin* (1997–98) 1 CCLR 512, 525.

'in need' who is found to have a substantial need for support.[37] An authority may of course choose to meet the need in the cheapest possible way, but providing the need is met and human rights standards are complied with, this will not be objectionable. A important exception to this is the duty to place 'looked after' children in the most appropriate placement available: see para 5.85.

## Resources

1.25    Any discussion of local authority support inevitably involves consideration of resources. In the context of support for children 'in need', there are two broad points. First, as Lord Laming observed after his inquiry in the death of Victoria Climbié, existing resources were not being utilised.[38] Supporting children 'in need' properly may therefore require utilising existing resources more effectively, particularly in a time of financial austerity. Management of children's services departments is also a pressing concern. Too often case files reveal management decisions (at times overriding decisions of social workers) which are inconsistent with the statutory obligations and are resource- rather than needs-led.

1.26    This leads to the second point, which is that parliament has enacted a statutory scheme which places a series of duties on children's services authorities which must be met regardless of resource considerations. These duties include the duty to:

1) take reasonable steps to identify the extent of children 'in need' in their area;[39]
2) assess a child if he or she is or may be in need of services;[40]
3) provide services to meet assessed needs if the assessment demonstrates that it is necessary to do so (see chapter 4);
4) produce a care plan setting out how assessed needs are to be met;
5) provide accommodation if the authority considers that the criteria set out in CA 1989 s20(1) are met (see chapter 5);
6) appoint a personal adviser for a child over 16 who has been looked after by children's services for more than 13 weeks;[41] and

---

37   Whether this will remain the case in the austere fiscal climate which exists at the time of writing remains to be seen.
38   See fn 22.
39   CA 1989 Sch 2 para 1.
40   Assessment Framework, see chapter 4.
41   CA 1989 Sch 2 para 19C.

7) prepare a pathway plan, setting out the support to be provided for a child leaving care up to the age of 21.[42]

1.27 As Lord Brown-Wilkinson said in response to an argument advanced by a local authority that it was not required to provide suitable education to a disabled child who could not attend school, 'to permit a local authority to avoid performing a statutory duty on the grounds that it prefers to spend the money in other ways is to downgrade a statutory duty to a discretionary power ... If Parliament wishes to reduce public expenditure on meeting the needs of sick children then it is up to Parliament so to provide'.[43] Given that there is no apparent public or political will to remove the duties owed to children 'in need', children's services authorities will continue to be bound to continue to discharge their duties towards these children and their families regardless of resource considerations.

1.28 Whereas there can be no doubt that children's services authorities have to meet many of the duties towards children 'in need' whatever their financial position, the position with respect to services provided to children under CA 1989 s17 is less clear. Under this section, children's services have a general but not a specific duty (see chapter 2) to provide services to meet the needs of children. In an attempt to cut back on expenditure on services provided under this section, some children's services have sought to mimic the adult social care scheme by introducing eligibility criteria to focus resources where there is perceived to be the greatest need.[44] Many authorities have therefore attempted to introduce eligibility criteria for children's services, perhaps supplemented by imposing 'thresholds' for accessing services or even (wholly unlawfully) assessments.

1.29 Despite the superficial attractiveness of such eligibility or threshold criteria, their introduction should be resisted. First, unlike the adult social care scheme there is no support for such criteria in the relevant statutory guidance. Second, it is impossible to see how having conducted an assessment under the Assessment Framework and found that a child has a particular need for services, a local authority could rationally refuse to provide that service on the basis of rigid

---

42 CA 1989 Sch 2 para 19B.

43 *R v East Sussex County Council ex p Tandy* [1998] AC 714, 749. See also chapter 2 at para 2.35.

44 *Prioritising need in the context of Putting People First: a whole system approach to eligibility for social care, England 2010*, February 2010.

criteria unrelated to the needs of the individual child.[45] The statutory scheme for the provision of services to children 'in need' does not permit barriers to be put in the way of meeting the needs of vulnerable children. As Lord Laming has pointed out, 'this undermines the very purpose of Section 17 of the Children Act 1989, which is to provide early support to children and families and prevent the escalation of risk'.[46] We are of the view that eligibility criteria or thresholds for services which do not display a high degree of sensitivity to the needs of individual children will be unlawful.[47]

1.30   One recent development that is less controversial is the increasing use of the private or voluntary sector to provide services more cost-effectively for children 'in need'.[48] Although the latest available figures show that only approximately 7 per cent of services provided for children 'in need' were provided by the private or voluntary sector in the year 2009/2010, this is likely to increase significantly in future.[49]

## Areas of concern

1.31   We have highlighted above that a principal concern is the general lack of understanding of the obligations of local authorities towards vulnerable children. It is for that reason that in chapter 2 we set out some of the fundamentals underpinning these obligations. This begins with a discussion of the relevant sources of law, followed by an explanation of the different types of duties owed by local authorities, in particular 'specific' and 'general' duties. (More detail is provided about these duties in the context of services to children 'in need' generally in chapter 4.) Chapter 2 also deals with the structures in place for the delivery of children's services and concludes with a section about avenues of redress. On this latter point we would em-

---

45  It was for this reason that the Black J found eligibility criteria employed by Islington LBC to restrict access to respite care for a disabled child to be unlawful: *R (JL) v Islington LBC* [2009] EWHC 458 (Admin), (2009) 12 CCLR 322.

46  'The Protection of Children in England: A Progress Report', The Lord Laming Report, March 2009, p30. Also see 'The Summary and Recommendations of the Inquiry into the Death of Victoria Climbié', p18.

47  For a more extensive discussion of the use of eligibility criteria in children's services, see chapter 4, paras 4.72–4.80.

48  Allen and Duncan-Smith, 'Early intervention: good parents, great kids, better citizens', Centre for Social Justice/Smith Institute, 2008, p102.

49  *Children in need in England, including their characteristics and further information on children who were the subject of a child protection plan (children in need census – final) year ending 31 March 2010*, table 23.

phasise that in seeking to resolve a dispute about services to children 'in need', the most important consideration is which of the possible means of resolution would provide the most effective remedy for the child, always bearing in mind that it is crucial that disputes about services to vulnerable children need to be resolved as quickly as possible. In the experience of the authors this means that it is frequently necessary to seek a court order to protect the child's interests. As a court order to require a local authority to provide support for a vulnerable child can only be made in judicial review proceedings, advisers will need to engage specialist lawyers. Where appropriate, court orders can be obtained at any time of the day or night and 'out-of-hours' interim orders are often sought and obtained by the authors of this book in situations where a child 'in need' requires urgent support, as, for example, in the case of a homeless 16-year-old or a child leaving custody with nowhere to go.

1.32     We have already mentioned the apparent lack of support for disabled children. There appears to be a huge number of such children who have not had their needs assessed and who in consequence do not receive the support that they require to live ordinary and decent lives. The specific duties owed to disabled children are considered in more detail in *Disabled children: a legal handbook*, also published by Legal Action Group.[50]

1.33     In the following chapters we deal with some specific areas of concern. Unaccompanied asylum-seeking children (UASC) are amongst the most vulnerable of children. By definition they have no one to provide parental support, generally have no means of sustaining themselves and usually have little or no English. We have seen in recent years how the routine response of the authorities (Home Office and local authorities) has been to assert that young people who say that they are under 18 are in fact adults and so are not entitled to services under the CA 1989. The obvious unfairness in a children's services authority deciding whether a young person is a child and therefore entitled to services from that authority was an important factor in the Supreme Court deciding that where such a dispute arises, that dispute should be resolved by the court taking the decision for itself.[51] This additional hurdle faced by UASC demonstrates the tenacity necessary for ensuring that the needs of vulnerable children are met. The consequences of *R (A) v Croydon LBC* and subsequent judgments are analysed in chapter 3.

---

50   S Broach, L Clements and J Read, *Disabled children: a legal handbook*, LAG, 2010.
51   *R (A) v Croydon LBC* [2009] UKSC 8, [2009] 1 WLR 2557, (2009) 12 CCLR 552.

1.34     Another major battle that has raged in the courts over recent years has been over the duties to accommodate children under CA 1989 s20. Children's services authorities have used every ingenious argument available to them to evade their duties towards homeless 16- and 17-year-olds, the principal argument being that there was no duty under CA 1989 s20 if the child was referred to the housing department. As with UASC they fought the point all the way to the House of Lords and lost. The law is now clear: the Children Act scheme has primacy over the Housing Act scheme when it comes to looking after homeless children, and the specific duty owed under CA 1989 s20(1) cannot be displaced by reliance on the general duty found in CA 1989 s17.[52] Disappointingly, despite the judgment of the House of Lords in the *Southwark* case being delivered in May 2009, the evidence suggests that the majority of local authorities are still not complying with their duties under CA 1989 s20.[53] It is hoped that the discussion of this issue in chapter 5 will help advisers persuade authorities to comply with their legal duties towards vulnerable teenagers under CA 1989 s20 and put an end to present pervasive and unlawful practices. Chapter 5 also considers the controversial power for local authorities to detain children in secure accommodation under CA 1989 s25.

1.35     The legal battles to ensure that obligations towards UASC and homeless 16- and 17-year-olds are met has been mirrored in the efforts to secure the legal entitlements for migrant children and their families. Once more the case-law has revealed that the legislation has been poorly understood, local authorities have sought to evade their responsibilities and vulnerable children have been denied the support to which they are entitled.[54] Chapter 6 seeks to explain in the clearest possible terms this particularly contentious area of the law.

1.36     Yet another battleground has been the enforcement of duties owed to children under the leaving care provisions, discussed in detail in chapter 7. These first came to the attention of the High Court in *R (P) v Newham LBC* when it became clear that the local authority had no appreciation of its statutory duties towards care leavers.[55] It was, however, the judgment of Munby J in *R (J) v Caerphilly CBC*

---

52  *R (G) v Southwark LBC* [2009] UKHL 26, [2009] 1 WLR 1367, (2009) 12 CCLR 437 at [10].

53  See fn 30.

54  See, for example, *R (Clue) v Birmingham City Council* [2010] EWCA Civ 460, [2010] 1 WLR 99, (2010) 13 CCLR 276 and *R (SO) v Barking and Dagenham LBC* [2010] EWCA Civ 1101, (2010) 13 CCLR 591.

55  *R (P) v Newham LBC* [2004] EWHC 2210, (2004) 7 CCLR 553.

that clarified the full extent of the duties towards this group of vulnerable young people.[56] Chapter 7 details these duties. The *Caerphilly* case was one of many cases brought by the Howard League for Penal Reform which have been concerned with the obligations of children's services authorities to young people in and leaving custody.[57] It is vital to recognise that this particularly vulnerable cohort of young people are owed important duties which need to be enforced if they are not to get caught up in a cycle of recurring imprisonment. The authors have dealt with many cases of children and young people leaving custody where it is apparent that had children's services engaged with them at an early age (as they should have done) there is a real possibility that the children would not have been drawn into the criminal behaviour which led to their imprisonment. The duties owed to these young people are the same duties owed to all children 'in need' which are discussed throughout this book.

1.37     We have emphasised above that children are 'in need' not through any fault on their part but due to the circumstances in which they find themselves. The law does not permit value judgments to be made as to whether a child deserves support or whether their behaviour is such that support should not be provided. An objective assessment of the needs of a child who may be in need of support is required. If a child is in need of support, the support should be provided, taking into account the wishes and feeling of the child to the greatest extent possible. Despite the plethora of court cases, the law is essentially very straightforward: support for vulnerable children must be provided if it is necessary to meet the child's needs. Nothing less is required to ensure proper respect for the dignity of the child.

---

56  *R (J) v Caerphilly CBC* [2004] EWHC 2210, (2004) 7 CCLR 553.
57  See also *R (Howard League for Penal Reform) v Secretary of State for the Home Department* [2002] EWHC 2497, (2003) 6 CCLR 47 and *R (K) v Manchester City Council* [2006] EWHC 3164, (2007) 10 CCLR 87.

# CHAPTER 2

# Legal fundamentals

### Key points

- The law of England and Wales comes from a number of sources, including statutes, secondary legislation, case-law and statutory guidance.
- In addition, human rights law – as laid down in the European Convention on Human Rights and other international conventions – plays an increasingly important role in court decisions relating to children 'in need'.
- Where a local authority is subject to a 'specific duty' in law, a breach of that duty will be challengeable by an individual in the courts.
- However, if the law imposes a 'general duty', this is owed to a group as a whole and not to any particular individual and a breach of the duty cannot therefore be challenged in the courts unless there is other unlawfulness.
- Local authorities' functions are also governed by the 'powers' with which they are provided in legislation; these powers may not be exceeded and must be exercised in a reasonable and fair way.
- Following reforms contained in the Children Act 2004, structures now exist at local authority level to ensure that all public bodies concerned with children operate in a way which is co-operative and safeguards children.
- Challenges to local authority decisions in relation to children 'in need' can be undertaken by various means including the statutory complaints procedure; a complaint to the local government ombudsman; or judicial review.
- The choice of which route of redress to use will depend on the facts of each case; for a judicial review challenge, assistance from a specialist solicitor is highly advisable, for which legal aid may be available.

## Introduction

2.1    As this book demonstrates, the law relating to children 'in need'[1] is contained in a wide range of domestic and international sources. Before these sources of law are addressed in their specific context later in the book, this chapter will introduce the general context

1 For more on the legal meaning of this phrase, see chapter 4 at paras 4.10–4.13.

within which they operate. It will provide an overview of the structure of English law and of children's services, with particular consideration of the way in which the law imposes binding duties on local authorities in relation to children 'in need'. There will also be discussion of the differences between duties and powers to provide support to such children. Finally, the internal structure of children's services will be examined, along with procedures for challenging their decisions, including by way of complaints and through applications for 'judicial review' in the High Court.

## Sources of law

2.2    The law in relation to children 'in need' and their families derives from several sources, each of which may be given different degrees of weight by the courts. While, therefore, courts are required strictly to apply the terms of an Act of parliament, a less authoritative source of law, such as 'statutory guidance', may be treated more flexibly. In addition, instruments of international law, such as the United Nations Convention on the Rights of the Child (UNCRC), may in certain circumstances be relied on by individuals in domestic courts. This section will identify the key legal sources and how the courts apply the rules they contain. For the sake of clarity, it will start with legislation and statutory guidance, before proceeding to case-law and finishing with human rights and EU law.

### Legislation and guidance

2.3    Legislation, or 'statute law', can be divided into two types: 'primary legislation', which refers to the law passed by parliament in the form of Acts; and 'secondary' or 'delegated legislation', which is law made by a public body (such as a government minister) under powers given to him or her in an Act of parliament. Linked to both of these are the various forms of guidance which contain explanations as to how legislation should be interpreted and public duties performed. These sources of law will be examined in turn below.

2.4    Primary legislation, such as the Children Acts of 1989 and 2004, has historically been regarded as the highest form of law in England and Wales. While recent developments in EU law and human rights law have modified this view,[2] it is generally the case that courts are re-

2  See below, paras 2.12–2.29.

quired to apply the terms of an Act of parliament ahead of any other source of law and that, outside certain very limited exceptions, no challenge can be made to an Act in the courts. Consideration of the rights of any individual child should therefore start with the relevant parts of any applicable Act.

2.5    Secondary legislation is often used as a convenient mechanism for fleshing out the rules in an area already covered in a more general way by an Act. This allows a decision-maker to set detailed standards and procedures in a given area without the need for full parliamentary debate. However, a public body (generally a minister) may only legislate in this way under powers conferred on it by an Act. Therefore, while secondary legislation must in most cases be strictly applied by the courts in the same way as an Act, it is possible to challenge the validity of a piece of secondary legislation by arguing that, for instance, a minister in making the legislation has exceeded the powers given to him or her in the relevant Act (ie has acted 'ultra vires') or has acted in a procedurally unfair way.[3]

2.6    There are many types of secondary legislation or 'statutory instruments', with the most relevant for present purposes being 'regulations' and 'rules'. The former are often the means by which substantive requirements contained in an Act are given a fuller content. Therefore, while the Children (Leaving Care) Act (CLCA) 2000 sets out in broad terms the duties owed towards young people who have previously been looked after by a local authority, the Children (Leaving Care) (England) Regulations (CLCE Regs) 2001[4] contain greater detail as to who is eligible for support under the Act, and how their needs should be met.[5] The particular type of secondary legislation known as 'rules' often stipulate the procedures which should be followed in a specific context, such as the Tribunal Procedure (First-tier Tribunal) (Health, Education and Social Care Chamber) Rules 2008[6] which govern the procedure of the Tribunal with responsibility for children with special educational needs.

2.7    'Guidance' is not legislation and is not strictly speaking binding, although it can impose obligations on local authorities if it is 'statutory guidance' issued under an Act which specifies that the guidance

---

3  See, for instance, *R (British Waterways Board) v First Secretary of State* [2006] EWHC 1019.

4  Separate regulations for Wales, entitled the Children (Leaving Care) (Wales) Regulations 2001, have also been made.

5  For more on the contents of the CLCA 2000 and the CLC Regs 2001, see chapter 7.

6  SI No 2699.

must be followed or considered (see para 2.8 below). Guidance is usually contained in documents published by central government departments (and now almost always accessible online), which expands upon statutory duties in order to regulate the functions of other public bodies, such as local authorities. The key division in this context is between 'statutory guidance' and 'non-statutory guidance'.

2.8      As the name suggests, statutory guidance is made under powers conferred by statute, such as section 7 of Local Authority Social Services Act (LASSA) 1970 or section 11(4) of the Children Act (CA) 2004. The first of these two provisions requires local authorities, in the social services context, to act 'under the general guidance of the Secretary of State', while the latter obliges a range of public bodies with responsibilities relating to children to 'have regard to any guidance given to them for the purpose by the Secretary of State'. The courts have interpreted the LASSA 1970 s7 duty to mean that local authorities may deviate from the terms of statutory guidance only 'where the local authority judges on admissible grounds that there is good reason to do so, but without freedom to take a substantially different course'.[7] As a result, and as the later chapters of this book demonstrate, the courts will regularly require local authorities to comply with obligations imposed by and set out in the key statutory guidance relating to children 'in need'. These include:

- *Framework for the assessment of children in need and their families* ('Assessment Framework')[8];
- *Statutory guidance on the duty to cooperate under section 10 of the Children Act 2004*; and
- *Statutory guidance on making arrangements to safeguard and promote the welfare of children under section 11 of the Children Act 2004.*

2.9      By contrast, non-statutory guidance is not underpinned by any duty found in legislation. It often consists of best practice approaches to the provision of services which may be read alongside relevant statutory guidance and can assist professionals and practitioners to put the statutory guidance into effect. This is the case with the *Assessing children in need and their families* practice guidance (June 2000) and the *Safeguarding disabled children* practice guidance (July 2009), which are intended to supplement, respectively, the Assessment Framework and *Working together to safeguard children* statutory guidance through the specification of further detailed procedures and standards. However, while the guidance in documents of this sort

7   *R v Islington LBC ex p Rixon* (1997–98) 1 CCLR at 119 per Sedley J.
8   See chapter 4 at para 4.25.

may be important in informing the court's view of the reasonableness, fairness or 'proportionality'[9] of the conduct of a local authority
(and therefore the lawfulness of their actions), it does not, of itself,
give rise to binding obligations. In general it will be far harder for a
child or a child's parents to win a case by relying on an alleged breach
of practice guidance than it will be to win by relying on an alleged
breach of statutory guidance.

## Case-law

2.10   Given the diversity of legal sources and the complexity which arises
in applying legislation to individual cases, the interpretative role of
the courts has always been central to the operation of the law in England and Wales. It is through examining the 'plain meaning' of a
legislative provision, but also the purpose of a given statute and the
legislative context in which it appears, that courts seek to apply legislation to individual cases. In addition, courts are bound by the principle of '*stare decisis*', which requires them to follow the statements
of law, or 'precedents', produced by superior courts. Thus, previous
cases in which a relevant statutory provision or factual scenario was
considered will be of key importance in resolving any legal dispute.
Although the courts do not 'make' the law, the common law tradition
means that certain rights, for instance the right to proper consultation,[10] stem from court judgments rather than Acts of parliament or
other legislation.

2.11   'Judicial review' is the legal mechanism by which most cases challenging the acts or omissions of local authorities will come to court.[11]
This procedure embodies the core 'rule of law' principle that everyone (including local and central government) is equal under the law,
and that courts will therefore hold local authorities to their legal obligations just as they would any individual.[12] Applications for judicial
review are heard in the first instance in the Administrative Court,
part of the Queen's Bench Division within the High Court, where
cases will generally be heard by a single judge or occasionally two
judges sitting as a 'Divisional Court'. Appeals from the High Court

---

9   See para 2.15.
10   See, for example, *R v North and East Devon Health Authority, ex p Coughlan*
[2001] QB 213.
11   See paras 2.67–2.70.
12   For a highly accessible and informative discussion of the concept of the 'rule of
law' from one of the greatest recent judges and jurists, see T Bingham, *The rule
of law*, Allen Lane, 2010.

go to the Court of Appeal, with onward appeals in cases of signifi-cant public importance to the Supreme Court, which has replaced the House of Lords at the apex of the domestic court system. Cases involving human rights issues may be taken to the European Court of Human Rights (ECtHR) in Strasbourg once domestic remedies have been exhausted, in other words once an individual has lost in the UK courts and exhausted all rights of appeal.

## Human rights law

### The ECHR and the Human Rights Act 1998

2.12   Where human rights law is referred to in the UK context, this is likely to be a reference to the law contained in the European Convention on Human Rights (ECHR), which is given effect in domestic law by the Human Rights Act (HRA) 1998. The ECHR, an international treaty to which the UK has been a party since 1951, contains a number of fundamental rights which the contracting states have agreed to respect, subject to certain well-defined exceptions (see below at paras 2.13 and 2.20).

2.13   Prior to 2000, UK citizens could only rely directly on ECHR rights before the ECtHR in Strasbourg. This entailed a time-consuming and expensive process which was poorly understood by most lawyers in the UK, never mind individuals who may have had their rights violated. The intention and effect of the HRA was to 'domesticate' these rights by making them enforceable in UK courts. Of particular importance are sections 3, 4 and 6 of HRA 1998. The first of these (section 3) requires domestic courts to interpret domestic legislation compatibly with these rights insofar as it is possible to do so. The second (section 4) obliges courts to declare legislation to be incom-patible with the ECHR where a convention-compliant reading is not possible.[13] The third (section 6) prohibits 'public authorities' (includ-ing local authorities and almost all other bodies with responsibility

13   Following such a 'declaration of incompatibility' parliament is likely to amend the offending piece of legislation to bring it in line with the ECHR, potentially under the special procedure established by HRA 1998 s10. See *R (Royal College of Nursing and others) v Secretary of State for the Home Department and another* [2010] EWHC 2761 (Admin) for a recent example of a declaration of incompatibility, made in this case in relation to the 'auto barring' provisions of the Safeguarding Vulnerable Groups Act 2006 which, to the extent that they required workers to be placed on lists of individuals barred from working with children and vulnerable adults without being given the chance to make representations, were declared to be incompatible with articles 6 (right to fair trial) and 8 (right to private and family life) ECHR.

for children 'in need') from acting in a way that is inconsistent with a convention right. While the constitutional changes brought about by sections 3 and 4 of HRA 1998 have been hugely significant, section 6 generally has more practical application in cases challenging the acts of public bodies since it requires compliance with the ECHR rights in the day-to-day provision of services and support to children 'in need'.

2.14    Of all the rights contained in the ECHR, articles 3 (the prohibition against torture and inhuman or degrading treatment), 8 (the right to respect for private and family life) and 14 (the prohibition on discrimination) may be most relevant in cases relating to children 'in need'. It is, however, the rights protected under article 8 ECHR which have the greatest potential to improve the services and support made available to children and families.

2.15    Article 8 prohibits interference with 'the right to respect for private and family life' except in the pursuit of one of a series of specified aims.[14] Further, even where the 'interference' relates to one of the specified aims, it will still breach article 8 ECHR unless it is 'in accordance with the law' and 'proportionate'. It is the second of these requirements which is frequently relied upon in individual cases since a decision that is 'not in accordance with the law' for article 8 ECHR purposes is likely to be otherwise unlawful under domestic law and thus amenable to challenge as such. Proportionality demands that an interference must bear a 'reasonable relationship' to the objective pursued and that the means used to achieve the objective must be no more restrictive of the right to family and private life than is necessary.[15] It is a concept which therefore entails a particularly high degree of scrutiny by a court of the way in which the state, including local authorities, interacts with individuals.[16] The ultimate question on a proportionality review is whether a 'fair balance has been struck between the rights of the individual and wider public interest.

2.16    The 'right to respect for private and family life' has been interpreted broadly by the Strasbourg and domestic courts. 'Private life'

14  The specified aims being 'national security', 'public safety', 'the economic well-being of the country', 'the prevention of disorder or crime', 'the protection of health or morals' or 'the protection of the rights and freedoms of others'.

15  See *de Freitas v Permanent Secretary of Ministry of Agriculture, Fisheries, Lands and Housing* [1999] 1 AC 69, [1998] 3 WLR 675 and *Huang v Secretary of State for the Home Department* [2007] UKHL 11 per Lord Bingham at [19].

16  *R (Daly) v Secretary of State for the Home Department* [2001] UKHL 21, [2001] 2 AC 532 per Lords Bingham, Steyn and Cooke.

encompasses 'personal autonomy' and includes a person's 'physical and psychological integrity', aspects of his or her 'physical and social identity', his or her 'personal development', and his or her 'right to establish and develop relationships with other human beings and the outside world'.[17] The prohibition on unjustified 'interference' with this right under article 8 does not only impose negative obligations by forbidding the state from taking active steps which run counter to a person's private and family life. In certain cases, article 8 also requires positive action to safeguard a person's rights,[18] particularly where there is a 'direct and immediate link between the measures sought by an applicant and the latter's private and/or family life'.[19] Where the welfare of children is at stake, article 8 may require the provision of welfare support in a manner which enables family life to continue.[20]

2.17    The courts have found breaches of the 'negative' obligations under article 8 ECHR where, for instance:

- children of blind parents were placed in care in circumstances where no actual harm to the children had been recorded and decisions were based on the evidence of occasional visits by the authorities, uncorroborated by independent evidence and without consideration of other, less drastic, means of improving the children's welfare;[21] and
- a Jamaican national was detained under immigration powers, resulting in her separation from her young children without regard having been had to the best interests of those children.[22]

2.18    Similarly, findings of violations of the 'positive' obligation under article 8 have been made where:

- prosecuting authorities refused to bring proceedings against an individual accused of raping a mentally disabled girl, in part because the girl was legally incapable of making the criminal complaint and no one was permitted to make it on her behalf;[23] and
- a local authority failed to adapt the housing occupied by a physically disabled woman making it impossible for her to access the

17  *Pretty v United Kingdom* (2002) 35 EHRR 1 at [61].
18  *Kroon v The Netherlands* (1994) 19 EHRR 263 at [31].
19  *Botta v Italy* (1998) 26 EHRR 241 at [34].
20  *Anufrijeva v Southwark LBC* [2003] EWCA Civ 1406, [2004] 1 QB 1124.
21  *Saviny v Ukraine* (2010) 51 EHRR 33.
22  *R (MXL) v Secretary of State for the Home Department* [2010] EWHC 2397 (Admin).
23  *X and Y v Netherlands* (1986) 8 EHRR 235.

toilet, to leave the house or go upstairs without her husband's assistance, which severely impacted upon her family life with her husband and children.[24]

2.19   Article 8 also imposes important procedural obligations on the state. In, for example, *Re X: Barnet LBC v Y and X*[25] Munby J (as he then was) held that local authorities must carefully consider all information relevant to the assessment decision to ensure adequate regard is had to the family's convention rights, including adequate participation in the process. A court must examine whether the decision-making process leading to any interferences with the right to respect for private and family life was fair and afforded due respect to the individual's interests which are safeguarded under article 8; *Connors v UK*.[26] The Strasbourg court held in the landmark case of *W v UK*[27] that the pre-CA 1989 child protection scheme breached parents' article 8 rights by failing to ensure a fair procedure for taking children into public care.

## EU law, the EU Charter and the Lisbon Treaty

2.20   By virtue of HRA 1998, most of the rights contained in the ECHR are now part of UK law.[28] As a result of the European Communities Act (ECA) 1972, European Union law also has effect in UK law, in a somewhat more direct manner. In fact, in contrast to HRA 1998, ECA 1972 has been interpreted as requiring courts to 'disapply' a piece of primary legislation which is inconsistent with directly effective rights provided for in EU law,[29] thus setting EU law above statute law in the legal hierarchy. So far, EU law has not proven to be significant to the protection of children 'in need' in domestic courts. However, given the entry into force in 2009 of the Lisbon Treaty, which gives the Charter of Fundamental Rights of the European Union ('the charter')

---

24   *R (Bernard) v Enfield LBC* [2002] EWHC 2282, (2002) 5 CCLR 577. See also *R (Hughes) v Liverpool CC* [2005] EWHC (Admin), (2005) 8 CCLR 243.

25   [2006] 2 FLR 998.

26   (2005) 40 EHRR 9 at [83].

27   (1987) 10 EHRR 29 at [63].

28   One exception is article 13 ECHR, the 'right to a remedy', which is excluded from the HRA 1998. This is one reason why cases involving breaches of ECHR rights by the UK may still be heard by the ECtHR.

29   See *R v Secretary of State for Transport ex p Factortame* [1991] 1 AC 603, [1990] 3 WLR 818.

equal status to the EU treaties,[30] it may be that the charter rights will provide additional grounds on which the rights of children in need can be safeguarded. The charter will only apply where a domestic authority is implementing, or acting within the scope of, EU law and so will only assist in cases with the necessary EU connection.

2.21    Of the rights contained in the charter, article 24 on 'the rights of the child' and article 26 on the 'integration of persons with disabilities' may be the most relevant.[31]

2.22    The former (article 24) states:

> 1.  Children shall have the right to such protection and care as is necessary for their well-being. They may express their views freely. Such views shall be taken into consideration on matters which concern them in accordance with their age and maturity.
>
> 2.  In all actions relating to children, whether taken by public authorities or private institutions, the child's best interests must be a primary consideration.
>
> 3.  Every child shall have the right to maintain on a regular basis a personal relationship and direct contact with both his or her parents, unless that is contrary to his or her interests.

2.23    The latter (article 26) provides:[32]

> The Union recognises and respects the right of persons with disabilities to benefit from measures designed to ensure their independence, social and occupational integration and participation in the life of the community.

## The UNCRC and the Disability Convention

2.24    The position is somewhat different again as regards the international agreements concerning the rights of children to which the UK is party but which have not been given effect in domestic law. The key instruments in this context are the UNCRC, ratified by the UK in

---

30  There is a UK protocol to the charter, widely described in the media as an 'opt out', but the government has conceded in the Court of Appeal in *R (NS) v Secretary of State for the Home Department* [2010] EWCA Civ 990 that the protocol merely explains the effect of the charter provisions which limit its application to cases falling within the scope of EU law. The rights in the charter can thus be directly relied on in domestic law where the matter at issue falls within the scope of EU law.

31  Article 7, which is intended to reflect article 8 ECHR, will also be relevant, as will the right to dignity under article 1.

32  Note, however, that article 26 embodies a 'principle' rather than a 'right' under the charter and therefore may be relied upon only when an EU legislative or executive act is being interpreted or applied.

1991,[33] and, in relation to disabled children, the UN Convention on the Rights of Persons with Disabilities ('the Disability Convention'), ratified in 2009. Since these treaties are not underpinned by domestic legislation, they cannot be directly applied by English courts. However, whilst the UNCRC is an international law instrument, it is applicable in domestic law as it is taken into account by the European Court of Human Rights when assessing the parameters of and applying article 8 ECHR, and it thus, by virtue of section 2(1) of the Human Right Act 1998 (HRA), has a place in the interpretation of Convention rights by the courts in this jurisdiction.[34] The courts have also on a number of occasions confirmed the centrality of the UNCRC to interpretative questions of domestic law concerning children.[35] Furthermore, in appropriate cases courts will be strongly influenced by the rights both of these treaties contain, regardless of article 8 ECHR. This is because it has been a long-standing principle of the common law that legislation is, in the absence of express words to the contrary, presumed to be in accordance with international law.[36] In a case concerning the UNCRC itself and its application to two regulations dealing with child support, Baroness Hale stated:[37]

> Even if an international treaty has not been incorporated into domestic law, our domestic legislation has to be construed so far as possible so as to comply with the international obligations which we have undertaken. When two interpretations of these regulations are possible, the interpretation chosen should be that which better complies with the commitment to the welfare of children which this country has made by ratifying the United Nations Convention on the Rights of the Child.

---

33 And indeed by every other member nation of the UN except Somalia and the USA. A UK reservation in relation to immigration control was removed in 2008.

34 See eg *R (P) v SSHD; R (Q) v SSHD* [2001] EWHC 357 (Admin), [2001] 2 FLR 383 at [33], *R (SR) v Nottingham Magistrates' Court* [2001] EWHC 802 (Admin) at [65]–[67].

35 See eg *R (Williamson) v Secretary of State for Education and* Employment [2005] 2 AC 246 at [81]; *R (SR) v Nottingham Magistrates' Court* [2001] EWHC 802 (Admin) at [65]–[67].

36 See, for example, *R v Secretary of State for the Home Department ex p Brind* [1991] 1 AC 696, [1991] 2 WLR 588.

37 *Smith v Smith* [2006] UKHL 35, [2006] 1 WLR 2024. In *R (Howard League for Penal Reform) v Secretary of State for the Home Department* [2002] EWHC 2497 (Admin), [2003] 1 FLR 484, Munby J (as he then was) stated in relation to the UNCRC and the EU Charter that they can 'properly be consulted insofar as they proclaim, reaffirm or elucidate the content of those human rights that are generally recognised throughout the European family of nations, in particular the nature and scope of those fundamental rights that are guaranteed by the European Convention'.

Therefore, while the rights detailed below in the unincorporated UNCRC and Disability Convention are not self-standing, they can be called upon to inform the domestic courts' interpretations of legislation and the ECHR[38] (or, in the case of the Disability Convention, give rise to a separate route of redress through the UN Committee on the Rights of Persons with Disabilities).[39]

2.25    Among the key provisions contained in the UNCRC for present purposes are:

- article 2, which prohibits discrimination in the securing of rights for children;
- article 3, which requires states to ensure that the best interests of the child are a 'primary consideration' in all actions concerning children;
- article 4, which obliges states to take all measures 'to the maximum extent of their available resources' for the implementation of children's economic, social and cultural rights;
- article 9, which prohibits separation of child and parents against their will, except where it is necessary in the child's best interests;
- article 12, which gives children the right to express their views in matters concerning them;[40]
- article 23, which recognises a range of rights envisaged by mentally or physically disabled children (see para 2.26); and
- articles 28 and 29, which recognise the right to education 'on the basis of equal opportunity' and with a view to '[t]he development of the child's personality, talents and mental and physical abilities to their fullest potential'.

2.26    Returning to article 23, a number of key principles are set out in relation to disabled children, who are recognised as belonging to a particularly vulnerable group. Recognition is given to the right of disabled children to 'a full and decent life, in conditions which ensure dignity, promote self-reliance and facilitate the child's active participation in the community'. Further, states are required to 'encourage and ensure' the provision of assistance (free whenever possible, subject to carers' finances) to the child and the child's carers, 'subject

---

38  See, for instance, *Maslov v Austria* [2009] INLR 47 and *ZH (Tanzania) v Secretary of State for the Home Department* [2011] UKSC 4.

39  See paras 2.28–2.29.

40  The 'right to participation' under UNCRC article 12 is of particular importance and underpins the duties on public bodies under domestic legislation to engage meaningfully with children 'in need' when decisions are taken about their lives; see, for example, CA 1989 s17(4A) and para 2.27 below.

to available resources'. This is with a view to ensuring that the child receives 'education, training, health care services, rehabilitation services, preparation for employment and recreation opportunities in a manner conducive to the child's achieving the fullest possible social integration and individual development, including his or her cultural and spiritual development'.

2.27 As is well known, when a court determines any question with respect to the 'upbringing' of a child, the child's welfare 'shall be the court's paramount consideration'.[41] By contrast, until the passage of CA 2004 (see paras 2.36 and 2.42) local authorities were under no common-law or statutory duty to promote children's welfare generally. There is no general statutory principle in the CA 1989 applicable to local authorities similar to that in CA 1989 s1(1)(a) which binds the courts.[42] However the Supreme Court in *ZH (Tanzania) v Secretary of State for the Home Department*[43] has recognised that the right to respect for private and family life under ECHR article 8 must be interpreted in the light of articles 3 and 12 UNCRC (see para 2.25 above). Therefore in carrying out any of their functions, public authorities are expected to treat the best interests of the child as a 'primary consideration' and where possible give 'due weight' to the child's views in accordance with his or her age and maturity.

2.28 The Disability Convention, which entered into force in 2008, can be seen as building on several of the UNCRC provisions detailed above. Among the significant principles and rights provided for in this instrument are the following:

- article 3, which sets out a number of general principles, including '[r]espect for the evolving capacities of children with disabilities and respect for the right of children with disabilities to preserve their identities';
- article 4, which imposes general obligations on states, including to take into account the human rights of disabled persons 'in all policies and programmes';
- article 7, which requires states to take all necessary measures to secure the full enjoyment of disabled children's human rights and ensure that disabled children's views are given due weight;

41  CA 1989 s1(1)(a). The welfare 'paramountcy principle' does not govern the application of CA 1989 Part III; see *Re M (Secure Accommodation Order)* [1995] 3 All ER 407, [1995] Fam 108.

42  *R (Howard League for Penal Reform) v Secretary of State for the Home Department and another* [2002] EWHC 2497 (Admin), [2003] 1 FLR 484 per Munby J (as he then was) at [35].

43  [2011] UKSC 4.

- article 9, which requires states to take appropriate measures to ensure that disabled people can gain access to the physical environment, information and communications;
- article 19, which recognises the equal right of disabled people to live independently and participate fully in society;
- article 23, which recognises the rights of disabled people to respect for their home and family, including the right of disabled children and their families to 'early and comprehensive information, services and support' with a view to preventing 'concealment, abandonment, neglect and segregation of children with disabilities'; and
- article 24, which enshrines the right of disabled people to education 'without discrimination and on the basis of equal opportunity'.

2.29 The Optional Protocol to the Disability Convention, which the UK ratified in 2009, provides for a Committee on the Rights of Persons with Disabilities, which may hear complaints from individuals claiming a breach of the Disability Convention. Any such complaint may generally only be brought once all domestic legal remedies have been exhausted.[44]

## Duties and powers

2.30 Local authorities are the bodies principally responsible for delivering support and services under Part III of CA 1989 as 'social services authorities'.[45] As bodies whose structure and operation is founded in legislation, they are legally required to act in accordance with any statutory provision imposing a duty and are prohibited from acting outside the limits of any power conferred on them. It is the phrasing of a statutory provision which is key to identifying whether it creates a duty or a power, with the word 'shall' or 'must' indicating a duty, and the word 'may' establishing a power. Many cases involving children 'in need' will turn on the scope and application of the relevant duty or power. It is therefore necessary to be as clear as possible as to the precise nature and scope of each provision. This can only be achieved after consideration of some important general principles.

---

44 Article 2(d).
45 Meaning (in England) county councils, metropolitan districts ('unitary authorities') and London boroughs and (in Wales), county councils and county boroughs; LASSA 1970 s1. See paras 2.36–2.41 below in relation to the duties imposed on other public bodies in this context by CA 2004 ss10 and 11.

## Duties

2.31   The notion of a public law duty is not straightforward. Even where a duty has arisen in law, it may not be enforceable on behalf of an individual child. This is because public law duties come in two forms, termed 'specific' duties and 'general' (or 'target') duties. The first, more clear-cut, type is owed to each individual falling within the category set out in the relevant provision. A key example in relation to CA 1989 Part III comes in section 20(1), which, as was held in *R (G) v Southwark LBC*,[46] mandates a duty on a local authority to accommodate each and every child 'in need' where he or she requires accommodation for the reasons set out in the subsection.[47] Where a specific duty such as this arises, an individual can meaningfully be said to have a 'right' to the provision. This is because any failure to fulfil a specific duty in an individual case should be declared unlawful by the courts on an application for judicial review (see paras 2.67–2.70 below) and if necessary the public body should be compelled to fulfil its duty or duties by way of a mandatory order.

2.32   By contrast, a general duty is owed to the relevant population as a whole and cannot (without more) be relied upon by an individual before the courts to establish a 'right' to particular treatment. Thus, the 'general' duty under CA 1989 s17(1) 'to safeguard and promote the welfare of children within their area who are in need; and ... so far as is consistent with that duty, to promote the upbringing of such children by their families, by providing a range and level of services appropriate to those children's needs' does not provide for a specific duty equivalent to that in section 20(1).[48] Rather, it sets out general requirements as to the way in which a local authority should approach the provision of services and support to children in need and does not bestow a legal right on any one child. 'General' or 'target' duties however remain of higher legal importance than powers as public bodies should always strive to comply with their duties but need not exercise their powers unless they deem it necessary to do so.[49]

2.33   Distinguishing between different types of duties is centrally im-

46   [2009] UKHL 26, [2009] 1 WLR 1299.
47   See chapter 5 on the duty to accommodate children under CA 1989 s20(1).
48   *R (G) v Barnet* [2003] UKHL 57, [2004] 2 AC 208; see more detailed discussion below at paras 4.37 and 6.32–6.40.
49   'A power need not be exercised, but a duty must be discharged'; *R (G) v Barnet LBC* [2003] UKHL 57, [2004] 2 AC 208 per Lord Nicholls at [12]. See also *R v Inner London Education Authority ex p Ali* (1990) 2 Admin LR 822 per Woolf LJ; a target duty may be enforced by the courts against a public body if it is not at least working towards compliance with that duty.

portant, not least at a time such as this when there is intense pressure on the resources of public bodies. As Lord Nicholls stated in *R (G) v Barnet LBC*, 'the extent to which a duty precludes a local authority from ordering its expenditure priorities for itself varies from one duty to another'.[50] The precise nature of each of the different duties which may arise in relation to an individual child 'in need' is identified throughout this book.

## Powers

2.34    On the other hand, where a 'power' to do something (for instance, the broad 'well-being' power under Local Government Act 2000 s2) is conferred on a local authority by parliament, no general obligation to exercise it arises since the authority has a 'discretion' as to the circumstances and manner of its performance. However, in accordance with well-established public law principles, a local authority must not act beyond the limits of the power as set out in legislation and must also not 'fetter its discretion' by ruling out the exercise of a power without giving consideration to each individual case.[51] Furthermore, any such consideration must be made in a way that is reasonable, procedurally fair and in accordance with relevant human rights requirements and statutory guidance (where appropriate). Failure to consider exercising a power or an unreasonable refusal to do so, particularly in a context where not to do so may lead to a breach of an ECHR right, is likely to result in a court declaring the act or omission of the public body to be unlawful.

2.35    The courts have repeatedly reiterated the central importance of distinguishing between 'powers' and 'duties'. A central example of this is the speech of Lord Browne-Wilkinson in *R v East Sussex County Council ex p Tandy*, where his Lordship stated that 'Parliament has chosen to impose a statutory duty, as opposed to a power ... In my judgment, the courts should be slow to downgrade such duties into what are, in effect, mere discretions over which the court would have very little real control'.[52]

50  [2003] UKHL 57, [2004] 2 AC 208 at [13].
51  See, for instance, *British Oxygen v Minister of Technology* [1969] 2 Ch 174, [1969] 2 WLR 877.
52  [1998] AC 714 at 749E–F. See also the speech of Lord Scott in *R (G) v Barnet LBC* [2003] UKHL 57, [2004] 2 AC 208 at [133], stating 'no doubt it is right that a statutory duty must not be downgraded to a mere discretionary power'. Lord Scott was in the majority which held that the duty under CA 1989 s17 was 'general' rather than 'specific'; see chapter 4 at para 4.37.

# Key local structures and processes[53]

2.36    The regulation and organisation of local authority departments with responsibility for children's services was significantly reformed as a result of the *Every child matters* green paper (2003) and the subsequent enactment of the CA 2004. In particular, new requirements were imposed with a view to ensuring co-operation and a child-centred focus across local authorities and other public bodies in the delivery of support to children.[54]

2.37    Therefore, although CA 1989 s27 had already conferred powers and duties on each local authority to request (and, where appropriate, receive) help from a variety of local government and healthcare bodies in their exercise of functions under Part III of the Act, the CA 2004 extended and deepened the scope of interagency co-operation designed to safeguard and promote children's welfare (see para 2.42 below).

2.38    In accordance with the statutory guidance on inter-agency co-operation to improve children's wellbeing, published in November 2008, this co-operation between public bodies in the interests of children's welfare has been formalised by various innovations, including:

- Children's Trusts, which are the setting for the co-operation arrangements and partnerships between the relevant bodies, under the oversight of a Children's Trust Board (but see para 2.41 below);
- Children and Young People's Plans (CYPPs), which detail how the bodies participating in the Children's Trust will co-operate to safeguard children's wellbeing (but see para 2.41 below);
- the Director of Children's Services,[55] which is an appointed post with professional responsibility and accountability for children's services at local authority level; and
- the Lead Member for Children's Services,[56] who is the elected member within the local authority with political responsibility and accountability for children's services.

2.39    A further important duty was imposed on local authorities by the Apprenticeships, Skills, Children and Learning Act 2009, which

---

53  This section sets out the reforms to children's services in England. Detailed coverage of developments in Wales is outside the scope of this book.

54  CA 2004 ss10 and 11. See also Childcare Act 2006 s4 in relation to the duty on local authorities and health authorities to co-operate to secure the provision of integrated early childhood services.

55  As required by CA 2004 s18.

56  As required by CA 2004 s19.

amended the Childcare Act 2006 to require authorities to arrange, so far as is reasonably practicable, sufficient provision of children's centres[57] to meet local need.[58] 'Local need' is defined as 'the need of parents, prospective parents and young children in the authority's area'.[59] The Childcare Act 2006 also imposes a duty on local authorities to improve the well-being of young children[60] in their area, and to reduce inequalities between young children in their area in relation to the *Every child matters* outcomes.[61]

2.40 These additional duties on local authorities to safeguard and promote children's welfare have been mirrored in a general duty on the Secretary of State (now the Education Secretary) to 'promote the well-being of children in England'.[62]

2.41 Shortly after entering office in 2010, the new coalition government signalled its intention to reform some of the new structures implemented by the CA 2004.[63] Since then it has, as of 31 October 2010, withdrawn the Children's Trust statutory guidance and removed the duty for Children's Trust Boards to produce a CYPP.[64] It has also announced its intention to use the forthcoming Education Bill to remove schools, non-maintained special schools, academies and further education authorities from the list of bodies with a duty to cooperate within Children's Trust Board. In future, the government intends to promote legislation to end the requirement for local areas to have a Children's Trust Board and to divest the Job Centre Plus of the duty to cooperate within the Board. As it stands, therefore, local areas remain free (though not obliged) to produce a CYPP

---

57 A place, or group of places, providing integrated early childhood services; Childcare Act 2006 s5A(4). This supplements the duty to provide integrated early childhood services in Childcare Act 2006 s3.

58 Childcare Act 2006 s5A, as amended by Apprenticeships, Skills, Children and Learning Act 2009 s198.

59 Childcare Act 2006 s5A(2).

60 In relation to this duty a child is a 'young child' during the period from the child's birth to the 1 September following the date on which the child attains the age of five; Childcare Act 2006 s19.

61 Childcare Act 2006 s1(1).

62 Children and Young Persons Act 2008 s7.

63 See 'Reform of Children's Trusts', Department for Education, 22 July 2010, www.education.gov.uk/childrenandyoungpeople/earlylearningandchildcare/a0063158/reform-of-childrens-trusts.

64 Under CA 2004 ss17 and 17A, inserted by Apprenticeships, Skills, Children and Learning Act 2009 s194. The regulations requiring a Children's Trust Board to be established were revoked on 31 October 2010 by the Children's Trust Board (Children and Young People's Plan) (England) (Revocation) Regulations 2010 SI No 2129.

and are under a duty to have a Children's Trust Board[65] (although the statutory guidance is no longer in effect). The government has confirmed that it has no plans to seek the abolition of the duty to co-operate under CA 2004 s10 or the requirement for a Director of, and a Lead Member for, Children's Services.

## Safeguarding and child protection

### Overview

2.42   In addition to the general and specific duties outlined elsewhere in this book, there are important overarching safeguarding and welfare duties on local authorities and their 'relevant' partners imposed by the Children Act 2004. The CA 2004 was passed following the inquiry into the death of Victoria Climbié which exposed significant failings on the part of children's services authorities. Accordingly, CA 2004 s 10 places a duty on each children's services authority to make ar-rangements to promote co-operation between itself and a range of bodies with responsibilities relating to the welfare of children. The relevant bodies include the police authority, the probation board, the youth offending team and the Strategic Health Authority and Pri-mary Care Trust,[66] and the aim of such arrangements is to improve the well-being of children in relation to the five outcomes identified by *Every child matters.*[67] CA 2004 s11 goes on to place further duties on a similar list of public bodies to have regard to the need to 'safe-guard and promote the welfare of children' in the performance of their respective functions. The secretary of state may also impose 'safeguarding targets' on local authorities, but it is unclear whether the coalition government will exercise this power.[68]

2.43   In addition, under CA 2004 s16 and the Local Safeguarding Child-ren Boards Regulations 2006,[69] provision is made for the establish-ment of organisations called Local Safeguarding Children Boards (LSCBs), which are composed of representatives from the local

---

65   Under CA 2004 s12A, inserted by Apprenticeships, Skills, Children and Learning Act 2009 s194.

66   After the passage of the Health and Social Care Bill 2011 into law, the relevant health partners will be the NHS Commissioning Board and GP commissiioning consortia.

67   CA 2004 s10(2).

68   CA 2004 s9A, as inserted by Apprenticeships, Skills, Children and Learning Act 2009 s195(1).

69   SI No 90.

authority and its various partner bodies, and have the function of setting, communicating and monitoring policies and procedures for safeguarding and promoting the welfare of children within each local authority area.

2.44    By virtue of these provisions, the duties under CA 1989 s17 and the Assessment Framework (see para 4.25 below) are now reinforced by the general duty to safeguard and promote the welfare of all children in the authority's area under the CA 2004, and in particular s11.[70] The statutory guidance[71] to the 2004 Act deals with the application of the duty to individual cases and describes the 'key functions of an effective system' as including that:

> Following assessment, relevant services are provided to respond to the identified needs of children and to support parents/carers in effectively undertaking their parenting roles.[72]

2.45    Further statutory guidance has been issued to reinforce the safeguarding and welfare obligations owed by local authorities to particular groups of children, for instance the guidance issued in June 2009 entitled 'Safeguarding children and young people from sexual exploitation'.[73] In accordance with this guidance, action to prevent sexual exploitation 'should be proactive',[74] a principle which should underpin the way in which local authorities work with all children in need. This guidance was held to have been unlawfully breached in *R (B) v Barnet LBC*[75] where an authority had failed to put in place any services to address the risk of sexual exploitation in relation to a girl with complex needs who had been assessed as 'at very high risk of sexual abuse or statutory rape'.

70  Section 28 in Wales.
71  Department for Education and Skills, *Statutory guidance on making arrangements to safeguard and promote the welfare of children under section 11 of the Children Act 2004*, TSO, 2005. CA 2004 s11(4) provides that all agencies 'must in discharging their duty under this section have regard to any guidance given to them for the purpose by the Secretary of State'.
72  See guidance at para 2.15. For children under five, the duty to improve the well-being of young children and reduce inequalities between young children in Childcare Act 2006 s1(1) also applies. Targets in relation to this duty may be set by the secretary of state under Childcare Act 2006 s1(3); see further Local Authority Targets (Well-Being of Young Children) Regulations 2007 SI No 1415 (as amended).
73  Issued under LASSA 1970 s7 and which therefore must be followed unless there is good reason not to do so, see guidance at para 1.13.
74  Guidance para 2.3.
75  [2009] EWHC 2842 (Admin), (2009) 12 CCLR 679.

## Working together to safeguard children

2.46   The proper procedures to be followed in relation to safeguarding children 'in need' can be found in a document entitled *Working together to safeguard children*,[76] issued in its revised form in 2010 by the (former) Department for Children Schools and Families. It sets out how organisations and individuals should work together to safeguard and promote the welfare of children and young people in accordance with the CA 1989 and the CA 2004. *Working together* is split into two parts: part one contains eight chapters of statutory guidance issued under LASSA 1970 s7, which should therefore be followed unless there is good reason not to; and part two contains four chapters which act as practice guidance in relation to safeguarding children.[77] The document is supplemented by a separate piece of practice guidance focusing specifically on disabled children.[78]

2.47   The statutory guidance section of *Working together* defines safeguarding and promoting the welfare of children as:[79]

- protecting children from maltreatment;
- preventing impairment of children's health or development; and
- ensuring that children are growing up in circumstances consistent with the provision of safe and effective care.

2.48   The guidance makes clear that a wide range of bodies are subject to safeguarding and welfare duties.[80] While each of these bodies has its own role within the child safeguarding structure, all of the bodies must also meet various common standards relating to their infrastructure and governance,[81] co-operation with other bodies and

---

76   HM Government, *Working together to safeguard children: a guide to inter-agency working to safeguard and promote the welfare of children* (2010) ('*Working together*').

77   In addition chapters 3, 4, 7 and 8 are issued under CA 2004 s16 which also means that they must be complied with unless there is good reason not to.

78   Department for Children, Schools and Families (DCSF), *Safeguarding disabled children – practice guidance* (2009).

79   Guidance para 1.20.

80   These include: children's services departments (2.18–2.27), adult social services (2.18), housing authorities and registered social landlords (2.29–2.32), youth and community workers (2.34–2.35), Connexions (2.36–2.38), a range of health bodies and professionals (2.39–2.122), the police (2.123–2.133), probation (2.133–2.134), prisons (2.135–2.139), young offenders' institutions, secure training centres and youth offending teams (2.140–2.148), the UK Border Agency (2.149–2.154), schools and further education institutions (2.155–2.165) and a number of other bodies concerned with children.

81   Guidance para 2.11.

sharing of information[82] both in the assessment of children's needs and in the meeting of those needs.[83]

2.49 In relation to managing individual cases where there are concerns about a child's safety and welfare, *Working together* sets out a number of key principles which apply to work with children. These are that agencies' involvement with children must be child-centred, focus on outcomes for the child, be multi- and inter-agency in approach, engage children and families, pursue an ongoing process rather than a single event and be informed by evidence.[84] There is also an emphasis on the fundamental importance of the assessment process (replicated in other statutory guidance[85]), which should be undertaken in a holistic context, involving consultation with parents and carers in most cases, and often calling upon specialist professional involvement.[86] This process entails a decision by a local authority on what steps to take within a day of referral,[87] an initial assessment within ten working days of referral,[88] and if necessary a core assessment within 35 days.[89] Throughout this period, the local authority should be alert to any immediate protection needs.[90]

2.50 In addition, *Working together* recognises particular risks in relation to certain vulnerable groups of children. It highlights children affected by gang activity[91] and disabled children[92] as among those

---

82 Guidance paras 2.12–2.14.
83 Guidance para 2.1.
84 Guidance para 5.5.
85 See, for instance, the Assessment Framework, discussed at para 4.25 below.
86 Guidance paras 5.60–5.64.
87 Guidance para 5.34.
88 Guidance paras 5.38–5.39. Confusingly, the requirement to undertake an initial assessment within *ten* days contradicts the Framework Guidance, which stipulates, at para 3.9, that the initial assessment must be within *seven* days. This is despite the fact that para 5.38 of *Working together* states that '[t]he initial assessment should be undertaken in accordance with statutory guidance, the *Framework for the Assessment of Children in Need and their Families*'. It may be that this new timeframe was intended to supersede that contained in the Assessment Framework, since page 28 of *Working together* states that the 'timescale for initial assessments being undertaken within 10 working days comes into force on 1 April 2010', although the guidance is by no means clear on this point.
89 Guidance para 5.120.
90 Guidance paras 5.51–5.55.
91 Guidance para 6.5.
92 Guidance paras 6.43–6.48.

groups who may have particular needs.[93] In relation to disabled children, the guidance emphasises the need to give due consideration to children's wishes and feelings and draw upon the expertise of specialist disability workers in any child protection investigations.[94] There is recognition of the increased risk of abuse in this context (particularly of disabled children away from home) and a requirement that agencies promote 'a high level of awareness of the risks of harm and high standards of practice' and strengthen 'the capacity of children and families to help themselves'.[95] This brings us back to the core purpose of Part III of CA 1989 – to provide support to children and families to help them lead ordinary lives.

## Parents and child protection[96]

2.51   The Children Act 1989 confers a wide range of powers and duties on local authorities to protect children from harm, including by way of care proceedings under Part IV of the Act. This highly important subject falls outside the scope of Part III of CA 1989, and therefore beyond the remit of this book.[97] Nevertheless, in approaching a local authority for support it may be that parents of, or others with responsibility for, children 'in need' have worries about the type of intervention that an authority may undertake, especially if there is disagreement about the appropriate steps required.

2.52   In the first place, it is important to note that it would be unlawful for a local authority to use its powers under Part III of the CA 1989 in a way which is incompatible with the general purpose of this part of the legislation, which has been identified as being 'that local authorities should provide support for children and families'.[98] Both the high court and the ombudsman have recently been called upon to

---

93  Other highlighted groups include sexually exploited children (6.2–6.4), girls subject to female genital mutilation (6.14–6.19), children subject to forced marriage and 'honour-based violence' (6.20–6.31), children abused for reasons related to 'spirit possession' (6.49–6.53) and trafficked children (6.54–6.66).

94  *Working together* (2010) at 1.30–1.31.

95  *Working together* (2010) at 6.45.

96  The material for this section (paras 2.51–2.55) is taken, with minor amendments, from S Broach, L Clements and J Read *Disabled children: a legal handbook* (LAG, 2010) at paras 3.94 to 3.97.

97  For more on this topic, reference should be made to White, Carr and Lowe, *The Children Act in Practice*, Lexis Nexis Butterworths, 5th edition, 2008.

98  *R(M) v Gateshead Metropolitan Borough Council* [2006] EWCA Civ 221 per Dyson LJ at [42].

consider the interplay between the duties of local authorities to safeguard children and the statutory purpose of supporting families.

2.53      *Re A*[99] concerned two separate cases relating to the care of individuals (called 'A' and 'C' in the court's judgment: the first of whom was a child, the second an adult) with significant behavioural difficulties. As a protective measure, their parents who, the court found, provided 'devoted and exemplary care', would lock the children in their bedrooms at night to safeguard against the considerable risks posed by their night-time behaviour. The court was asked to consider whether this amounted to a deprivation of liberty under article 5 ECHR such that the local authority was thereby required to intervene. Munby LJ held that the parents' approach represented 'a reasonable, proportionate and entirely appropriate regime implemented by devoted parents in the context of a loving family relationship with the single view to the welfare, happiness and best interests' of the two individuals concerned. It could not therefore come close to engaging article 5.

2.54      In addition, Munby LJ provided general guidance as to the approach to be taken by local authorities in cases of this nature. In response to the suggestion that a local authority 'is not merely "involved" with people in the situation of A and C and their families but that it may also have "complete and effective control ... through its assessments and care plans',[100] he stated that this suggestion, which 'worryingly some local authorities seem almost to assume and take ... for granted' was 'simply wrong in law'.[101] Munby LJ went on:

> 52 Moreover, the assertion or assumption, however formulated, betrays a fundamental misunderstanding of the nature of the relationship between a local authority and those, like A and C and their carers, who it is tasked to support – a fundamental misunderstanding of the relationship between the State and the citizen. People in the situation of A and C, together with their carers, look to the State – to a local authority – for the support, the assistance and the provision of the services to which the law, giving effect to the underlying principles of the Welfare State, entitles them. They do not seek to be "controlled" by the State or by the local authority. And it is not for the State in the guise of a local authority to seek to exercise such control. The State, the local authority, is the servant of those in need of its support and assistance, not their master ...

> 53 This attitude is perhaps best exemplified by the proposition that "in the event that the parents were to disagree with the *decisions* of the local authority (which will always be based upon the opinion of relevant

99 [2010] EWHC 978 (Fam).
100 At para [50].
101 At para [51].

professionals) it would seek to *enforce its decisions* through appropriate proceedings if necessary" (emphasis added). This approach, which to repeat is not the approach of the local authority in this case, though reflecting what I have come across elsewhere, reflects an attitude of mind which is not merely unsound in law but hardly best calculated to encourage proper effect being given to a local authority's procedural obligations under Article 8 of the Convention ... Moreover, it is likely to be nothing but counter-productive when it comes to a local authority 'working together', as it must, with family carers. 'Working together' involves something more – much more – than merely requiring carers to agree with a local authority's 'decision' even if, let alone just because, it may be backed by professional opinion ...

2.55   The local government ombudsman has also made trenchant criticism of ineffective and insensitive interventions by local authorities in children 'in need' cases. In a complaint from 2008,[102] the ombudsman considered the case of a young man with cerebral palsy and epilepsy, who by the time of the complaint had turned 21 years old. Because of local authority delays in the provision of a hoist for the young man, his father had to carry him upstairs to be bathed. The local authority responded to this approach by making a referral under its protection of vulnerable adults procedures. The ombudsman recognised the hurt caused by this procedure and stated: '[i]t beggars belief that the referral was made at all.' In another case of maladministration,[103] a local authority delayed for several years the provision of suitable accommodation to a family with two seriously disabled children. During this time, the mother of the children was faced with the choice of strip-washing them in a downstairs toilet, risking serious injury by taking them to a small and inadequate bathroom upstairs or washing them with a hose in the garden. Despite its failure to provide any sufficient cleaning facilities, the local authority told the children's mother that it would be 'abusive' to wash the children outside. The ombudsman considered that the council's approach showed 'breathtaking insensitivity' and 'institutionalised indifference' and recommended the issuing of a personal apology along with the payment of compensation.

## Means of redress

2.56   As stated below (paras 2.67–2.70), the courts are most likely to intervene in a case involving a child in need by way of the judicial review

102  Case number 07 B 07665 (10 September 2008).
103  Case number 07 C 03887 (14 October 2009).

procedure. However, local authority decisions can also be challenged outside the courts: indeed, where 'alternative remedies' are 'convenient and effective'[104] there is an important presumption that these will be pursued before resort to judicial review is made. Any failure to explore alternative remedies may result in the High Court refusing permission, the first stage of any application for judicial review. Alternatively, the courts may refuse to grant any relief at full hearing if there has been no or insufficient consideration of alternative remedies, as relief in judicial review proceedings is always at the court's discretion. This section therefore discusses both judicial review and the available alternative remedies as they may apply in cases concerning children 'in need'.

## Complaints procedures under Children Act 1989

2.57    By virtue of CA 1989 s26 and in accordance with regulations passed under section 26,[105] local authorities are obliged to set up systems for considering any complaint in relation to the discharge of their functions under Part III of CA 1989, and certain of their functions under Parts IV and V of the Act,[106] with complaints able to be submitted by a parent or others with an interest in the child's welfare. In practice, this means that the local authority functions covered in this book are subject to the section 26 complaints procedure.

2.58    Consideration of a complaint proceeds in a three-stage process. The first step, where a complainant and the local authority consent, is to consider the complaint through 'local resolution', which can be undertaken internally by the local manager of the relevant service. In all but complex cases, this stage must be completed within ten working days.[107]

2.59    Where the parties do not consent to local resolution, or where the complainant is not content with the outcome of the procedure, the complaint will proceed to stage two, an 'investigation' or (in Wales) a 'formal consideration'. This will be undertaken by an 'independent person' and must be completed within 25 working days (which may be extended to a period of up to 65 working days).[108]

---

104 *Kay v Lambeth LBC* [2006] UKHL 10, [2006] 2 AC 465 per Lord Bingham at [30].
105 Children Act 1989 Representation Procedure (England) Regulations (RPE Regs) 2006 SI No 1738 and Children Act 1989 Representation Procedure (Wales) Regulations (RPW Regs) 2005 SI No 3365.
106 CA 1989 s26(3) and (3A).
107 RPE Regs 2006 reg 14; RPW Regs 2005 reg 15.
108 RPE Regs 2006 reg 17; RPW Regs 2005 regs 17 and 18 – note that there is no formal time limit in the Welsh legislation.

2.60    If the outcome of the investigation is unsatisfactory, the complainant may (in England) request the appointment of a review panel to consider the complaint. This consists of three independent panel members who must meet within 30 working days of the receipt of the complainant's request in order to consider the representations of the complainant, the local authority and any other interested parties. The panel will then, within five working days, send a written report containing recommendations to the complainant and local authority. The authority must, along with the independent person appointed in stage two, then notify the complainant as to how it will respond to the recommendations.[109]

## The ombudsman

2.61    The local government ombudsman (LGO) (in England) and the public services ombudsman (PSO) (in Wales) are charged with conducting independent investigations of complaints about maladministration and service failures by local authorities and certain other public bodies. They examine complaints relating to failures and inadequacies in decision-making or in the delivery (or non-delivery) of services, including delay, unfairness, incompetence, impropriety and other instances of fault on the part of local authorities.

2.62    Procedurally, the ombudsman will (except in urgent cases) expect complaints to be made directly to the local authority in the first instance (for example, by the complaints procedure identified above). If the complainant is unsatisfied with the outcome or if no response is made by the local authority within a reasonable time, a complaint may then be directed to the ombudsman. Normally, a complaint should be made within 12 months of the complainant becoming aware of the instance of maladministration. It can be submitted to the ombudsman over the phone or online.[110]

2.63    The ombudsman is then likely to request representations from the complainant and the local authority as well as taking further investigatory steps, such as requests for documents and site visits, if necessary. The LGO completes most investigations within three months, although complex cases may take up to a year. The ombudsman may make findings of 'no fault', 'insufficient injustice' (where the harm caused is too minor to justify continued investigation),

109 RPE Regs 2006 regs 19 and 20.
110 See www.lgo.org.uk/making-a-complaint/submitting-a-complaint (England) or www.ombudsman-wales.org.uk/en/fact-sheets (Wales).

'local settlement' (where the local authority consents to the recommendations proposed by the ombudsman) or a 'report'. It is the last of these which is likely to result in the most significant consequences, with ombudsman reports often delivering robust criticisms of local authority conduct and recommending substantial remedies, including financial compensation.

2.64    Recent examples of such reports include:

- A case involving the London Borough of Waltham Forest and a child who had been the victim of very serious abuse.[111] Although the girl had repeatedly sought help from the local authority, she had been either sent away or subject to inadequate assessments, which meant that services to which she was entitled were withheld and her schooling suffered. The LGO found maladministration causing injustice and recommended that the local authority apologise, pay £7,000 in compensation to the girl and conduct reviews of its assessments and complaints procedures.

- A case in which Liverpool City Council, in assessing the age of a girl of Cameroonian nationality who said she was 15 years old, had breached relevant guidance, ignored important medical evidence and failed to clarify uncertainties with the girl herself.[112] As a result, the council had wrongly assessed the girl as an adult and therefore deprived her of services to which she was entitled as a child over a period of 15 months, during which time she had fallen pregnant and been subject to sexual abuse. In March 2010, maladministration and injustice was found by the LGO and compensation of £5,000 was recommended, as well as reviews of the local authority's age assessment procedures.

- A case in which the London Borough of Lambeth failed properly to assess, take account of or plan for the needs of a young man who had been looked after by the local authority while a child and subsequently left its care.[113] The young man had suffered distress, frustration and uncertainty as a consequence of the shortcomings in the assessment of his needs, the pathway plans formulated to meet those needs and the information passed to his personal adviser. The LGO found service failures, failures to provide a service or maladministration which caused injustice and recommended a review of the young person's pathway plan, the

111  Case number 08 016 986 (December 2009).
112  Case number 08 005 858 (March 2010).
113  Case number 08 013 283 (May 2009).

payment of £5,000 compensation and £2,000 to be paid to a charity which had assisted him in the absence of adequate support from the local authority.

2.65   LGO reports, which are published unless special reasons apply, are not binding on local authorities but are usually complied with.[114] While challenges involving a dispute on legal issues may best be made through judicial review (see paras 2.67–2.70 below), an ombudsman is nevertheless likely to consider the relevant legal standards in examining a complaint. Where, for instance, a complaint relates to disability discrimination, the ombudsman should apply the relevant discrimination law in assessing the conduct of a local authority.[115] Any error of law in an ombudsman's decision can be challenged by way of judicial review (see paras 2.67–2.70 below).

2.66   The complaints procedures, particularly through the ombudsman, may therefore provide a child with a significant remedy in the form of a recommendation for substantial financial compensation which will normally be complied with by the public body. However, a complaint is unlikely to be a 'convenient' and 'effective' remedy in cases whether there is an *ongoing* breach (or alleged breach) of a public body's duties towards a vulnerable child and/or their family. In such serious and urgent cases the courts are likely to accept that the appropriate remedy is judicial review, as the judgments referred to throughout this book amply demonstrate.

## Judicial review

2.67   As has been indicated over the course of this chapter, local authorities are subject to the oversight of the courts primarily by means of the judicial review procedure, which permits courts to review the

---

114   See *R (Gallagher) v Basildon DC* [2010] EWHC 2824 (Admin), which reinforced both the non-binding nature of ombudsman reports and the general expectation that local authorities will act on their conclusions.

115   See, for instance, the challenge to the report of the Parliamentary and Health Service Ombudsman into the healthcare provided to six people with learning difficulties in the case of *R (Mencap) v Parliamentary Health Service Ombudsman* [2010] EWCA Civ 875 at [11]. In remitting this case to be considered again in the High Court, the Court of Appeal stated that it was at least arguable that a finding by the ombudsman of a breach of the duty to make reasonable adjustments on behalf of disabled people would in itself amount to service failure, a failure to provide a service or maladministration. This question will therefore be reconsidered by the High Court in 2011.

lawfulness of the conduct of public bodies. The senior courts[116] have the power to provide various forms of remedy in the event of unlawful action or inaction, including a 'declaration' (a statement that unlawfulness has occurred), a 'quashing order' (which quashes or nullifies a particular decision, generally requiring the decision to be taken again), a 'mandatory order' and an 'injunction' (which require particular acts to be taken, or prohibit acts from being taken), and, in very limited categories of cases, financial damages.[117]

2.68   Judicial review is particularly appropriate for cases involving potential unlawfulness on the part of a public body where a degree of legal analysis is required to resolve the dispute, or where a particular urgency exists (in which case the claimant can ask that the matter be dealt with expeditiously[118]). As stated above, if 'convenient' and 'effective' alternative avenues are not pursued prior to a claim for judicial review, the court may not consider the case. Where, however, any such alternative route would be inadequate or inappropriate, judicial review should be used. It is possible, indeed routine, for the High Court to order 'interim relief' and require a public body to act to protect a child's interests while the case waits to come before the court (which even on urgent cases can be several months). This is a very powerful tool for children and families to obtain vital services from an authority which may not be acting swiftly or at all to safeguard and promote their welfare.

2.69   An important consideration for any potential claimant is the costs necessarily involved in any judicial review claim. It remains the case that the losing party in a judicial review claim will be required to pay not only his or her own legal costs but also, normally, those of his or her opponent (generally here a local authority but also potentially a health body or one of the secretaries of state). In the absence of entitlement to funding (or 'legal aid') from the Legal Services

---

116 High Court, Court of Appeal and Supreme Court. In certain cases, the Upper Tribunal has this power; see Tribunals, Courts and Enforcement Act 2007 s15.

117 The only situation in which a child 'in need' is likely to obtain any damages on an application for judicial review is in relation to a breach of the ECHR (most likely article 8), and any such damages are likely to be modest in all but the most exceptional cases.

118 Applications for urgent consideration using form N463 are likely to need to be made in most cases involving a child 'in need' – as unless the matter needs to be considered urgently it is likely that the dispute should be dealt with by way of a complaint.

Commission (LSC), which carries with it 'costs protection',[119] costs implications may well dissuade claimants from proceeding to judicial review. However, because cases involving children 'in need' are usually brought in the name of the child, and entitlement to legal aid is generally considered by reference to the child's financial resources, legal aid may be more readily available in these cases than in other cases involving vulnerable people. Importantly, the consultation on the future of legal aid issued in November 2010 proposes to retain full legal aid funding for all judicial review applications, including those brought on behalf of children 'in need', and for community care, which will include cases brought to enforce the duties under CA 1989 Part III.

2.70    Given the complex nature and importance of any judicial review claim, advice from a specialist solicitor should be sought by any child or family who is contemplating such a step. It is also important to note that any judicial review challenge is subject to strict time-limits: a claim is expected to be brought 'as soon as possible' and, in any event, within three months of the decision under challenge, with extensions of time granted by the court only where there is a good reason to do so.[120] Although time may be extended when a child or family has not had access to specialist legal advice, and although, alternatively, a court may allow a claimant to challenge an 'ongoing' failure by a public body, there is no guarantee of either of these things happening in an individual case. Families and their advisers therefore need to be alive to the possibility of bringing a judicial review claim as soon as it appears there is a significant legal dispute with a public body – while at the same time not acting too quickly and ignoring potentially available alternative remedies. This is one of the reasons why specialist legal advice is so important at the earliest possible stage in any proposed application for judicial review.

119 Access to Justice Act 1999 s11 provides that, except in certain circumstances, a costs order against a publicly funded party shall not exceed a 'reasonable amount' in all the circumstances, having regard to the parties' financial resources and their conduct in the proceedings. For a child with no financial resources in their own name their contribution should be zero. However, there is a residual risk to any parent who has a substantial income and who acts as a child's litigation friend. Solicitors and other advisers should always highlight this theoretical costs risk to families.

120 Civil Procedure Rules 54.5. See White Book 2010 at 54.5.1 for commentary on circumstances where time is likely to be extended. Any application for judicial review made out of time should be accompanied by an application for a direction that time for the claim form to be issued be extended to the date of issue. Such a direction will often be made by the judge considering the papers either in relation to an application for urgent consideration or at the permission stage.

# Age disputes – child or not?

## Key points

- Correctly determining the age of a young person is an issue of the utmost importance, both to the young person's sense of identity and also to the support to which the young person may be entitled.
- However, determining a young person's age is in no way an exact science, and disputes regularly arise between a young person who claims to be a child and a public body (normally a local authority or the Home Secretary) who considers that the young person is in fact an adult.
- The correct approach to determining age was set down by the Supreme Court in *R (A) v Croydon LBC*. Prior to this judgment, assessing a young person's age was a matter for the local authority or the Home Secretary subject to review by the courts on public law grounds. Following *R (A) v Croydon LBC*, where a dispute arises the question of a young person's age must be determined as a matter of fact by the court.
- As a result of the Supreme Court's decision, age assessment challenges continue to proceed as applications for judicial review but the courts must engage in an extensive 'fact finding' exercise, where necessary hearing oral evidence.
- Medical evidence and documentary evidence may be relevant, but no single piece of evidence is likely to be determinative, with the courts required to determine a young person's age having regard to all the available evidence.
- The Home Office will normally accept a local authority's assessment of a young person's age, but questions remain as to the extent to which one public body is bound by the assessment of another public body.
- Current practice is that age disputes are being transferred from the Administrative Court to the Immigration and Asylum Chamber of the Upper Tribunal, exercising its judicial review jurisdiction.

## The issue and its importance

3.1   'Man or boy?' How to determine the correct age of young asylum-seekers and other migrants coming to the UK (generally, but not always, young men) has become a thorny issue for the courts, engaging judges from the High Court all the way up to the Supreme Court. As Lady Hale explained in the Supreme Court's decision in *R (A) v Croydon LBC and R (M) v Lambeth LBC:*[1]

> The problem of determining age has come to prominence with the recent increase in migration and particularly in unaccompanied young people coming to this country, some of them to claim asylum for their own benefit but some of them also having being trafficked here for the benefit of others.[2]

3.2    Determining the age of this cohort of young people arriving in the UK is important for two reasons. First, if a young person is an unaccompanied child there will invariably be a duty upon the local authority in which the child finds himself or herself to assess the child's needs and to provide the child with accommodation and support under Children Act (CA) 1989 s20(1).[3] As services under Part III of CA 1989 are only available to children under 18 and their families, the assessment of a young person's age is obviously a central issue for unaccompanied asylum-seekers claiming to be children. Secondly, if a young person's claim for asylum has been rejected, it is the current policy of the UK Border Agency (UKBA) to grant the young person discretionary leave to remain in the UK for three years or until the young person reaches 17.5 years old, whichever is the earlier, unless there are adequate arrangements to look after the young person in his or her country of origin.[4]

3.3    The first contact which a young person will have regarding his or her age will almost always be with the UKBA when the young person claims asylum. This will usually be followed by contact with the social services department of the local authority in which the young person is located. It is local authorities which have taken the lead in assessing the age of young persons, with social work assessments routinely being accepted as a correct determination of an individual's age by the UKBA.[5]

1  [2009] UKSC 8, [2009] 1 WLR 2557.
2  Judgment at [3].
3  Section 20(1) provides that 'Every local authority shall provide accommodation for any child in need within their area who appears to them to require accommodation as a result of [amongst other matters] — (c) the person who has been caring for him being prevented (whether or not permanently, and for whatever reason) from providing him with suitable accommodation or care'. See chapter 5 for a detailed discussion of duties to accommodate children under CA 1989 s20.
4  UKBA APU Notice 3/2007. See chapter 6 at paras 6.62–6.65
5  See paras 3.56–3.60 below for more details on the Home Office's policy with regards to assessing age.

3.4    For an unaccompanied asylum-seeking child the consequences of being age disputed and wrongly treated as an adult are extremely significant. Disputes over age have important implications for the ability of young people to access appropriate social welfare, health and educational support. In addition to the practical consequences and child protection risks of being age disputed, there is evidence of significant mental health difficulties associated with the fact that a young person's past and identity are brought into question.[6]

3.5    Furthermore, an age disputed child does not benefit from any of the procedures that the Home Office has put in place to ensure that children's experiences and vulnerabilities are taken into account during the asylum determination process. The application may be refused and the child detained and removed without ever having his or her age formally assessed. There is evidence that age disputed applicants are likely to be considered less credible and refused asylum as a result.[7]

3.6    In the light of the decision of the Supreme Court in *R (A) v Croydon LBC*, the question of whether an individual is a child or not is now ultimately a matter to be resolved by the courts at a fact finding hearing. This was a landmark decision because previously challenges against assessments of age were limited to grounds based on conventional judicial review principles. As of January 2011 there were approximately 64 outstanding cases of age disputed individuals awaiting the determination of their age by the Administrative Court.[8]

## The position prior to *R (A) v Croydon LBC*

3.7    The issue of how to assess an individual's age first came to prominence following the High Court's decision in *R (B) v Merton LBC*.[9] 'B' was an asylum-seeker from the Ivory Coast. He claimed to be 17 years old, however the local authority assessed him to be at least 18. In reaching his judgment and quashing the local authority's assessment of the claimant's age, Stanley Burnton J noted that there

---

6   See Immigration Law Practitioners' Association research report *When is a child not a child? Asylum, age disputes and the process of age assessment*, Heaven Crawley, May 2007, at 7.4.

7   Immigration Law Practitioners' Association research report *When is a child not a child? Asylum, age disputes and the process of age assessment*, Heaven Crawley, May 2007 at 2.4.

8   See para [4] of the Court of Appeal's judgment in *R (FZ) v Croydon LBC* [2011] EWCA Civ 59.

9   [2003] EWHC 1689 (Admin), [2003] 4 All ER 280, [2003] 2 FLR 888.

was no statutory procedure or guidance to assist local authorities in how to conduct an assessment of the age of a person who was claiming to be under 18 years of age.

3.8 The judge set out a number of principles which he considered local authorities should adopt when assessing age. These were:

a) Given the impossibility of any decision-maker being able to make an objectively verifiable determination of the age of an applicant who may be in the age range of (for example) 16–20, it was necessary to take a history from him or her with a view to determining whether it was true. A history that was accepted as true and was consistent with an age below 18 would enable the decision-maker in such a case to decide that the applicant was a child. Physical appearance and behaviour could not be isolated from the question of the veracity of the applicant: appearance, behaviour and the credibility of his account were all matters that reflected upon each other.[10]

b) The decision-maker could not determine age solely on the basis of the appearance of the applicant. In general, the decision-maker had to seek to elicit the general background of the applicant, including family circumstances and history, educational background and activities during the previous few years. Ethnic and cultural information might also be important. If there was reason to doubt the given age, the decision-maker would have to make an assessment of credibility by questions designed to test credibility.[11]

c) A social services department of a local authority could not simply adopt a decision made by the Home Office. It had itself to decide whether an applicant was a child. A local authority could take into account information obtained by the Home Office; but it had to make its own decision, and for that purpose have available to it adequate information.[12]

d) A local authority was obliged to give adequate reasons for its decision that an applicant claiming to be a child was not a child.[13]

e) Procedural fairness required those assessing age to put to the young person matters which they were minded to hold against him so that the young person had an opportunity to rectify any misunderstandings that may have arisen.[14]

---

10 Judgment at [28].
11 Judgment at [37].
12 Judgment at [38].
13 Judgment at [45].
14 Judgment at [55].

3.9    Stanley Burnton J also noted his view that although the assessment
of age in borderline cases was a difficult matter, it was not complex.
The judge remarked, 'it is not an issue which requires anything approaching a trial, and judicialisation of the process is ... to be avoided.
It is a matter which may be determined informally, provided safeguards of minimum standards of inquiry and fairness are adhered
to'. As will be seen, this view was not borne out by the ultimate decision of the Supreme Court in *R (A) v Croydon LBC*.

3.10   In his judgment, Stanley Burnton J also referred to a draft document which had been formulated by the London Boroughs of Croydon and Hillingdon, as to how local authorities should conduct age
assessments. This document was finalised as the 'Practice guidelines
for age assessment of young unaccompanied asylum seekers'. These
guidelines are now commonly used by local authorities throughout
England and Wales when carrying out age assessments.

3.11   The guidelines represent local authorities' practice and policy
when assessing age. They materially provide that:

> The task of the assessing worker is to assess from a holistic perspec-
> tive, and in the light of the available information, to be able to make
> an informed judgment that the person is probably within a certain
> age parameter. It is a process of professional judgment.
>
> Age assessments are sometimes undertaken at the port of entry and the
> asylum screening unit where a decision is required in a short period
> of time, or sometimes at a later stage. In circumstances of age uncer-
> tainty, the benefit of the doubt should always be the standard practice.
> When practical, two assessing workers is beneficial. Age assessments
> are also undertaken following the acceptance of a referral to social
> services to ascertain if the person is entitled to a service as a child.
> However, in some Local Authorities age assessments are undertaken
> on presentation when the stated age is disputed. Here the assessment
> can sometimes be undertaken over a period of time, and involve other
> professionals, for example residential social work staff, foster carers,
> doctors, panel advisors, teachers and other young people.
>
> It is very important to ensure that the young person understands
> the role of the assessing worker, and comprehends the interpreter.
> Attention should also be paid to the level of tiredness, trauma, bewil-
> derment and anxiety that may be present for the young person. The
> ethnicity, culture and customs of the person being assessed must be
> a key focus throughout the assessment.
>
> It is also important to be mindful of the 'coaching' that the asylum
> seeker may have had prior to arrival, in how to behave and what to say.
> Having clarified the role of social services, it is important to engage
> with the person and establish as much rapport as the circumstances

will allow. The process is sometimes known as 'joining'. The assessing worker needs to acknowledge with the young person that they will have had to already answer many questions, and that it may be difficult and distressing to answer some of the questions.

In utilising the assessment framework, the practitioner should ask open-ended non-leading questions. It is not expected that the form should be completed by systematically going through each component, but rather by formulating the interview in a semi structured discussion gathering information at different stages. The use of circular questioning is a useful method, as it is less obvious to the person being assessed that the questions relate directly to age, and hence may reveal a clear picture of age-related issues.

3.12   Therefore, in the light of the decision in *Merton* the position was that although a local authority was obliged to take certain matters into account when assessing a young person's age, its decision could only be reviewed on conventional judicial review grounds.[15] The question for the court was therefore in essence: Did the local authority reach a rational conclusion which took account of all relevant factors? It was not: Did the authority get the individual's age right? Authorities were therefore free to make incorrect decisions, so long as they did not act irrationally, perversely or contrary to other recognised public law principles.

3.13   The restricted scope of challenges under the *Merton* approach is best evidenced by the judgment of Collins J in the now overturned case of *R (A) v Croydon LBC and (WK) and Kent CC.*[16] At paragraph [8] Collins J stated:

Parliament has made clear that the decision is that of the relevant authority. Judges have frequently warned against the judicialisation of matters which have been left to be decided by an authority. It is for them to decide the facts which lead to a decision. It is only if they reach a conclusion of fact which is unreasonable (as Lord Brightman put it in *Puhlhofer v Hillingdon LBC* (1986) 84 LGR 385 at 413–414 in a different context 'verging on absurdity') or they fail to have regard to a material consideration that their decision can be impugned. The decision is not for the court but is for the Secretary of State or the local authority.

3.14   In the light of the fact that challenges to local authorities' age assessments were limited to a review on conventional judicial review principles, this in turn meant that where an assessment was

15   An age assessment taking into account the factors set out by Stanley Burnton J subsequently became termed as a 'Merton compliant' assessment.
16   [2009] EWHC 939 (Admin), [2010] 1 FLR 193.

successfully impugned as defective and unlawful by a young person, the remedy would be for a new assessment to be carried out by that local authority. In many cases this had the effect of local authorities carrying out multiple age assessments of individuals, each assessment reaching the same conclusion on the young person's age but for different reasons.

3.15     Prior to the Supreme Court's decision, the grounds for a successful challenge against a local authority's determination of age were varied. They included a local authority's failure to allow the young person to be given an adequate opportunity to answer points which the local authority was minded to hold against the young person;[17] an assessment being procedurally unfair because the questioning of the young person conducted by the assessors had been 'unduly hostile';[18] and a review by a local authority of its early assessment of age being defective because of its failure to take account of a keyworker's opinion that the young person was likely to be younger than his or her assessed age.[19]

3.16     There were also a number of successful challenges, which were centred upon medical evidence in support of the young person's age. The issue of the relevance of medical evidence is considered further below at paras 3.39–3.50.

## The Supreme Court's decision in *R (A) v Croydon LBC*

3.17     The whole approach to the assessment of age was transformed by the judgment of the Supreme Court in *R (A) v Croydon LBC*. The claimants 'A' and 'M' were both asylum-seekers who upon their arrival in the UK claimed that they were children. The London Borough of Croydon carried out an assessment of A's age and determined that he was in fact an adult. Lambeth did the same in respect of M.

3.18     A and M brought judicial review proceedings challenging the lawfulness of the local authorities' decisions. This was, among other factors, on grounds that: (1) the local authorities' procedure for assessing age was in breach of A and M's rights under article 6 of the European Convention on Human Rights (ECHR); and (2) whether an individual was a child or not was a precedent fact to the exercise of the local authorities' powers, which was not reviewable on

17  *R (B) v Merton LBC*, see fn 9 above.
18  *R (T) v Enfield LBC* [2004] EWHC 2297 (Admin).
19  *R (P) v Croydon LBC* [2009] EWHC 1993 (Admin).

conventional judicial review grounds but instead was a question for the court to determine for itself as a matter of fact.

3.19 In respect of the article 6 ECHR argument, it was contended by A and M that the determination of their age by social workers employed by a local authority, which had a vested interest in whether accommodation and support were to be provided to them, was not independent and impartial and therefore breached the article 6 safeguards in the determination of their civil rights. The civil right in question was their ability to access accommodation under CA 1989 s20(1).

3.20 The claim was dismissed in the High Court[20] and the Court of Appeal.[21] In the High Court Bennett J found that article 6 ECHR was not engaged as in assessing a young person's age a local authority did not determine a civil right, for the purposes of that article.[22] Bennett J found that even if a decision on age did constitute a determination of civil rights, and if it were to be assumed that social workers were not independent, judicial review proceedings provided a sufficient mechanism/procedure to remedy this.

3.21 As to the precedent fact argument, Bennett J held that the construction of CA 1989 s20(1) was such that parliament intended local authorities to evaluate the age of young persons and that 'It is not appropriate therefore for the doctrine of precedent fact to be applied in respect of an assessment, part of which necessitated determining their ages'.[23]

3.22 The Court of Appeal decided that the language of CA 1989 s20(1) did not allow the precedent fact argument to succeed because the words 'child in need' constituted a composite phrase which did not admit of being a limiting condition stated in wholly objective terms. A local authority was required to determine whether an individual was a 'child in need', a matter which required judgment.[24]

3.23 As to article 6 ECHR, the Court of Appeal agreed with Bennett J that accommodation provided under CA 1989 s20 did not constitute a civil right.[25] The court also concluded that even if article 6 were engaged, the composite process of an age assessment conducted by social workers, which could be reviewed on conventional judicial review principles, satisfied the requirements of the ECHR.[26]

20 [2008] EWHC 1364 (Admin), [2008] 2 FLR 1026.
21 [2008] EWCA Civ 1445, [2009] 1 FLR 1325.
22 Judgment at [86]–[89].
23 Judgment at [148].
24 Judgment at [19]–[34].
25 Judgment at [50]–[60].
26 Judgment at [84] and [85].

3.24    A and M succeeded in their appeal to the Supreme Court. In giving the lead judgment of the court, Lady Hale distinguished between whether an individual was a 'child' and whether they were 'in need'. In respect of the latter, this required a number of different value judgments. Lady Hale then explained:

> But the question whether a person is a 'child' is a different kind of question. There is a right or a wrong answer. It may be difficult to determine what that answer is. The decision-makers may have to do their best on the basis of less than perfect or conclusive evidence. But that is true of many questions of fact which regularly come before the courts. That does not prevent them from being questions for the courts rather than for other kinds of decision-makers.[27]

3.25    Lady Hale continued:

> The word 'child' is undoubtedly defined in wholly objective terms (however hard it may be to decide upon the facts of the particular case). With a few limited extensions, it defines the outer boundaries of the jurisdiction of both courts and local authorities under the 1989 Act. This is an Act for and about children. If ever there was a jurisdictional fact, it might be thought, this is it.[28]

3.26    Lady Hale also rejected the argument that such a decision by the Supreme Court would be practically difficult to put into effect:

> The final arguments raised against such a conclusion are of a practical kind. The only remedy available is judicial review and this is not well suited to the determination of disputed questions of fact. This is true but it can be so adapted if the need arises: see *R (Wilkinson) v Broadmoor Special Hospital Authority* [2002] 1 WLR 419. That the remedy is judicial review does not dictate the issue for the court to decide or the way in which it should do so, as the cases on jurisdictional fact illustrate. Clearly, as those cases also illustrate, the public authority, whether the children's services authority or the UK Border Agency, has to make its own determination in the first instance and it is only if this remains disputed that the court may have to intervene. But the better the quality of the initial decision-making, the less likely it is that the court will come to any different decision upon the evidence. If the other members of the court agree with my approach to the determination of age, it does not mean that all the other judgments involved in the decision whether or not to provide services to children or to other client groups must be subject to determination by the courts. They remain governed by conventional principles.[29]

27  Judgment at [27].
28  Judgment at [32].
29  Judgment at [33].

3.27    In the light of the decision on the construction of CA 1989 s20(1), Lady Hale did not express a firm view on the article 6 ECHR argument. However, she stated that she was inclined to hold that if CA 1989 s20(1) did confer a civil right, it was at the periphery of such rights, with a local authority assessment coupled with judicial review on conventional grounds, being adequate to result in a fair determination.[30] Lord Hope found that it could be asserted with 'reasonable confidence' that section 20(1) did not give rise to a civil right, whilst in his speech Lord Walker stated that he wished to leave the point open. Lords Scott and Neuberger agreed with Lady Hale's speech.

## The effect of *R (A) v Croydon LBC*

3.28    In the light of the Supreme Court's decision, whether or not someone is a child, and what their correct age is, is a matter to be ultimately resolved by the courts by way of a fact finding hearing.

3.29    In *R (F) v Lewisham LBC and others*,[31] Holman J considered how a number of age dispute claims were to proceed in the light of the Supreme Court's decision. He explained that permission to apply for judicial review was still required in age dispute cases. The judge stated:

> I cannot stress strongly enough that, as the Supreme Court has made quite clear (see paragraph 33 of the judgment of Lady Hale), proceedings such as this remain firmly proceedings for judicial review. Accordingly, in common with all claims for judicial review, permission is required before the claim can proceed. Further, in my view, the familiar discretionary grounds for refusal to grant permission may apply no less than in other cases. For example, delay or that the question is academic, or that for some other reason there is no useful purpose in the proposed proceedings. Permission must not become a matter of formality in these cases any more than in any others.[32]

3.30    Holman J formulated the following test for the grant of permission in an age dispute case:

> [T]he relevant test is: is there a realistic prospect, or arguable case that at a substantive fact-finding hearing the court will reach a relevant conclusion that the claimant is of a younger age than that assessed by the local authority and is or was on the relevant date a child?[33]

---

30  Judgment at [45].
31  [2009] EWHC 3542 (Admin).
32  Judgment at [15].
33  Judgment at [15].

3.31   In a recent judgment of the Court of Appeal, *R (FZ) v Croydon LBC*,[34] the test formulated by Holman J in *R (F) v Lewisham LBC* was reconsidered. Sir Anthony May, giving the judgment of the court, held that:

> At the permission stage, the claimant has to show that he has a properly arguable case on the facts in the light of the evidence before the court, the local authority's assessment and other relevant facts or circumstances. We are wary lest reformulation of, or discussion about, Holman J's unchallenged formulation may muddy the waters by substituting one necessarily general formulation for another.[35]

3.32   The court then noted:

> We consider that at the permission stage in an age assessment case the court should ask whether the material before the court raises a factual case which, taken at its highest, could not properly succeed in a contested factual hearing. If so, permission should be refused. If not, permission should normally be granted, subject to other discretionary factors, such as delay. We decline to attach a quantitative adjective to the threshold which needs to be achieved here for permission to be given.

3.33   Once the threshold for permission is crossed, it is now clearly established that at a final 'fact finding' hearing a court will consider more than just the assessment of age by a local authority, and instead will wish to hear evidence from the claimant, and other relevant witnesses, and consider other relevant evidence, such as medical or documentary evidence as to the claimant's age.[36]

3.34   Who is the relevant defendant for the purposes of a fact finding hearing? On first analysis this would appear to be a question with a simple answer: the local authority which has carried out the age assessment. However, it is not uncommon for individuals to move area after their age has been assessed by a local authority, most commonly because, where they are deemed to be an adult, they are provided with accommodation by the UKBA in another part of the country. In these circumstances, if the individual were subsequently accepted to be a child, it is arguable that the local authority which carried out the age assessment would no longer owe a duty to accommodate and support that individual because he was no longer in their area. If this

---

34  [2011] EWCA Civ 59.

35  Judgment at [7].

36  See paras 3.39–3.50 in respect of medical evidence and paras 3.51–3.55 on the relevance of documentary evidence.

is correct, this begs the question why that local authority should be forced to defend its age assessment in circumstances where the outcome will not result in it looking after the child.

3.35　　Nevertheless, it is the authors' view that in the absence of any new evidence in support of the individual's age, the relevant defendant must be the local authority which carried out the assessment of age. Although following a successful fact finding hearing that authority may not be responsible for providing the child with services under CA 1989, as it is that authority's assessment which stands in the way of the individual receiving CA services, it must be the relevant defendant. However, where new evidence has come to light in support of the young person's claimed age, the young person should approach the local authority in which he or she resides for it to carry out a new assessment of the young person's age, rather than bring a challenge against the local authority which initially assessed his or her age. Given that any judicial review challenge will relate to the ongoing need for services, it is likely that where the individual is challenging a local authority in whose area he or she is no longer present, the local authority in which he or she is present should be joined as an interested party to the claim.

3.36　　The standard of proof in age dispute cases is the ordinary civil standard of the balance of probability. With whom the burden of proof lies has been a more controversial issue. In *R (F) v Lewisham LBC*, Holman J thought that the burden of proof may not necessarily always be upon claimants seeking to establish their age and may depend on the facts and circumstances of the individual case.[37] In the first age assessment fact finding hearing conducted after the decision in *R (A) v Croydon*, the proposition that the burden of proof lay with one party or the other was rejected because 'the process is one of assessment'. In other words, because age was now a matter for the court itself to decide, the burden of proof was irrelevant.[38] In another fact finding hearing the court declined to resort to the burden of proof in the case, as the material before it was clear.[39]

3.37　　However, in a decision of the High Court, *R (CJ) v Cardiff CC*[40] Ouseley J held that the burden of proof in age dispute cases lay with the claimant. In doing so the judge remarked:

---

37　*R (F) v Lewisham LBC* at [16].

38　*R (MC) v Liverpool CC* [2010] EWHC 2211 (Admin) at [5].

39　*R (A) v Camden LBC* [2010] EWHC 2882 (Admin) at [35]. The court rejected the claimant's claimed age.

40　[2011] EWHC 23 (Admin), handed down on 17 January 2011.

127. ... First in judicial review proceedings it is for the Claimant to show that the public authority has erred in its duties. Second, but obviously related, it is the Claimant who is asserting that the duty is owed; the authority is not asserting a power to do something. It is not crucial but supportive nonetheless that the readier means of knowledge lies with the Claimant on this issue.

...

130. It is not for the authority to disprove the jurisdictional fact asserted by a Claimant as the basis for the duty alleged. It is for the authority to prove the jurisdictional fact which it needs to assert against a disputing Claimant in order to give it the power it exercises.

3.38    Ouseley J justified his resort to the burden of proof on the basis that *CJ's* case involved 'a stark choice' between competing cases which had been advanced.[41] However, it is the authors' view that the better view remains that reliance upon the burden of proof in age dispute cases is unhelpful, because as correctly noted in the earlier fact finding hearings, the court's role post the Supreme Court's decision in *R (A) v Croydon LBC* is one of assessment. The role of the court is to identify the claimant's age, as best it can, not to determine whether the claimant has discharged the burden of proving his or her age.

## The relevance of medical evidence

3.39    Prior to the Supreme Court's decision in *R (A) v Croydon LBC* there were a number of High Court decisions in which it was held that medical evidence was clearly a relevant factor when assessing age. In some cases, reliance upon medical evidence was decisive in the local authority's assessment being found unlawful.

3.40    In *R (C) v Merton*,[42] Davis J quashed the local authority's assessment of the claimant's age because the local authority had failed properly to assess the expert opinion of a general paediatrician, Dr Michie, which was supportive of the claimed age. In *R (I and O) and SSHD*,[43] Owen J held that in the light of an expert report from Dr Michie the Secretary of State for the Home Department had erred in his decision on the claimants' ages because he had, without good reason, preferred the assessment of the local authority over the reports of Dr Michie. At [53] he stated: 'Dr Michie's reports derived further authority from his extensive specialist expertise, and most

41  See para [82] of the judgment.
42  [2005] EWHC 1753 (Admin).
43  [2005] EWHC 1025 (Admin).

importantly from the fact that unlike the social workers he was qualified to undertake dental examinations, giving an estimate of age "accurate to within +/– two years for 95% of the population" (ie those up to 18 year of age).' In R *(A) v Liverpool City Council* an age assessment was deemed unlawful because the local authority, which had obtained its own report from a dental surgeon in order to counter a paediatric report supplied by the claimant in support of his claimed age, failed properly to consider the consequences of the dental surgeon's analysis.[44]

3.41    The high water mark of the successful deployment of medical evidence in support of a young person's claimed age came in *R (A) v Croydon LBC*,[45] a decision of a deputy High Court judge, Mr Steven Morris QC. In that case the young person had relied upon reports from another paediatrician, Dr Birch, in support of his age. The local authority had taken the position in response that, in general, paediatric reports provided limited assistance to the local authority in reaching its decision because, whilst such reports might possibly be able to give a guide as to the range of ages within which an applicant might fall, they could not assist as to where within that range the applicant fell.

3.42    The judge found that the local authority was not entitled to ignore Dr Birch's report because of a general objection, in the absence of any medical evidence to demonstrate the general unreliability of a paediatrician's report. At [31] the judge set out the following principles as to the relevance of medical evidence in assessing age, as it was then understood, by reference to the case-law which had developed:

> As regards the particular issue of medical opinion in age assessment, the current position is as follows:
> (a) Whilst it is not necessary for the local authority to obtain a medical report, a medical opinion will always be helpful ...
> (b) Reliable medical opinion on the issue can only be got from one of the few paediatricians with experience in the area, but they may be of limited help (as in that case Michie was) ...
> (c) When conducting or reviewing an age assessment, the local authority is under a duty to consider any medical report submitted ...
> (d) Where a local authority decides not to follow the views in a medical report, it is under a duty to give reasons for not following those view ...
> (e) A local authority should not 'rubber stamp' medical opinion, whether obtained by it or by an applicant: *R. v. Wandsworth Borough*

44  *R (A) v Liverpool CC* [2007] EWHC 1477 (Admin), (2007) 10 CCLR 716.
45  [2008] EWHC 2921 (Admin), [2009] 2 FLR 173. This is a different case from *R (A) v Croydon LBC* which went to the Supreme Court.

Council ex parte Banbury (1987) 19 HLR 76 at 84–85; *Osmani v. Camden LBC* [2004] EWCA Civ 1706 at para. 38(8). On the other hand, local authorities cannot be expected to make their own critical evaluation of applicants' medical evidence and should have access to independent specialist advice, if they wish to disagree *on medical grounds, Shala v. Birmingham City Council* [2007] EWCA Civ 624 per Sedley LJ at para. 19. In my judgment, this passage supports the proposition that, in such circumstances, the local authority is not only entitled, but is required to, obtain its own specialist advice.

3.43   In the light of this judgment, there was a proliferation of claims against local authorities in which individuals sought to rely upon medical evidence in support of their claimed age.

3.44   The issue of the relevance of medical evidence came before the court once again in *R (A) v Croydon LBC and R (WK) v Kent CC*,[46] which was set up as a test case on this issue. As Collins J stated at [2] the claims came before him:

> ... in order to enable guidance to be given on the proper approach to be applied by the Secretary of State or local authorities who, having made their assessment of age, are presented with a report from a paediatrician whose opinion is that their assessment was wrong. For obvious reasons, this arises when the assessment made was that the individual was over 18. The opinion obtained from the paediatrician asserts that in the doctor's view he (or in rare instances she) is under 18. I was told that there were more than 70 claims for judicial review challenging the refusal of the relevant authority to follow the paediatrician's opinion or at least to accept that it raises a doubt and the benefit of that doubt should be given to the claimant in question.

3.45   The two claimants ('A' being the young person who eventually succeeded in the Supreme Court in establishing that age is a precedent fact) sought to rely upon the evidence of Dr Birch in support of their claimed age. In response, the local authorities filed evidence from a consultant paediatrician, Dr Stern. Although directions were initially made for live evidence from the paediatricians, in fact no live evidence was given at the trial.

3.46   In dismissing the claimants' claims, Collins J made the following remarks in respect of the relevance of evidence from a paediatrician:

> 32. ... The criticisms made by Dr Stern seem to me to be cogent and, as I have said, entirely in accordance with the views of paediatricians in general. I do not doubt that her [Dr Birch's] opinion is reached following careful observations and that she is not in any way consciously seeking to favour the individual upon whom she has been asked to

46  [2009] EWHC 939 (Admin), [2010] 1 FLR 193.

report. She is able to observe some physical developments which social workers, because they are not doctors, cannot. Sexual maturity, body hair insofar as not visible when the individual is dressed and the state of his teeth are not observable by social workers. Equally, they will not normally be aware of precise height and weight. But none of these can be a reliable basis for assessing age.

33. Thus I do not think that the existence of a report from Dr Birch can generally attract any greater weight than the observations of an experienced social worker. In order to comply with the Hillingdon and Croydon guidelines, the assessments of social workers will be made by two working together and based upon interviews and observations over a far greater time period than that available to Dr Birch or indeed any paediatrician instructed by [an unaccompanied asylum-seeking child (UASC)] representative.

3.47 Thus Collins J concluded that paediatric expert reports were of no greater weight than the observations of an experienced social worker but that local authorities could not in general disregard such reports, the weight to attach to that report being a matter for the local authority.[47]

3.48 A and WK appealed the judgment of Collins J. However, before the Court of Appeal could consider the matter the Supreme Court delivered its judgment on the preliminary issue of whether a local authority's assessment of age was limited to review on conventional judicial review principles. In the light of the Supreme Court's decision that age was ultimately a matter to be determined by the courts (see paras 3.24–3.27 above), it was apparent that the case before Collins J had been determined on the entirely wrong legal basis and the decision could not stand. As a result, by consent, the appeal was allowed and the decision of Collins J was set aside.

3.49 This means that the position in respect of the relevance of medical evidence when considering a young person's age remains uncertain. In *R (F) v Lewisham*,[48] Holman J made clear his view that in the light of the judgment of the Supreme Court, the relevance of medical evidence had to be revisited. This was because in his judgment Collins J had (wrongly, as it transpired) looked at the matter through a 'conventional judicial review perspective'.[49] Holman J remarked:[50]

Where does the issue of medical evidence currently stand? As I have said, in four out of the five cases there are already reports from Dr Birch. Collins J has said in terms, in a passage quoted above, that he

47 Judgment at [3]–[37].
48 *R (F) v Lewisham LBC and others* [2009] EWHC 3542 (Admin).
49 Judgment at [19].
50 Judgment at [25].

does not think that local authorities and the Secretary of State can in general disregard such reports. If that is true of local authorities, it seems to me that at this stage in the evolution of the approach to this type of case they cannot be disregarded either by the court. As I have said, Dr Birch did not give any oral evidence before Collins J. It seems to me that, at any rate in the cases with which I am concerned and which are currently before the court, and in which there is already paediatric evidence, reliance upon it at the fact-finding hearings cannot be excluded by some direction given at this stage.

3.50   At the time of writing (March 2011) there has not been an age assessment fact-finding trial on *R (A) v Croydon LBC* principles at which a paediatrician has given live evidence. However, in a decision of the High Court, *R (A) v Camden LBC*,[51] notwithstanding evidence from Dr Birch in support of the claimant's claimed age and supportive evidence in the form of separate dental reports, the judge preferred the local authority's assessment of age. In doing so, and despite the comments of Holman J in *F v Lewisham* and the fact that live evidence from Dr Birch had not been given, the judge accepted the criticisms made by Collins J of Dr Birch in his now overturned judgment in *A and WK v Croydon LBC and Kent CC*.[52] It is therefore arguable that *R (A) v Camden LBC* was wrongly decided and that the issue of the relevance of medical evidence in assessing a young person's age has yet to be conclusively determined.

## Documentary evidence

3.51   More often than not, unaccompanied asylum-seeking children will enter the UK without any documentary evidence in support of their age – for example, a passport or identification document. This is one of the reasons that age is so often disputed for such children. However, where there is such material it may be extremely important in helping establish an individual's claimed age.

3.52   In the context of asylum appeals, in *Tanveer Ahmed v SSHD*[53] Collins J set out three principles in respect of the relevance of documentary evidence. The judge held that:

1) in asylum and human rights cases it was for the applicant to show the reliability of a document on which he or she wished to rely;

51   *R (A) v Camden LBC* [2010] EWHC 2882 (Admin).
52   At [42].
53   [2002] UKIAT 439, [2002] Imm AR 318.

2) the decision-maker should decide whether the document was reliable after looking at all the available evidence; and

3) it would only rarely be necessary to allege forgery. The failure to establish such an allegation did not show that the document was reliable; the decision-maker still had to apply the principles set out at (1) and (2) above.

3.53 Since *Tanveer Ahmed* there have been three reported decisions in the context of individuals challenging decisions as to their age, where reliance upon documentary evidence has been placed. In *R (NA) v Croydon*[54] the claimant, who was an Afghani, in seeking to challenge the local authority's assessment of his age, relied upon an ID card. In quashing the local authority's assessment of age, Blake J rejected the approach set down in *Tanveer Ahmed*. He stated:

> In the skeleton argument lodged by the defendant in this case there is reference to the approach of the Asylum and Immigration Tribunal with respect to documents generally in the case of *Tanveer Ahmed v Secretary of State for the Home Department* [2002] Imm App R 318. That submission was wisely not renewed in oral submissions by Mr. McGuire, but, in any event, I conclude that that point is not well-founded in this particular case. Unlike in an asylum case a claimant is not seeking to make out a claim to protection where the burden is upon him to establish his case. Here the local authority is engaged in an age assessment where, to some extent, the obligation is upon them to provide cogent reasons after a fair procedure as to why the claimed age, particularly where it is supported by the document that would normally be indicative of age, is to be objected.

3.54 However, in *R (Prenga) v LB Barnet*,[55] another decision of Blake J, the judge made clear that although a birth certificate or ID evidence by itself was a starting-point for the assessment of age, and, depending upon the country and the material in the document, may well be a very important piece of evidence in the assessment of age, it might not always be conclusive. That case concerned an Albanian national who had entered the UK and sought asylum, claiming to have been born in December 1992 and so aged 17, as evidenced by a document in the style of a birth certificate. However, the certificate had only recently been obtained and bore a photograph of the claimant clearly taken some years before. Furthermore, in his narrative given to the local authority in the course of two age assessments the claimant had contradicted himself on an important issue which affected his

54 [2009] EWHC 2357 (Admin).
55 [2010] EWHC 1765 (Admin).

credibility. Blake J held that, notwithstanding the birth certificate, the local authority was entitled to conclude that the claimant was born in December 1990, therefore meaning he was over 18 years old.[56]

3.55    In *R (CJ) v Cardiff County Council*[57] the claimant relied upon three documents: a residence card, a letter from the hospital in which he had been born and a vaccination card. Both parties relied upon experts who gave evidence at the fact finding hearing in support of their competing claims as to the authenticity of the documents. In reaching his decision not to accept the claimant's claimed age, Ouseley J rejected the evidence of the claimant's document expert, although he stated that this did not mean that the documents could simply be ignored. However, the judge held that the documentary evidence, of which he made no firm findings as to their authenticity, was insufficient to counter the 'strong reservations' he had in respect of the claimant's truthfulness.[58]

## The UKBA's approach to age disputes

3.56    The UKBA has a published policy entitled *Age dispute cases*.[59] This states that where an individual first comes to the attention of the UKBA and claims to be a child, it will dispute the individual's age if his or her physical appearance and/or general demeanour very strongly suggests that he or she is aged 18 or over, unless there is credible or documentary or other persuasive evidence to demonstrate the age claimed.[60] In borderline cases, the UKBA's policy is to give the applicant the benefit of the doubt and treat the applicant as a child. However, if the applicant's physical appearance/demeanour very strongly suggests that he or she is *significantly* over 18 years of age, the applicant will be treated as an adult and considered under the process instructions for adults.

3.57    If the individual's age is disputed, the individual is then referred on to the relevant local authority for it to carry out a Merton compliant

---

56  It should be noted that the claimant in *Prenga* was neither present nor represented at the final hearing of his claim.

57  See fn 40 above.

58  See paras [108] and [125] of the judgment.

59  First published in August 2007, see www.ukba.homeoffice.gov.uk/sitecontent/ documents/policyandlaw/asylumprocessguidance/specialcases/guidance/ assessing-age?view=Binary.

60  *Age dispute cases*, p4.

age assessment.[61] The UKBA's *Age disputes* policy states: 'It is [UKBA] policy to accept a local authority (in England and Wales) Merton compliant age assessment as evidence of age where we are satisfied that such an assessment has been carried out.' In other words, it is the UKBA's stated policy to defer to a local authority's decision on an individual's age.[62]

3.58    However, the policy also states that it will not accept a local authority's assessment of age in certain circumstances. These include where there is documentary evidence that has not been taken into account or the UKBA is satisfied that a full assessment had not in fact been carried out. Furthermore, where a local authority assessment has already been completed and the applicant then produces evidence of age which conflicts which that assessment, the Home Office's policy is that the case must be reviewed, although '[i]t is Border and Immigration Agency policy to give prominence to a Merton compliant age assessment by a local authority, and it is likely that in many cases that the authority's decision will be decisive'.[63]

3.59    Notwithstanding its policy, it is the practice of the UKBA to accept a decision on an applicant's age made in the First-tier Tribunal (Immigration and Asylum Chamber) in the context of an asylum appeal. This is so even if the decision of the immigration judge as to the individual's age is in conflict with an existing local authority's assessment. As a respondent to such an appeal, the UKBA is bound by the First-tier Tribunal's decision on age in the absence of a compelling reason not to follow it.

3.60    However, in assessing an individual's age, a local authority is not bound by a decision of the First-tier Tribunal on an individual's age, or a decision by the UKBA.[64] In respect of the First-tier Tribunal, it has been held that it does not have jurisdiction in an asylum appeal to make a determination of age that is binding against the world.[65]

---

61  The policy provides at p5 that in such circumstances all applicants must be served with an IS.97M form immediately after the UKBA disputes their age. This document informs the applicant that their age has been disputed and advises them of the procedure to follow in order to obtain an age assessment.

62  Page 5.

63  Page 21.

64  In respect of a decision by the UKBA, see Stanley Burnton J in *R (B) v Merton* at para [38].

65  *R (PM) v Hertfordshire County Council* [2010] EWHC 2056 (Admin) at [57].

## Transfer to the Upper Tribunal

3.61   At the time of writing, the Administrative Court has begun transferring individual age dispute judicial reviews to the Upper Tribunal,[66] which now has a judicial review jurisdiction and is empowered to hear such claims.[67] At the present time there is no ability for an age-disputed young person to originate a claim in the Upper Tribunal. A claim must still be brought by way of judicial review and issued in the Administrative Court. It will then be for the court to transfer the case to the Upper Tribunal.

3.62   The Upper Tribunal has the same powers in respect of the grant of relief as the Administrative Court. It can make mandatory, prohibiting and quashing orders.[68] It can grant declarations and injunctions.[69] It is able to award damages[70] where the High Court can, as well as award costs.[71]

3.63   Some reasoning for transferring age dispute cases was provided by the Court of Appeal in *FZ*[72] in which it stated:

> The Administrative Court does not habitually decide questions of fact on contested evidence and is not generally equipped to do so. Oral evidence is not normally a feature of judicial review proceedings or statutory appeals. We would therefore draw attention to the power which there now is to transfer age assessment cases where permission is given for the factual determination of the claimant's age to the Upper Tribunal ... Transfer to the Upper Tribunal is appropriate because the judges there have experience of assessing the ages of children from abroad in the context of disputed asylum claims.[73]

3.64   There is yet to be a reported decision of an age assessment case heard by the Upper Tribunal. It therefore remains to be seen what impact the transfer of these cases to that forum will have.

---

66  Pursuant to the Senior Courts Act 1981 s31A(3), as inserted by section 19 of the Tribunal, Courts and Enforcement Act (TCEA) 2007.
67  Pursuant to TCEA 2007 s15 and the First-tier Tribunal and Upper Tribunal (Chambers) Order 2001 SI No 2655.
68  TCEA 2007 s15(1)(a)–(c).
69  TCEA 2007 s15(1)(d)–(e).
70  TCEA 2007 s16(6).
71  Tribunal Procedure (Upper Tribunal) Rules 2008 SI No 2698 r10.
72  See fn 34 above.
73  Judgment at [31].

## Conclusion

3.65   In the light of the decision of *R (A) v Croydon LBC*, young people now have an opportunity to have the issue of their age resolved once and for all by the courts. The finality which this affords in individual cases is to be welcomed. It is hoped that as an individual can now present a range of evidence in support of his or her age, which must be weighed and considered by a court, the decision as to the individual's age will be fairer and more accurate than when such decisions rested with social workers subject only to review by the courts on public law principles. However, important issues remain outstanding, such as the weight to be given to medical evidence, in particular evidence from paediatricians. It is too early to tell whether the Supreme Court's decision will lead to a greater number of individuals having their claimed age accepted, but it must at the very least lead to a fairer procedure and more carefully considered decision-making in relation to an issue which is of central importance to a particularly vulnerable group of young people. This represents significant progress from the previous position.

## CHAPTER 4

# Services for children 'in need'[1]

*continued*

---

1   Much of the content of this chapter derives from S Broach, L Clements and J Read, *Disabled children: a legal handbook*, LAG, 2010, chapter 3 'Children's services'. The authors are grateful to the authors of that work for permitting its re-use in this context. Where content in this chapter is particularly closely related to that in *Disabled children: a legal handbook* this is specifically noted.

## Key points

- The duties under Children Act (CA) 1989 s17 are at the heart of the scheme providing support to children and families. The key tests for a child to be eligible for services (such as that they are 'in need' and in an authority's area) will generally be interpreted broadly and in children's favour.
- Services to children 'in need' are generally provided under CA 1989 s17, with the important exception that most services to disabled children are provided under Chronically Sick and Disabled Persons Act (CSDPA) 1970 s2.
- There is a duty to assess all children who are or may be 'in need' in accordance with the *Framework for the assessment of children in need and their families* ('the Assessment Framework'), the requirement being to produce either an 'initial' or 'core' assessment.
- Following assessment, a decision must be taken as to whether it is 'necessary' to provide services to the child and/or family. If that decision is positive then a duty arises (under either the Assessment Framework or CSDPA 1970 s2) to provide services to meet the assessed need.
- Support for children 'in need' can be provided by way of a direct service or a 'direct payment', a financial sum which can be used to purchase the services a child needs.
- Local authorities are increasingly moving towards 'personal budgets' for children's services – although the law underpinning such budgets remains solely that governing direct payments.
- The use of 'eligibility criteria' to limit access to children's services is problematic and such criteria will only be lawful if they are constructed with great care.
- Any services provided to children 'in need' must be specified in a care plan which should amount to a 'realistic plan of action' to show who will do what, where and when to help the child.

## Introduction

4.1    The provision of services to children 'in need' is at the heart of local authority duties towards children and families. The majority of such services will be provided under Children Act (CA) 1989 s17. However, services for disabled children will generally be provided under

Chronically Sick and Disabled Persons Act (CSDPA) 1970 s2, as discussed below.[2]

4.2    The duty to provide services to children 'in need' and their families arises following an assessment, which must be conducted in accordance with the relevant statutory guidance.[3] It is only following assessment that a local authority can rationally and reasonably decide whether or not it is 'necessary' to provide a child or family member with services, such a decision if positive giving rise to a duty to provide. Further, assessment, planning, intervention and review all have to take place in 'real partnership' with parents.[4]

4.3    Once an assessment is completed, a local authority may decide that it is necessary to provide a very wide range of services to meet the child's needs. This can include additional support to access mainstream services such as those provided in playgroups and children's centres and specialist services to meet a child's individual needs. Further, a child's needs may be met by providing services or in the form of a 'direct payment',[5] a financial allocation used to purchase services from independent providers. There are also important obligations on local authorities to secure a sufficient supply of specific services, for instance childcare under Childcare Act 2006.

4.4    This chapter is concerned primarily with the provision of services to children 'in need' by local authorities. It sets out the duties to assess the needs of children who may be 'in need' and considers the important and unhelpfully complex question of when an authority has a duty to provide services to meet the child's assessed needs. This chapter should be read alongside chapter 5, which deals with duties to accommodate children under CA 1989 s20. The specific needs of migrant children and families, in particular their needs for accommodation, are considered in chapter 6.

4.5    The duties towards children 'in need' summarised in this chapter are onerous, and local authority officers may frequently be taken aback when they are informed of the nature and extent of their duties

---

2   Detailed consideration of the duties owed to disabled children and their families can be found in *Disabled children: a legal handbook*, LAG, 2010.

3   Department of Health, *Framework for the assessment of children in need and their families*, 2000.

4   Department for Children, Schools and Families (DCSF), *Short breaks: statutory guidance on how to safeguard and promote the welfare of disabled children using short breaks*, April 2010, para 3.1. See also CA 2004 s10(3): 'In making arrangements under this section a local authority in England must have regard to the importance of parents and other persons caring for children in improving the well-being of children'.

5   Pursuant to CA 1989 s17A, see paras 4.63–4.70 below.

towards this client group. There is, however, good reason for these duties being so onerous, as they are the central legal protection given to vulnerable children and their families. Local authorities must ensure that they 'secure the provision of adequate staff'[6] to discharge these duties, and where harm results from delay or non-provision of services caused by staff shortages, it will constitute maladministration.[7] Furthermore, social workers who may be accustomed to working with children who have suffered significant harm, may have to remind themselves of the 'fundamentally different relationships with families' seeking support under CA 1989 Part III.[8] Recent statutory guidance describes partnership with parents and consultation with children on the basis of careful joint planning and agreement as the 'guiding principle' for the provision of such services.[9]

## Statutory scheme – Children Act 1989 s17 and Sch 2

4.6    The legislation governing the provision of services to children 'in need' in CA 1989 Part III[10] is supplemented in relation to disabled children by the important duties in CSDPA 1970. Part III of CA 1989 was intended to reflect the obligation under article 18(2) of the UN Convention on the Rights of the Child (UNCRC) for the state to render appropriate assistance to parents and legal guardians and to ensure the development of facilities for the care of children.[11] The CA 1989 and the related statutory guidance[12] establishes the assessment duty and also requires the provision of services where they are deemed necessary to 'secure the well-being' of the child. It further requires local authorities to make enquiries if they have 'reasonable cause to suspect' that a child 'is suffering, or is likely to suffer, significant

6  Local Authority Social Services Act 1970 s6(6).
7  Report on complaint no 05/C/18474 against Birmingham City Council, 4 March 2008 where the ombudsman referred to Birmingham's 'corporate failure to ensure adequate resourcing and performance of its services to highly vulnerable people' (para 55).
8  DCSF, *Short breaks: statutory guidance on how to safeguard and promote the welfare of disabled children using short breaks*, April 2010, para 3.1.
9  DCSF, *Short breaks: statutory guidance on how to safeguard and promote the welfare of disabled children using short breaks*, April 2010, para 3.1.
10  CA 1989 Part III is headed 'Local authority support for children and families'.
11  Speech of Lord Hope in *R (G) v Barnet LBC* [2003] UKHL 57, [2004] 2 AC 208 at [68].
12  Department of Health, *Framework for the assessment of children in need and their families*, 2002; see further para 4.25 below.

harm'.[13] For disabled children, CSDPA 1970 s2 establishes a duty to provide most of the services which they will need. An assessment carried out under the duties established by CA 1989 in relation to a disabled child should also determine whether a child is eligible for support under CSDPA 1970.[14]

4.7   CA 1989 Part III begins with section 17(1), which creates a general duty on local authorities to safeguard and promote the welfare of children within their area who are 'in need'. Section 17 is 'not just a statement of general principle' but explicitly confers a duty on local authorities.[15] The duty reads as follows:

> **17 Provision of services for children in need, their families and others**
> (1) It shall be the general duty of every local authority (in addition to the other duties imposed on them by this Part)—
>   (a) to safeguard and promote the welfare of children within their area who are in need; and
>   (b) so far as is consistent with that duty, to promote the upbringing of such children by their families,
> by providing a range and level of services appropriate to those children's needs.

4.8   It can therefore be seen that so far as is consistent with a child's welfare, local authorities must promote the upbringing of children 'in need' by their families.[16] This establishes immediately that the purpose of Part III of CA 1989 is to ensure that families are supported by local authorities to continue to care for their children. This duty constituted a 'fundamental shift' in the provision of children's services which recognised the 'valuable contribution' made by family life to a child's welfare.[17] It is only if it is not possible to provide support to families under the powers and duties contained in CA 1989 Part III in order to secure the well-being of children within their family that local authorities should consider exercising their child protection powers.

---

13  CA 1989 s47(1)(b). 'Harm' means ill-treatment or the impairment of health or development; CA 1989 ss31(9) and 105(1). Where the question of whether harm suffered by a child is 'significant' turns on the child's health or development, the child's health or development shall be compared with that which could reasonably be expected of a similar child; CA 1989 s31(10).

14  As specifically provided for by CA 1989 Sch 2 para 3(a).

15  *R (G) v Barnet LBC* [2003] UKHL 57, [2004] 2 AC 208 per Lord Nicholls at [25]. See, however, the somewhat different perspective of Lord Hope, who was in the majority, at [85]; 'It [CA 1989 s17(6)] is an overriding duty, a statement of general principle'. In the view of the authors it is hard to reconcile these two concepts put forward jointly by Lord Hope, as a duty which is 'overriding' must be more than merely a statement of principle.

16  CA 1989 s17(1)(b).

17  Speech of Lord Hope in *R (G) v Barnet LBC* [2004] 2 AC 208 at [68].

Therefore the work of authorities under CA 1989 Part III should be directed at (amongst other things) avoiding the need for care proceedings under CA 1989 Part IV by providing effective family support.[18]

4.9    As Lord Nicholls noted in *R (G) v Barnet LBC*, the language of CA 1989 s17(1) 'deliberately eschews references to particular types of services ... because the needs of children vary widely'.[19] Although the duty in section 17(1) is 'general' not 'specific' (see further para 4.37 below), it will impose important constraints on the actions of local authorities in relation to children 'in need'; see by analogy the quashing of Manchester's policy limiting the amount that could be paid to certain foster carers in *R (L and Others) v Manchester CC*[20] because of a breach of a duty to 'safeguard and promote' children's welfare elsewhere in CA 1989 Part III.[21]

## 'In need'

4.10   Under the general duty in CA 1989 s17(1), local authorities are empowered[22] to provide 'a range and level of services' to meet the needs of children 'in need'. The definition of 'in need' is to be found at CA 1989 s17(10), which provides that a child is to be taken as 'in need' if:

(a) he is unlikely to achieve or maintain, or to have the opportunity of achieving or maintaining, a reasonable standard of health or development without the provision for him of services by a local authority ...; or

(b) his health or development is likely to be significantly impaired, or further impaired, without the provision for him of such services; or

(c) he is disabled.

4.11   At subsection (11) the definition of 'disabled' for the purposes of CA 1989 Part III is given as follows:

For the purposes of this Part, a child is disabled if he is blind, deaf or dumb or suffers from mental disorder of any kind or is substantially and permanently handicapped by illness, injury or congenital deformity or such other disability as may be prescribed.

18  CA 1989 Sch 2 para 7(a)(i). See further J Murphy, 'Children in need: the limits of local authority accountability', (2003) 23 Legal Studies 103, cited in the speech of Lord Hope in *R (G) v Barnet LBC* at [68].

19  *R (G) v Barnet LBC* [2003] UKHL 57, [2004] 2 AC 208 at [29].

20  [2001] EWHC Admin 707, (2001) 5 CCLR 268.

21  In that case the relevant duty was that in CA 1989 s22(3).

22  And may be required; see 'Duty to provide services' at para 4.36.

4.12   The definition of 'in need' for the purposes of CA 1989 s17 is therefore very broadly drawn. Non-disabled children will be 'in need' if there is any 'likelihood' that achieving or maintaining a reasonable standard of health and/or development will require the provision of services by the local authority. Children with recognised physical and/or mental impairments will be 'in need' either under this definition or under the definition of 'disabled' in section 17(11), which, although outdated and lacking in respect for the 'social model' of disability, is also helpfully extremely broad. In particular, the phrase 'mental disorder of any kind' within CA 1989 s17(11) encompasses a wide range of conditions, including Asperger syndrome/high-functioning autism, attention deficit hyperactivity disorder (ADHD) and attention deficit disorder (ADD) as well as impairments such as a learning disability, mental illness or personality disorder. It will therefore be unlawful for any group of children with a particular condition or impairment to be excluded from assessments and/or services for children 'in need' by reason of their diagnosis.

4.13   The policy reason for such a broad statutory definition of a child being 'in need' is obvious, as this is merely the first hurdle that a child must clear in order to be entitled to services from a local authority. It is therefore essential that local authorities do not seek to restrict eligibility at this stage by operating exclusions in relation to assessments of particular groups of children, for instance children with ADHD. Such group-based exclusions are highly likely to be unlawful both under CA 1989 s17 itself (as a fettering of the local authority's discretion) and under the Equality Act 2010 as discrimination.[23] It should also be remembered that there is generally a low threshold for social care assessments,[24] which should be carried out if a child *may be* 'in need' (one of the potential outcomes of the assessment being a decision that he or she is not in fact 'in need').

## 'Within their area'

4.14   The wording of CA 1989 s17(1) also makes clear that the duties contained in this section are only owed to children who are 'within the area' of a particular local authority. It is, however, important to remember that the 'ordinary residence' provisions of the adult

---

23   See *Disabled children: a legal handbook* at chapter 9 for more on the Equality Act 2010 duties in relation to disabled children.

24   See *R v Bristol CC ex p Penfold* (1997–98) 1 CCLR 315 in relation to the duty to assess adults who may be in need of community care services.

community care legislation do not apply to the CA 1989.[25] Under CA 1989 s17(1), the approach is far broader and it is possible, indeed in areas such as London likely, that a child will be a child 'in need' in the area of more than one local authority. For example, in *R v Wandsworth LBC ex p Sandra Stewart*,[26] Jack Beatson QC (as he then was) held that 'within their area' meant simply that the 'physical presence' of a child within the authority's area is required.[27] In that case, the children were held to be 'within the area' of both Lambeth, where the hostel in which they lived was located, and Wandsworth, where they went to school. However, they were not held to be 'within the area' of a third authority, Hammersmith, which had placed the family outside their own area in the hostel, having done so as a temporary measure whilst making enquiries pursuant to their duties to homeless families under the housing legislation. Importantly, this was held not to have been a decision taken to avoid ongoing CA 1989 duties, otherwise the outcome of the case may well have been different.

4.15    As a result of the imperative to ensure that children 'in need' are not neglected while authorities argue amongst themselves as to which should meet their needs,[28] CA 1989 s27 permits an authority to ask another authority (or another body such as a Primary Care Trust) for assistance in carrying out its Part III functions.[29] The duty to co-operate also applies to other public bodies such as housing authorities.[30] Any authority that receives such a request has a duty to comply with it if the request is compatible with its own statutory duties and does not 'unduly prejudice the discharge of any of their

---

25  See L Clements and P Thompson, *Community care and the law*, LAG, 4th edn, 2007 at chapter 6 for a summary of the law in relation to 'ordinary residence' in particular as it applies to the provision of adult community care services.

26  [2001] EWHC Admin 709, [2002] 1 FLR 469.

27  Judgment at [23], where the concept is described as having a 'geographical or physical meaning'. See also *R (M) v Barking & Dagenham LBC and Westminster CC* (interested party) [2002] EWHC 2663 (Admin), (2003) 6 CCLR 87.

28  See *R (M) v Barking & Dagenham LBC and Westminster CC* (interested party) [2002] EWHC 2663 (Admin), (2003) 6 CCLR 87 per Crane J at [17]: 'To put it shortly, the needs should be met first and the redistribution of resources should, if necessary, take place afterwards'.

29  CA 1989 s27(1).

30  *R (G) v Barnet LBC* [2003] UKHL 57, [2004] 2 AC 208 per Lord Nicholls at [62], emphasising on the facts of one of the cases before the House of Lords (the case of A) that 'disabled children, with their special housing needs, cannot be permitted to fall between these two stools' (referring to children's services authorities and housing authorities).

functions'.[31] Considering this duty in *Sandra Stewart*, the deputy judge stated:

> In a case where more than one authority is under a duty to assess the needs of a child, there is clearly no reason for more than one authority to in fact assess a child's needs and there is a manifest case for co-operation under section 27 of the Children Act and a sharing of the burden by the authorities.[32]

4.16　The ratio in *Sandra Stewart* was applied in *R (Liverpool CC) v Hillingdon LBC*,[33] where James Goudie QC held that Liverpool's initial responsibility for a young failed asylum-seeker, AK, ceased when he was no longer within their area, having been detained and removed to adult immigration detention facilities in the Hillingdon area.[34] Once an immigration judge had concluded that AK was in fact a child,[35] Hillingdon then owed the CA 1989 duties to AK, given that he was present in their area.[36] However, when AK then moved back to Liverpool of his own volition, he again became Liverpool's responsibility and it did not matter that he had received assistance from Hillingdon to make this move.[37] As a child 'in need' within Liverpool's area who required accommodation as a result of there being no person who had parental responsibility for him, Liverpool then owed the duty to accommodate AK under CA 1989 s20(1) (see chapter 5).

## Children in custody – whose responsibility?

4.17　Particular consideration must be given to the duties on local authorities in relation to children 'in need' who are in custody. The landmark *Howard League* case[38] established that the duties which a local

---

31　CA 1989 s27(2).
32　Judgment at [28].
33　[2008] EWHC 1702 (Admin). See further chapter 5 at paras 5.28–5.29.
34　Judgment at [50].
35　See chapter 3 in relation to age assessments where a dispute arises as to a young person's age.
36　Judgment at [53]–[54].
37　Judgment at [67]–[69].
38　*R (Howard League for Penal Reform) v Secretary of State for the Home Department and another* ('the *Howard League* case') [2002] EWHC 2497 (Admin), [2003] 1 FLR 484. In this case, Munby J (as he then was) was specifically concerned with children in Young Offender Institutions (YOIs). At that time, there were 3,000 children in YOIs, around 1,000 of whom were aged either 15 or 16. Munby J stated that 'they are, on any view, vulnerable and needy children. Disproportionately they come from chaotic backgrounds. Many have suffered abuse or neglect'. Over half had been in local authority care; see judgment at [10]–[11].

authority would otherwise owe to a child, either under CA 1989 s17 or under CA 1989 s47,[39] do not cease to be owed merely because the child is detained in custody.[40] As such, CA 1989 continues to apply to children in Young Offender Institutions (YOIs), Secure Training Centres and other custodial settings, albeit that the duties operate subject to the necessary requirements of imprisonment. So, for example, a local authority could not, in the purported exercise of its powers under the CA 1989, remove a child from a YOI and place the child in local authority accommodation.[41] However, both the 'home' authority (ie the authority in whose area the child was living when arrested for the relevant offence) and the 'host' authority (ie the authority in whose area the custodial setting is located) will owe duties under Part III of the CA 1989 to children in custodial settings.

4.18    Following the *Howard League* judgment, the primary responsibility to the child lies with the 'host' authority,[42] however the obligations on the 'home' authority, for example to children who were 'looked after'[43] prior to the imposition of a custodial sentence, subsist during the sentence.[44] The *Working together to safeguard children* statutory guidance (see paras 2.46–2.50) states that 'It is important that agreed procedures between the secure establishment and the local authority ... with that establishment in its geographical area are in place outlining how to deal with and undertake child in need assessments'. *Working together to safeguard children* states further (at 11.43) that 'Where a looked after child who is the subject of a care order, meaning that their responsible authority shares parental responsibility for them, enters a young offender institution (YOI), either on sentence or on remand, the responsible authority has continuing responsibilities as a corporate parent to visit and continue to assess their needs'.

4.19    Children who were 'looked after' having been accommodated pursuant to CA 1989 s20 (see chapter 5) lose that status on entering custody, however the home authority must appoint a representative to visit all children and young people who have ceased to be

---

39  The duty to investigate where a child may be at risk of 'significant harm'.
40  Judgment at [136].
41  Judgment at [148].
42  *Howard League* case at [154].
43  See chapter 5 at paras 5.76–5.98 for the definition of 'looked after' status.
44  See *Howard League* case at [136]: 'The duties which a local authority would otherwise owe to a child ... do not cease to be owed merely because a child is currently detained'. This is emphasised by the *Working together to safeguard children* statutory guidance (see paras 2.46–2.50) which states (fn 23, p46) that 'The home local authority of a child or young person in custody retains continuing responsibility for safeguarding them and promoting their welfare'.

accommodated. The representative will be responsible for assessing the child's needs in order to make recommendations about the support the child will need whilst detained, and, in particular, the support necessary on release which could include planning for the child to become looked after again; see *Working together to safeguard children* at 11.44. See further chapter 5 at para 5.92.

## 'Specific' duties – Schedule 2

4.20   CA 1989 s17(2) states that for the purpose of facilitating the discharge of their 'general' duty under section 17(1), local authorities shall have the 'specific' duties and powers set out in CA 1989 Sch 2 Part I. In *R (G) v Barnet LBC; R (W) v Lambeth LBC and R (A) v Lambeth LBC* (*'R (G) v Barnet LBC'*), Lord Nicholls memorably described these duties and powers as a 'motley collection' and it is true to say that as a package of measures to safeguard and promote the well-being of vulnerable children they lack focus and coherence.[45] They do, however, contain important powers and duties which are frequently overlooked or ignored.

4.21   It is suggested that the term 'specific' in this context should be read as meaning 'specified' rather than read in the public law sense of being a duty owed to an individual which gives rise to enforceable entitlements; see paras 2.31–2.33 above. This is obvious from their wording which shows that the majority (though not all) of these provisions are 'general' and owed to all children in an authority's area.[46] These include:

- a duty to take 'reasonable steps'[47] to identify 'the extent to which there are children in need' in the authority's area;[48]

- a duty to 'open and maintain a register of disabled children within their area',[49] although presently this duty is routinely ignored by local authorities;

---

45   Judgment at [21].

46   As Lord Nicholls states in *R (G) v Barnet LBC* at [21], some of these duties and powers are obviously 'general in their impact on children'.

47   'Reasonable steps' in the context of CA 1989 Sch 2 means everything 'within the bounds of what is reasonably practicable'; *R v Brent LBC ex p S* [1994] 1 FLR 203 at 215C–F per Peter Gibson LJ.

48   CA 1989 Sch 2 para 1. This duty is part of the reason why the House of Lords implied an assessment obligation into CA 1989 s17 in *R (G) v Barnet LBC* [2003] UKHL 57, see para 4.24 below.

49   CA 1989 Sch 2 para 2.

- a duty to take 'reasonable steps, through the provision of services under Part III of this Act, to prevent children within their area suffering ill-treatment or neglect';[50]
- a duty to inform another authority if a child in their area who is likely to suffer harm moves or is likely to move to the second authority's area;[51]
- a power to assist a person who is causing a child to suffer or to be likely to suffer ill-treatment to move to alternative premises;[52]
- a duty to provide services 'to minimise the effect on disabled children within their area of their disabilities'[53] and to give disabled children 'the opportunity to lead lives which are as normal as possible';[54]
- a duty to take reasonable steps designed to reduce the need to bring care proceedings,[55] criminal proceedings,[56] any other family proceedings[57] or proceedings under the inherent jurisdiction of the High Court[58] with respect to children within their area;
- a duty to take reasonable steps 'to encourage children within their area not to commit criminal offences';[59]
- a duty to take reasonable steps 'to avoid the need for children within their area to be placed in secure accommodation';[60]
- a duty to make 'make such provision as they consider appropriate' for the following services to children 'in need' living with their families including:
  - advice, guidance and counselling;[61]
  - occupational, social, cultural or recreational activities;[62]

---

50  CA 1989 Sch 2 para 4(1).
51  CA 1989 Sch 2 para 4(2).
52  CA 1989 Sch 2 para 5. Such assistance may include cash payments; para 5(2).
53  CA 1989 Sch 2 para 6(1)(a).
54  CA 1989 Sch 2 para 6(1)(b). A third duty, to assist individuals who provide care for disabled children to continue to do so, or to do so more effectively, by giving them breaks from caring (para 6(1)(c)), was introduced by Children and Young Persons Act 2008 s25, in force from 1 April 2011.
55  CA 1989 Sch 2 para 7(a)(i).
56  CA 1989 Sch 2 para 7(a)(ii).
57  CA 1989 Sch 2 para 7(a)(iii).
58  CA 1989 Sch 2 para 7(a)(iv).
59  CA 1989 Sch 2 para 7(b).
60  CA 1989 Sch 2 para 7(c).
61  CA 1989 Sch 2 para 8(a).
62  CA 1989 Sch 2 para 8(b).

- home help (including laundry facilities); [63]
- assistance with travelling to and from home for the purpose of taking advantage of any other service;[64] and
- assistance to enable the child and his or her family to have a holiday;[65]

- a duty to provide 'such family centres as [local authorities] consider appropriate in relation to children within their area';[66]

- a duty to 'take such steps as are reasonably practicable' to enable children 'in need' who are not 'looked after' but are living apart from their families to enable them to live with their families[67] or to promote contact between such children and their families,[68] if, in their opinion, it is necessary to do either of these things in order to safeguard or promote the child's welfare; and

- a duty to 'have regard to the different racial groups to which children within their area who are in need belong' in making arrangements for day care and in promoting fostering in their area.[69]

4.22    A further important duty is in force with effect from April 2011 in respect of 'accommodated children', being children who are accommodated under health or education legislation and are therefore not 'looked after' (see chapter 5).[70] The duty is to 'make provision for such services as [authorities] consider appropriate' for these children, including advice, guidance and counselling, services necessary to enable the child to visit, or to be visited by, members of the family and assistance to enable the child and members of the family to have a holiday together.[71]

4.23    The 'specific' duties contained in Schedule 2 therefore significantly amplify the general duty to safeguard and promote children's welfare established by CA 1989 s17(1). However, their existence in

63  CA 1989 Sch 2 para 8(c).
64  CA 1989 Sch 2 para 8(d).
65  CA 1989 Sch 2 para 8(e). See also the duty under CSDPA 1970 s2 to arrange holidays for disabled children, discussed at para 4.53 below.
66  CA 1989 Sch 2 para 9. See chapter 2 at para 2.39 for the duty to establish and maintain sufficient children's centres.
67  CA 1989 Sch 2 para 10(a).
68  CA 1989 Sch 2 para 10(b).
69  CA 1989 Sch 2 para 11.
70  'Accommodated' children are those children for whom the local authority has received a notification under CA 1989 s85 or s86 from another agency that is providing the child with accommodation.
71  CA 1989 Sch 2 para 8A, inserted by Children and Young Persons Act 2008 s19.

no way undermines the broad and purposive interpretation of the general duty in section 17(1), which essentially empowers (and may, depending on the facts of the case, require) a local authority to do *anything* which it considers is necessary to safeguard and promote the welfare of children 'in need' in its area. Further, as with the general duty under CA 1989 s17(1), the 'specific' duties in the Schedule can only be enforced in relation to an individual child once an authority has decided that it is 'necessary' to provide the service in question. Such a judgment can only be rationally and reasonably exercised when it is informed by the outcome of an assessment.

## Duty to assess[72]

4.24    Effective assessment is an essential prerequisite to the provision of appropriate services and support to children 'in need'. The purpose of an assessment is to provide the understanding necessary for appropriate planning and action.[73] As a matter both of law and of common sense, authorities must ensure a child's needs are properly understood before any attempt is made to produce a care plan for the child; see, for example, *R (LH and MH) v Lambeth LBC*.[74] Although CA 1989 contains no explicit duty on local authorities to assess the needs of children 'in need' and their families,[75] the House of Lords in *R (G) v Barnet LBC and others*[76] held that there is such a specific obligation implied in CA 1989 s17, read with Sch 2.[77] Lord Hope referred

---

72    The content in this section derives from the assessment section of *Disabled children: a legal handbook* at paras 3.13–3.24. A number of paragraphs are reproduced here verbatim or with minor amendments.

73    *Framework for the assessment of children in need and their families*, see fn 79 below.

74    [2006] EWHC 1190 (Admin), (2006) 9 CCLR 623.

75    There is such an express duty to assess in the primary legislation for adult social care; see NHS and Community Care Act 1990 s47.

76    [2003] UKHL 57: the view was expressed by Lord Hope, Lord Nicholls and Lord Scott and influenced in part by the requirement in CA 1989 Sch 2 para 1 that 'Every local authority shall take reasonable steps to identify the extent to which there are children in need within their area'. See chapter 6 at paras 6.32–6.40 for further discussion of the decision in *R (G) v Barnet LBC* in the context of migrant families without accommodation.

77    See speeches of Lords Nicholls, Scott and Hope. The issue in *R (G) v Barnet LBC* was whether CA 1989 s17 created a specific duty to provide services, in particular accommodation. Lord Nicholls was in the minority who held that such a duty did arise; however, his view that there was also a duty to assess was shared by Lord Hope and Lord Scott, who were in the majority.

to CA 1989 Sch 2 para 3, which allows a local authority to assess the needs of a child who appears to be in need at the same time as any assessment under CSDPA 1970 and Education Act 1996 Part IV (a special educational needs assessment). Lord Hope stated that compliance with this duty 'will involve assessing the needs of each child who is found to be in need in their area as paragraph 3 [of CA 1989 Sch 2] makes clear'.[78]

4.25    Any lingering doubt as to whether there is a duty to assess the needs of children who are or may be 'in need' is resolved by the relevant statutory guidance, *Framework for the assessment of children in need and their families* ('the Assessment Framework')[79] which requires local authorities to undertake assessments adopting a child- and family-centred approach. The Assessment Framework is statutory guidance (see para 2.8 above) issued under Local Authority Social Services Act (LASSA) 1970 s7 and as such children's services departments are bound to follow it unless there is good reason not to do so.[80] It is over 100 pages in length and has annexed to it model care plans which themselves occupy 40 pages. The Assessment Framework is the product of considerable research and seeks to ensure that social workers when undertaking an assessment address all aspects of the child's life. Its purpose is therefore to ensure that provision for children in need is not arbitrary or left to chance. As it states, assessment requires 'a systematic approach which ... discriminates effectively between different types and levels of need'.[81] The Assessment Framework states further that its primary purpose is to 'improve outcomes for children in need'.[82]

4.26    In the following section we detail the duties of local authorities in relation to assessment. There are, however, some very basic principles which should underpin all assessments of children 'in need' and their families:

- assessments should be needs-led rather services-led; in other words, the assessment must objectively identify a child's needs rather than shaping the description of those needs around available services;

---

78  Judgment at [77].
79  Department of Health, Department for Education and Employment and Home Office, *Framework for the assessment of children in need and their families* (policy guidance), TSO, 2000: very similar guidance has been issued in Wales by the Welsh Assembly, *Framework for assessing children in need and their families*, TSO, 2001, although in this chapter, reference is made to the English guidance.
80  *R v Islington LBC ex p Rixon* (1997–98) 1 CCLR 119, 123 J–K.
81  Assessment Framework at 2.1.
82  Preface at para xi.

- any assessment must be a genuinely participatory process conducted in partnership with all the children and adults concerned;[83]
- assessments should adopt a 'social model' of disadvantage, identifying first which barriers inhibit the child and family living an 'ordinary' life and only then what can be done by statutory agencies and others to tackle these problems;[84]
- assessments must be holistic, both in terms of looking at the 'whole child' but also in taking account of the needs of the whole family and all the individuals within it. It is important to note that pursuant to CA 1989 s17(3), services may be provided to any member of a child's family, if they are provided with a view to safeguarding or promoting the child's welfare. This emphasises the importance of considering the child's needs in the family context, where possible;
- agreed provision or arrangements following assessment need not necessarily take the form of what are usually seen as 'social care' services;[85]
- assessments should adopt an outcome focus. The professional, together with the children and adults in the family, should identify a range of outcomes that are important to help the family to live a more 'ordinary' life (particularly in relation to disabled children) or will promote positive outcomes. All involved should then agree on the provision that could make those outcomes happen.[86] The effectiveness of any intervention is judged on the extent to which the identified outcomes are achieved;
- assessments should be undertaken and provision put in place at the earliest opportunity and children and families should not have to wait for services, particularly once they have been assessed as necessary. Early intervention is recognised to be critically important in order to avoid families reaching crisis point;[87] and

83  See Assessment Framework at para 3.41 for the obligations to involve children 'in need' in assessments concerning them.
84  See, for example, Department for Education and Skills, *Together from the start: practical guidance for professionals working with disabled children (birth to third birthday) and their families*, 2003.
85  Department of Health, *Carers and disabled children act: practice guidance*, TSO, 2001.
86  See, for example, Department of Health, *Carers and disabled children act. practice guidance*, TSO, 2001; J Cavet and P Sloper, 'Participation by disabled children in individual decisions about their lives and in public decisions about service development', *Children and society* 18, 278–290, 2004.
87  The preface to the Assessment Framework at [xi] states that 'early intervention is essential to support children and families before problems ... escalate into crisis or abuse'.

- assessment should not be seen as a one-off event, but should be repeated as required to reflect children's growth and development and their changing family circumstances. However, it is essential to avoid the burden that unnecessary and repetitious assessments imposes on children and families.

## Assessments – minimum requirements

4.27    The Assessment Framework sets out mandatory requirements of the assessment process, described as the first stage in helping vulnerable children,[88] which include the following:[89]

- A decision as to whether to assess should be made within *one working day* of a referral being received. A 'referral' is defined as a request for services to be provided, and may be made by the family, a professional or indeed anyone involved in or concerned about the care of a child. A decision following a referral may be to take no action, but this remains a decision and should be recorded as such. All decisions should be communicated, with reasons, to the referrer, the parents or caregiver and the child, if appropriate (Assessment Framework, para 3.8).

- If there is a need to gather more information, an initial assessment must be completed *within a maximum of seven working days* (although see para 2.49 in relation to the extension of this timescale to 10 workings days by more recent guidance). An initial assessment can be brief if the child's circumstances allow, but must address all the 'dimensions' set out in the Assessment Framework (see para 4.25 below). It should determine whether the child is in need, the nature of any services required, who will provide these services and within what timescales. It should also state whether a further, more detailed core assessment should be undertaken. As part of any initial assessment, the child should be seen[90] (Assessment Framework, paras 3.9–3.10).

- A core assessment is an in-depth assessment which 'addresses the central or most important aspects of the needs of a child'.

---

88  Assessment Framework at para 3.1.
89  This summary is adapted from the summary of the assessment process in *Disabled children: a legal handbook* at 3.15.
90  The authors would contend that any assessment where the child is not seen is almost certain to be held to be unlawful if challenged in the courts, absent exceptional circumstances.

Although led by children's services, it will invariably involve other agencies, for example in the case of disabled child most likely the Primary Care Trust.[91] The conclusion of a core assessment should involve analysis of the findings to inform planning, case objectives and service provision. The entire process should be completed within a *maximum of 35 working days* (from the date the initial assessment ended). Appropriate services should be provided while awaiting the completion of the core assessment (Assessment Framework, para 3.11).

- At the conclusion of the assessment the child or the parent should be asked to record their views and comment on the assessment (Assessment Framework, para 3.13).

- Assessments must be 'ecological' in that 'an understanding of a child must be located within the context of the child's family (parents or caregivers and the wider family) and of the community and culture in which he or she is growing up' (Assessment Framework, para 1.39).

- If there are concerns about neglect, maltreatment or any other risk of significant harm, these concerns need to be addressed through the 'section 47 enquiry' route prescribed in the Assessment Framework at paras 3.15–3.19. It is essential to note that if these concerns are unfounded and there is no risk of significant harm to the child, the case must progress through the child 'in need' route – see the flowchart set out in the Assessment Framework at figure 5, p35.

- Direct work with the child is 'an essential part of assessment'. Assessments of disabled children or other children whose needs are more subtle, profound or complex may therefore require more preparation, more time and potentially specialist expertise in communication (Assessment Framework, para 3.41[92]).

4.28 This obligation to engage with the child in the assessment process is reinforced by CA 1989 s17(4A),[93] which requires an authority to ascertain and give due consideration to a child's wishes and feelings before deciding what (if any) services to provide to that child.[94] The

---

91 Or, once the Health and Social Care Bill 2011 is enacted, the relevant GP commissioning consortia.
92 Assessment Framework, para 3.128.
93 As inserted by CA 2004 s53.
94 See also *CF v SSHD and another* [2004] EWHC 111 at [158] on the ECHR obligation to engage with children.

High Court has stressed that even if a disabled person was felt to be 'completely' prevented from communicating their wishes and feelings, the assessors had a duty to ascertain those wishes and feelings by any possible means.[95] In the context of the provision of residential accommodation, a child's wishes should normally be determinative of a choice between two otherwise equally suitable placements.[96] In *R (CD) v Isle of Anglesey*[97] a care plan which proposed that a severely disabled girl should remain at a residential school for further nights was held to be unlawful primarily because it ran contrary to the child's wishes and feelings without sufficient consideration having been given to whether those wishes and feelings could be complied with through an alternative course. The Assessment Framework (para 3.42) sets out the five 'critical components' of direct work with children; seeing, observing, engaging, talking and activities. In any given case it may be necessary for *all* these components to have been in place for the assessment to be in compliance with the guidance and thereby lawful.

4.29    The assessment process can best be represented in the form of a triangle or pyramid with three 'domains', with the child's welfare at the centre.[98] Both an initial assessment and a core assessment must cover the three 'domains' and 20 'dimensions' set out in the Assessment Framework. The 'domains' are:

1) the child's developmental needs;
2) parenting capacity; and
3) family and environmental factors.[99]

Important 'dimensions' within these domains are likely to include health, education, emotional and behavioural development and self-care skills (child's developmental needs), ensuring safety (parenting capacity) and housing, family's social integration and community resources (family and environmental factors). 'Involving disabled children in the assessment process' is also listed as a separate

---

95   *R (A and B) v East Sussex CC* [2003] EWHC 167 (Admin), (2003) 6 CCLR 194.
96   *R (Twomey) v Calderdale MBC* [2004] EWHC 1998 (Admin), (2005) 8 CCLR 101.
97   [2004] EWHC 1635, (2004) 7 CCLR 589.
98   Assessment Framework, fig 2, p17 and para 2.2.
99   The needs of parents can be recorded under the dimension of family functioning within the Assessment Framework; see DCSF, *Short breaks: statutory guidance on how to safeguard and promote the welfare of disabled children using short breaks*, April 2010 at para 3.14. This supplements the duty to carry out carer's assessments for parent carers of children 'in need'; see *Disabled children: a legal handbook* at chapter 8.

'domain' under family and environmental factors, demonstrating the importance of a genuinely participatory approach to assessment, including assessments of children with significant communication or other impairments.

4.30    The Assessment Framework is silent as to precisely when authorities should move from an initial assessment to a core assessment. The presumption seems to be that if a child has needs which require the involvement of more than one agency, then a core assessment should be carried out – because a central point of a core assessment is the multi-agency approach it entails. However, as even an initial assessment requires a consideration of the three 'domains' and 20 'dimensions' and must result in a care plan[100] (see paras 4.87–4.92 below), there may be little practical difference between the outcome of these different types of assessment – unless the child's needs are such that other agencies should be involved in the provision of services to them.

4.31    The Assessment Framework is a very prescriptive document and there is an obvious danger that form may trump substance – that is, that a document which has all the correct headings for the different 'dimensions' may be produced but there may still be no proper assessment of the child's needs. This is the opposite of the intention of the Assessment Framework and any such document will be unlawful. What is therefore important is not that the assessment *looks* like an initial or core assessment, but that it carefully and accurately sets out and evaluates all the child's needs so that a proper decision can be made as to what services (if any) are required to be provided to the child and/or family to meet those needs (see para 4.36 below for the duty to provide services to meet assessed needs).

## Assessment – key case-law

4.32    The assessment duties under the Assessment Framework have been the subject of significant litigation, which has reinforced their nature as being duties of substance rather than form. In *R (AB and SB) v Nottingham City Council*[101] it was held that a failure by an authority to

---

100  Although it is possible for the 'plan' at the end of the initial assessment to be to complete a 'core assessment', the assessment should still identify whether, and if so, what services are required pending completion of that assessment. This is a necessary requirement of the plan being 'realistic'; see Assessment Framework at para 4.1.

101  [2001] EWHC 235 (Admin), (2001) 4 CCLR 294 at 306G–I.

have in place a 'systematic approach' involving collaboration between all relevant agencies so as to achieve a full understanding of the child in his or her family and community context was unlawful.[102] A failure to achieve this in relation to a core assessment was held to be an 'impermissible departure from the guidance'. The High Court held further that at the end of the assessment process 'It should be possible to see what help and support the child and family need and which agencies might be best placed to give that help'. The court further made clear in *R (G) v Nottingham CC*[103] that 'assessment goes beyond mere identification of needs; it involves analysis and evaluation of the nature, extent and severity of the child's needs'.[104] In *R (S) v Sutton LBC*[105] the court found that the assessment was 'vague and unsubstantiated' and that there was not a 'realistic plan of action' as required by the Assessment Framework (see para 4.87 below).

4.33　　The High Court has also established that assessments must address foreseeable future needs as well as present needs; *R (K) v Manchester*.[106] This will be particularly important for children who are scheduled to come out of custody and will require local authority assistance, including accommodation, on their release. It will be unlawful for an authority to wait to conduct an assessment of a child in custody until after they are released.[107] Instead, the 'home' and 'host' authorities should co-operate to ensure that the child's needs are assessed during their sentence and a 'realistic plan of action' is put in place to ensure that these needs are met both during their time in custody and upon release.

4.34　　A failure to carry out a lawful assessment according to the Assessment Framework may result in the court requiring that a new assess-

---

102　Judgment at [41].

103　[2008] EWHC 400 (Admin), (2008) 11 CCLR 280.

104　Judgment at [36].

105　[2007] EWHC 1196 (Admin), [2007] 2 FLR 849.

106　[2006] EWHC 3164, (2007) 10 CCLR 87.

107　The *Working together to safeguard children* statutory guidance (see paras 2.46–2.50) states (at 11.39) that 'Continuity of services when children and young people transfer into and out of the secure estate is a vital element of good safeguarding practice and good resettlement planning. This includes ensuring that young people have suitable supported accommodation, help with mental health and substance misuse issues and with identifying appropriate education, training or employment'. It should of course be remembered that the usual requirement for an initial assessment to be completed in seven working days applies to children in custody. See further paras 5.129–5.134 in relation to the National Standards for youth justice.

ment be undertaken.[108] A failure to involve a child in his or her assessment may be sufficient on its own to render the process unlawful. Equally, in *R (J) v Caerphilly CBC*,[109] under the heading 'The problem of the un-cooperative child', Munby J (as he then was) held that severely challenging behaviour exhibited by a young man did not absolve the authority of its duties to undertake the required assessment and care planning process (in that case to produce a 'pathway plan' for a care leaver, in relation to which see paras 7.60–7.66 below). Thus even where a child refuses to engage with the assessment process the authority must do its best to comply with its statutory duties to the child.

4.35    Since the Assessment Framework was published, there has been an attempt by central and local government to move away from detailed assessments of children 'in need' towards a more flexible approach, often using what has been termed the Common Assessment Framework (CAF).[110] The policy behind this is to streamline the assessment process for the benefit of all concerned. While such an approach may have practical advantages, the fundamental legal duty towards children 'in need' is to assess their needs in a manner consistent with the Assessment Framework. If the needs of children and families are met while adopting a less rigorous approach, this may be acceptable in practice – although this itself begs the question as to whether the needs will be properly identified without a full and lawful assessment. However, any authority that neglects its assessment duty where a child or family is less than happy with the outcome is likely to find itself criticised by the High Court and potentially required by a mandatory order to conduct a lawful initial or core assessment.

---

108  *R (G) v Barnet LBC* per Lord Nicholls at [32].

109  [2005] EWHC 586 (Admin), (2005) 8 CCLR 255. This case is discussed in detail in chapter 7 – see, for example, paras 7.40–7.41.

110  Department for Children, Schools and Families (2006), Common Assessment Framework. The recent statutory guidance on short breaks for disabled children (see para 4.62) suggests (at 3.7) that a CAF can 'form the basis' for an initial assessment. While this is no doubt correct as a proposition of law it is hard to see what benefit could be derived from completing a CAF rather than simply completing an initial assessment in the first instance – particularly given the overriding requirement to provide necessary support to children 'in need' without undue delay.

## Duty to provide services[111]

4.36   There is an expectation in the law and guidance that where children are assessed as having substantial needs, these needs will be met through the provision of services. However, and particularly in the current context of significant public spending cuts, it is important for there to be clarity as to precisely when there is an enforceable *duty* on an authority to meet need following assessment.

4.37   Both CA 1989 s17 and the specific duties subsequent to this general duty contained in Schedule 2 clearly reinforce this general expectation that assessed needs will be met. However, the House of Lords held in *R (G) v Barnet LBC* that the duty under CA 1989 s17 was a 'general' duty (see paras 2.31–2.33 in relation to different types of duties) and on its own could not require the provision of services to a child 'in need'. The majority held (3–2) that the correct analysis of CA 1989 s17(1) was that it set out duties of a general character which were intended to be for the benefit of all children 'in need' in the local authority's area. As Lord Hope stated, a child 'in need' is eligible for the provision of services under CA 1989 s17(1), 'but he has no absolute right to them'.[112] This is despite the force of the dissenting judgment of Lord Nicholls, who suggested that:

> the duty to promote the welfare and upbringing of all [children 'in need'] makes little sense unless it is a duty in respect of the welfare and upbringing of each such child. Indeed, if this were not so section 17(1) would be a poor sort of additional general duty.[113]

4.38   Although all three of the cases heard by the House of Lords concerned requests for the provision of accommodation pursuant to CA 1989 s17(6), as a result of the *R (G) v Barnet LBC* judgment any specific individual duty to provide any type of service to children 'in need' must now be found elsewhere than on the face of CA 1989 s17. The source of this duty for most children is the Assessment Framework, although for disabled children the duty is generally under CSDPA 1970 s2, as discussed below.

4.39   For all children 'in need', the Assessment Framework requires services to be provided if an initial or core assessment demonstrates that such services are necessary to 'secure the wellbeing of the child

---

111  The content of this section derives from the equivalent section of *Disabled children: a legal handbook* at paras 3.25–3.77.

112  Judgment at [85].

113  *R (G) v Barnet LBC* [2003] UKHL 57, [2004] 2 AC 208 at [28].

or young person'. This is demonstrated by para 4.1 of the Assessment Framework (emphasis added):

> The conclusion of an assessment should result in:
> - an analysis of the needs of the child and the parenting capacity to respond appropriately to those needs within their family context;
> - identification of whether and, if so, where *intervention will be required to secure the wellbeing of the child or young person*;
> - a *realistic plan of action (including services to be provided)*, detailing who has responsibility for action, a timetable and a process for review.

4.40 Under the Assessment Framework, therefore, the essential question that governs whether a duty arises to provide a service to a child 'in need' is whether intervention is necessary 'to secure the well-being of the child'. It is for the authority to exercise its judgment in answering this question. However, the language of the Assessment Framework, read with the general duty under CA 1989 s17, makes plain that if that judgment falls in favour of services being necessary there is then no *discretion* – the services must be provided. As a matter of public law, that judgment must be applied rationally, reasonably and fairly and with proper regard to all the relevant evidence and considerations.

4.41 It is important to note that although the Assessment Framework featured in the argument before the House of Lords in *R (G) v Barnet LBC*, its provisions were not addressed in the speeches of Lords Hope, Millett and Scott who held that CA 1989 s17(1) on its own did not impose specific individual duties. Furthermore, the majority judgments do not consider the implications of the safeguarding and welfare duties under CA 2004 ss10 and 11[114] or indeed the child's rights under relevant international conventions read through the prism of the Human Rights Act 1998.[115] It therefore remains open to courts to find, as they have routinely done (see below), that intervention is required to 'secure the well-being of the child' and to order an authority that has failed to put in place a 'realistic plan of action' to provide the necessary services.

4.42 It is centrally important here not to confuse the decision that a need must be met with the decision on the *way* to meet the need. For example, a local authority may conclude that there is a need for

---

114 See further paras 2.36 and 2.42 above.
115 Most obviously article 8 of the European Convention on Human Rights (see paras 2.14–2.19 above) and the UN Convention on the Rights of the Child (see paras 2.24–2.27 above).

a child and his or her carers to have a short break from each other. This need can be met in a variety of ways – for example, by way of a sitting service in the child's home, by the child attending a day service or activity away from the home, and so on. The decision that intervention is required (and hence that the duty to provide services arises) does not mandate that any particular service should follow. The nature and extent of the service required to meet an assessed need is a further question upon which the authority must exercise its judgment – but again, it has no discretion *not* to provide a service or to provide less than has been assessed as necessary to secure the child's well-being.

4.43    A suggested overview of how authorities should approach the service provision decision in relation to an individual child 'in need' is set out in the flowchart at figure 1.[116] The specific duty to meet the needs of disabled children under CSDPA 1970 s2 is discussed below at paras 4.46–4.53. Duties to accommodate children under CA 1989 s20 are dealt with in chapter 5. See also paras 4.54–4.62 below in the context of residential short breaks.

4.44    Situations where a child's needs require the provision of accommodation will be relatively infrequent. Much more frequently, the local authority will be under a duty to provide services under the Assessment Framework (for non-disabled children) or CSDPA 1970 s2 (for disabled children). Whether it is 'necessary' to provide a service to secure an individual child's well-being is an entirely case-specific decision for the authority to make, subject always to the general public law requirements to act rationally, reasonably and fairly, to take account of all relevant considerations, and so forth.

4.45    The more severe the consequences of not meeting a need, the more 'anxiously' will the courts and the ombudsmen scrutinise the reasons given by the council for not responding to that need, any actions taken in trying to meet the needs and the process by which the council arrived at its decision. In addition, where a fundamental human right is likely to be violated by a failure to provide support – such as, in particular, the right to respect for personal dignity or family life under article 8 of the ECHR – the 'positive obligations' of the state may mean that an authority has no choice but to meet its general duty and provide the service; see paras 2.16 and 2.18 above.

116 See *Disabled children: a legal handbook* at pp80–81 for the original version of this diagram in relation to the operation of the service provision decision-making process in relation to disabled children. The authors are particularly grateful to the authors of that work for permission to reproduce this diagram in its amended form.

# Figure 1: Assessment and service provision decision – stages and questions

## Assessment

If a child presents who may be 'in need', the local authority must undertake an assessment and identify what needs for support or services the child and/or the family have (see paras 4.24–4.35 above).

Following the assessment, the local authority must decide which of the various needs that have been identified it is 'necessary' to respond to – ie, where 'intervention will be required to secure the child's wellbeing' (see para 4.39 above). If it is accepted that intervention is required, the nature and extent of this intervention must then be set out in a care plan, which must constitute a 'realistic plan of action, including services to be provided'.

## Service provision

If the local authority decides that support is 'necessary', then the following questions should be asked in sequence:

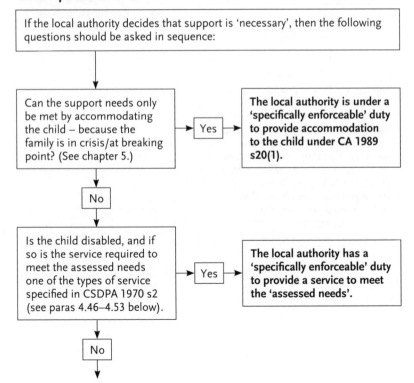

Can the support needs only be met by accommodating the child – because the family is in crisis/at breaking point? (See chapter 5.)

→ Yes → The local authority is under a 'specifically enforceable' duty to provide accommodation to the child under CA 1989 s20(1).

No

Is the child disabled, and if so is the service required to meet the assessed needs one of the types of service specified in CSDPA 1970 s2 (see paras 4.46–4.53 below).

→ Yes → The local authority has a 'specifically enforceable' duty to provide a service to meet the 'assessed needs'.

No

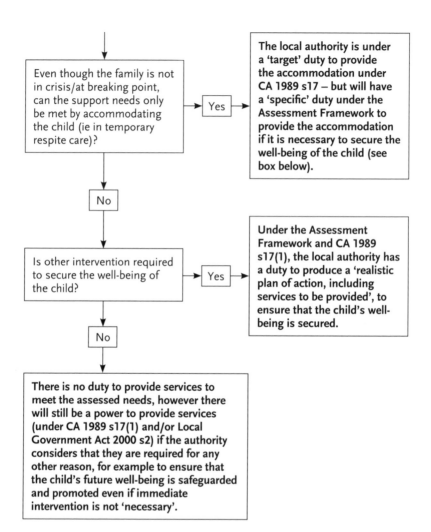

Even though the family is not in crisis/at breaking point, can the support needs only be met by accommodating the child (ie in temporary respite care)?

Yes → The local authority is under a 'target' duty to provide the accommodation under CA 1989 s17 – but will have a 'specific' duty under the Assessment Framework to provide the accommodation if it is necessary to secure the well-being of the child (see box below).

No ↓

Is other intervention required to secure the well-being of the child?

Yes → Under the Assessment Framework and CA 1989 s17(1), the local authority has a duty to produce a 'realistic plan of action, including services to be provided', to ensure that the child's well-being is secured.

No ↓

There is no duty to provide services to meet the assessed needs, however there will still be a power to provide services (under CA 1989 s17(1) and/or Local Government Act 2000 s2) if the authority considers that they are required for any other reason, for example to ensure that the child's future well-being is safeguarded and promoted even if immediate intervention is not 'necessary'.

## Services under the CSDPA 1970[117]

4.46  As noted above, most services to disabled children will be provided not under CA 1989 s17, but under CSDPA 1970 s2. If a service can be provided under either CA 1989 or CSDPA 1970, then the settled legal position is that it is provided under CSDPA 1970.[118] In essence, the reason for this is that the more enforceable duty under CSDPA 1970 'trumps' the lesser duty under CA 1989. This prevents parliament's intention to create a specific duty to provide services being undermined by any purported reliance by a local authority on a more general provision.[119]

4.47  As a matter of law, the relationship between CA 1989 and CSDPA 1970 is perplexing and complex. Thankfully this is a technical complexity that is not of relevance in practice. The difficulty arises from the link between CSDPA 1970 s2(1) and National Assistance Act (NAA) 1948 s29, one of the key legislative provisions in relation to adult social care. CSDPA 1970 s2(1) states that any services provided under that section are to be provided in the 'exercise of [the authority's] functions' under NAA 1948 s29. In relation to disabled children, this raises two difficulties. The first is that although services under CSDPA 1970 s2 can be provided to disabled children,[120] services under NAA 1948 s29 can only be provided to disabled adults. The second concerns the fact that the duty to provide services under NAA 1948 s29 is generally considered to be a 'target' duty, whereas the duty to provide under CSDPA 1970 s2 has been held to be 'specifically enforceable' (see paras 2.31–2.33 above). In a series of cases the courts have sought to make sense of these problems[121] and in *R (Spink) v Wandsworth LBC*[122] the Court of Appeal held that: (1) services provided to children under CSDPA 1970 s2 are in fact provided by a local authority in the 'exercise of their functions' under Part III of CA 1989; and (2) such services when so provided are provided under a

---

117  For a more extensive discussion on the duties to disabled children under CSDPA 1970 s2, see *Disabled children: a legal handbook* at 3.48–3.57. Some of the content of that section is repeated here verbatim or with minor amendments.

118  *R v Bexley LBC ex p B* (2000) 3 CCLR 15; *R (Spink) v Wandsworth LBC* [2005] EWCA Civ 302, [2005] 1 WLR 2884.

119  See by analogy the attempts by local authorities to avoid the duty to accommodate homeless teenagers under CA 1989 s20(1) by reliance on the lesser duties in CA 1989 s17, as discussed in chapters 1 and 5.

120  CSDPA 1970 s28A.

121  For a review and analysis of the relevant case-law, see L Clements and P Thompson, *Community care and the law*, LAG, 2007, paras 9.134–9.136.

122  [2004] EWHC 2314 (Admin), [2005] 1 WLR 258 at [34]–[35].

specifically enforceable duty. Following *R (Spink) v Wandsworth LBC* therefore, the position in practice is now clear.

4.48   CSDPA 1970 s2 provides a list of services that councils must make available to disabled people (children[123] and adults). In practice this includes services of great importance, such as short breaks (also known as 'respite care', although many disabled people and families object to this language), day activities, equipment, adaptations and so on. The list of services which can be provided under CSDPA 1970 s2 is summarised below, and more detail can be found in *Disabled children: a legal handbook*:[124]

### Home-based short breaks

4.49   Short breaks are one of the most valued services provided to disabled children and their families. Home- and community-based short breaks take a wide variety of forms such as sitting and befriending schemes for children and young people of all ages. Home-based short breaks are provided under CSDPA 1970 s2(1)(a) (ie as 'practical assistance in the home') and community-based support is provided under section 2(1)(c) (ie as recreational/educational facilities 'outside his home'). Some short breaks are linked to a disabled child's preferred leisure activities, for instance a playscheme at a local football club, horse riding, swimming etc. If a child has a need for short break/respite care which cannot be provided in his or her own home or a community-based setting, and which has to be provided in a care home or foster placement (ie away from the child's home) then it cannot be provided under CSDPA 1970 and will be provided under CA 1989 (see paras 4.54–4.62 below).

### Practical assistance in the home

4.50   The provision covers a very wide range of home-based (sometimes called 'domiciliary') care services, although it does not cover healthcare services even if these do not have to be provided by qualified health professionals.[125]

### Recreational/educational facilities

4.51   This covers community-based activities such as day centres and after-school or school holiday clubs, as well as specific recreational/

123 CSDPA 1970 s28A.
124 See *Disabled children: a legal handbook* at paras 3.48–3.57.
125 *R (T, D and B) v Haringey LBC* [2005] EWHC 2235 (Admin), (2006) 9 CCLR 58.

educational support activities that the assessment of need identifies as necessary to meet the child's needs. Services under this provision include those which assist the disabled person 'in taking advantage of educational facilities' that are available to him/her. Although this does not cover the actual provision of education, it is aimed at providing support that enables the disabled person to access education – for example, help with their personal care requirements whilst they pursue their studies,[126] as well as escorted travel to and from their studies, and possibly the provision of additional facilities at the institution[127] (although these might also be required under the Equality Act 2010).

## Home adaptations, fixtures and fittings

4.52    This important provision requires a local authority to make such adaptations to the home in which a disabled child lives as is assessed are necessary. Such adaptations can include ramps, grab handles or accessible washing facilities, and can extend to major works such as lifts and ground-floor extensions. Frequently the authority may ask the family to apply for a Disabled Facilities Grant to meet some or all of the cost of this work –these grants are considered in detail in chapter 6 of *Disabled children: a legal handbook*. It is, however, important to note that the fact that a grant may be available does not detract from the core duty to make the adaptations under CSDPA 1970 s2(1).

## Holidays

4.53    The authority must consider if a child's needs can and should be met by the provision of (or assistance in obtaining) a holiday.[128] Holidays are likely to be of great importance to a child's development and a family's sense of well-being and as such should not be viewed as a luxury item but as a potentially necessary service.[129]

---

126  See Department of Health LAC(93)12 – Further and Higher Education Act 1992.

127  *R (M) v Birmingham CC* [2009] EWHC 688 (Admin).

128  The duty under CSDPA 1970 s2(1)(f) to facilitate the taking of holidays by a disabled person includes a power to meet the basic cost of the holiday and it will be unlawful for an authority to refuse to consider meeting such costs; *R v North Yorkshire County Council ex p Hargreaves* (1997) 96 LGR 39.

129  One week's holiday a year away from the home is a core criteria within the Townsend Deprivation Index – see P Townsend, P Phillimore and A Beattie, *Health and deprivation: inequality and the north*, Croom Helm, 1988.

## Residential short breaks

4.54   While the majority of short break care for disabled children is provided under CSDPA 1970 as a service in the home or community (or via a direct payment, see paras 4.63–4.70 below), it may also be provided overnight in settings other than the family home, for example in hospices or by foster carers. In *R (JL) v Islington LBC*[130] the High Court confirmed that residential and other overnight short break care could not be provided under CSDPA 1970 and that as a general rule such support is provided by councils under CA 1989 s17(6) or s20(4).[131] The relevant statutory guidance notes that while most users of short breaks are disabled children, 'non-disabled children in need may also receive short break services'.[132]

4.55   The duty to provide short-break care under CA 1989 has been reinforced by an important amendment[133] such that CA 1989 Sch 2 para 6(1)(c)[134] further requires authorities to:

> Assist individuals who provide care for such children to continue to do so, or to do so more effectively, by giving them breaks from caring.

4.56   Regulations[135] have now been published to further particularise the new duty. The regulations:

- specify the needs to which local authorities must have regard when exercising their new duty (regulation 3);

- require authorities to provide, 'so far as is reasonably practicable, a range of services which is sufficient to assist carers to continue to provide care or to do so more effectively'. These services must

---

130 [2009] EWHC 458 (Admin), (2009) 12 CCLR 322.

131 Subsection 20(4) reads: 'A local authority may provide accommodation for any child within their area (even though a person who has parental responsibility for him is able to provide him with accommodation) if they consider that to do so would safeguard or promote the child's welfare.' See HM Government, *The Children Act 1989 guidance and regulations, volume 2: care planning, placement and case review*, March 2010 at 6.4, headed 'The legal basis for short breaks'. This guidance amends Local Authority Circular (2003) 13: Guidance on accommodating children in need and their families, by clarifying the decision-making process in respect of providing residential short breaks to children. The guidance does not amend the circular for other purposes; see para 6.6.

132 HM Government, *The Children Act 1989 guidance and regulations, volume 2: care planning, placement and case review*, March 2010 at para 6.2.

133 Introduced by Children and Young Persons Act 2008 s25.

134 In force from 1 April 2011.

135 Breaks for Carers of Disabled Children Regulations 2011 SI No 707.

include daytime care, overnight care and 'educational or leisure activities for disabled children outside their homes' (regulation 4); and

- require authorities to prepare a 'short breaks services statement' by 1 October 2011, setting out details of the range of services provided in accordance with regulation 4, any criteria by which eligibility for those services will be assessed and how the range of services is designed to meet the needs of carers in their area (regulation 5). It is perhaps of some concern that the short breaks services statement is not required to set out how the services will meet the needs of children but merely how they will meet carer's needs, as this tends to introduce unhelpful confusion as to whether a short break is provided to a disabled child or their carer. As a matter of law it is the firm view of the authors that any service that is provided to that child is a service provided under either CA 1989 or CSDPA 1970 rather than a carer's service.

4.57    In *R (JL) v Islington LBC*,[136] a centrally important judgment on the law in relation to disabled children, the judge (Black J) considered that in limited circumstances residential and other overnight short breaks care might be provided in the exercise of a council's duty under CA 1989 s20(1) (see chapter 5). The importance of this is that the duty under CA 1989 s20(1) is specifically enforceable (see paras 2.31–2.33). Black J decided, however, that the section 20(1) duty would only arise when a parent was 'immediately' prevented from providing a disabled child with suitable care and accommodation.[137] This means that residential short breaks are only provided under CA 1989 s20(1) if there is an 'actual crisis', not a 'possible or prospective' crisis.[138] As such, the vast majority of short breaks which involve accommodating the child will be provided under CA 1989 s17(6) or s20(4).

4.58    Any placement made under CA 1989 s20(1) and s20(4) until 31 March 2011 must accord with the requirements of the Arrangements for Placement of Children (General) Regulations 1991.[139] These

136 [2009] EWHC 458 (Admin), (2009) 12 CCLR 322.
137 Judgment at [95]–[96].
138 Judgment at [96].
139 SI No 890. Regulation 2(1)(a) states that the regulations apply to placements by a local authority of any child. In Wales, the 1991 regulations were amended by the Arrangements for Placement of Children (General) and the Review of Children's Cases (Amendment) (Wales) Regulations 2002 SI No 3013, particularly in relation to health assessments.

regulations are replaced in England from 1 April 2011 by the Care Planning, Placement and Case Review (England) Regulations 2010,[140] which have far more detailed requirements in relation to placements of children in need, including disabled children.[141] However, any residential short breaks provided under CA 1989 s17(6) will not be caught by the requirements of the 1991 or 2010 Regulations because the child will not be 'looked after'. The statutory guidance prescribes a list of factors which should be considered during an assessment to determine whether a short break should be provided pursuant to CA 1989 s17(6) or s20(4), which are as follows:

- particular vulnerabilities of the child, including communication method;
- parenting capacity of the parents within their family and environmental context;
- the length of time away from home and the frequency of such stays – the less time the child spends away from home, the more likely it is to be appropriate to provide accommodation under section 17(6);
- whether short breaks are to be provided in more than one place – where the child spends short breaks in different settings, including residential schools, hospices and social care placements, it is more likely to be appropriate to provide accommodation under section 20(4);
- potential impact on the child's place in the family and on primary attachments;
- observation of the child (especially children who do not communicate verbally) during or immediately after the break by a person familiar with the mood and behaviour of the child (for example, the parent or school staff);
- views of the child and views of parents – some children and parents may be reassured by and in favour of the status of a looked after child, while others may resent the implications and associations of looked after status;
- extent of contact between short break carers and family and between child and family during the placement;
- distance from home; and

---

140  SI No 959.
141  See chapter 5 for more on the duties to accommodate children under CA 1989 Part III and particularly s20(1).

- the need for an Independent Reviewing Officer (IRO) to monitor the child's case and to chair reviews.[142]

4.59 It can therefore be seen that the decision as to whether a residential short break is to be provided under CA 1989 s17(6) or s20(4) is one that requires the most careful consideration by the assessing social workers. In all of this the best interests of the child must be a primary consideration – not least to ensure compliance with UNCRC article 3 (see para 2.25 above).

4.60 If short break accommodation is provided under CA 1989 s20(4) for a continuous period of more than 24 hours, then the child is 'looked after' for the period in which the child is accommodated. If the child is placed for a weekend short break which lasts from Saturday morning until Sunday evening, this should count as two placement days.[143]

4.61 For a child who is 'looked after' during a residential short break provided under CA 1989 s20(4), then the placement must be a placement with local authority foster carers, in a registered children's home or in other appropriate arrangements.[144] Any such placement must comply with the relevant placement regulations for 'looked after' children.[145] However, if that child receives a pre-planned series of short breaks in the same setting[146] under section 20(4), the care planning arrangements under the 2010 regulations are modified in respect of that child by regulation 48 'to reflect the continuing central role played by the parents'.[147] In these circumstances the 2010 regulations apply subject to the following modifications:

---

142 HM Government, *The Children Act 1989 guidance and regulations, volume 2: care planning, placement and case review*, March 2010 at para 6.8. From the preface: 'Volume 2 of the Children Act 1989 Guidance and Regulations provides guidance, primarily addressed to local authorities and their staff in England, about their functions under Part 3 of the Children Act 1989. It is issued as guidance under section 7 of the Local Authority Social Services Act 1970 which requires local authorities in exercising their social services functions, to act under the general guidance of the Secretary of State'.

143 HM Government, *The Children Act 1989 guidance and regulations, volume 2: care planning, placement and case review*, March 2010 at para 6.13.

144 CA 1989 s22C.

145 Care Planning, Placement and Case Review (England) Regulations 2010.

146 Where a child receives short breaks in more than one setting including, for example, a residential school or a hospice, regulation 48 cannot apply. HM Government, *The Children Act 1989 guidance and regulations, volume 2: care planning, placement and case review*, March 2010 at para 6.19.

147 HM Government, *The Children Act 1989 guidance and regulations, volume 2: care planning, placement and case review*, March 2010 at para 6.15.

- The authority must make a 'short break care plan' addressing issues key to the safe care of the child. The short break care plan should be linked to the child in need plan (see paras 4.87–4.92 below), which should include all the key information about the child. These should not be separate plans which duplicate information.[148] The statutory guidance on short breaks requires proper engagement with both children and parents in the development of the short break care plan.[149]

- An IRO must be appointed, however the visiting and review requirements are less onerous than for children who are looked after for longer periods. The first visit must take place within three months of the first placement day or as soon as practicable thereafter. Subsequent visits must be at intervals of no more than six months. The child's case must be reviewed within three months of the start of the first placement and then at intervals of no more than six months.[150]

4.62    Further guidance[151] published by the then-Department for Children, Schools and Families in April 2010, entitled *Short breaks: statutory guidance on how to safeguard and promote the welfare of disabled children using short breaks,* describes in greater detail the processes of assessment, planning and review which apply to disabled children and their families in receipt of such services. This guidance states (at 1.4) that further guidance will be forthcoming to support the new duty on local authorities to provide a 'short breaks service' (see para 4.55 for this new duty) in April 2011. The guidance states (at 1.7) that there has been a 'worrying degree of non-compliance' with the law designed to safeguard and promote the welfare of disabled children in receipt of short breaks. It further describes a change in the pattern of short breaks away from longer periods of residential care to shorter periods of care at home or in the community, often delivered by way of direct payments. It should therefore be remembered that residential short breaks are only one option for a child 'in need' and their family, and may well be a less preferable option that

148  HM Government, *The Children Act 1989 guidance and regulations, volume 2: care planning, placement and case review,* March 2010 at para 6.21.

149  DCSF, *Short breaks: statutory guidance on how to safeguard and promote the welfare of disabled children using short breaks,* April 2010 at para 2.24.

150  There is a helpful table setting out the different consequences when regulation 48 of the 2010 regulations does or does not apply at HM Government, *The Children Act 1989 guidance and regulations, volume 2: care planning, placement and case review,* March 2010, table 2, p109.

151  Issued under Local Authority Social Services Act 1970 s7, see para 2.8.

community-based activities provided under CSDPA 1970, see para 4.51 above. Although the guidance suggests that for relatively low levels of short break provision a formal assessment may not be necessary for families to access such services, if these arrangements are not satisfactory, the right to a formal assessment in accordance with the Assessment Framework remains; see paras 4.24–4.35 above.[152]

## Direct payments

4.63  Where an authority has decided that it is necessary to provide services, parents (or a child aged 16 or 17) can insist (if certain conditions are met) on having support by way of a 'direct payment' which can then be used to purchase services from independent providers. A direct payment takes the place of support from the authority's in-house services or (more commonly now) having the authority commission the service directly from a third party. The right to insist on a direct payment applies regardless of whether the support is provided under CSDPA 1970 or the CA 1989.[153] Where a parent opts for direct payments, local authorities retain their responsibilities under CA 1989 to assess and review the needs of children 'in need' and their families in the normal way.[154]

4.64  The statutory scheme governing direct payments derives from CA 1989 s17A and its operation is established by regulations[155] and detailed guidance[156] ('the direct payments guidance') issued under the Health and Social Care Act 2001 which place a duty on local

---

152  DCSF, *Short breaks: statutory guidance on how to safeguard and promote the welfare of disabled children using short breaks,* April 2010 at paras 3.4–3.6.

153  This derives from the fact that services provided under CSDPA 1970 s2 are technically provided in discharge of a local authorities' functions under CA 1989 Part III; see para 4.47 above.

154  Department of Health (2009) *Guidance on direct payments for community care, services for carers and children's services England* 2009, para 163. In Wales, the relevant guidance is the *direct payments guidance community care, services for carers and children's services (direct payments) guidance Wales* 2004. References in the remainder of this chapter are to the English guidance.

155  Community Care, Services for Carers and Children's Services (Direct Payments) (England) Regulations 2009 SI No 1887 and the Community Care, Services for Carers and Children's Services (Direct Payments) (Wales) Regulations 2004 SI No 1748 (W.185). The English regulations have been amended by the Community Care, Services for Carers and Children's Services (Direct Payments) (England) (Amendment) Regulations 2010 SI No 2246) but these amendments do not relate to children's services.

156  Department of Health (2009) *Guidance on direct payments for community care, services for carers and children's services England* 2009.

authorities to make a direct payment in certain situations. The relevant conditions which must be met for a family to be able to insist on a direct payment are that:

- the person appears to the responsible authority to be capable of managing a direct payment by himself or herself, or with such assistance as may be available to him or her;
- the person consents to the making of a direct payment;
- the responsible authority is satisfied that the person's need for the relevant service can be met by securing the provision of it by means of a direct payment; and
- the responsible authority is satisfied that the welfare of the child in respect of whom the service is needed will be safeguarded and promoted by securing the provision of it by means of a direct payment.[157]

4.65   Although direct payments cannot be used to purchase prolonged periods of residential respite care (being capped at a maximum of four consecutive weeks in any period of 12 months[158]), as long as the residential care periods are less than four weeks long and are separated by at least four weeks of non-residential care, then successive such periods are permitted.[159]

4.66   The direct payments guidance notes (at para 124) that individuals receiving direct services may wish to switch to direct payments, and councils should raise this possibility proactively. However, receiving support by way of a direct payment remains a *choice*; there is no mechanism by which a council can force a parent or child to take a direct payment rather than to receive a direct service from the council or from a third party commissioned by the council. This does not of course undermine a council's entitlement to select the most cost-effective direct service to offer to the family in place of direct payments – so long as the service meets the assessed needs and is otherwise compatible with the child's human rights.

4.67   A related question is how the value of any given direct payment should be determined. The answer is that any direct payment made

---

157 Community Care, Services for Carers and Children's Services (Direct Payments) (England) Regulations 2009 SI No 1887 reg 7(1)(c).

158 Community Care, Services for Carers and Children's Services (Direct Payments) (England) Regulations 2009 SI No 1887 reg 13 and the Community Care, Services for Carers and Children's Services (Direct Payments) (Wales) Regulations 2004 SI No 1748 (W.185) reg 8.

159 Department of Health (2009) *Guidance on direct payments for community care, services for carers and children's services England* 2009, paras 101–103.

must be sufficient for the parent or child to purchase support that will ensure that assessed eligible needs are met. Health and Social Care Act 2001 s57(4)(a) prescribes that direct payments should be calculated on the basis of the 'reasonable cost of securing the provision' of the necessary service. Similarly, the direct payments guidance states (at para 111) that the amount of a direct payment should be 'sufficient to enable the recipient lawfully to secure a service of a standard that the council considers is reasonable to fulfil the needs for the service to which the payments relate'. The direct payments scheme is therefore intimately linked to, rather than being a replacement for, the assessment and service provision decision-making processes – as without proper assessment it will be impossible to know whether the level of any direct payment is reasonable and sufficient to meet the child's needs.

4.68    The regulations[160] restrict the use of direct payments to pay a relative who lives in the same household as the child. There is, however, no restriction if the relative lives elsewhere. Accordingly, paying such a relative, who may well know and have a good relationship with the child, to provide care may be a very attractive option for families. If, however, the relative lives in the same household, the presumption is that he or she may not be paid with the direct payment – unless the authority 'is satisfied that securing the service from a family member is necessary for promoting the welfare of the child'. This means that the council can agree to such a payment, if it is satisfied that it is necessary –a relatively low threshold.

4.69    The guidance states (para 26) that in the vast majority of cases, 'it is expected that councils will have a duty to make direct payments to people with eligible needs'. However, once a direct payment is agreed, an authority can terminate it (wholly or partially) if in all the circumstances it considers it appropriate to do so.[161] The fact of a direct payment does not affect the duty on councils to carry out a regular review of the individual's care package[162] and if a child's needs change, they should be reassessed and the level of direct payment reviewed.[163]

---

160  Reg 11 in England; reg 7 in Wales.

161  Reg 17(2)(b).

162  Department of Health (2009) *Guidance on direct payments for community care, services for carers and children's services England* 2009, para 225.

163  Department of Health (2009) *Guidance on direct payments for community care, services for carers and children's services England* 2009, box at para 242, p87.

## Individual budgets and personalisation

4.70   Many children and families will now be told that their entitlement
to services will take the form of an 'individual budget' or 'personal
budget'. These budgets are financial allocations which are typically
generated through the application of a model known as a Resource
Allocation System (RAS). This is a core part of the 'personalisation'
agenda, which is a dominant theme in adult community care services and is starting to take hold in children's services. However, it
is essential to note that the only legal basis for 'personalisation' is
the Direct Payments legislation, and any attempt to use personalised
approaches to avoid the assessment and service provision duties set
out above will be unlawful.

4.71   The application of RAS and other 'personalisation' approaches
familiar from adult social care is problematic in relation to children's services. The fundamental problem with the RAS approach
is that it can break the link between the assessment of need and
the service provision decision by inserting a process by which an
'indicative budget' is determined, very often based on a self assessment questionnaire rather than a lawful assessment (which in the
children's services context must be an initial or core assessment
which complies with the Assessment Framework, see paras 4.24–
4.35 above). The judgment of the Court of Appeal in *R (Savva) v
Royal Borough of Kensington and Chelsea*[164] makes clear that while
RAS schemes may be used as a 'starting point' to give an indication
of the level of funding which may be required, they cannot dispense
with a local authority's 'absolute duty' to meet assessed needs with
services or direct payments once it has concluded that such services
are necessary.[165]

## Eligibility criteria[166]

4.72   The use of eligibility criteria in children's services is a highly contentious issue. The process of deciding whether services are necessary
and hence that there is a duty to provide them requires authorities
to act rationally, follow agreed procedures which are explained to the
child/family in question and to produce a decision for which clear

164   [2010] EWCA Civ 1209. *Savva* is a case concerning the use of RAS schemes
in adult social care but the principles established by the Court of Appeal are
directly applicable to their use in children's services.

165   Judgment at [7].

166   This section derives from *Disabled children: a legal handbook* at 3.36–3.44.

and logical reasons are provided. At law, there is a distinction between the process of deciding what services are required (the 'service provision decision') and the duty to provide those services if the
necessary threshold is crossed. These distinct issues are sometimes
unhelpfully confused. The confusion relates to the use of eligibility
criteria – which in itself is not surprising, since, as Lord Laming observed in his Victoria Climbié Inquiry Report,[167] their use 'to restrict
access to services is not found either in legislation or in guidance,
and its ill-founded application is not something I support'.

4.73     The confusion in this area relates to precisely for what issues set
criteria may be used to determine eligibility. As we have seen above,
local authorities are under a statutory duty to assess all children who
are or may be 'in need'. Accordingly, it would be unlawful for a local
authority to impose its own 'eligibility criteria' for *assessments*. This
would constitute an extra hurdle for a child to cross which is not
permitted in the law or statutory guidance. However, as we have
also seen above, once a child has been assessed, the law does not
require that services be provided in every case – only when (put
shortly) such services are judged to be 'necessary' as a result of the
assessment.

4.74     It follows that it is reasonable for an authority to state that a child
will not as a general rule be 'eligible' for support services unless the
authority is satisfied that these are necessary. This, however, then
requires that the authority explain the process by which it will decide
whether or not a child is 'eligible' – ie the criteria it uses to make this
judgment. The use of 'eligibility criteria' in this context has been held
to be lawful by the courts.[168]

4.75     Such criteria must, however, promote the objects of the legislation, ie that so far as possible children should be brought up by their
families[169] and, if the child is disabled, that services provided should
seek to minimise the effects of their disabilities and give them the
opportunity to lead lives which are 'as normal as possible'.[170] Given
that resources are limited, the criteria should also contain an element of 'prioritisation' – ie it is legitimate for authorities to target
those in most need and to devote resources where they can have the
most positive impact, providing always that any eligibility criteria do

---

167  Lord Laming, *The Victoria Climbié inquiry: report of an inquiry*, Cm 5730 (TSO,
     2003).
168  *R v Gloucestershire CC ex p Barry* [1997] 2 WLR 459, (1997–98) 1 CCLR 40 and
     more recently *R (JL) v Islington LBC* [2009] EWHC 458 (Admin).
169  CA 1989 s17(1)(b).
170  CA 1989 Sch 2 para 6.

not preclude the provision of services that the authority has a duty to provide.[171] As Lord Nicholls noted in *R (G) v Barnet LBC*, 'cost is also an element which may properly be taken into account in deciding what is "appropriate" in a particular case' – although this approach can only apply to services provided under CA 1989 s17, not services provided under CSDPA 1970 s2 as set out above (para 4.46).[172]

4.76    The human rights obligations on public bodies (particularly article 8 ECHR, see paras 2.14–2.19 above) additionally require that any criteria they operate must not be so strict as to deny support where there is a real risk of significant harm[173] to the child or family if support is not provided ('significant harm' being harm that is more than minor or trivial).[174]

4.77    The lawfulness of one example of eligibility criteria for disabled children's services was tested in *R (JL) v Islington LBC*[175] where the court held the criteria to be unlawful for a variety of reasons. Following *R (JL) v Islington LBC*, lawful eligibility criteria for children's services must (i) only limit the pool of children who are eligible for provision, not the amount of provision to be made to eligible children (in relation to CSDPA 1970 s2 services); (ii) not prescribe a fixed maximum amount of support; (iii) be applied *after* (not instead of) a lawful assessment of needs; and (iv) be set with due regard to the

---

171  In this context see also L Clements and P Thompson, *Community care and the law*, LAG, 2007, para 24.35–24.36.

172  *R (G) v Barnet LBC* [2003] UKHL 57, [2004] 2 AC 208 at [30].

173  'Significant harm' is not defined in the CA 1989, but does not include 'minor shortcomings' or 'minor defects' in care being provided; *CA 1989 guidance and regulations, volume 1, court orders* (1991) Department of Health, para 3.12. See R White, AP Carr and N Lowe, *The Children Act in practice*, LexisNexis, 4th edn, 2008 at 8.43–8.44 and HM Government, *Working together to safeguard children: a guide to inter-agency working to safeguard and promote the welfare of children* (2010) at 1.26–1.31 for more on the 'significant harm' threshold.

174  In *R v Gloucestershire CC ex p Mahfood* (1997–98) 1 CCLR 7, DC (a pre-Human Rights Act 1998 judgment) McCowan LJ expressed this proposition in the following way: 'I should stress, however, that there will, in my judgment, be situations where a reasonable authority could only conclude that some arrangements were necessary to meet the needs of a particular disabled person and in which they could not reasonably conclude that a lack of resources provided an answer. Certain persons would be at severe physical risk if they were unable to have some practical assistance in their homes. In those situations, I cannot conceive that an authority would be held to have acted reasonably if they used shortage of resources as a reason for not being satisfied that some arrangement should be made to meet those persons' needs.'

175  [2009] EWHC 458 (Admin), (2009) 12 CCLR 322.

general equality duty in Equality Act 2010 s149. Breaches of the requirements summarised above persuaded Black J to strike down Islington's eligibility criteria (and resulting service provision decision in JL's case) as unlawful.[176]

4.78    It should again be noted that although services must be provided if the duties under CA 1989 or CSDPA 1970 are triggered, there is no duty to provide 'Rolls Royce' services; the duty will be to provide an adequate service to meet the assessed needs and comply with the child's human rights. If there are two suitable and adequate services available, both of which meet the assessed need, it is open to an authority to choose the less expensive of the two services. As the Court said in *R v Kirklees MBC ex p Daykin*[177] (in relation to the CSDPA 1970 s2 duty):

> Once needs have been established, then they must be met and cost cannot be an excuse for failing to meet them. The manner in which they are met does not have to be the most expensive. The Council is perfectly entitled to look to see what cheapest way for them to meet the needs which are specified.

4.79    It follows that councils cannot, in such situations, seek to delay or attempt further rationing – for instance, by placing a person on a waiting list[178] or suggesting that the case needs to go to a 'panel'.[179] Similarly, local authorities cannot adopt general exclusions or rigid limits or lists of services that will not be provided – for example, excluding all children with Asperger syndrome from disabled children's services, having a cap or ceiling on the amount of service to be provided (eg a maximum of 100 hours per year of short breaks, as Islington contended in JL's case), or stating that 'out of county residential respite will not be provided'. To do any of these things would, at the very least, be to 'fetter their discretion' to meet their general duties in such cases.[180] It may also be an unlawful refusal to discharge specific duties, for instance to assess or to determine whether services are necessary to meet the needs of the child, depending on the facts of the individual case.

---

176  Judgment at [126].
177  (1997–98) 1 CCLR 512 at 525D.
178  See, for example, Local Government Ombudsman Complaint no 00/B/00599 against Essex, 3 September 2001.
179  See L Clements and P Thompson, *Community care and the law*, LAG, 2007, para 3.183 for further discussion about the questionable legality of such panels.
180  See, for example, *R v Bexley LBC ex p Jones* [1995] ELR 42, p55.

4.80    Whilst the use of eligibility criteria is well developed in relation to adult community care under a centralised approach[181] this is not the case in relation to children's services, where such criteria have developed locally on an ad hoc basis. In *R (JL) v Islington LBC*,[182] Black J stressed the 'pressing need' for government guidance on eligibility criteria for children services, given that many local authorities have, at best, imperfect, and, at worst, unlawful criteria. It is understood that such guidance, at least in relation to disabled children's services, will be forthcoming in relation to the new short break duties in force from April 2011; see para 4.55.

## Reducing or withdrawing services

4.81    This book is being published (early 2011) at a time of widespread and wholesale cuts to children's services budgets. As such, many children and families will be concerned that the service package they have been receiving may be reduced or withdrawn altogether. Local authorities and other public bodies should also be concerned to ensure that any cuts deemed necessary as a result of the current fiscal situation are made lawfully – to ensure both that resources are not wasted in defending legal challenges, and, more importantly, that essential services continue to be provided to vulnerable members of the communities that they exist to serve.

4.82    There are two important dimensions to any consideration of the lawfulness of reducing or withdrawing services that are being provided to a child 'in need'. The first dimension is whether the decision is in accordance with the authority's specific duties to that child under the Assessment Framework and (if disabled) CSDPA 1970 s2 – or in the case of children being provided with accommodation, under CA 1989 s20. While this question can only sensibly be answered on the facts of an individual case, some general observations can be made. Firstly, it will be very difficult for an authority to justify reducing a child's service package (for example, cutting the number of short break hours a disabled child receives from eight to four each week) unless a re-assessment shows that the child's needs have changed. A

181   See, for example, Department of Health, *Prioritising need in the context of Putting People First: A whole system approach to eligibility for social care. guidance on eligibility criteria for adult social care, England 2010* (2010) and the equivalent Welsh Assembly Government policy guidance *Creating a unified and fair system for assessing and managing care*, 2002: see also L Clements and P Thompson *Community care and the law*, LAG, 2007, para 3.163.
182   [2009] EWHC 458 (Admin), (2009) 12 CCLR 322.

change in the child's circumstances was what saved the decision to reduce the respite care provision from 20 to six hours in *R v Bexley LBC ex p B*[183], where the medical evidence was held to have shown that the child B no longer had any need for the extra hours of home care.[184] In the absence of such a change in circumstances the authority is unlikely to be able to lawfully reduce a service package because the existing level of service will remain 'necessary'. By contrast, however, an authority *may* lawfully be able to *withdraw* services to an individual child completely if its budget is reduced, as this may entitle an authority to reduce the pool of children for whom it deems it 'necessary' to provide services, a question in relation to which (under the CSDPA 1970 at least[185]) the authority is entitled to take account of resources. This somewhat perverse outcome is a necessary result of the complexities of the law governing the provision of services to children 'in need'. It should be stressed, however, that even in this factual scenario the authority will still be required to re-assess each child to determine whether their needs are eligible under the new criteria.

4.83    The second dimension of this question relates to the wider duties imposed on local authorities – not to act in a way that breaches a person's ECHR rights, to consult properly on any decisions which affect important services to vulnerable groups, to have due regard to the general equality duty (Equality Act 2010 s149),[186] to have regard to the need to safeguard and promote children's welfare (CA 2004 s11) and so on. A decision to withdraw services to an individual child or group of children can potentially be challenged in the courts in relation to any or all of these provisions, albeit that a local authority is likely to be given greater leeway by the courts in these areas (although not in relation to whether the decision is disproportionate in the context of article 8 ECHR,[187] a decision which the court as a public authority must take for itself).

---

183   (2000) 3 CCLR 15.

184   Per Latham J at 23E.

185   *R v Gloucestershire CC ex p Barry* [1997] 2 WLR 459, (1997–98) 1 CCLR 40.

186   See *Disabled children: a legal handbook* at paras 9.73–9.85 for the new public sector equality duty in the context of disabled children's services.

187   See above, paras 2.14–2.19.

## Charging for children's services[188]

4.84    Local authorities have the power to charge for most services provided under the CA 1989 Part III. Authorities may recover 'such charge as they consider appropriate' (CA 1989 s29(1)) and in so doing, if the child is under 16, can take into account the financial circumstance of the parents, and if 16 or over, can take into account the child's means (section 29(4)).[189] However, no person can be charged while in receipt of income support or a range of other benefits (section 29(3)). Further, an authority cannot require a person to pay more than he or she can reasonably be expected to pay (section 29(2)). Local authorities can also charge for services provided under CSDPA 1970 s2.

4.85    In practice, few authorities do charge parents or children for services provided either under CA 1989 Part III or CSDPA 1970 s2.[190] Any authority contemplating introducing charges for children's services will need to be careful to avoid this frustrating the discharge of its duties to children 'in need' or conflicting with its duties under the Equality Act 2010.

# Duty to produce a care plan

4.86    Regardless of the duty under which a local authority is providing services, it is essential that the nature and extent of the services to be provided are clearly set out in a care plan.[191] The Assessment Framework (at para 4.1) expresses this as an obligation to produce 'a realistic plan of action (including services to be provided)'. Wherever possible, there should be a single plan which includes the full range of family support services on a multiagency basis.[192] Care plans must be 'realistic' and should not be dependent upon resources which are known to be scarce or unavailable.[193] It is 'good practice' for an

---

188  This section derives from *Disabled children: a legal handbook* at 3.92–3.93.

189  See *R (Spink) v Wandsworth London Borough Council* [2005] EWCA Civ 302, [2005] 1 WLR 2884.

190  See Clements and Thompson, *Community care and the law*, 4th edn, 2007 at 24.68–24.73 and chapter 10 for further information on charging.

191  See Assessment Framework at 4.32–4.37, 'Plans for children in need'.

192  DCSF, *Short breaks: statutory guidance on how to safeguard and promote the welfare of disabled children using short breaks*, April 2010, para 3.16. This paragraph contains detailed specification of the requirements for a care plan for a disabled child in receipt of short breaks.

193  Assessment Framework at para. 4.34.

authority to review a child's care plan every six months[194] and reviews should take place whenever the child's circumstances significantly change, with particularly significant changes potentially resulting in a requirement for a re-assessment. The 'areas in which clarity is required in child care planning' are specified by the Assessment Framework[195] and include the objectives of the plan, what services will be provided by whom and the purpose of services to be provided to the child and/or family.

4.87    The importance of the assessment leading to a 'realistic plan of action' where a child's well-being so requires has been demonstrated in a number of cases. In *R (J) v Caerphilly CBC*,[196] the court held that a 'detailed operational plan' should result from the assessment process (in that case the pathway planning process for a young person leaving care, see paras 7.60–7.66 below). Similarly, in *R (AB & SB) v Nottingham CC*[197] the council's assessment and care plan were struck down by the court because 'there was no clear identification of needs, or what was to be done about them, by whom and when'.[198] The same approach was followed by the court in *R (S) v Plymouth CC*,[199] where the assessments were quashed because they failed to result in a 'realistic plan of action' to meet the child's needs in relation to housing and short-break care.

4.88    In *R v Ealing LBC ex p C*,[200] a case heard before the publication of the Assessment Framework, the Court of Appeal considered the care planning in relation to a boy with visual impairment and a range of specific learning difficulties and other problems. The Court of Appeal held that the decision-making was flawed and that there had been no proper consideration of the accommodation problems faced by the family. As such, the authority had acted unreasonably within the meaning set out in the seminal public law case of *Tameside*,[201] in essence by failing to ask and answer the right questions. As such, 'important practical problems were simply not addressed' and the authority had therefore acted unlawfully.[202]

194  Assessment Framework at para. 4.36.
195  Figure 7, p62.
196  [2005] EWHC 586 (Admin), (2005) 8 CCLR 255.
197  [2001] EWHC 235 (Admin), (2001) 4 CCLR 294.
198  [2001] EWHC 235 (Admin), (2001) 4 CCLR 294 at [43].
199  [2009] EWHC 1499 (Admin).
200  (2000) 3 CCLR 122.
201  *Secretary of State for Education and Science v Tameside MBC* [1977] AC 1014.
202  Per Judge LJ at 129K.

4.89    The question posed by the court in *Ex p C*, adapting the formula proposed by Lord Diplock in *Tameside*, was 'did the council ask themselves the right question and take reasonable steps to acquaint themselves with the relevant information to enable them to answer it correctly?'. The answer to both questions on the facts of the case was held to be 'no'. Lord Justice Judge concluded that:

> ... both the decision and the decision-making process were flawed. Unless the repetition of an assertion is to be regarded as a proper manifestation of a reasoning process, there was none here. Certainly there was no analysis of the accommodation problems faced by this disabled boy and his mother and brother. The decision is therefore susceptible to judicial review on the basis that it is unreasonable in the *Wednesbury* sense.[203]

4.90    It can therefore be seen that the duty to undertake proper care planning stems not only from the Assessment Framework but also from the general public law obligations placed on local authorities, including the duty to act rationally and reasonably and to have regard to all relevant considerations in their decision-making.

4.91    Care plans must be kept up-to-date and reviewed as often as the circumstances of the child and family demand. However, the level of service should not be varied (and certainly not downward) without a full re-assessment of the child's needs. A review for a child who is not 'looked after' (see paras 5.76–5.96) should:

- ensure the service(s) provided meet the needs identified in the child in need;
- plan and safeguard and promote the welfare of the child;
- focus on outcomes for the child and family;
- see the child's development and progress in the round and therefore be a multi-agency review whenever possible;
- include the ascertainable wishes and feelings of the child and the views of the family; and
- take place at least every six months.[204]

---

203 Judgment ar 130E–H.
204 DCSF, *Short breaks: statutory guidance on how to safeguard and promote the welfare of disabled children using short breaks*, April 2010, para 3.19. Although this guidance specifically relates to care plans for disabled children in receipt of short breaks it is clearly applicable to other plans for children 'in need'.

# Timescales for assessments and providing services

4.92 As noted above (para 3.15) the Assessment Framework lays down detailed and tight timescales for the completion of assessments – just eight working days for an initial assessment and accompanying care plan. See, for example, *R (J) v Newham LBC*[205] for an example of a case where an authority was criticised by the court for excessive delay in the assessment of (in that case) a disabled child. Where delay occurs, children and families may use the complaints process[206] or, if the situation is sufficiently urgent (as it often will be), may challenge failures to comply with the timescales prescribed by the Assessment Framework through an application for judicial review.

4.93 In relation to the provision of services, the Assessment Framework states that a plan of action must be 'realistic' and this obviously requires the provision of services within a reasonable time. What constitutes 'reasonable' in such a context will depend entirely on the facts of the case. Where the delay appears excessive, then again the remedy lies either in a complaint, or an application for judicial review if the matter is sufficiently urgent and serious.

4.94 Where a delay arises because there is a physical shortage of services (for example, no place available at a day centre) the court will require that short-term alternative arrangements be made to meet the identified need as well as steps taken by the council to address the structural 'supply side' problem, if there is one (eg the shortage is not a 'one-off' but a chronic problem).[207] In general, if the shortage is due to a budgetary problem it will not be an acceptable excuse – as the Court of Appeal has noted (in the context of CSDPA 1970 s2):[208]

> Once a local authority has decided that it is necessary to make the arrangements, they are under an absolute duty to make them. It is a duty owed to a specific individual and not a target duty. No term is to be implied that the local authority are obliged to comply with the duty only if they have the revenue to do so. In fact, once under that duty resources do not come into it.[209]

---

205 [2001] EWHC Admin 992, (2002) 5 CCLR 302.
206 See chapter 2 at paras 2.57–2.60.
207 *R v Islington LBC ex p Rixon* (1997–98) 1 CCLR 119 at p128.
208 *R v Gloucestershire CC ex p Mahfood* (1997–98) 1 CCLR 7, DC per McCowan LJ; and see also *R v Kirklees MBC ex p Daykin* (1997–98) 1 CCLR 512 at 525D.
209 Judgment at 16G–H.

## Conclusion – the need for services to promote dignity

4.95   To conclude on the provision of services to children 'in need', it should be remembered that the purpose of assessment and care planning must be to promote and protect the inherent dignity of the child. In *R (A, B, X and Y) v East Sussex CC*[210] the High Court stated (at [86]) that:

> The recognition and protection of human dignity is one of the core values – in truth the core value – of our society and indeed all societies which are part of the European family of nations and which have embraced the principles of the [European Convention on Human Rights].

4.96   The obligations on local authorities to provide services to meet children's assessed needs must therefore be seen in the context of the state's ECHR obligations, in particular the positive obligations under article 8 ECHR, to ensure decent and dignified standards of living for children and where possible to allow children to remain with their families. The service provision decision in relation to any individual child therefore needs to be taken with due regard to all the general principles and human rights standards set out in chapter 2. At a time when the budgets for children's services face massive reductions, this may become ever more difficult, but it is nothing less than what the law requires.

210 [2003] EWHC 167 (Admin), (2003) 6 CCLR 194.

# CHAPTER 5

# Duties and powers to accommodate children

*continued*

## Key points

- Part III of the Children Act (CA) 1989 contains a number of duties and powers to accommodate homeless children, and children in unsuitable accommodation.
- The most commonly used provision is CA 1989 s20(1)(c). Local authorities have a specific duty to provide suitable accommodation to any child who falls within this provision.
- A child who is the subject of a care order, or accommodated under section 20, section 25 or a number of other CA 1989 provisions, is 'looked after' by the local authority and entitled to a range of further support.
- A child provided with accommodation under CA 1989 s17 or the Housing Act 1996 is not a 'looked after' child.
- If a child accumulates sufficient 'looked after' time, he or she becomes entitled to long-term support from the local authority, potentially stretching until the age of 25 (see chapter 7).
- CA 1989 s20(1)(c) has been controversial in recent years but the law is now clear: local authorities cannot sidestep their statutory duties by labelling section 20 accommodation as some other form of accommodation.
- Section 20 accommodation may take any form, according to the child's needs. An assessment will always be needed to inform the decision as to what type accommodation should be provided.
- Some forms of accommodation, for example bed and breakfast (B&B) or hostels are accepted to be unsuitable for *all* children 'in need'.
- Local authorities may use accommodation to restrict children's liberty in certain circumstances, which are tightly defined by CA 1989 s25.
- Local authorities have a number of discretionary powers to accommodate children and young adults until the age of 21.
- A child may be in need of accommodation before he or she actually becomes homeless, for example if an address is needed in advance to secure release from custody.
- Accommodation may also be provided under CA 1989 s17(6). This provision allows for the accommodation of homeless children with their families, unlike section 20 which applies to lone children only.

*continued*

- Joint protocols between children's services and housing departments or authorities are essential, but unfortunately are not always in place.
- Important changes concerning accommodation under CA 1989 Part III are in force as of 1 April 2011.

## Introduction

5.1 In recent years, the duties on and powers of local authority children's services departments to accommodate children in need have been much debated and hotly contested. This contest has primarily focussed on section 20 of the CA 1989, which contains a number of duties and powers to accommodate children without the child being made the subject of a care order.

5.2 This chapter explains local authorities' duties and discretionary powers to accommodate under Part III of CA 1989, and details precisely what duties are owed to such accommodated children. We outline key practical considerations for legal representatives in dealing with such cases. There are a number of specific issues arising for particular categories of children requiring accommodation, such as children in custody and children at risk of gang violence. We note the additional guidance and case-law of particular relevance to these groups of children. Finally, we deal with the likely impact of new regulations and guidance (made pursuant to the Children and Young Persons Act 2008), in force from April 2011.

5.3 The controversy about local authorities' duties and powers to accommodate derives from a number of factors, including local authorities' tight budgets, and related disputes between children's services and housing departments/authorities[1] regarding who should pay to accommodate homeless 16- and 17-year-olds. Crucially, if a child is accommodated by children's services, or 'looked after', for a particular period of time, the authority may owe that child longer-term duties – which run into adulthood – under the Children (Leaving Care) Act (CLCA) 2000. There are thus substantial long-term resource implications to recognising that a child needs to be looked after. The

---

1 In unitary authorities and London boroughs, the children's services department and the housing department will be part of the same council. However in other areas, children's services will be under the auspices of the county council and the housing authority will be the district council.

leaving care regime is addressed in detail in chapter 7 of this book. Given the budget implications for local authorities, it is perhaps unsurprising that the duty to accommodate under section 20 has been a flashpoint for debate concerning Part III of the CA 1989.

5.4    In addition to the resource implications, a high number of 'looked after' children in the care of a local authority appears to be seen in some quarters as a sign that the authority is failing and it may be that this in itself makes children's services reluctant to accommodate children under this provision.

5.5    Another reason why these issues have achieved such prominence in recent years is because many of the judicial reviews issued pursuant to Part III of the CA 1989 concern urgently needed accommodation, as the practical importance to a child of having a roof over his or her head will usually necessitate the issue of proceedings rather than extensive pre-action negotiations. In contrast, many potential cases concerning the adequacy of an assessment to provide other services under CA 1989 s17 – for instance, in relation to disabled children – will be suitable for more extended pre-action negotiations, with the issue of proceedings being a last resort.

5.6    Disputes over the meaning of the key duty to accommodate contained in CA 1989 s20(1) twice reached the country's highest court within the space of 12 months, in the landmark cases of *R (M) v Hammersmith and Fulham LBC*[2] and then *R (G) v Southwark*[3] (although their Lordships in the latter case expressed some understandable surprise that the issue had returned so quickly given the clarity and detail of the former decision[4]).

5.7    The law concerning the duties and powers contained in CA 1989 s20 is now clear, following these two judgments of the House of Lords, but unfortunately despite this it is often necessary to send formal pre-action correspondence, or even issue proceedings, to secure appropriate accommodation for child clients who are street homeless, 'sofa-surfing' or in unsuitable accommodation. The majority of these cases tend, however, to settle at an early stage post-issue due to the clear guidance given by the House of Lords in these two important cases.

5.8    To put this chapter into context, it is useful to bear in mind the statistics cited in the guidance which is in force as of April 2011 (they relate to England only):

2   [2008] UKHL 14, [2008] 1 WLR 535.
3   [2009] UKHL 26, [2009] 1 WLR 1299.
4   *R (G) v Southwark LBC* [2009] UKHL 26, [2009] 1 WLR 1299 at [5].

At any one time around 60,000 children are looked after, representing roughly 0.5% of all children. As many as 85,000 children will spend some time being looked after over the course of a year, with many entering and leaving the system very rapidly. Forty per cent of children remain looked after for less than six months and only 13% are looked after for five years or more.[5]

It should be remembered that many children are not presently being accommodated as required under CA 1989 s20 and hence are not included in these statistics; see chapter 1 at para 1.16 and footnote 30.

## Section 20: duties to accommodate

5.9    Of central importance to Part III of CA 1989 is section 20, concerning accommodation. Section 20 includes both mandatory duties to accommodate (in section 20(1) and (3)) and wider discretionary powers (in section 20(4) and (5)).

5.10   The duty to accommodate under section 20 should be thought of as a twin duty, twinned to the duty to assess under CA 1989 s17 (dealt with extensively in chapter 4 of this book). There is a substantial crossover between the issues of assessment and accommodation. This is because, first, before the duty to accommodate under either section 20(1) or (3) can be triggered, it must be established that the child is a child 'in need' within the local authority's area. Finding a child to be 'in need' is a prerequisite to the duty to accommodate, and of course as we have seen there is a duty to assess the needs of any child who is or may be 'in need'. Second, the case-law makes clear that a child without accommodation is a child in need: *R v North-avon District Council ex p Smith*,[6] cited by Lord Nicholls in *R (G) v Barnet LBC*.[7] Third, the issues of assessment and accommodation are in any event inextricably linked as, without a detailed, lawful assessment of a child's needs, a local authority cannot reach sensible, lawful decisions regarding a child's accommodation. As Baroness Hale has recognised, a homeless child or child without suitable accommodation will require 'more than a roof over his head',[8] and so proper assessment is key to the services the child will require and be provided with, either in supported accommodation of some kind,

---

5   *Sufficiency: statutory guidance on securing sufficient accommodation for looked after children*, Department for Children, Schools and Families (DCSF), 2010, para 2.1.

6   [1994] 2 AC 402, 406.

7   [2004] 2 AC 208, 224 at [32].

8   *R (M) v Hammersmith and Fulham LBC* [2008] UKHL 14, [2008] 1 WLR 535 at [4].

a foster placement, or as part of a package of floating support while the child is in independent or semi-independent accommodation.

5.11 At this point it should be noted that the duty to accommodate children 'in need' can be discharged by placing a child in any type of accommodation that is suitable to the child's needs. Despite popular misconceptions to the contrary, there is no such thing as 'section 20 accommodation' in the sense of a specific type of accommodation to which children 'in need' are restricted. However, some forms of accommodation – for example, B&B, hostels or foyers – are accepted to be unsuitable for *all* children 'in need', see para 5.24 below.

## Children Act 1989 s20(1)

5.12 CA 1989 s20(1) places local authorities under a 'specific'[9] statutory duty to provide accommodation for any child in need within their area who requires accommodation as a result of:

(a) there being no person who has parental responsibility for him;
(b) his being lost or having been abandoned; or
(c) the person who has been caring for him being prevented (whether or not permanently, and for whatever reason) from providing him with suitable accommodation or care.

Paragraphs (a), (b) and (c) are alternatives, rather than cumulative requirements. The authors are aware of internal guidance or a protocol prepared by one local authority which wrongly described these as cumulative requirements; and it has sometimes been incorrectly asserted by other authorities that no section 20(1) duty can be owed because the parent still has parental responsibility.

5.13 In practice, the vast majority of section 20(1) cases will concern 20(1)(c), rather than the more extreme scenarios envisaged in (a) or (b), although unaccompanied asylum-seeking children will generally also fall within (a) and/or (b). In any event, any child arguably falling within (a) or (b) would need also to contend that section 20(1)(c) is made out, in the event that he or she cannot establish lack of parental responsibility or abandonment to the court's satisfaction.

5.14 Section 20(1) applies to all children, ie up to the age of 18. The statutory predecessors to section 20(1), in the Children Act 1948 and the Child Care Act 1980, applied only up to the age of 17.[10]

---

9  See chapter 2 at paras 2.31–2.33.
10  *R (M) v Hammersmith and Fulham LBC* [2008] UKHL 14, [2008] 1 WLR 535 at [16].

*Section 20(1)(a): no person with parental responsibility*

5.15    Reliance on this provision in establishing a CA 1989 s20 duty will be extremely rare, in large part because in any situation where there is no person with parental responsibility for a child it is highly likely that the matter will be dealt with through care proceedings. Claimants are advised in any event to plead section 20(1)(c) as a fall-back in any such cases. The section 20(1)(a) duty may, however, be relevant for unaccompanied asylum-seeking teenagers who may have lost their parents in conflict or otherwise.

5.16    Parental responsibility is dealt with in CA 1989 s2. More than one person may have parental responsibility for a child at the same time (section 2(5)). Responsibility may be shared, for example, between a child's mother and father, or between a parent and a local authority where there is an interim care order in place. Section 2 details a range of situations and scenarios, including parenthood under the Human Fertilisation and Embryology Act 2008, and details the allocation of parental responsibility.

*Section 20(1)(b): lost or abandoned*

5.17    There is no specific definition provided of the terms 'lost' or 'abandoned'. Again, reliance on this paragraph will be rare, and in any event claimants are advised to plead section 20(1)(c) as a fall-back in any such cases. The term 'abandoned' should be construed strictly: a child who requires accommodation because his or her family is in crisis should generally be accommodated under section 20(1)(c).

*Section 20(1)(c): prevented*

5.18    In contrast to the narrowly drawn paragraphs 20(1)(a) and (b), paragraph 20(1)(c) has obviously broad phrasing: the local authority must accommodate the child in need if the child requires accommodation due to 'the person who has been caring for him being prevented (whether or not permanently, and for whatever reason) from providing him with suitable accommodation or care'. This requires establishing who was previously 'caring' for the child; and whether that person is in a position to provide the child with 'suitable accommodation or care'. This alternative phrasing indicates that even if the person is in a position to provide the child with suitable accommodation, but not suitable care, or vice versa, the section 20(1)(c) duty will be triggered.

5.19    It is clear from the statutory language and the case-law that section 20(1)(c) is to be given a broad and purposive interpretation. As

Lord Nicholls put it in *R (G) v Barnet LBC*, '"prevented ... for whatever reason" in paragraph (c) is to be interpreted widely'.[11] Burton J followed this wide, purposive approach in *R (L) v Nottinghamshire County Council*, stating that in interpreting the term 'prevented' in section 20(1)(c), the court should adopt an approach of 'fact and common sense'.[12] In that case, which also involved a difficult and occasionally violent parent–child relationship, he held:

> It seems to me plain that L's mother in this case was prevented from continuing to provide care to her daughter by the fact of her having been assaulted by the daughter and by the fact that the relationship had so badly broken down that she was not prepared to continue to accommodate the child and indeed the child was not prepared to be accommodated by the mother. This was not a question of choice, it was, in my judgment, a question of force of events.[13]

5.20　Similarly, Stanley Burnton J in *R (S) v Sutton LBC* also referred to the 'prevented' test being capable of being satisfied when circumstances have arisen where 'people are so incompatible that they simply cannot live together'.[14] (The case reached the Court of Appeal, but not on this point.[15]) This encompasses the kinds of situation which, with adults, might lead to a finding of intentional homelessness in a housing case.

5.21　This broad, purposive approach has since been endorsed by the Court of Appeal and House of Lords. In *R (RO) v East Riding of Yorkshire Council and Secretary of State for Education*[16] the Court of Appeal adopted such a broad purposive approach, drawing heavily on the judgment of the House of Lords in *R (M) v Hammersmith and Fulham*. In that case, Baroness Hale , delivering the single judgment of the House, stated:

> For what it is worth, it will be obvious from what has gone before that I agree with the broad approach to the interpretation of when a parent is 'prevented' from providing suitable accommodation or care under section 20(1)(c), which was favoured by Michael Burton J in the Nottinghamshire case and by Stanley Burnton J at first instance in the *Sutton London Borough Council* case [2007] EWHC 1196 (Admin), [2007] 2 FLR 849, rather than with the narrow approach favoured by

---

11　[2003] UKHL 57, [2002] 2 AC 208 at [24].
12　[2007] EWHC 2364 (Admin) at [34].
13　[2007] EWHC 2364 (Admin) at [34].
14　[2007] EWHC 1196 (Admin), (2007) 10 CCLR 485 at [40].
15　*R (S) v Sutton LBC* [2007] EWCA Civ 790, (2007) 10 CCLR 615.
16　[2011] EWCA Civ 196.

Lloyd LJ in this case. This mother may not have been prevented from providing her daughter with any accommodation or care but she was surely prevented from providing her with suitable accommodation or care.[17]

## Duty to provide accommodation

5.22    Once section 20(1)(a), (b) or (c) is triggered, the local authority is obliged to provide accommodation to the child. This is an absolute duty.

5.23    No definition of 'accommodation' is provided in section 20(1), although it is suggested that it must be 'suitable accommodation', meaning that it must, so far as practicable, meet the needs of the particular child, and take his or her wishes into account. This is the necessary implication of the phrase 'suitable accommodation or care' being used in section 20(1)(c). Further, this is supported by a definition of 'suitable accommodation' as it appears elsewhere in CA 1989 (s23B(10)), and in the Children (Leaving Care) (England) Regulations 2001 reg 11(2). The question of the suitability of accommodation is also informed by articles 27 and 39 of the UN Convention on the Rights of the Child (UNCRC) (the right to a standard of living adequate for the child's development, and state parties undertaking to take all appropriate measures to promote social reintegration of children who have suffered any form of neglect).

5.24    It is now widely recognised that certain types of accommodation are unsuitable for homeless 16- and 17-year-olds. In particular, B&B or hostel accommodation will not be suitable for these young people. This is recognised in the *Homelessness code of guidance 2006.*[18] This guidance makes clear that 16- and 17-year-olds who are homeless will be particularly vulnerable and in need of support;[19] that housing solutions are unlikely to be successful if appropriate support is not provided, so close liaison between housing, social services and other agencies 'will be essential';[20] and that B&B accommodation is unlikely to be suitable for children of 16 or 17 in need of support.[21] Baroness Hale in the *M* case echoed these concerns regarding B&B

---

17  [2008] UKHL 14, [2008] 1 WLR 535 at [43].

18  As detailed in paras 1 and 2 of the introduction to the code, local authority social services departments (including children's services) are obliged to have regard to the code under Housing Act 1996 s182(1).

19  Para 12.12.

20  Para 12.13.

21  Para 12.14.

accommodation.[22] They are further reinforced by the statutory guidance issued in the aftermath of the *G* case, which states that 'Bed and breakfast accommodation is not considered suitable for 16 and 17 year olds even on an emergency accommodation basis'.[23]

5.25    If representing a homeless child, it is imperative that clear instructions are received at an early stage regarding the child's wishes and feelings as to their needs, particularly regarding location and type of accommodation. As regards location of accommodation, it should not unduly disrupt the child's access to education, or the child's support network; and it should not place the child at risk in any way, for example if there are issues concerning gang membership or threats. As regards type of accommodation, many young people may have strong views regarding foster care, for example, or may require support which would prevent them living alone. If there is a history of sexual abuse or exploitation, or drug use, these may be important factors in ascertaining whether accommodation on offer is suitable for the child. A full initial or core assessment under CA 1989 s17 (see chapter 4) should of course deal with all of these matters, but often accommodation will need to be provided urgently, either by agreement or on the basis of a court order, prior to the completion of the assessment.

5.26    As we noted in the introduction to this chapter, of much concern to the authors is the popular – and unfortunately, on occasions, judicial[24] – misconception that 'section 20 accommodation' involves only certain types of accommodation, such as children's homes or foster care. The section 20 duty to accommodate homeless children 'in need' can be discharged by placing a child in *any* type of accommodation that is suitable to the child's needs. Despite misconceptions to the contrary, there is no such thing as 'section 20 accommodation' in the sense of a specific type of accommodation to which children 'in need' are restricted. This may be a children's home or foster care, but it may also be a placement with a family friend or relative, semi-independent or independent accommodation – whatever the

22  *R (M) v Hammersmith and Fulham LBC* [2008] UKHL 14, [2008] 1 WLR 535 at [27].

23  DCSF/DCLG, *Provision of accommodation for 16 and 17 year old young people who may be homeless and/or require accommodation: guidance to children's services authorities and local housing authorities about their duties under Part 3 of the Children Act 1989 and Part 7 of the Housing Act 1996 to secure or provide accommodation for homeless 16 and 17 year old young people*, April 2010 at para 2.16; see also paras 2.10 and 3.1. For Wales, see Welsh Assembly Circular 025/2010, *Provision of accommodation for 16 and 17 year old young people who may be homeless*, September 2010, at paras 2.14 and 2.18.

24  See, eg, *R (AH) v Cornwall CC* [2010] EWHC 3192 (Admin).

child's needs require. With older children, particularly 17-year-olds who have been street homeless or 'sofa-surfing' for some time, their independence will be of considerable importance to them, and foster placements or children's homes are unlikely to be suitable for, or desirable to, them. For a local authority to conclude that a child who wishes to live in independent accommodation (such as his or her own flat) necessarily falls outside section 20, is quite wrong.

## Section 20(6): child's wishes and feelings

5.27    CA 1989 s20(6) provides that:

> Before providing accommodation under this section, a local authority shall, so far as is reasonably practicable and consistent with the child's welfare –
> (a) ascertain the child's wishes and feelings regarding the provision of accommodation; and
> (b) give due consideration (having regard to his age and understanding) to such wishes and feelings of the child as they have been able to ascertain.

5.28    The section 20(6) duty does not entail the child's views being determinative; it instead amounts to a duty to give due consideration (having regard to the child's age and understanding) to the child's wishes and feelings. This clause was considered carefully by the Court of Appeal in *R (Liverpool CC) v Hillingdon LBC*,[25] in which it was held that Hillingdon LBC had acted unlawfully and failed to discharge its statutory duty under CA 1989 s20 by failing to conduct an age assessment of an asylum-seeker who claimed to be a child, and failing to provide him with accommodation pending such assessment, and instead removing him to another local authority (Liverpool County Council, the claimant), albeit that the move was in accordance with the young person's expressed wishes and feelings. The court stated that the requirement to have regard to a child's wishes was not determinative of a local authority's duty to provide accommodation to a child in need. The emphasis of the CA 1989 was on a child's welfare, and, as Dyson LJ pointed out, 'children are often not good judges of what was is in their best interests'[26] (later cited by Baroness Hale in the G case[27]). It was recognised by the Court of Appeal in the *Liverpool* case that there might be cases where the child's wishes were

25  [2009] EWCA Civ 43, [2009] 1 FLR 1536.
26  [2009] EWCA Civ 43, [2009] 1 FLR 1536 at [32].
27  *R (G) v Southwark LBC* [2009] UKHL 26, [2009] 1 WLR 1299 at [28].

decisive, but a local authority should reach the conclusion that the child's wishes were decisive only as part of its overall judgment, which included an assessment of the child's welfare needs and the type and location of accommodation that would meet those needs. A section 17 assessment would always be required, as otherwise the authority would not be able to give due consideration to the question whether it was consistent with the child's welfare needs to accede to his or her wishes.

5.29    In the circumstances of that particular case, Hillingdon LBC had not given any consideration to the young person's welfare needs. It had not made any assessment of his needs, nor of what kind of accommodation would meet those needs. It had not taken account of his age, because it had not known what his age was. It had made no assessment of his understanding, and made no enquiry of what accommodation would be available in Liverpool CC's area and whether it would be suitable for his needs. Hillingdon LBC had not applied the nuanced approach to the wishes and feelings of a child which was mandated by section 20(6), and had instead taken the simplistic view that the fact that he said that he wanted to live in Liverpool was determinative of the matter. That was not a proper discharge of the section 20 duty.

5.30    Critically, if a child is provided with accommodation under section 20, he or she falls within the definition of a 'looked after' child, but not if that accommodation is provided under CA 1989 s17, or under the Housing Act 1996 (CA 1989 s22; see further paras 5.76–5.96 below). The implications of 'looked after' status are profound; if the child accumulates sufficient looked after time, his or her 'corporate parent' (the local authority) will then be obliged to provide leaving care services for him or her until the age of at least 21. Put shortly, the central aim of the leaving care regime is to ensure that young people who have spent a substantial period of time in the care of the local authority are supported with their transition to adulthood and independence, with the authority providing, 'broadly, the support that a good parent might be expected to give' when a child is preparing to leave and actually leaving home.[28] The leaving care regime is discussed in detail in chapter 7.

5.31    As detailed throughout this chapter, the courts have now repeatedly made clear that local authorities cannot sidestep their long-term duties to vulnerable young people under the leaving care regime

28  *Children (Leaving Care) Act 2000 regulations and guidance*, DoH, 2001, chapter 4 para 3.

by labelling accommodation which should be provided pursuant to their section 20 duties as 'section 17 accommodation', 'Housing Act accommodation', a 'private fostering arrangement' or any other form of arrangement that avoids the child being considered a 'looked after' child.

5.32    However, there is an open question regarding the implications of CA 1989 s20(6) in this regard. The issue is whether, on the basis of section 20(6), a child can 'waive' his or her right to be looked after. This is an area of real concern, particularly as the local authority, the body that would ultimately have to pay for the accommodation for the child, and the resulting 'leaving care' support, would be the same body presenting the competing options to the child, and ascertaining the child's views, which gives rise to a clear conflict. In the authors' view, CA 1989 s20(6) should properly be read as concerning the *type* of accommodation – for example, if the child wishes to be as independent as possible, or refuses to accept a foster placement – and not the legal label it attracts.

5.33    Baroness Hale touched on this issue in *R (M) v Hammersmith and Fulham LBC*.[29] She noted (obiter, or outside the main judgment) that she had 'reservations' about the 'narrow approach' adopted by Stanley Burnton J in *R (S) v Sutton LBC*[30] to the significance of the child's wishes under section 20(6), a matter about which the Court of Appeal in the *Sutton* case had declined to express a concluded view.[31] She continued:

> It seems to me that there may well be cases in which there is a choice between section 17 and section 20, where the wishes of the child, at least of an older child who is fully informed of the consequences of the choices before her, may determine the matter. It is most unlikely that section 20 was intended to operate compulsorily against a child who is competent to decide for herself. The whole object of the 1989 Act was to draw a clear distinction between voluntary and compulsory powers and to require that compulsion could only be used after due process of law.

5.34    Regrettably, the authors are aware of multiple instances in which section 20(6) is being used to justify a conclusion that section 20(1) does not apply, on the basis that the child has expressed a view that he or she does not want to become 'looked after'. The explanations provided to the child tend to focus on the type of accommodation on offer, so

29  [2008] UKHL 14, [2008] 1 WLR 535 at [43].
30  [2007] EWHC 1196 (Admin), [2007] 2 FLR 849.
31  [2007] EWCA Civ 790, (2007) 10 CCLR 615.

the child understands that he or she is being offered either restrictive accommodation (children's home or foster care) under section 20, or alternatively 'independent' accommodation under the Housing Act 1996. This is far from the fully free and informed consent envisaged by Baroness Hale in her obiter comments in the *Hammersmith and Fulham* case.

## Has the section 20(1) duty been triggered?

5.35 In the recent, and leading, case of *R (G) v Southwark LBC*, Baroness Hale summarised the recent case-law concerning section 20(1), and set out how that provision is to be approached. She referred to a series of judgments set out by Ward LJ in *R (A) v Croydon LBC*,[32] and drew on his analysis to construct seven questions to ascertain whether or not a duty is owed under section 20(1). This is a useful checklist for legal advisers and local authorities. The seven questions are set out in the box below. However, note our concerns regarding questions six and seven being considered as part of the eligibility test, as they both relate to section 20(6) which we consider to perform a very different statutory function (see para 5.32 above).

---

### Has the CA 1989 s20(1) duty been triggered?

- Question 1: Is the applicant a child, ie under the age of 18 (CA 1989 s105(1))?
- Question 2: Is the applicant a child 'in need', ie does the child meet the definition in CA 1989 s17(10)? Bear in mind that a child without accommodation is a child 'in need' (see para 5.10 above).
- Question 3: Is the child within the local authority's area? (See paras 4.14–4.19 above.)
- Question 4: Does the child appear to the local authority to require accommodation?
- Question 5: Is that need the result of:
  (a) there being no person who has parental responsibility for the child; or
  (b) the child's being lost or having been abandoned; or
  (c) the person who has been caring for the child being prevented (whether or not permanently and for whatever reason) from providing the child with suitable accommodation or care?

---

32  [2008] EWCA Civ 1445, [2009] LGR 24 at [75].

- Question 6: What are the child's wishes and feelings regarding the provision of accommodation for him or her? This question is based on CA 1989 s20(6). Note the difficulty with including this as part of the eligibility test, as distinct from it informing decisions on suitability of accommodation (see para 5.32 above).
- Question 7: What consideration (having regard to the child's age and understanding) is duly to be given to those wishes and feelings?

5.36   The section 20(1) duty may be triggered before the child becomes homeless. The reason why advance planning is so essential is that the duty under section 20 is to provide *suitable* accommodation (see para 5.23 above). Last-minute accommodation often unfortunately involves B&Bs or hostels, despite such accommodation being widely recognised as unsuitable for children. In particular circumstances, it may also be essential to secure an address in advance, for example where a child is entitled to early release from custody on an electronic tag but cannot be released without the address first being confirmed (see paras 5.116–5.141 below).

## Section 20(3)

5.37   Section 20(3) of the CA 1989 provides that every local authority shall provide accommodation for any child within their area who has reached the age of 16 and whose welfare the authority considers likely to be seriously prejudiced if the authority does not provide the child with accommodation. This subsection is rarely relied upon in practice, as any child falling within the section 20(3) definition will usually fall within the far broader and now well-established section 20(1)(c) duty – if the child's welfare will be 'seriously prejudiced' without accommodation being provided, it stands to reason that the person who has been caring for the child must in some way be 'prevented' from providing him or her with 'suitable accommodation or care'. The main use for the section 20(3) duty will be in situations where a teenager has been living independently for a period and then requires accommodation.

5.38   If legal advisers are relying upon section 20(3), our view is that section 20(1)(c) should generally be included in the alternative.

5.39   If a child is accommodated pursuant to section 20(3), this will also result in the child being considered 'looked after', as with section 20(1) (see paras 5.76–5.98 below). The concerns we have raised regarding the implications of section 20(6) also apply to section 20(3) (see para 5.32 above).

## Children Act 1989 s20: powers to accommodate

5.40 In addition to the duties to accommodate, detailed in section 20(1) and (3), there are discretionary powers to accommodate contained in section 20(4) and (5).

### Section 20(4)

5.41 Section 20(4) of the CA 1989 provides that:

> A local authority may provide accommodation for any child within their area (even though a person who has parental responsibility for him is able to provide him with accommodation) if they consider that to do so would safeguard or promote the child's welfare.

5.42 Given the breadth of the section 20(1)(c) duty, this is very much a residual power, as in the vast majority of cases a child falling into this category will also fall within that provision.

5.43 Despite its discretionary nature, once a child is accommodated pursuant to section 20(4), the same implications flow from it for the local authority and the child in terms of the child's looked after status, and accumulation of sufficient time will result in entitlement to leaving care support. The only exception to this is some residential short-break care for (generally) disabled children; see chapter 4 at para 4.61 for the modifications to 'looked after' status in such cases.

### Section 20(5)

5.44 Section 20(5) of the CA 1989 is of more significance than section 20(4). It provides that:

> A local authority may provide accommodation for any person who has reached the age of sixteen but is under twenty-one in any community home which takes children who have reached the age of sixteen if they consider that to do so would safeguard or promote his welfare.

5.45 As the upper age limit to this subsection is 21, it provides a potential protection for vulnerable young people between the ages of 18 and 21, in addition to other community care and housing provisions. In relation to this group, the power to accommodate must be considered in every case, and the decision as to whether it should be exercised taken rationally, reasonably and fairly in the light of all the evidence. As regards 16- and 17-year-olds, again, the category of children likely to fall within the reach of section 20(5) but not section 20(1)(c) is very limited.

5.46   Despite its discretionary nature, once a child is accommodated pursuant to section 20(5), the same implications flow from it for the local authority and the child in terms of the child's looked after status, and accumulation of sufficient time will result in entitlement to leaving care support.

## Parental veto

5.47   Subsections 20(7)–(11) concern circumstances in which a parent may, in effect, 'veto' what would otherwise be a section 20 placement. Legal advisers to children and young people should ensure that where these provisions are relied upon, the parent(s) have truly objected in this way, and that there has been no misunderstanding regarding the effect of a child becoming a 'looked after' child. Care must also be taken to ensure that a person with parental responsibility who objects to a child being placed under section 20 is 'able' to accommodate the child.

5.48   Section 20(7) provides that a local authority may not provide section 20 for any child if any person who:

(a) has parental responsibility for him; and
(b) is willing and able to –
   (i)  provide accommodation for him; or
   (ii) arrange for accommodation to be provided for him,
objects.

5.49   In similar terms, section 20(8) provides that any person who has parental responsibility for a child may 'at any time' remove the child from accommodation provided by, or on behalf of, the local authority under section 20. Thus, section 20(7) provides a right of parental veto prior to the placement, and section 20(8) allows for the parent to terminate the placement at any time. 'Parental responsibility', the phrase used in both subsections, is defined in CA 1989 s2.

5.50   However, subsections 20(7) and (8) do not apply in two circumstances. First, and most significantly, they have no application to children aged 16 and over, where the children agree to be provided with accommodation (section 20(11)). Second, the veto provisions do not apply if there is agreement to the section 20 accommodation from a special guardian of the child, a person who has care of the child pursuant to a court order 'made in the exercise of the High Court's inherent jurisdiction with respect to children', or a person in whose favour a residence order with respect to the child (section 20(9)). If there is more than one person falling within the section 20(9) categories, they must all agree (section 20(10)).

5.51     If section 20(7) or (8) are relied upon by a person with parental responsibility, yet the local authority consider that the child's welfare would be seriously prejudiced by remaining in the family home, it may be necessary to utilise the provisions of Part IV of CA 1989 to protect the child (for example, by securing an interim care order).

## Practical issues in section 20 litigation

5.52     For practitioners representing claimants, there are a number of important practical features of CA 1989 s20 cases of which they should be aware:

- Often these issues are litigated through urgent judicial reviews, within a very tight timeframe.

- Such judicial reviews will be publicly funded in the vast majority of cases, based on the child's means rather than the parents'; due to the timeframe, they will often require the use of devolved or emergency funding powers to secure funding to issue proceedings and seek interim relief.

- The claimant child will often be street homeless or staying in unsafe or unstable accommodation, and so securing interim relief from the Administrative Court (either on the papers or out-of-hours from the duty judge) will be crucial. Interim relief may be obtained prior to the issue of proceedings,[33] usually from the duty judge by telephone subject to an undertaking to issue proceedings the following day. A preferable approach, if time allows, is to issue proceedings, even if with only outline grounds of review, seeking interim relief 'on the papers', potentially with an early hearing to review the position.

- If applying for interim relief on an urgent and ex parte[34] basis, the claimant's solicitor and counsel must ensure that they comply with the minimum requirements specified in *R (Lawer) v Restormel BC*, a Housing Act 1996 case in which Munby J (as he

---

33  Civil Procedure Rules (CPR) 25.1.
34  Legal action that is by a single party.

then was) found that there had been serious non-disclosure to the duty judge.[35] In the pre-action correspondence the claimant's solicitor must put the authority on notice of the intention to apply for interim relief on an ex parte basis, preferably including a copy of the draft order to be sought; must ensure his or her out-of-hours contact details are provided; and must request equivalent details from the local authority, including a fax number (this is important in order to fax the authority a copy of any order obtained from the duty judge). Counsel or the solicitor making any duty judge application should disclose all adverse material and should keep a full attendance note. Many Queen's Bench duty judges will now request that an attendance note of the telephone application be filed and served; even if this is not requested, it is best practice that it should be offered and an undertaking to this effect included in the draft order.[36]

- It is sensible for the claimant's solicitor to attempt to secure a suitable address for the child in advance if at all possible, so that a fall-back address can be included within the draft order in the event that the local authority cannot secure suitable accommodation for the child within a specific timeframe (eg by 6pm that evening). There are a number of private providers who specialise in accommodation for vulnerable children and who will accept queries from legal representatives directly.

- Legal representatives must also consider whether or not the child needs a litigation friend, and if there is a suitable adult in his or her life to perform this role. Part 21 of the Civil Procedure Rules (CPR) requires that a child has a litigation friend unless the court dispenses with the requirement by order.[37] Often it will be necessary to approach the Official Solicitor (OS) as there is no suitable adult available. Sometimes with older and 'streetwise' children, the solicitor may consider that there is no need for a litigation friend, so an application can be made to dispense with the requirement. Often, even if a litigation friend is necessary, proceedings will need to be issued and/or urgent interim relief sought prior to securing one. In those circumstances the duty judge should be asked to make an order under CPR 21.2(3) dispensing with the need for a litigation friend for the time being, for practical reasons, while the solicitor approaches the OS or any suitable adult identified.

---

35 [2007] EWHC 2299 (Admin).
36 See further CPR PD 25A, paras 4.5 and 5.1.
37 CPR 21.2(2) and (3).

- As the law concerning section 20 is now clear, the majority of cases settle post-issue, with a high percentage of inter partes[38] costs orders (either by consent or following costs submissions).

5.53 Further, claimants' legal representatives should consider whether to include a claim for damages under the Human Rights Act (HRA) 1998, for example if the child has been street homeless as a consequence of a failure by the local authority to comply with its section 20 duty, or if the child's life has been put at risk through remaining in an unsafe estate when he or she is at risk of gang violence.

5.54 As regards disclosure, the authors consider that there are certain types of documents that will always be of relevance in section 20 cases. In the authors' view, in pre-action correspondence claimants' solicitors should routinely request sight of the following documents:

1) *The child's social services/children's services file(s).* They may disclose, for example, that the child or any siblings have previously been on the child protection register, or other concerns regarding the family home. They may also disclose that the local authority has been aware of accommodation difficulties in the past or that accommodation has been provided by the local authority in the past.

2) *The child's housing file.* Again, this may reveal information regarding the family home, and communications between housing and children's services.

3) *Any draft or final inter-agency protocol concerning homeless 16- and 17-year-olds, between children's services and the housing department or any housing authorities.* There may not be any such protocol in place, which is unlawful in itself (see para 5.108 below); or when disclosed it may become apparent that the protocol is unlawful, or the decision-making of the local authority in refusing to recognise a section 20 duty was flawed in light of the protocol.[39]

## Section 21

5.55 Section 21 of the CA 1989 concerns the provision of accommodation by local authorities for children in police protection, detention or on remand. The section commences with a general duty: it is mandatory for every local authority to 'make provision for the reception and

---

38 Between parties, as opposed to ex parte.
39 Under the common law obligation for public bodies to comply with stated policies absent good reason not to do so.

accommodation' of children who are removed or kept away from home on this basis (section 21(1)).

5.56    Section 21(2) then specifies circumstances in which the designated local authority must 'receive' children, and provide them with accommodation:

(a) children in police protection, whom the authority is requested to receive under CA 1989 s46(3)(f);

(b) children whom they are requested to receive under section 38(6) of the Police and Criminal Evidence Act 1984 (detention overnight post-charge due to the custody officer having 'reasonable grounds for believing' that the child 'ought to be detained in his own interests');

(c) children who are on remand,[40] or remanded to local authority accommodation for breach of referral orders or reparation orders,[41] youth rehabilitation orders,[42] or breach of certain orders under the Street Offences Act 1959;[43]

(d) children who are the subject of a youth rehabilitation order imposing a local authority residence requirement, or a fostering requirement.

## Section 25

5.57    CA 1989 s25 makes provision for local authorities to use accommodation to restrict liberty in certain tightly defined circumstances. This provision is designed for extreme circumstances, where a child poses a serious risk to himself or herself or others – in other words, it is a form of preventative detention. It must be interpreted in the context of the importance attached to liberty by article 5 of the European Convention on Human Rights (ECHR) and the common law. In a controversial decision, the Court of Appeal in *K (A Child) (Secure Accommodation Order: Right to Liberty)*[44] accepted that a secure accommodation order amounted to a deprivation of the child's liberty, but held that it was not incompatible with article 5 ECHR, as article 5(1)(d) rendered permissible the detention of a child 'by lawful order for the purpose of educational supervision'. The local authority had a statutory obligation to provide 'K' with education at the secure unit

---

40  Children and Young Persons Act 1969 s23(1).
41  Powers of Criminal Courts (Sentencing) Act 2000 Sch 1 para 4 or Sch 8 para 6.
42  Criminal Justice and Immigration Act 2008 Sch 2 para 21.
43  Street Offences Act 1959 s1(2A) and para 10 of the Schedule.
44  [2001] 2 All ER 719.

where he was detained, it was held; and furthermore, 'educational supervision' was to be interpreted widely so as to encompass many aspects of the exercise by a local authority of parental rights over a child.

5.58     Section 25 is supplemented by a number of statutory instruments, most notably the Children (Secure Accommodation) Regulations (CSA Regs) 1991.[45]

5.59     Section 25(1) is drafted in negative terms:

(1) Subject to the following provisions of this section, a child who is being looked after by a local authority may not be placed, and, if placed, may not be kept, in accommodation provided for the purpose of restricting liberty ("secure accommodation") unless it appears–
(a) that –
(i)   he has a history of absconding and is likely to abscond from any other description of accommodation; and
(ii)  if he absconds, he is likely to suffer significant harm; or
(b) that if he is kept in any other description of accommodation he is likely to injure himself or other persons.

5.60     The section 25 power is subject to section 20(8), the parental veto described above at para 5.49 above, and which is in turn subject to section 20(9)–(11). There is a duty to inform the child's parents and other significant persons of the exercise of the section 25 power (CSA Regs 1991 reg 14), plainly essential if the section 20(8) veto is to be meaningful.

5.61     'Secure accommodation' is defined in section 25(1) as 'accommodation provided for the purpose of restricting liberty'. However, as White, Carr and Lowe have noted, it is not so much the *purpose* for which the accommodation is used as whether, on the facts, it *is* actually secure accommodation.[46] For example, a patient held in a hospital maternity ward which could only be accessed using a key or pass, being treated by nursing staff who had been instructed to prevent her leaving so that her health and life were not endangered, was considered to be held in secure accommodation.[47]

5.62     The test laid down under section 25(1)(a) refers to both the likelihood of the child absconding and the likelihood of him or her suffering significant harm if he or she does abscond. There is no definition of 'likely' provided, and so the question arises whether it means 'a

---

45  SI No 1505.

46  R White, AP Carr and N Lowe, *The Children Act in practice*, LexisNexis, 4th edn 2008, para 9.8.

47  *A Metropolitan Borough Council v DB* [1997] 1 FLR 767.

real possibility' (as in CA 1989 s31, where the words 'likely to suffer significant harm' are used[48]), or 'more likely than not'. This issue was addressed in *S (A Child) v Knowsley BC*.[49] The applicant, 'S,' sought to challenge the lawfulness of secure accommodation orders made against her. She had been the subject of successive secure accommodation orders over the years. In the course of the last order she was diagnosed with cancer requiring intensive chemotherapy. She asserted that, if she were not removed from secure accommodation, she would refuse treatment, in which case her prognosis was very poor. The court concluded that 'likely' in the phrase 'likely to abscond' should be construed in the same way as in the threshold criteria in section 31, 'namely, in the sense of a real possibility or a possibility that cannot sensibly be ignored'.[50] It proceeded to reject S's application for judicial review, and her HRA claim, on the basis that, given her past history, there was a real possibility or a possibility that could not be ignored that she would abscond in the absence of an order.

5.63     The double requirement in section 25(1)(a) is thus diluted significantly in practice: all that is required is a 'possibility that cannot sensibly be ignored' that the child will abscond, and, if so, a 'possibility that cannot sensibly be ignored' that the child will suffer significant harm.

## Age at which a child may be subject to a section 25 order

5.64     The upper age limit is 18, as section 25 refers to a 'child' and the general definition in the CA 1989 applies (section 105(1)).

5.65     There is no specified lower age limit, but in the case of a child aged under 13, CSA Regs 1991 reg 4 must be complied with:

> **4 Placement of a child aged under 13 in secure accommodation in a children's home**
> A child under the age of 13 years shall not be placed in secure accommodation in a children's home without the prior approval of the Secretary of State to the placement of that child and such approval shall be subject to such terms and conditions as he sees fit.

---

48   *Re H and Others (Minors) (Sexual Abuse: Standard of Proof)* [1996] AC 563.
49   [2004] EWHC 491 (Fam), [2004] 2 FLR 716.
50   [2004] EWHC 491 (Fam), [2004] 2 FLR 716 at [37].

## Exclusion from section 25

5.66    By virtue of CA 1989 s25(7)(a), the CSA Regs 1991 provide for the exclusion of certain categories of children from the section 25 power. It is unlawful to exercise the section 25 power in respect of any young people falling within these excluded categories. These exclusions are detailed in regulation 5, and they are:

1) a child detained under the Mental Health Act 1983 (regulation 5(1));
2) a child in respect of whom an order has been made under section 90 or section 91 of the Powers of the Criminal Courts (Sentencing) Act 2000 (detention at Her Majesty's pleasure or for a specified period) (regulation 5(1));
3) a person who is being accommodated pursuant to CA 1989 s20(5) (accommodation of persons over 16 but under 21, dealt with at paras 5.44–5.46 above) (regulation 5(2)(a));
4) a child who is being kept away from home due to an order made pursuant to CA 1989 s43 (child assessment order) (regulation 5(2)(b)).

## Modified application of section 25

5.67    Section 25(7)(b) authorised the making of regulations which would modify the application of section 25 to certain categories of child. The CSA Regs 1991 make such modifications, in regulations 6 and 7.

5.68    Regulation 6 makes a number of modifications to the section 25 regime in respect of detained and remanded children. As regards remanded children, regulation 6 includes additional requirements before the section 25 power may be used. There are two such requirements, but they are alternatives:

a) the child must have been charged with or been convicted of a violent or sexual offence, or an offence punishable in the case of an adult with imprisonment for 14 years or more; or
b) the child has a recent history of absconding while remanded to local authority accommodation, and is charged with or has been convicted of an imprisonable offence alleged or found to have been committed while he was so remanded.

5.69    Regulation 7 extends the application of section 25 to children who are not looked after by a local authority, but are accommodated by health authorities, Primary Care Trusts, National Health Service Trusts, or local education authorities (regulation 7(1)(a)), or children accommodated in care homes or independent hospitals (regulation

7(1)(b)). There are a number of modifications to the system detailed in regulation 7.

## Time limits under section 25 and court authorisation

5.70   Given the profound consequences of a section 25 order, it is necessarily subject to judicial supervision. The maximum period for which
a child may be kept in secure accommodation without the authority
of a court is an aggregate of 72 hours (whether or not consecutive) in
any 28-day period (CA 1989 s25(2) and CSA Regs 1991 reg 10(1)).

5.71   A court may authorise longer periods, but there are limitations in
the CSA Regs 1991. In general, the maximum initial period which the
court may authorise is three months (regulation 11), but for children
on remand the maximum is 28 days at any one time and the period
may not exceed the remand period (regulation 13). Rather oddly,
despite these initial restrictions regulation 12 allows for the court to
authorise further periods of up to six months (provided, in the case of
children on remand, this does not exceed the remand period).

5.72   A court may only exercise powers under section 25 if the child is
legally represented, or 'having been informed of his right to apply for
representation funded by the Legal Services Commission ... and having had the opportunity to do so, he refused or failed to apply'.[51] For
this to be meaningful, the court must be satisfied that the opportunity
to apply was meaningful, the implications of not applying were fully
understood, and it was an informed decision to proceed without legal
advice. Given the extreme and often chaotic circumstances which will
be in play in section 25 cases, and the profundity of the consequences
for the child, it is the authors' view that the courts must be particularly alert to this restriction on the exercise of the section 25 power by
local authorities.

## Review of section 25 order

5.73   In addition to oversight by the court, regulation 15 of the CSA Regs
1991 provides that each local authority looking after a child in secure
accommodation must appoint a panel of at least three persons, at
least one of whom must be independent of the authority, to review
the section 25 placement. The first review must take place 'within
one month of the inception of the placement' and thereafter reviews
must take place at maximum three-month intervals.

---

51   CA 1989 s25(6).

5.74    The nature of these reviews is mandated by regulation 16. The panel must, if practicable, 'ascertain and take into account' the views of the following people, and subsequently inform them of the outcome of the review:

(a) the child,
(b) any parent of his,
(c) any person not being a parent of his but who has parental responsibility for him,
(d) any other person who has had the care of the child, whose views the persons appointed consider should be taken into account,
(e) the child's independent visitor if one has been appointed, and
(f) the person, organisation or local authority managing the secure accommodation in which the child is placed if that accommodation is not managed by the authority which is looking after that child.

5.75    On review, the panel 'shall satisfy themselves' (a) that the criteria for keeping the child in secure accommodation continue to apply, (b) that the placement continues to be necessary, and (c) of whether or not there is any less restrictive option available, ie is there any other form of accommodation which would be suitable for the child. In conducting this exercise the panel must have regard to the welfare of the child whose case is being reviewed.[52]

## 'Looked after' children

5.76    Section 22(1) of the CA 1989 provides the definition of a looked after child:

> In this Act, any reference to a child who is looked after by a local authority is a reference to a child who is–
> (a) in their care; or
> (b) provided with accommodation by the authority in the exercise of any functions (in particular those under this Act) which are social services functions within the meaning of the Local Authority Social Services Act 1970, apart from functions under sections 17, 23B and 24B ...

5.77    'Accommodation' in section 22(1) means accommodation provided for a continuous period of more than 24 hours.[53]

---

52  CSA Regs 1991 reg 16(1).
53  CA 1989 s22(2).

5.78    Falling within this definition has both immediate and longer-term implications for a child. There are a series of duties owed by the local authority to 'looked after' children, detailed in CA 1989 ss22–23ZB. Longer-term, depending on the age of the child when looked after, and the duration of the period for which he or she is looked after, the local authority may owe him or her duties until the age of 25 under the leaving care regime, detailed in full in chapter 7.

## Local authority duties towards looked after children

### General duties

5.79    CA 1989 ss22–23ZB detail the duties local authorities owe towards children who are looked after by them. A number of these duties have been introduced by the Children and Young Persons Act (CYPA) 2008; these changes are in force as of 1 April 2011. Important changes arising from CYPA 2008 are dealt with below in paras 5.143–5.160.

5.80    The general duties are detailed in CA 1989 s22, subsection (3) onwards. First, and underpinning all other duties, is the welfare requirement (section 22(3)):

> It shall be the duty of a local authority looking after any child –
> (a) to safeguard and promote his welfare; and
> (b) to make such use of services available for children cared for by their own parents as appears to the authority reasonable in this case ...

5.81    This duty to safeguard and promote the child's welfare is owed to the individual child and includes an explicit requirement to 'promote the child's educational achievement' (section 22(3A)).

5.82    Before making any decision concerning a looked after child, the local authority should ascertain the wishes and feelings of key individuals, including in particular the child and the child's parents or anyone with parental responsibility (section 22(4)), and give due consideration to those wishes and feelings (section 22(5)(a) and (b)), and 'to the child's religious persuasion, racial origin and cultural and linguistic background' (section 22(5)(c)).

5.83    Section 22B was introduced by CYPA 2008. It provides that it is the duty of the local authority to maintain a child they are looking after 'in other respects apart from the provision of accommodation'. This echoes the requirements of CA 1989 s17, whereby the local authority is obliged to assess the needs of the child, and provide services to meet those needs (see chapter 4).

## Accommodation and maintenance duties

5.84 Section 23 of CA 1989 previously mandated a general duty on local authorities both to accommodate looked after children, and to maintain them in other ways. This has now been substituted by the new sections 22A–22F.

5.85 Section 22C details ways in which looked after children are to be accommodated and maintained. The 'overriding factor' is that the placement must be the most appropriate placement available.[54]

5.86 The local authority must make arrangements for the child to live with a parent, someone with parental responsibility, or a person in whose favour a residence order was made (section 22C(3)), unless such an arrangement would be inconsistent with the child's welfare or not reasonably practicable (section 22C(4)). This means that a child may be 'looked after' even in circumstances where he or she returns to live in the family home. This is described in one of the related pieces of statutory guidance as the 'rehabilitative duty,' reflecting

> the principle that state intervention in family life should be kept to the minimum necessary to protect the child from harm – ultimately a child should be brought up by his/her family if that is a safe place for him/her to be.[55]

5.87 If the local authority is unable to place the child with a parent or other category of person falling within section 22C(3), the authority must place the child 'in the placement which is, in their opinion, the most appropriate placement available' (section 22C(5)). Pursuant to section 22C(6), such a placement may be with a friend or relative who is a local authority foster parent, a different foster parent, a children's home, or any other placement, provided the arrangements comply with any relevant regulations (this may involve independent accommodation, semi-independent accommodation, a placement with a private care provider, and so on). For disabled children in particular, the most appropriate placement may be a residential special school: see *R (RO) v East Riding of Yorkshire Council and Secretary of State for Education.*[56] In deciding upon placement, the local authority should give preference to a known adult, ie a friend or relative who is a local authority foster parent (section 22C(7)).

---

54 *Sufficiency: statutory guidance on securing sufficient accommodation for looked after children* ('Sufficiency Guidance'), Department for Children, Schools and Families, 2010, para 2.17.

55 *The Children Act 1989 regulations and guidance: vol 2, care planning, placement and case review,* HM Government, 2010, para 3.2.

56 [2011] EWCA Civ 196.

5.88 Insofar as it is reasonably practicable, the local authority must ensure that the placement allows the child to live near the family home (section 22C(8)(a)), does not disrupt the child's education or training (section 22C(8)(b)), and allows for siblings to live together (section 22C(8)(c)). As discussed above at para 5.23, the duty under section 20(1) is in any event to provide 'suitable' accommodation, and it stands to reason that, in order to be suitable, these requirements should be met.

5.89 In the case of a disabled child, the accommodation should be suitable to meet the child's needs arising from disability (section 22C(8)(d)).

5.90 If reasonably practicable, the placement should be in the local authority's area (section 22C(7)(c) and (9)). However, in certain circumstances there will be a conflict between this requirement and the requirement of suitability. For example, if a child is in danger in a particular area due to gang involvement, it may be essential for the accommodation to be out-of-borough.

5.91 This is recognised in the Sufficiency Guidance, in force as of 1 April 2011. It recognises that children who require highly specialist services, or children for whom there is a safeguarding issue, may need to be placed in a neighbouring borough, but it emphasises the importance of placing the child 'as close to their existing family networks and support systems as is possible and appropriate'.[57]

## Other duties

### Visits and contact

5.92 By virtue of section 23ZA, local authorities have a duty to ensure visits to, and contact with, looked after children and others. The section applies to looked after children, but provision is also made for it to apply more widely, to children previously looked after but who no longer are due to certain prescribed circumstances (section 23ZA(1)). The Visits to Former Looked After Children in Detention (England) Regulations 2010 now provide for this duty to apply to those children who have ceased to be looked after as a result of being remanded or sentenced to custody, but who are not eligible for leaving care support.[58]

5.93 Section 23ZA is already partially in force in England, but not yet in Wales at time of writing. The requirements in this section are supplemented by two sets of regulations, in force as of 1 April 2011: the Care Planning, Placement and Case Review (England) Regulations (CPPCR

---

57 *Sufficiency: Statutory guidance on securing sufficient accommodation for looked after children*, Department for Children, Schools and Families, 2010, paras 2.19 and 2.20.

58 SI No 2797.

Regs) 2010;[59] and the Visits to Former Looked After Children in Detention (England) Regulations 2010. There is also supporting statutory guidance for both sets of regulations, in force as of 1 April 2011.

5.94 Section 23ZA(2) places two statutory duties on the local authority: first, to ensure that the young person is visited by a representative of the authority; and second, to ensure that arrangements are made for 'appropriate advice, support and assistance' to be available to a looked after young person who seeks this from them. These duties are to be exercised in accordance with any relevant regulations. The likely impact of the CPPCR Regs 2010 is discussed at paras 5.149–5.157 below.

### Independent visitors

5.95 Again, section 23ZB has already been in force for certain purposes since 1 September 2009, but its impact is reliant on the CPPCR Regs 2010, in force only as of April 2011. It requires the local authority to appoint 'independent visitors' for looked after children if required to do so by the regulations (section 23ZB(1)(a)), or if it appears it would be in the child's interests to do so (section 23ZB(1)(b)). A person so appointed 'must visit, befriend and advise the child' (section 23ZB(2)) and may recover expenses from the local authority for this.

5.96 The child may object to the appointment or continuation of the appointment of a particular visitor, and the local authority is required to terminate the appointment if the child objects and they believe he or she has sufficient understanding to appreciate the implications of this (section 23ZB(6) and (7)). If the child's objection is specific to the particular person, it appears that a fresh appointment should then be made; but if the child objects generally to having any visitor at all, 'the authority does not have to propose to appoint another person ... until the objection is withdrawn' (section 23ZB(8)).

### Wider implications of being looked after

5.97 Being 'looked after' by the local authority has potentially very great significance for the child's future. If the child accumulates sufficient looked after time (13 weeks between the ages of 14 and 18, at least one day of which must be after the child's 16th birthday) the child becomes entitled to a 'leaving care' package after his or her 18th birthday. This gives (in law if not always unfortunately in practice) a panoply of support to the young person as they enter adulthood, intended to replace the support that would otherwise be provided by family. This support runs until the age of at least 21, and may

59  SI No 959.

run until 24 or 25 in certain circumstances. Thus there is 'all the difference in the world'[60] between the services which a young person entitled to the full leaving care package may expect from social services, to make up the shortfall in parental support or guidance in his or her childhood or to compensate for his or her disabilities or other needs, and the sort of help available to a homeless or vulnerable young adult. Even if the child does not accumulate the full 13 weeks, having been looked after may nevertheless have more limited benefits: entitlement to an ongoing 'advice and assistance' package from social services, and 'priority need' status as a young adult for the purposes of securing housing. All of these issues are considered in more detail in chapter 7.

5.98    Excluded from the definition of being 'looked after' is accommodation provided pursuant to CA 1989 s17, or accommodation provided pursuant to the Housing Acts. It is now beyond doubt that local authorities cannot lawfully evade the implications of section 20 by claiming that accommodation is provided pursuant to CA 1989 s17 or the Housing Acts when, in fact, the section 20(1) or (3) duty has been triggered.

## Children Act or Education Act?

5.98A    To similar effect, the Court of Appeal in *R (RO) v East Riding of Yorkshire Council* has recently confirmed that it is also unlawful for a local authority to attempt to side-step its obligations under CA 1989 s20 by reference to the Education Act 1996.[61] In that case, the appellant was a vulnerable 15-year-old boy with severe autism and severe attention deficit hyperactivity disorder. His 'looked after' status under s20 had been terminated on the basis that a suitable residential school had been named in part 4 of his statement of special educational needs (SEN) issued under section 324 of the Education Act (EA) 1996, an institution capable of meeting his social as well as his educational needs. The court stated that it was 'impossible' to regard the EA's 'SEN regime as supplanting rather than supporting the Children Act's LAC regime.'[62]

---

60   *R (M) v Hammersmith and Fulham LBC* [2008] UKHL 14, [2008] 1 WLR 535 per Baroness Hale at [24].
61   *R (RO) v East Riding of Yorkshire Council and Secretary of State for Education* [2011] EWCA Civ 196
62   Judgment at [117].

## Section 17 or section 20 accommodation?

5.99   Accommodation may be provided to children under section 20, as we have seen above, or section 17. Section 17(6) states that (emphasis added), 'the services provided by a local authority in the exercise of functions conferred on them by this section may include *providing accommodation and* giving assistance in kind or in cash' (see chapter 6 at para 6.30). The words 'providing accommodation and' were inserted as of November 2002 by the Adoption and Children Act 2002.[63] See chapter 6 for a more detailed discussion of the law in relation to accommodating families together under CA 1989 s17(6).

5.100   The distinction between the status of children accommodated under CA 1989 s17 and s20 was made following amendments to sections 17 and 22 of the CA 1989. It was necessitated, in the government's view, by a series of cases which cast doubt on the ability of local authorities to provide accommodation to homeless families with children (falling outside the section 20(1) criteria) under section 17.

5.101   Local Authority Circular LAC (2003) 13 describes the interaction of sections 17 and 20 in the light of these amendments (emphasis added):

> The amendment to section 17 did not affect the duties and powers of local authorities to provide accommodation for lone children under section 20 of the Children Act 1989, or under a care order. Accordingly, *the power to provide accommodation under section 17 will almost always concern children needing to be accommodated with their families.* However, there may be cases where a lone child who needs *help with accommodation,* but does not need to be looked after, might appropriately be *assisted under section 17* ... [In certain cases] section 17 may be used for support, including *help with accommodation,* without making the child a looked after child.

5.102   Holman J in *R (H and others) v Wandsworth LBC and Others* carefully dissected the statutory provisions and LAC (2003) 13 in light of a submission that the Circular was erroneous in its guidance as to the law in that it suggested local authorities could 'choose' to accommodate a child under section 17 despite the apparent existence of a section 20(1) duty.[64] He noted that the circular's phrasing is misleading, and that it appeared to mislead one of the defendant local authorities in that particular case. He made clear that, once the section 20(1) criteria were met, local authorities could not evade their

---

63   Sections 116(1) and 148(1) with Sch 4 paras 6–8.
64   [2007] EWHC 1082 (Admin).

statutory duty by purporting to classify the child's status as being accommodated under section 17 instead.

5.103    Holman J's judgment was expressly approved by the Court of Appeal in *R (S) v Sutton LBC*,[65] and was approved (obiter) by Baroness Hale in the case of *R (M) v Hammersmith and Fulham LBC*. In *R (G) v Southwark LBC*, now the leading case, the House of Lords made clear that local authorities cannot sidestep their duties under section 20 by labelling accommodation as 'Housing Act accommodation' (see further below) or 'section 17 accommodation'.[66]

5.104    The standard scenario in section 17(6) cases involves a homeless single parent, often a failed asylum-seeker or overstayer, with children, although any homeless family will fall within the parameters of this power. The accommodation needs of migrant families are considered in detail in chapter 6.

## Children Act or Housing Act accommodation?

5.105   It is also clear that the Housing Act 1996 cannot be lawfully used as a means of avoiding CA 1989 s20 duties. This is the effect of articles 2 and 3 of the Homelessness (Priority Need for Accommodation) (England) Order 2002.[67] As the Court of Appeal recognised in *R (S) v Sutton LBC*, if a local authority advises a child in custody who will be homeless on release that he or she should await release and then report to the Homeless Persons Unit (HPU) or otherwise apply to the housing department (or housing authority, in non-unitary authorities) for accommodation, that would be 'quite wrong'.[68] As the Master of the Rolls put it in that case, to categorise the claimant's accommodation as accommodation provided under the Housing Act would 'fly in the face of reality, and result in the local authority sidestepping its obligations under s 20'.[69]

5.106    The House of Lords has now confirmed this position, in the *M* and *G* cases. This may result in advisers being able to secure mandatory or declaratory relief from the courts to the effect that a child was in fact accommodated pursuant to section 20 for a period of time, despite the authority at the time claiming that this was Housing Act or section 17 accommodation.

---

65  [2007] EWCA Civ 790, (2007) 10 CCLR 615 at [56].
66  [2009] UKHL 26, [2009] 1 WLR 1299.
67  SI No 2051.
68  [2007] EWCA Civ 790, (2007) 10 CCLR 615 at [45] per Hooper LJ.
69  [2007] EWCA Civ 790, (2007) 10 CCLR 615 at [66].

5.107   However, there is a practical difficulty for claimants arising from the *M* case: if the housing department or housing authority fail to notify children's services about a child who reports to them as homeless, it will not be possible subsequently to fix a section 20 duty on children's services. Although the duty under section 20(1) may have been triggered had they been aware, the courts are unwilling to re-write history in this way when the department simply never knew of the child's existence or circumstances. It is therefore vital that advisers advise children in need of accommodation to contact children's services rather than the authority generally. It is also why it is essential for legal advisers to secure disclosure of the child's social services and housing records, as often a detailed review of these documents will reveal that children's services were in fact put on notice of the child's lack of accommodation at the relevant time.

## *Joint protocols*

5.108   The need for co-operation between housing departments or authorities and children's services is emphasised in many policy documents, particularly in respect of homeless 16- and 17-year-olds. There is now a mandatory requirement for 'joint protocols' between children's services and housing (either between departments in unitary authorities, or between housing authorities and local authorities in non-unitary areas). The *Homelessness code of guidance* mandates that there must be in existence a joint protocol between these entities, dealing with how homeless 16- and 17-year-olds should be assessed and dealt with.[70]

5.109   The importance of such joint protocols was emphasised by the House of Lords in the *M* case, Baroness Hale drawing on the then applicable guidance:

> **What ought to have happened in this case**
> The Homelessness Code of Guidance for Local Authorities (Office of the Deputy Prime Minister, 2002, para 8.37) which was current at the time was clear:
>
> > 'Responsibility for providing suitable accommodation for a relevant child or a child in need to whom a local authority owes a duty under section 20 of the Children Act 1989 rests with the social services authority. In all cases of uncertainty as to whether a 16 or 17 year old applicant may be a relevant child or a child in need, the housing authority should contact the relevant social services authority. It is recommended that a framework for joint

70   Department for Communities and Local Government, 2006, para 10.39.

assessment of 16 and 17 year olds is established by housing and social services authorities to facilitate the seamless discharge of duties and appropriate services to this client group.'[71]

5.110　Baroness Hale explained the practical importance of joint protocols: 'not only to avoid a young person being passed from pillar to post, but also to ensure that the most appropriate agency takes responsibility for her'.[72]

5.111　Following their Lordships' decisions in the *M* and *G* cases, on 1 April 2010 statutory guidance was issued to local authorities jointly by the Secretary of State for Children, Schools and Families and the Secretary of State for Communities and Local Government. The guidance is aimed at clarifying the roles and responsibilities for children's services and housing departments or local housing authorities about their respective duties in securing and providing accommodation to homeless 16- and 17-year-old children. Again, it mandates the use of joint protocols.[73]

5.112　Despite these clear requirements, it is the authors' experience that often these joint protocols do not exist, or they are unlawful. Legal advisers for claimants or potential claimants should always request the joint protocol in pre-action correspondence and the absence of any lawful protocol should be pleaded as a separate ground of challenge should it be necessary to issue proceedings.

## Private fostering arrangements

5.113　Another mechanism for evading the short- and long-term implications of CA 1989 s20 is for a placement to be classified as a private fostering arrangement. It will be a question of fact in each individual case as to whether or not the arrangements have in fact been arranged by the local authority, and whether in so doing they have been discharging their section 20 duties. In *Southwark LBC v D*,[74] for example, the child could no longer live in the family home due to violence from her father. A Southwark social worker arranged for

---

71　*R (M) v Hammersmith and Fulham* [2008] UKHL 14, [2008] 1 WLR 535 at [25] and [26].

72　*R (M) v Hammersmith and Fulham* [2008] UKHL 14, [2008] 1 WLR 535 at [31].

73　*Provision of accommodation for 16 and 17 year old young people who may be homeless and/or require accommodation: guidance to children's services authorities and local housing authorities about their duties under Part 3 of the Children Act 1989 and Part 7 of the Housing Act 1996 to secure or provide accommodation for homeless 16 and 17 year old young people*, April 2010, at para 5.2.

74　[2007] EWCA Civ 182, [2007] 1 FLR 2181.

her to live with a woman who had previously been her father's partner. The court considered that a section 20 duty had in fact arisen, and Southwark LBC had been discharging that duty in making the arrangements it did. Relevant facts in reaching this conclusion included the social worker having prevented the father from taking his daughter home from school; children's services taking the lead in making arrangements; and assurances given to the woman regarding financial support.

## Special cases

5.114 This chapter provides a general outline of local authority duties and powers to accommodate vulnerable children. There are additional issues arising for certain categories of children, including in particular those in and leaving custody. Particular accommodation issues that arise for that very vulnerable group are detailed below. Relevant additional guidance and case-law concerning children at risk of gang violence are also noted in brief (see para 5.142 below).

5.115 Chapter 6 deals with two other categories of children who may require accommodation from local authorities and who will have particular additional needs: trafficked or abused children (paras 6.73–6.89) and unaccompanied minors (paras 6.61–6.72).

### Accommodation for children in and leaving custody

5.116 Children in custody are an inherently vulnerable group. Key statistics in relation to this group include:

---

**Vulnerabilities of children in custody**

- A high proportion of the children in custody have been involved with, or are in the care of, children's services prior to entering custody – 71 per cent in recent research.[74]
- 85 per cent of children in prison show signs of a personality disorder.[75]

---

75 Youth Justice Board (YJB), *Accommodation needs and experiences* (2007).
76 Children's Rights Alliance for England (CRAE), *Rethinking child imprisonment* (2002). See also YJB, *Female health needs in Young Offender Institutions* (2006): 86 per cent of young women surveyed for this report had current psychiatric disturbance or a long-standing psychiatric disorder.

- One in ten shows signs of a psychotic illness.[76]
- Children in prison are 18 times more likely to commit suicide than their counterparts in the community.[77]
- It is estimated that 36 per cent of girls in custody have self-harmed in the past month, the majority by cutting themselves.[78]
- 75 per cent of children in custody have lived with someone other than a parent at some time (compared to only 1.5 per cent of children in the general population).[79]
- 40 per cent of children in custody have previously been homeless.[80]
- Two in five girls and one in four boys report suffering violence at home.[81]
- One in three girls and one in 20 boys in prison report sexual abuse.[82]
- One in ten girls in custody has been paid for sex.[83]
- At least ten per cent of children in prison are from minority ethnic communities (compared to two per cent of the general population).[84]

5.117   The transition from custody to the community is difficult for most prisoners, regardless of their age. Many are at high risk of self-harm, suicide, and reoffending if they do not have appropriate support, care and accommodation upon their release. Child prisoners are, in this sense, no different to adult prisoners. However, there are three key differences between child and adult prisoners: first, children are inherently more vulnerable than adults, and of course tend to be particularly vulnerable on release; second, for many child prisoners their release is actually contingent upon suitable accommodation being in place for them in advance; and third, there is a clear legal framework setting out the duties placed upon children's services departments, custodial institutions and Youth Offending Teams (YOTs) from the

77  CRAE, *Rethinking child imprisonment*, 2002.
78  S Fruhwald and P Frottier, 'Suicide in prison' *The Lancet*, Vol 366, Issue 9493, 8 October 2005 (results publicised September 2005).
79  YJB, *Female health needs in Young Offender Institutions*, 2006.
80  YJB, *Accommodation needs and experiences*, 2007.
81  YJB, *Accommodation needs and experiences*, 2007.
82  YJB, *Accommodation needs and experiences*, 2007.
83  YJB, *Accommodation needs and experiences*, 2007.
84  YJB, *Female health needs in Young Offender Institutions*, 2006.
85  CRAE, *Rethinking child imprisonment*, 2002.

moment of the child's entry into custody until his or her release back into the community.

5.118 Regrettably, despite this clear framework many children remain in custody unnecessarily past their release dates due to lack of accommodation and planning, and upon their release many children are either homeless, or provided with inadequate or no support to assist them with resettlement.

5.119 Further, unfortunately local authority children's services departments on occasion fail to comply with their statutory duty to assess such children's needs, sometimes purportedly 'delegating' this duty to other agencies, such as a YOT or Connexions; and some go so far as to attempt to side-step their duties to vulnerable homeless children, directing them instead to housing departments or housing authorities, or Homeless Persons Units (HPUs). These approaches are plainly unlawful in the light of the statutory framework and recent case-law.

## Children in custody

5.120 Although article 37 of the UN Convention on the Rights of the Child (UNCRC) provides that children should only be imprisoned as a last resort, and for the shortest possible time, England and Wales has the dubious honour of imprisoning more children and young people than any other Western European country.[86] At any one time there are approximately 3,000 children under the age of 18 held in custody – in secure children's homes, Secure Training Centres (STCs) or Young Offender Institutions (YOIs). However, this number fell in 2010, and as of March 2010 there were only 2,209 young people detained in the secure estate, the lowest figures in a decade.[87]

5.121 Child prisoners tend to come from troubled backgrounds, often involving homelessness, sexual and physical abuse, domestic violence, drug and alcohol use, literacy difficulties and school exclusion: see para 5.116 above. As Munby J (as he then was) has noted, they 'are, on any view, vulnerable and needy children'.[88] They are more likely to have physical and mental health problems than their counterparts outside prison, and 18 times more likely to commit suicide.

---

86 'England and Wales lead the pack on European imprisonment rates', Howard League for Penal Reform press release, 18 January 2006.

87 YJB, *Annual report and accounts, 2009/2010*, 26 July 2010, HC 273, p 5.

88 *R (on the Application of the Howard League for Penal Reform) v Secretary of State for the Home Department and the Department of Health* [2003] 1 FLR 484, paras 10 and 11.

The majority of child prisoners also have a history of accommodation disruption and previous contact with children's services. It is fair to say the children who are sent to prison represent some of the most damaged and vulnerable members of society.

## Sentencing and release regime for children

5.122   In order to understand the accommodation issues arising for imprisoned children, it is necessary to appreciate the different types of custodial sentence which may be imposed. Children can be sentenced to five different terms of imprisonment, two determinate and three indeterminate:[89]

- Determinate:
    - Detention and training order (DTO)
    - Section 91 detention
- Indeterminate:
    - Indefinite detention for public protection (IPP)
    - Detention for life
    - Detention during Her Majesty's pleasure

### Determinate sentences

5.123   DTOs are available for children aged between 12 and 17.[90] They may be of between four and 24 months' duration. The first half of the DTO is served in a custodial establishment, and the second half in the community.

5.124   A child serving a DTO must be released at the half-way point of his or her sentence, but for most DTO prisoners there is a presumption of early release either two months before the mid-point (for DTOs of 18 to 24 months) or one month beforehand (for DTOs of eight, ten or 12 months).

5.125   For those convicted of a 'grave crime',[91] a determinate sentence under Powers of Criminal Courts Sentencing Act 2000 s91 is available. A section 91 prisoner is released at the half-way point of the sentence, or earlier if a successful application for home detention curfew (HDC) is made.

---

89  For a detailed explanation of these sentences see Ashford, Chard and Redhouse, *Defending young people in the criminal justice system*, LAG, 3rd edn, 2006, chapter 24.

90  Powers of Criminal Courts (Sentencing) Act 2000 s100(1) and (2).

91  Defined in Powers of the Criminal Courts (Sentencing) Act 2000 s91(1)(a)–(e). This definition includes certain sexual offences and any offence punishable for an adult defendant by a term of imprisonment of 14 years or more.

5.126    Both forms of early release require the child to be placed on an electronic 'tag.' This requires a suitable address, and in practice a child will not be released unless this is in place in advance.

### Indeterminate sentences

5.127    For certain serious offences, children can be sentenced to extended[92] and indeterminate[93] sentences if they are found to be 'dangerous' within the meaning of the Criminal Justice Act (CJA) 2003. A life sentence is also available for child offenders in limited circumstances, and when a child is convicted of murder the mandatory sentence is detention during Her Majesty's pleasure.

5.128    With the exception of the extended sentence, all of these indeterminate sentences require the deliberation of the parole board before the child can be released. The suitability of the resettlement package in these cases is especially crucial – release may be entirely dependent on this given the close relationship between risk and a stable living environment. Those serving the extended sentence will be eligible for parole at the half-way point but automatically released at the end of their custodial period.

5.129    It is clear that release is often heavily dependent on the availability of suitable accommodation, and for early release this is an essential pre-requisite.

## Accommodation on release: legal framework

5.130    The duties and powers relating to the release of children and young people from custody is governed by a web of legislation, guidance and case-law. In addition to the Children Acts 1989 and 2004, the Crime and Disorder Act 1988, National Standards on Youth Justice Services (National Standards), Local Authority Circulars and statutory guidance interact to map out a clear timetable which children's services departments, YOTs and custodial institutions must comply with from the moment children are sentenced in order to protect and promote the welfare and safety of this extremely vulnerable group of prisoners.

5.131    The National Standards were issued jointly by the Secretary of State for the Home Department (SSHD) and the Youth Justice Board (YJB) in 2004. They were issued following advice from the YJB pursuant to section 41(5)(b)(iii) of the Crime and Disorder Act 1998, and after consultation with the then Department for Education and Skills

92  CJA 2003 s228.
93  CJA 2003 s226.

(DfES), Department of Health, Lord Chancellor's Department (as it then was), the Welsh Assembly Government and the Information Commissioner. The National Standards are framed around the 'principal aim' set out in section 37 of the Crime and Disorder Act 1998 (to prevent offending) and the UNCRC.

5.132   Unsurprisingly given the wide-ranging and extensive consultation process, the introduction to the National Standards makes clear that they were issued in the expectation that they would be binding on all agencies within the youth justice system (emphasis added):

> National Standards ... are the required standards of practice which practitioners who provide youth justice services are expected to achieve. They provide:
> * A basis for promoting effective work with children and young people who have offended or are at risk of offending, and also their families and victims;
> * Benchmarks against which the effectiveness of youth justice services can be measured and inspected.
>
> ... They provide for *the minimal level of service required by those working in the delivery of youth justice services* ... [They] require that YOTs and secure facilities ensure exchange of information relating to young people in custody within *prescribed timescales*, and that work begun in custody is carried on following release. Any departure from these standards as they relate to the delivery of youth justice services needs to be appropriately authorised by the YOT Manager, Governor or Head of Establishment and the reasons recorded.[94]

5.133   The binding nature of the National Standards is confirmed by the Crime and Disorder Act 1998 s42(3), which provides that:

> In carrying out any of their duties under those provisions, a local authority ... shall act in accordance with any guidance given by the Secretary of State.

'Those provisions' refers to sections 37–42 of the Crime and Disorder Act 1998, the youth justice provisions, and the statutory context makes clear that 'guidance' undoubtedly refers to the National Standards (they are the only form of SSHD guidance referred to in the relevant sections).

5.134   The National Standards provide that professionals should interact to ensure a 'seamless transition' for children from custody to the community, planning for which should start at the very beginning of the child's sentence.[95] CA 1989 duties to assess and accommodate

94   *National Standards on Youth Justice Services*, 2004, paras 2, 4, 6.
95   National Standard 11, para 11.9.

also apply to this group, supplemented by specific references in the National Standards. National Standard 4 deals with assessment within the secure estate, with standard 4.7 imposing a duty on both the YOT and the relevant social services department to check the child's name with social services records and the Child Protection Register before a YOT assessment ('Asset') is undertaken. Existing child in need assessments must also be taken into account (standard 4.9). These duties ensure interaction between professionals, an informed assessment of the child's needs and vulnerabilities, and early identification of likely post-release difficulties.

5.135 National Standard 11 concerns integrated work with young offenders sentenced to DTOs. It addresses the need for planning for release commencing from the date of sentence. In particular, it includes the following requirements, which amount to a detailed timetable to protect the child's welfare, both in custody and post-release, and to minimise the risk of re-offending:

> 11.3  Secure establishment staff must undertake a reception interview within one hour of the offender's arrival that assesses the offender's needs and level of vulnerability ... Staff undertaking the interview must see information about the offender that will have been already been sent to the secure establishment by ... YOT staff involved in court proceedings.

> 11.5  A sentence planning meeting must be convened within 10 working days of admission. The offender's parent(s) or carer(s) should *be encouraged to attend the meeting, including the local authority social worker if the young person is a looked after child ...*

> 11.9  Education, health and accommodation needs on transfer to the community must be addressed from the beginning of the sentence and firm arrangements agreed for accommodation and education, training or employment arrangements to form a seamless post-release transition. The supervising officer must ensure the plan is distributed, that the offender and the parent(s) or carer(s) understand it, and that the offender has indicated the extent of his or her agreement with the plan by signing it ...

> 11.13  One month before the discharge date a resettlement review meeting will be held to confirm arrangements for discharge including arrangements for education, training, employment, offending behaviour work, accommodation, health provision and other relevant issues. Within 10 days of discharge a review should be undertaken to ensure all the necessary arrangements are in place and going to plan ...

> 11.14  The final review meeting must detail the specific release arrangements, including reporting details and where the young person will

be living in the community. If the young person is a looked after child or without suitable supported accommodation the Local Authority must make suitable accommodation arrangements for the young person in advance of the release into the community ...

11.16  Young offenders serving a DTO of 12 months or less must be visited at least monthly by a YOT member ... The Supervising Officer must make regular contact with secure establishment staff to discuss progress, and must maintain regular contact with the parent(s) or carer(s) ...

11.18  On transfer to the community the training plan must be reviewed within 10 working days ...

5.136   Given the profile and characteristics of many children leaving custody, articles 5 and 8 of the ECHR[96] often come into play. Further, the general duty to prevent offending set out in section 37 of the Crime and Disorder Act 1998 should be borne in mind. It provides that the principal aim of the youth justice system is to prevent offending by children and young persons (section 37(1)). Section 37(2) casts the net wide, stating that, in addition to any other duty to which they are subject, 'it shall be the duty of all persons and bodies carrying out functions in relation to the youth justice system to have regard to that aim'. This clearly applies to YOTs, the police, the courts and so on, but in the authors' view it also applies to children's services given their recognised role in the youth justice system. As poor resettlement planning is undoubtedly linked to reoffending by children and young people, this general duty should be borne in mind and potentially relied upon in any proceedings it may be necessary to issue.

### Duty to assess the needs of child prisoners

5.137   The application of CA 1989 s17 duty to assess the needs of children in custody is dealt with at paras 4.17–4.19 and 4.33. As we noted above, an unfortunately common problem is that children's services departments may be unwilling to assess a young person while they are in custody, instead deciding to do so post-release. There is no lawful basis for delaying assessments in this way. The landmark *Howard League* judgment put beyond doubt that the Children Act 1989 applies to children in prison,[97] and so section 17 obliges local authorities to assess their needs while in custody and plan appropriately

96  Rights to liberty and respect for private and family life.
97  *R (Howard League for Penal Reform) v Secretary of State for the Home Department and the Department of Health* [2003] 1 FLR 484.

for their release. As noted above (at para 5.134), National Standard 4 supplements the CA 1989 s17 duty in relation to these children.

5.138   As the case of *R (K) v Manchester CC* confirmed, a 'lawful assessment under section 17 of the Children Act must necessarily examine not only the immediate, current circumstances of the child concerned but must also look to imminent changes in those circumstances',[98] chief amongst which will be the question of accommodation.

5.139   Further, as all sentences for children of eight months and over involve an opportunity for early release which is subject to the need to have suitable accommodation, their liberty will often be dependent on their local authority complying with its statutory duties to assess, plan and agree in advance to provide suitable accommodation. This raises serious questions about the compatibility of failures to assess and plan with article 5 (right to liberty) of the ECHR.

## Duty to arrange accommodation for child prisoners

5.140   As noted above at para 5.36, CA 1989 s20(1) duty may be triggered before the child becomes homeless. The child may appear to be in need of accommodation prior to the actual date on which homelessness occurs.[99] For children in custody, such advance arrangements will often be essential, as without a definite address in place they cannot secure early release to which are otherwise entitled (as a definite address is needed for the electronic tagging scheme); or without a definite accommodation and support package they will be unable to persuade the parole board of their suitability for release. The absence of an open estate for child prisoners makes the latter issue all the more pressing.

5.141   Failures to make appropriate and timely arrangements for the release of children from custody not only does a disservice to the children themselves, but there are also wider societal implications. Recent research suggests that the combination of a package of support both in custody and on release could result in a reduction of 35 per cent in frequency and ten per cent in seriousness of offending. Further, the savings for the total number of young people aged 15 to 17 given DTOs in one year in England and Wales (approximately 6,500) would be over £80 million.[100]

---

98  [2006] EWHC 3164 (Admin) para 39.
99  *R (S) v Sutton LBC* [2007] EWCA Civ 790, (2007) 10 CCLR 615.
100 RESET, *The costs and benefits of effective resettlement*, available at www.catch-22. org.uk/publications.

*Children at risk from gang violence*

5.142    If working with or representing children at risk from gang violence, including members of gangs who may be at risk from rivals, former gang members, and girls who have been subjected to or threatened with sexual violence, there are two specific additional pieces of guidance to take into account. These may inform the application of the test under, for example, section 20(1)(c) or section 20(3) of the CA 1989, as they detail the nature of the risks to these children. The two additional documents are:

- Joint guidance, London Safeguarding Children Board and the London Serious Youth Violence Board, *Safeguarding children affected by gang activity/serious youth violence* (October 2009); and
- HM Government, *Safeguarding children and young people who may be affected by gang activity* (Home Office and Department for Children, Schools and Families, 2010)[101] (non-statutory practice guidance).

A key point to emerge from these documents is that affected young people are unlikely to offer information on these issues, due to fear, loyalty and other factors. They alert local authorities and other agencies to likely non-disclosure or reticence by affected young people, and signs to watch out for. To comply with this guidance requires pro-active, detailed and meaningful assessment, and looking behind the bare answers to questions which may be given by the young person.

# Changes from April 2011

5.143    From April 2011 onwards, a number of important changes are in force which will impact upon local authorities' exercise of their duties and powers to accommodate young people. Key changes are summarised below.

## Sufficiency duty

5.144    First, section 9 of CYPA 2008 inserted a new section 22G into the CA 1989. This creates a general duty on local authorities to secure sufficient accommodation for looked after children. This provision is in force from 1 April 2011 and the supporting guidance is also in force

---

101 Available at www.wlscb.org.uk/dcsf-00064-2011.pdf.

as of 1 April 2011 (the Sufficiency Guidance).[102] This is statutory guidance, which has been issued jointly under two provisions: section 7 of the Local Authority Social Services Act 1970, which requires local authorities, in the exercise of their social services functions, to act under the general guidance of the Secretary of State; and section 10(8) of the CA 2004, which requires all local authorities in England and each of their relevant partners to have regard to guidance from the secretary of state when exercising their functions in relation to their duty to co-operate to improve the wellbeing of children in the local area.

5.145 Section 22G(1) provides that it is the general duty of a local authority to take steps that secure, 'so far as reasonably practicable', the outcome in subsection (2). The required 'outcome' is that the local authority is able to provide looked after children who are not placed with a friend or relative with accommodation within the authority's area, which meets their needs. The key limiting phrase, 'so far as reasonably practicable', is explored in the Sufficiency Guidance, and it is made clear that:

> When the local authority takes steps to secure accommodation, a local authority should not assume that it is 'not reasonably practicable' to secure appropriate accommodation simply because it is difficult to do so or because they do not have the resources to do so. Any constraining factors should not be taken as permanent constraints on the local authority's requirements to comply with the sufficiency duty.[103]

5.146 Section 22G(4) provides that, in taking steps to secure the required outcome, the local authority must have regard to the benefit of having

> (a) a number of accommodation providers in their area that is, in their opinion, sufficient to secure that outcome; and
> (b) a range of accommodation in their area capable of meeting different needs that is, in their opinion, sufficient to secure that outcome.

5.147 Of concern, however, is the restrictive definition in section 22G(5), which defines 'accommodation providers' only as local authority foster parents and children's homes. These are forms of accommodation more suited to younger children, and there is nothing in section 22G to address the serious shortage of suitable supported, semi-supported

---

102 *Sufficiency: Statutory guidance on securing sufficient accommodation for looked after children*, Department for Children, Schools and Families, 2010.

103 *Sufficiency: Statutory guidance on securing sufficient accommodation for looked after children*, Department for Children, Schools and Families, 2010, para 2.16.

and independent placements for children, particularly 17-year-olds who are on the brink of adulthood. The Sufficiency Guidance emphasises that, 'having the right placement in the right place, at the right time, is a vital factor in improving placement stability, which in turn is a critical success factor in relation to better outcomes for looked after children'.[104] However, by restricting the statutory requirement to foster placements and children's homes only it is unlikely that the 'right placement' will be available for older children.

5.148    The Sufficiency Guidance also details how local authorities should modify their commissioning practices to ensure that they have sufficient local provision to meet their needs, and ensure they have a strategic plan for commissioning placements for their looked after child population. The authors anticipate that there may be challenges arising shortly regarding local authorities that have failed to comply with the duty under section 22G, or the supporting Sufficiency Guidance.

## Placements for looked after children and reviews

5.149    The CYPA 2008 has introduced a number of changes which involve review of a looked after child's case. For example, the CYPA 2008 inserted a new section 22D into the CA 1989, requiring a review of a child's case prior to a change in accommodation arrangements, unless there is urgency or another welfare-based reason; section 23ZA requires there to be visits to the child by a representative of the local authority; and section 23ZB introduces the independent visitor system.

5.150    As regards the placement of looked after children, the provisions in the CA 1989 are underpinned by the Care Planning, Placement and Case Review (England) Regulations (CPPCR Regs) 2010[105] and supporting statutory guidance (the CPPCR Guidance).[106]

5.151    Regulation 4 of the CPPCR Regs 2010 recognises the crucial link between assessment and accommodation, requiring that a care plan be prepared for a looked after child, and that, when assessing the child's needs, the authority 'must consider whether [the child's] placement meets the requirements of Part 3 of the 1989 Act' (regulation

---

104 *Sufficiency: statutory guidance on securing sufficient accommodation for looked after children,* Department for Children, Schools and Families, 2010, para 1.7.

105 SI No 959.

106 *The Children Act 1989 regulations and guidance: vol 2, care planning, placement and case review,* HM Government, 2010.

4(3)). A copy of the care plan must be provided to the person responsible for the placement, eg the foster carer (regulation 6(3)).

## Placement plan

5.152    Regulation 9 is central. It provides that, before making arrangements under section 22C for the child's placement, the responsible authority must prepare a placement plan which sets out how the placement will contribute to meeting his or her needs. The placement plan must include all the matters listed in the schedule to the regulations; must take account of the child's wishes and feelings; and a copy must be provided to the child's independent reviewing officer (IRO – see below at para 5.157).

5.153    If it is not reasonably practicable to prepare the placement plan in advance of the placement being made, there is a tight and mandatory timeframe: it must be prepared within five working days of the placement commencing (regulation 9(2)).

5.154    For looked after children placed already, before 1 April 2011, the duty on the local authority is to prepare the placement plan 'as soon as reasonably practicable' (regulation 9(4)).

## Placement guidance

5.155    Chapter 3 of the CPPCR Guidance deals with placements, including in particular sections 22A–22D of the CA 1989. It highlights the 're-habilitative duty,' requiring the child to be brought up by his or her family if this is safe, but otherwise requiring him or her to be placed in the most appropriate placement available. Further details regarding factors to be taken into account by the local authority are detailed in the CPPCR Guidance.

## Reviews and oversight

5.156    The new scheme requires reviews before changes are made to placement arrangements. The relevant statutory provision is CA 1989 s22D, but the CPPCR Regs 2010 include further detail. For example, regulation 10 sets out requirements which must be met before changes are made to a placement which will disrupt the child's education.

## Independent reviewing officer

5.157    The IRO has specific responsibilities to review the cases of looked after children, and must be informed of certain matters. The IRO will potentially have an important role to play regarding the appropriateness of placements, and proposed moves of placement. In addition to the CPPCR Guidance, there is additional specific guidance concerning the IRO role also in force as of April 2011.[107]

## Visits to former looked after children in custody

5.158   Both the Visits to Former Looked After Children in Detention (England) Regulations 2010 and the supporting guidance came into effect on 1 April 2011.[108] They concern children in custody who immediately before remand or sentence were looked after by the local authority and who are not eligible for leaving care support. The new provisions recognise that they may have very similar needs to other groups of children from care who end up in custody.

5.159   Section 23ZA of the CA 1989, the guidance and regulations set out how local authorities should carry out their responsibilities to this group of children in custody: the responsible local authority must appoint a representative to visit the child to assess their needs; and the representative must make recommendations about any appropriate advice, support and assistance needed by the child, which where necessary, could include arranging for their accommodation on release, which might involve planning for them to be looked after again.

## Guidance on short breaks

5.160   Statutory guidance entitled *Short breaks: statutory guidance on how to safeguard and promote the welfare of disabled children using short breaks* also came into effect in April 2011. It provides clarification on the legal framework for short breaks under Part III of CA 1989, in particular when to provide accommodation under sections 17(6) or 20(4) for children accommodated in short breaks. See further chapter 4 at para 4.62.

---

107  *IRO handbook: statutory guidance for independent reviewing officers and local authorities on their functions in relation to case management and review for looked after children*, Department for Children, Schools and Families, 2010.

108  *Statutory guidance to the Visits to Former Looked After Children in Detention (England) Regulations 2010*, Department of Education, 2010.

# Conclusion

5.161 The CA 1989 Part III duties and powers to accommodate vulnerable children and young people, outlined in this chapter, are an essential tool to secure their welfare. Accommodating a child may remove the child from an unsafe or unsuitable home environment, may ensure that the child is no longer sleeping on the streets or on a friend's sofa, or may even result in the child's release from custody when he or she would otherwise remain detained. It also provides an opportunity for the child to have his or her needs assessed and tailored services to be provided to meet those needs. The intention of Parliament in Part III of CA 1989 is clear: in the words of Baroness Hale, 'these children need more than a roof over their heads'.[109] This is why the requirement for a lawful assessment under section 17 is closely intertwined with local authorities' duties and powers to accommodate in sections 20, 21 and 25: without an understanding of the child's needs, and the child's wishes and feelings, no sensible or lawful decisions can be taken regarding accommodation placements.

5.162 The April 2011 changes are largely welcome, although the Sufficiency Guidance is a missed opportunity, as it focuses upon certain types of accommodation only (children's homes and foster placements), when in fact a wide range of types of accommodation must be available to local authorities in order truly to comply with their duties to provide suitable accommodation to vulnerable children and young people.

5.163 Particularly controversial in recent years has been the question of the respective duties owed to homeless 16- and 17-year-olds by children's services authorities and housing departments or authorities. It is now beyond doubt that children's services authorities cannot evade their statutory responsibilities by passing such young people over to local housing authorities or housing departments, or by wrongly classifying accommodation provided to a child in need as 'section 17 accommodation'. However, the authors are concerned that theory and practice in this field are very different, and regrettably these unlawful actions continue to occur. Indeed, why else would the *G* case[110] have reached the House of Lords only 12 months after their Lordships had given definitive guidance on these issues in the *M* case[111]?

---

109  *R (M) v Hammersmith and Fulham LBC* [2008] UKHL 14, [2008 1 WLR 535 at [4] and [31].

110  *R (G) v Southwark LBC* [2009] UKHL 26, [2009] 1 WLR 1299.

111  *R (M) v Hammersmith and Fulham LBC* [2008] UKHL 14, [2008 1 WLR 535.

5.164     Of particular concern to the authors is the increasing reliance by local authorities on CA 1989 s20(6) – a provision intended to enshrine children's autonomy – to justify failures to comply with Part III duties. This 'chink' in the *M* and *G* judgments is fast becoming a staple response in many section 20 cases. This was never the intention of section 20(6) when Part III was drafted; nor, the authors suggest, was it the intention of the House of Lords in the *M* case when they made reference to the right of a child to make a fully free and informed decision to reject section 20(1) accommodation otherwise available to him or her.[112] Over the past decade we have seen a number of attempts to side-step the long-term implications of looked after status: turning children away from children's services; referring children to HPUs, housing authorities or housing departments; or classifying what is truly section 20 accommodation as section 17 accommodation, Housing Act 1996 accommodation, Education Act 1996 accommodation, or private fostering arrangements. The use of section 20(6) is the latest in this long line of examples and must be resisted with the same vigour as its predecessors.

112 [2008] UKHL 14, [2008] 1 WLR 535 at [43].

# CHAPTER 6
# Services for migrant children and their families

## Key points

- Migrant families with children are among the most vulnerable and excluded in the UK.
- The UK Border Agency (UKBA) and local authorities are under a duty to safeguard and promote the welfare of children.
- Many migrant families will be excluded from mainstream benefits and provision for homeless people.
- Certain classes of migrant are also excluded from social services support, including under Children Act (CA) 1989 Part III, save to the extent that such support is necessary to prevent a breach of European Convention on Human Rights (ECHR) or EU rights.
- CA 1989 s17 provides a power for local authorities to accommodate children and their families together.
- Where such accommodation is necessary to prevent a breach of ECHR or EU rights, the local authority will have a duty to provide it.
- Where a family has a pending application for leave to remain which expressly or implicitly raises ECHR grounds, and which is not obviously hopeless or abusive, local authorities will normally need to provide accommodation and support.
- Unaccompanied children must be accommodated and supported by local authorities until they turn 18 and, if they then qualify for leaving care support (as most will), should continue to receive that support even if they might otherwise be eligible for asylum support.
- Local authorities can claim grants from UKBA to assist in meeting the costs of supporting unaccompanied asylum-seeking children.

## Introduction

6.1    Migrant children and their families are among the most socially excluded groups in modern Britain. There are no wholly reliable figures of the number of 'irregular' migrants – those who either entered illegally and remain in the country without status, or who have remained beyond the expiry of their leave to remain in the UK. An LSE study for the Mayor of London in May 2009, however, estimated that as at the end of 2007 there were approximately 618,000 irregular residents in the UK, including children born here.[1] Even migrant families with permission to be in the UK will often find themselves subject to a 'no recourse to public funds' (NRPF) condition restricting their access to most mainstream benefits and the range of support available to them from local authorities.

6.2     Many children who might be classed as 'migrants' for these purposes were in fact born in the UK, or came to the UK at a very early age and have known no other home.[2] They may be integrated into their local communities, attending school and be part of extensive family and social support networks, and some may never realise that they – or their parents – have no right to remain in the UK. Many such children never come to the attention of local authorities – either because their parents are able (legally or not) to work and support them, or because friends, family or the wider community provide accommodation (often overcrowded) and sufficient support to meet their essential needs.

6.3     Yet local authorities regard the provision of accommodation and other services to migrant children and their families as a very significant issue, and this is an area in which they are often particularly concerned to ensure that they only provide support where they are legally required to do so. It is often argued by local authorities that services provided to migrant families detract from their ability to meet the needs of other children 'in need' – but the courts are increasingly requiring local authorities to accept their responsibilities to this group to ensure that children's welfare is safeguarded and promoted; see, for example, *Birmingham CC v Clue*,[3] at paras 6.52–6.57 below.

6.4     This chapter is concerned with local authorities' duties to migrant children and their families under Children Act (CA) 1989 Part III. By 'migrant' in this context, we mean children and families where at least one family member has migrated to the UK from abroad. There are many subsets of this overarching category of 'migrant' families and the term as used in this chapter includes:

- families where one parent is a British citizen or has indefinite leave to remain in the UK but the other is a migrant, whether documented or not;

---

1   Greater London Authority (GLA) *Economic impact on the London and UK economy of an earned regularisation of irregular migrants to the UK*, May 2009, available at www.lse.ac.uk/collections/LSELondon/pdf/irregular%20migrants %20full%20report.pdf.

2   The LSE/GLA study referred to above increased its estimate of irregular residents by 12–20 per cent to take account of UK-born children.

3   [2010] EWCA Civ 460, [2010] 1 WLR 99.

- families with limited leave to remain, for example as students, or for employment;
- families who entered the UK illegally and have not regularised their status;
- families who have overstayed their leave to remain in the UK;
- European Union citizens; and
- children who were born in the UK but who may not have acquired British citizenship.

6.5    This chapter does not attempt to examine in detail the requirements for entitlement to mainstream benefits for migrant children and their families, nor does it consider in any detail the availability of asylum support under the Immigration and Asylum Act (IAA) 1999 for current and former asylum-seekers.[4] It is concerned solely with the provision of services under CA 1989 Part III and the potential differences in entitlement to access such services created by variations in immigration status.

6.6    Importantly, however, it should be noted that Borders, Citizenship and Immigration Act (BCIA) 2009 s55[5] places the UK Border Agency (UKBA) under a duty to have regard to the need to safeguard and promote the welfare of children in the exercise of its functions which is identical to that imposed on, among others, local authorities by Children Act (CA) 2004 s11.[6] In *ZH (Tanzania) v SSHD*,[7] Lady Hale emphasised that this obligation was intended to reflect 'the spirit, if not the precise language' of the obligation under article 3(1) of the UN Convention on the Rights of the Child (UNCRC) to treat the best interests of children as a primary consideration.[8] Lady Hale stated that while other considerations could outweigh a child's best interests, 'the important thing ... is to consider those best interests first'.[9] The Secretary of State conceded before the Supreme Court that the best interests obligation applied to decisions about removal from the UK as well as to decisions about the care of children while they are in the UK, and Lady Hale observed that:

---

4  For detailed coverage, see S Willman and S Knafler, *Support for asylum-seekers and other migrants*, LAG, 3rd edn, 2009 ('Willman and Knafler').
5  Which entered into force on 2 November 2009.
6  The same duty is imposed in relation to children's services authorities in Wales by CA 2004, s 28.
7  [2011] UKSC 4.
8  Judgment at [23].
9  Judgment at [26].

... any decision which is taken without having regard to the need to safeguard and promote the welfare of any children involved will not be 'in accordance with the law' for the purpose of article 8.2. Both the Secretary of State and the tribunal will therefore have to address this in their decisions.[10]

6.7    The interplay between the duties placed on UKBA and local authorities in the particular context of the provision of accommodation, support and other services for migrant children and their families has yet to be worked out by the courts and in practice. However, statutory guidance issued under BCIA 2009 s55(3) indicates that the primary function of UKBA in the safeguarding context is:

> ... to identify and act on their concerns about the welfare of children with whom they come into contact, perhaps during or following completion of a common assessment while others might be more involved in supporting a child once concerns have been identified.[11]

6.8    The strong implication of this guidance is that the function of providing appropriate support and services to children 'in need' remains that of specialised agencies, in particular children's services departments of local authorities, and not of the UKBA. That is an approach which has recently been endorsed by the courts in, for example, *R(O) v Barking & Dagenham LBC*,[12] which reaffirmed that UKBA's powers to provide accommodation and financial support (in that case to 'former relevant children', see chapter 7) are 'residual'. The section 55 Guidance also requires UKBA to take account of services being provided to meet children's assessed needs and support their parents when 'planning their future interaction with the family and children',[13] and to co-operate and share information with other agencies

---

10  Judgment at [24]; see also *R (MXL & Others) v SSHD* [2010] EWHC 2397, where the court held that a decision to maintain detention of a mother which necessarily involved separation from her minor children was both unlawful in 'domestic' law and not 'in accordance with the law' for the purposes of Articles 5 and 8 ECHR because of a failure to treat the welfare of the children as a primary consideration, and *R (Suppiah and Others) v SSHD* [2011] EWHC 2, where the court held that decisions taken to detain two families with children prior to their intended removal had been unlawful in part because of a failure to have regard to the BCIA 2009 s55 duty or to treat the children's interests as a primary consideration.

11  *Every Child Matters: Change for Children, Statutory Guidance to the UK Border Agency on making arrangements to safeguard and promote the welfare of children*, November 2009 ('The s55 Guidance'), para 1.6.

12  [2010] EWCA Civ 1101.

13  S55 Guidance at para 1.14.

involved in safeguarding the welfare of children.[14] In *R (TS) v Secretary of State for the Home Department*,[15] the High Court quashed a decision by the Home Secretary to remove an Afghan child to Belgium for his asylum claim to be considered there, because of a failure to have regard to the BCIA 2009 s55 duty. Given the time which the child had spent in the UK to date, it was the opinion of the local authority social services department which had been caring for him (Northamptonshire County Council) that it would be detrimental to his welfare and not in his best interests to be removed to Belgium. The local authority had put in place a care plan which involved it caring for TS until his 18th birthday. The UKBA's decision to remove was held to be unlawful because it had failed to consider the child's best interests as a primary consideration, which the Judge held was a requirement of the s 55 Guidance, and had failed to satisfy itself that there were adequate social welfare arrangements in place for him in Belgium.[16]

6.9     This chapter considers:

- the position of families with no recourse to public funds under CA 1989 s17(6);
- the impact of Schedule 3 to the Nationality, Immigration and Asylum Act (NIAA) 2002 on the ability of certain children and families to access CA 1989 Part III services;
- the existence of a power and/or duty to accommodate families together under CA 1989 s17(6) (see chapter 5 for duties to accommodate children away from their families under CA 1989 s20);
- other services to families and children with no recourse to public funds;
- services to unaccompanied minors; and
- specific obligations to trafficked children.

6.10    The question of age disputes is covered in chapter 3. Resolving such disputes in the young person's favour will be essential for families to be eligible for CA 1989 Part III services, although these issues are more likely to arise in the case of unaccompanied minors than of children who are in the UK as part of a family.

---

14  S55 Guidance at paras 2.29 – 2.33.
15  [2010] EWHC 2614 (Admin).
16  Note, however, that in *R (BT and others) v SSHD* [2010] EWHC 3572 (Admin), while expressly not criticising the decision in *TS*, Davis J held that the SSHD was generally entitled to assume that other EU Member States would make adequate provision for the care of such children while considering their asylum claims.

# Accommodation of families with no recourse to public funds – CA 1989 s17(6)

6.11 Although the powers and duties in CA 1989 s17 apply on their face equally to migrant children as to those with British citizenship or settled status, the ability to provide accommodation under this section for families with children who would otherwise be homeless has played a particular role for migrant families because of their exclusion from mainstream benefits and ineligibility for homelessness assistance and housing allocations under Housing Act (HA) 1996 Parts 6 and 7. This section will therefore consider, first, the legislative provisions which exclude migrant families from mainstream homelessness assistance and benefits, then the exclusions from social services provision in NIAA 2002 Sch 3, before addressing the history and scope of the power to provide accommodation under CA 1989 s17, and the extent to which there is a duty to do so where necessary to prevent a breach of a family's rights under the European Convention on Human Rights (ECHR).

## Exclusion of migrant families from mainstream housing and benefits

6.12 Ordinarily, and where immigration status is not an issue, children's services authorities will only be concerned with the provision of accommodation to homeless children (and not their families) under CA 1989 s20, which places a duty on the authority to accommodate children 'in need' where, most frequently, the person who would otherwise be responsible for their care is prevented from providing them with accommodation (see chapter 5 for a more detailed discussion of this duty).

6.13 Homeless families requiring accommodation together will ordinarily be the responsibility of the local housing authority under Part 7 of the HA 1996, and families with dependent children will always be regarded as in 'priority need' for the purposes of the duty to secure housing for the homeless in Part 7.[17] Families may only be excluded from homelessness assistance if they are:

- not eligible; or
- found to be intentionally homeless.

17 HA 1996 s189(1)(b). In many areas, the children's services authority and the housing authority will be the same local authority – for example, a London borough council. In rural areas in particular the children's services authority may be a county council while the housing authority is a district council.

6.14    However, many migrant families will not be eligible for homelessness assistance, housing allocations or mainstream benefits including housing benefit. The relevant provisions excluding migrant
families from accessing these benefits are summarised below:

- 'Persons subject to immigration control' (PSICs) for the purposes
of IAA 1999 s115, are normally excluded from access to all mainstream benefits, including housing benefit. This includes all non-
European Economic Area (EEA) nationals who require leave to
enter or remain in the UK and either (a) do not have it or (b) have
it, but either (i) their leave is subject to a condition prohibiting recourse to public funds[18] or (ii) they obtained their leave following
a 'maintenance undertaking'.[19]

- 'Persons from abroad' are excluded from housing allocations and
homelessness assistance under HA 1996 Parts 6 and 7.[20] In most
circumstances, PSICs – which for these purposes means persons
requiring leave to enter or remain in the UK, whether or not they
have it[21] – are treated as persons from abroad for the purposes of
HA 1996. There are a number of exceptions, including refugees,
those with exceptional or discretionary leave to enter or remain
granted outside the Immigration Rules, those with humanitarian
protection, those with indefinite leave to enter or remain, and
certain asylum-seekers who applied for asylum before 3 April
2000.[22] In certain circumstances, non-economically active EU

---

18  This is a standard condition for those granted limited leave to enter or remain
    in the UK, for example as students, for the purposes of employment, or as
    spouses during the initial 'probationary' period in which they are granted two
    years' leave to remain. It is not normally imposed on those granted refugee
    status, humanitarian protection or discretionary leave to remain. The UK
    Residence Permit or Entry Clearance endorsement in an individual's passport
    will normally state if this restriction applies.
19  For more detailed consideration, including of the circumstances when such
    persons are not excluded, see Wilman and Knafler, chapter 3.
20  Section 185(1). This includes those subject to immigration control, and those
    (such as British citizens coming to the UK from abroad) who, while not subject
    to immigration control, are not habitually resident in the common travel area.
21  The following groups do not require leave to enter or remain in the UK: British
    citizens and Commonwealth citizens with a right of abode (Immigration Act
    (IA) 1971 ss1 and 2); seamen, aircrews, diplomats and members of certain
    armed forces (IA 1971 s8); EEA nationals exercising an EU right of entry or
    residence (IA 1988 s7).
22  Allocation of Housing and Homelessness (Eligibility) Regulations 2006 SI No
    1294. The latter category is only eligible for homelessness assistance, not for
    housing allocations.

nationals will also be treated as persons from abroad for these purposes.[23]

6.15 Families falling within these exclusions are often described as having 'no recourse to public funds' (NRPF). For the purposes of eligibility for services under CA 1989 s17, including accommodation, migrant families with NRPF must be further divided into two sub-categories:

- those who are ineligible for CA 1989 s17 services save to the extent that such support is necessary for the purpose of avoiding a breach of their ECHR rights[24] or EU Treaty rights;[25]
- those who are eligible for CA 1989 s17 services.

## Ineligibility for CA 1989 services

6.16 The NIAA 2002 introduced a series of classes of person who are excluded from eligibility for a wide range of social services and other support, including under CA 1989 ss17, 23C, 24A or 24B.[26] Local authorities are prohibited from exercising their powers and duties under the listed provisions in respect of such persons.[27] Importantly, however, children are not excluded from eligibility even if they otherwise fall into one of the relevant classes,[28] for example as a dependant of an excluded person, and nor are those who are also British citizens.[29]

6.17 The main purpose of these provisions is therefore to exclude families and former relevant children (care leavers) from being supported under these provisions unless it is necessary to do so to avoid a breach of their rights. As Buxton LJ observed in *R (M) v Islington LBC*,[30] 'Schedule 3 is an instrument of the Secretary of State's immigration control policy'.[31]

---

23 For more detailed consideration of eligibility for homelessness assistance and housing allocations, see Willman and Knafler, chapter 8.
24 That is, their rights under Human Rights Act (HRA) 1998 Sch 1.
25 Under NIAA 2002 s54 and Sch 3.
26 Sch 3 para 1(1)(g).
27 Sch 3 para 1(2).
28 Para 2(1)(b).
29 Para 2(1)(a).
30 [2004] EWCA Civ 235.
31 Judgment at [21].

6.18        The excluded classes of adults are:

- people granted refugee status in other EEA states;[32]
- citizens of other EEA states;[33]
- former asylum-seekers who fail to co-operate with removal directions issued in respect of them.[34] This class includes both single adults and those with children born to a parent after they ceased to be an asylum seeker for support purposes;[35]
- former asylum-seekers with dependent children in respect of whom the Secretary of State for the Home Department (SSHD) has certified that they have failed to take reasonable steps to leave the UK voluntarily;[36]
- dependants of all of the above: 'dependant' for these purposes is defined in the Withholding and Withdrawal of Support (Travel Assistance and Temporary Accommodation) Regulations (WWS Regs) 2002[37] reg 2(2), and includes the spouse or civil partner (S) of a person (A), a child of A or of S, a member of A's or S's close family aged under 18, a child under 18 who has been living with A or S for six of the last 12 months or since birth, a person in need of care and attention by reason of a disability who would fall into one of the two preceding categories if he were not over 18, or a person with whom A has been living as an unmarried couple for two of the last three years;
- persons who are in the UK in breach of the immigration laws, other than (current) asylum-seekers.[38] A person is in the UK in breach of the immigration laws for these purposes if – in summary – the person requires leave to enter or remain[39] and does

---

32  Para 4.
33  Para 5.
34  Para 6.
35  Note that under IAA 1999 s94(1), a person who has claimed asylum ceases to be an 'asylum-seeker' for support purposes once his or her claim for asylum and any appeals have been determined, unless at any time while the person is still an asylum-seeker his or her household includes a dependent child under the age of 18, in which case he or she continues to be treated as an asylum-seeker for support purposes for so long as the child is under 18 and both the person and the child are in the UK; IAA 1999 s94(5).
36  Para 7A.
37  SI No 3078.
38  Para 7.
39  See fn 21 above.

not have it (whether or not he or she previously held it).[40] Note that a person will not be caught by this provision if the person has not 'entered' the UK as a matter of law[41] – this will mainly apply to asylum-seekers who applied on arrival in the UK and were granted temporary admission to the UK pending a decision on their asylum claim.[42]

6.19    In respect of all of these classes, the exclusion does not apply if and to the extent that support is necessary to prevent a breach of a person's ECHR rights, or of a person's rights under EU law.[43] The existence of such a breach will be the critical issue for such families. The position in respect of ECHR breaches is discussed further below but it should be noted that there may be situations in which the refusal of services under CA 1989 Part III may breach an EU national's rights under EU law. The EU's Residence Directive[44] article 24 entitles EU citizens to equal treatment when they are residing in accordance with the directive,[45] including in matters of social assistance, and article

40  Para 7(a), by reference to British Nationality Act 1981 s50A, as amended by BCIA 2009 s48, which also repealed NIAA 2002 s11
41  IA 1971 s11 and BNA 1981 s50A(6).
42  *R (AW) v Croydon LBC; R (A, D and Y) v Hackney LBC & SSHD* [2005] EWHC 2950 (Admin). The decision of Lloyd Jones J on this point was approved by the Court of Appeal in *R (M) v Slough BC* [2006] EWCA Civ 655, in the light of which the appellants conceded this aspect of the appeal to the Court of Appeal in *AW* [2007] EWCA Civ 266. The appeal to the House of Lords in *M v Slough* [2008] UKHL 52 was not concerned with this aspect of the Court of Appeal's decision. However, if the person in question fails to comply with the conditions of temporary admission (such as reporting or a prohibition on employment), or is detained and then released, the person is likely to be found to have 'entered' the UK for these purposes: *Akhtar v Governor of Pentonville Prison* [1993] Imm AR 424; *R v SSHD ex p Mostafa (Mohamed)* [1994] Imm AR 18.
43  Sch 3 para 3.
44  Directive 2004/38/EC on the right of residence for citizens of the EU and their family members to move and reside freely within the territory of the member states amending Regulation (EEC) No 1612/68 and repealing Directives 64/221/EEC, 68/360/EEC, 72/194/EEC, 73/148/EEC, 75/34/EEC, 75/35/EEC, 90/364/EEC, 90/365/EEC and 93/96/EEC.
45  This applies to workers, self-employed persons, students, self-sufficient people and their family members, and to certain other categories with retained or permanent rights of residence under the directive. It does not apply to EU nationals during the initial three months' unconditional right of residence granted by the directive, nor to those residing merely as 'jobseekers' – see eg *R (Conde) v Lambeth LBC* [2005] EWHC 62 (Admin) in which the court held that an EU national jobseeker could not rely on her EU law rights to claim an entitlement to accommodation and support under section 17 while she looked for work. For more detailed consideration of the EU rights of residence in this context, see Wilman and Knafler, chapter 2.

18 of the Treaty on the Functioning of the European Union (TFEU)[46] prohibits discrimination against EU citizens on nationality grounds within the scope of the treaty. These provisions are most obviously likely to be relevant in this context for families of EU nationals with a right of residence,[47] for example as a worker or self-employed person, where the family includes a child or children 'in need' who require services which would ordinarily be provided to British families under CA 1989 s17.[48] While the child would not in any event be excluded from such services by NIAA 2002 Sch 3, reliance on EU rights may be necessary for such services to be provided to his or her family members. This can include young people up to the age of 21.[49]

6.20    Paragraphs 8–10 of Schedule 3 and the WWS Regs 2002 created limited powers for local authorities to provide support to families who are made ineligible for support by the provisions of Schedule 3. These provide that:

- local authorities may pay for families to leave the UK where they are excluded because they have refugee status in another EEA state or are EEA nationals;[50]
- local authorities may provide very limited support to such families pending their departure,[51] and to families who are excluded because they are unlawfully present in the UK but who have not failed to co-operate with removal directions set by the UKBA.[52]

6.21    These powers only exist where the excluded person has with him or her a dependent child.[53] The WWS Regs 2002 prohibit the provision of assistance in cash, or in any way that would enable a supported person to obtain any other benefit or support,[54] and expressly require

---

46  Ex-article 12 EC.
47  On current domestic authority, only those with a right of residence in the UK are able to rely on the prohibition on discrimination in TFEU article 18: *Abdirahman v Secretary of State for Work and Pensions* [2007] EWCA Civ 657, [2008] 1 WLR 254; *Kaczmarek v Secretary of State for Work and Pensions* [2008] EWCA Civ 1310, [2009] 2 CMLR 3.
48  Such families are likely to be eligible for other welfare support, such as jobseekers' allowance and housing benefit. It is only social services as listed in Sch 3 para 1 for which they need to rely on their EU law rights to claim an entitlement.
49  Immigration (European Economic Area) Regulations 2006 SI No 1003 reg 7(1)(b).
50  Sch 3 para 8.
51  Sch 3 para 9.
52  Sch 3 para 10.
53  Sch 3 paras 9(2) and 10(2).
54  Reg 4(3).

accommodation to be provided as cheaply as practicable.[55] If an EEA national or EEA refugee fails to comply with travel arrangements, the local authority must normally terminate the accommodation, unless satisfied that the person failed to travel because he or she or a dependant was medically unfit to do so, or because transport failures prevented them from travelling despite having made reasonable efforts to do so.[56]

6.22　　Local authorities are required to comply with guidance issued by the SSHD in providing support and making travel arrangements under these provisions.[57] In *R (M) v Islington LBC*,[58] the Court of Appeal considered the impact of that guidance in a case involving a mother who was ineligible for CA 1989 services because she was unlawfully present in the UK, having stayed beyond the expiry of her visa. The guidance stated that it would be 'preferable' for accommodation to be provided only for ten days in such a case. The Court of Appeal held that the local authority was entitled – and indeed, on the facts of the case, bound – to provide accommodation for longer than ten days in circumstances where the UKBA had not yet issued directions for M's removal from the UK. It was unreasonable to withdraw accommodation because M had not been removed from the UK after ten days, when that was a matter entirely outside the control of both M and the local authority.

## Eligibility for CA 1989 services

6.23　　Other PSICs who are excluded from mainstream benefits and homelessness assistance may nonetheless be eligible for CA 1989 services without the need to establish that support is necessary to prevent a breach of ECHR or EU law rights. These will include:

- children, including unaccompanied children who are routinely accommodated under CA 1989 s20 and provided services under s17;

- asylum-seekers, although where the UKBA is providing support under IAA 1999 s95 (asylum support) to an asylum-seeker household which includes a dependent child under 18, has offered to do so, or there are reasonable grounds for believing that it would be required to do so if an application were made to it, local authorities

---

55　Reg 4(2).
56　Reg 6.
57　Reg 4(4).
58　[2004] EWCA Civ 235.

are prohibited from providing assistance for a child under CA 1989 s17.[59] 'Assistance' is defined as 'the provision of accommodation or of any essential living needs',[60] so local authorities are not prohibited from providing other services under section 17 to meet the assessed needs of such children and their families, for example needs relating to any disability a child may have;

- former asylum-seekers who are not in the UK in breach of the immigration laws and who have not failed to co-operate with removal directions or, in the case of families with dependent children, where the SSHD has not certified that they have failed to take reasonable steps to leave the UK voluntarily. This would only apply to those who sought asylum on arrival in the UK and were granted temporary admission;[61]

- migrant families with leave to remain subject to a condition prohibiting recourse to public funds.[62] The definition of 'public funds' in the Immigration Rules HC395 (as amended) (para 6) does not currently include services provided under CA 1989 Part III, so such a person will not be in breach of their conditions of leave by having recourse to CA 1989 support.

6.24    Following the Supreme Court decision in *ZO (Somalia)*,[63] a former asylum-seeker with an outstanding fresh claim for asylum *may* fall to be treated as a current asylum-seeker for these purposes. An argument to that effect at first instance in *R (SO) v Barking & Dagenham LBC*,[64] reliant on the earlier case of *BA (Nigeria)*,[65] was described by Calvert-Smith J as 'interesting' but he held that it was not necessary for him to decide it because of a concession by the local authority that support was in any event necessary to avoid a breach of SO's ECHR rights.[66]

6.25    In the case of these categories, there is in theory no need to show that the provision of services under CA 1989 s17 is necessary to avoid a

---

59  IAA 1999 s122(5).
60  IAA 1999 s122(6). Note that section 122 is to be substituted by NIAA 2002 s47, not yet brought into force, and the substituted text does not limit the prohibited 'assistance' to the provision of accommodation and essential living needs.
61  As they are deemed not to have entered the UK as a matter of law; see paras 6.18 and fns 41 and 42 above.
62  For example, spouses of British citizens during the initial probationary period of two years' leave to remain.
63  [2010] UKSC 36.
64  [2010] EWHC 634 (Admin).
65  [2009] UKSC 7, [2009] 3 WLR 1253.
66  Judgment at [16].

breach of a person's ECHR or EU rights. However, in practice, for the reasons set out below,[67] local authorities are very unlikely to agree to provide accommodation under section 17(6) in a case which would not otherwise result in a breach of ECHR rights, and the court is also unlikely to be persuaded to order them to do so, particularly on an interim basis which will be required in cases where a family is homeless.

## Power to provide accommodation under CA 1989 s17(6)

6.26    The historical controversy as to whether accommodation could be provided under CA 1989 s17 has been resolved in favour of families seeking such accommodation by both the courts and parliament.

6.27    The predecessor provisions to CA 1989 s17 were to be found in the Children and Young Persons Act 1963 s1,[68] which placed a duty on local authorities to provide 'such advice, guidance and assistance as may promote the welfare of children by diminishing the need to receive children into or keep them in care'. The clear policy behind this provision was that local authorities should endeavour, through the provision of 'advice, guidance and assistance' to prevent children from being separated from their parent unnecessarily. In *Attorney-General ex rel Tilley v Wandsworth LBC*,[69] the Court of Appeal held that given that purpose, the term 'assistance' clearly encompassed the provision of accommodation or of funds to pay for accommodation. In *R v Tower Hamlets LBC ex p Monaf*,[70] the Court of Appeal concluded that the deliberate exclusion of families with children who were found to be intentionally homeless from an entitlement to homelessness assistance under the Housing Act 1985 did not 'deprive the children, however, of receiving under section 1 of the [Child Care Act 1980] such assistance, where appropriate, in the form of accommodation as emergency short term relief to prevent the necessity to take them into care'.

6.28    The position then prior to the enactment of the CA 1989 was that local social services authorities had a power to provide accommodation to families with dependent children, even when they were not entitled to assistance from the local housing authority under the homelessness provisions. Section 17 as originally enacted – just as

---

67  Paras 6.29–6.36.
68  Subsequently re-enacted in Child Care Act 1980 s1.
69  [1981] 1 WLR 854.
70  (1988) 20 HLR 529.

with its predecessor provisions – did not expressly provide a power or duty for local authorities to provide accommodation to families whose children were in need. Section 17(6) stipulated only that:

> The services provided by a local authority in the exercise of the functions conferred on them by this section may include giving assistance in kind or, in exceptional circumstances, in cash.

6.29   In *R (A) v Lambeth LBC*,[71] however, the Court of Appeal held that neither a power nor a duty to provide accommodation could be implied into CA 1989 s17(6). This decision caused widespread concern and was swiftly overruled by the Court of Appeal in *R (W) v Lambeth LBC*.[72] However, the court was at pains to emphasise that a local authority 'is entitled, if it sees fit, to reserve this power to cope with extreme cases'.[73]

6.30   With effect from 7 November 2002, CA 1989 s17(6) was in any case amended by Adoption and Children Act (ACA) 2002 s116, so as expressly to provide that assistance provided in the exercise of a local authority's functions under section 17 might include accommodation. It now reads (emphasis added):

> The services provided by a local authority in the exercise of functions conferred on them by this section may include *providing accommodation* and giving assistance in kind or in cash.

## A duty to provide accommodation?

6.31   The judgment of the Court of Appeal in *W v Lambeth* and the amendments made by the ACA 2002 thus made it crystal clear that local authorities have a *power* to accommodate children in need and their families under CA 1989 s17(6). The question that then arose was as to whether there was in fact a duty to accommodate children in need and their families who were not entitled to mainstream housing, whether because they were intentionally homeless or because they were ineligible persons from abroad.

6.32   This issue was considered by the House of Lords in *R (G) v Barnet LBC; R (W) v Lambeth LBC and R (A) v Lambeth LBC*.[74] As discussed in chapter 4, the majority of the House concluded that the duty in section 17(1) to provide 'a range and level of services appropriate' to

---

71   [2001] EWCA Civ 1624.
72   [2002] EWCA Civ 613.
73   Judgment at [83].
74   [2003] UKHL 57, [2004] 2 AC 208.

meet the needs of children in need within a local authority's area was a general target duty, and did not impose an enforceable duty on the local authority to meet the assessed needs of any individual child.

6.33    The appellants G (who was a Dutch national who was not habitually resident in the UK and was ineligible for mainstream homelessness provision) and W (who had been held to be intentionally homeless) were single mothers who sought accommodation for themselves and their children from the local authority and claimed that they would otherwise be street homeless. It was accepted that the children were children 'in need' because they lacked suitable accommodation, and further that the local authority owed the children a duty under CA 1989 s20 to provide them with accommodation because their mothers were 'prevented ... for whatever reason' from providing them with such accommodation. The defendant local authorities had offered to provide accommodation for the children under CA 1989 s20, but refused to accommodate their mothers. G and W argued that in the circumstances, the local authority was under a duty by virtue of CA 1989 s23(6)[75] to place their children with them, and to provide them with accommodation in order that their children could be placed in their mothers' care. The House of Lords unanimously rejected this argument, finding that CA 1989 s23(6) was only concerned with the placement of looked after children with parents or relatives who already had accommodation, and not with the provision of accommodation.

6.34    The majority (Lords Hope, Scott and Millett) also concluded that CA 1989 s17 did not place a duty on the local authority in the case of any individual child to provide accommodation for the child and the child's parents together, in order to avoid separating them. The majority held that Lambeth's general policy of not providing accommodation in such circumstances was lawful, and that in particular local authorities were allowed to take account of their resources when considering how to meet their general duty under section 17. Local authorities were stretched financially and were entitled to regard their child protection and safeguarding duties as being their core functions, and to seek to preserve their resources for meeting those duties. Refusing to provide accommodation to families who were to some

75  Section 23(6) required local authorities who are looking after children to place them with their parent or a person with parental responsibility, or with a relative, friend or other person connected with them unless that would not be reasonably practicable or consistent with their welfare. This section was replaced with effect from 1 April 2011 by the amendments to CA 1989 introduced in the Children and Young Persons Act 2008. See chapter 5.

extent to be regarded as responsible for their predicament (whether because they were intentionally homeless or because they were not entitled to support) was not inconsistent with the general duty, providing always that the local authority was prepared to accommodate the children if they were genuinely faced with homelessness.

6.35   This decision is now widely relied on by local authorities to refuse to provide accommodation for children in need and their families who are excluded from homelessness assistance. Authorities will offer to provide accommodation for children alone under CA 1989 s20 if the family is genuinely facing homeless, but most local authorities now operate a policy similar to Lambeth's and as a general rule are not willing to accommodate children and their families together.

6.36   However, the position for families seeking accommodation under CA 1989 s17(6) is far from hopeless. First, the decision of the majority in *G v Barnet* was that a local authority is entitled to have a *general* policy of refusing to provide accommodation to such families. Lord Millett observed:

> It does not follow that the social services authority is not obliged to assess the needs of the individual child. The existence of a power to provide assistance to a class involves a duty to consider whether a particular individual is eligible for such assistance; and in the present context that involves assessing the needs of the child in order to decide whether and the extent to which the authority will meet his needs.[76]

6.37   Thus, the local authority is required to assess the needs of each specific child, and to consider whether and to what extent the authority will meet his or her needs. The local authority cannot simply rely on a general policy without having assessed and considered the needs of each individual child in accordance with the detailed process outlined in chapter 4. Such an approach would be incompatible with the general public law prohibition on the operation of an inflexible policy in the exercise of a discretion by a public authority;[77] it is also likely to be incompatible with the duties of the local authority to act compatibly with article 8 ECHR, which protects families' right to respect for their family life. Lord Hope accepted that 'The question whether decisions taken under Part III are compatible with the child's article 8 Convention rights must, of course, depend on the facts of each case'.[78] These observations are consistent with earlier authority. Thus, in *Anufrijeva*

---

76   Judgment at [110].
77   See Lord Scott's observation at para 139 that 'It is, of course, correct that each case must be considered on its merits'.
78   Para 69.

*v Southwark LBC*,[79] the Court of Appeal had accepted (only a week before the judgment in *G v Barnet*) that 'Where the welfare of children is at stake, article 8 may require the provision of welfare support in a manner which enables family life to continue'.[80]

6.38 Secondly, while the decision of the majority was that there is not in general a specific, mandatory duty to meet the assessed needs of each child, the court is still entitled to consider whether in the individual circumstances of a given case, the failure to meet those needs is lawful and rational. As Lord Scott said (emphasis added):

> If a mandatory order against a local authority to take some specific step is sought the applicant must either point to a specific duty to take the step imposed elsewhere in the Act (or in other legislation) or must invalidate the local authority's decision to decline to take the step *on the usual reasonableness and proportionality grounds available in judicial review challenges.*[81]

6.39 Thus the position now is that while CA 1989 s17 does not itself impose any specific duty on a local authority to accommodate children 'in need' and their families who have no other source of accommodation:

- an authority is still required to assess each individual child's needs and decide whether, and if so how, to meet them according to the approach prescribed by the *Framework for the assessment of children in need and their families* ('the Assessment Framework'), see chapter 4;

- if there is a separate, specific duty imposed either under CA 1989 or in other legislation, then the local authority must accommodate the family. This duty is most likely to be found in the Assessment Framework, which requires services to be provided where it is necessary to do so to secure the well-being of the child; see chapter 4 at para 4.36; and

- a refusal to accommodate a family together can be challenged on ordinary public law 'reasonableness and proportionality grounds' (see speech of Lord Scott at para 6.38 above) and under article 8 ECHR, which requires the court to determine for itself the proportionality of any failure to provide services (including accommodation) by a local authority.[82]

---

79 [2003] EWCA Civ 1406, [2004] QB 1124.
80 Judgment at [43].
81 Judgment at [135].
82 *Belfast City Council v Miss Behavin' Ltd* [2007] UKHL 19.

6.40   The judgment of the Court of Appeal in *Clue* (see paras 6.52–6.57 below) is important because it reiterates that local authorities cannot avoid a duty to accommodate a family together where it is necessary to do so to avoid a breach of a person's ECHR rights.

## The position of those who are ineligible for support under NIAA 2002 Sch 3

6.41   As discussed above,[83] for families who are in principle ineligible for support because they fall under one of the excluded categories in NIAA 2002 Sch 3 to qualify for the provision of accommodation (and other services) under CA 1989 s17(6), it must be shown that support is necessary to prevent a breach of a person's ECHR rights or EU Treaty rights. It should be noted that the legislation provides that support must be necessary to prevent a breach of *a person's* rights – not necessarily the *excluded person's* rights.[84] So in the case of a family comprising a mother who is excluded by Schedule 3 and a child who is not (because he or she is a child), if the refusal of support to the mother would breach the child's ECHR rights, the mother will be entitled to support.[85]

6.42   The combined effect of Schedule 3 to the NIAA 2002 and the duty under the Human Rights Act (HRA) 1998 s6 on public authorities to act compatibly with ECHR rights is that where support is necessary to prevent a breach of a person's ECHR rights, the local authority is under a duty to provide it: *R (AW) v LB Croydon*.[86]

6.43   The central issue in these cases is thus whether support is necessary to avoid a breach of ECHR rights. In *R (M) v Islington*, Buxton LJ held that this question was 'a condition precedent' to the exercise of the statutory function and that accordingly 'That test must be applied according to objective criteria, which the court retains the power to review'.[87] Since the judgment of the House of Lords in *Limbuela*,[88]

---

83   Paras 6.16–6.19.

84   As accepted by Buxton LJ in *R (M) v Islington LBC* at [45].

85   In practice, of course, a breach of the child's rights is also likely to involve a breach of the mother's rights.

86   [2005] EWHC 2950 (Admin); this part of the judgment of Lloyd Jones J was not appealed to the Court of Appeal.

87   Judgment at [47]. Although Maurice Kay LJ and Waller LJ did not agree with Buxton LJ on the construction of the WWS Regs 2002, so that his comments on the article 8 aspects of the appeal are strictly obiter (ie not binding), they both expressly agreed with his analysis of the position under article 8: see [53] and [80].

88   [2005] UKHL 66, [2006] 1 AC 396.

it has been clearly established that to make a person destitute and street homeless with no recourse to any public funds and no right to obtain employment can amount to inhuman and degrading treatment contrary to article 3 ECHR. In *Limbuela*, the claimants were asylum-seekers with pending claims for asylum. Thus there was no question of their being required to leave the UK in order to avoid the breach of article 3 at least until their asylum claims had been finally determined, and as such there was a duty to provide them with accommodation and support.

6.44     In the case of individuals who do not have pending asylum claims, the question that has arisen for consideration is whether it would be reasonable to expect the individual concerned to leave the UK in order to avoid the breach of convention rights which would ensue if they are refused any form of support. This will normally be so where it can be shown that requiring an individual to leave the UK would or may result in a breach of their ECHR rights, normally either article 3 (inhuman or degrading treatment or punishment) or article 8 (privacy and family life), or would breach the Refugee Convention. The central issue has been the extent to which the local authority is entitled to investigate such a claim for itself prior to accepting that the provision of support is necessary to avoid a breach of ECHR rights, or whether it should simply leave this question to the UKBA to resolve.

6.45     *Limbuela*[89] established that where a person's initial claim for asylum is unresolved, article 3 may be engaged by a refusal to provide any support, and such families will ordinarily be eligible for asylum support if they are destitute.[90] In the case of a person with a fresh claim for asylum, once the UKBA has accepted that any further representations do indeed amount to a fresh claim for the purposes of paragraph 353 of the Immigration Rules HC395, such a person is in the same position as an initial asylum claimant and is entitled to support under IAA 1999 s95.

6.46     What about a person who has made further representations, but these have not yet been accepted to be a 'fresh claim' for the purposes

---

89  [2005] UKHL 66, [2006] 1 AC 396.
90  Subject to the application of NIAA 2002 s55, the provision at issue in *Limbuela*, although this provision has never applied to those whose household includes dependent children: section 55(5)(b) and (c). It is now UKBA policy only to apply this provision to exclude applicants from asylum support where the application is for subsistence only support (ie where the applicant has an alternative source of accommodation so will not be made street homeless by the refusal of asylum support).

of paragraph 353 of the Immigration Rules by the UKBA? In *R (AW) v LB Croydon*,[91] Lloyd Jones J held that a refusal to provide support would not necessarily breach a person's ECHR rights in every such case. He considered that the local authority was entitled to consider the content of the representations and may be entitled to refuse support where it was apparent that the representations were merely repetitious or manifestly unfounded. However, he emphasised that 'it is only in the clearest cases that it will be appropriate for the public body concerned to refuse relief on the basis of the manifest inadequacy of the purported fresh grounds'.[92] As discussed above (para 6.24), following *ZO (Somalia)*, it is now arguable that such persons are also entitled to asylum support under IAA 1999 s95.

6.47    In a series of cases, the Court of Appeal has considered the question of when support is necessary to prevent a breach of convention rights for the purposes of NIAA 2002 Sch 3 where the family does not have a pending asylum claim, but claims that for other reasons it would be unreasonable to expect them to leave the UK to avoid destitution. These cases most frequently involve families who have been resident for long periods in the UK and are reliant in their immigration claim either expressly or impliedly on the right to respect for private and family life under article 8 ECHR. Although in many of the cases discussed below the courts have taken a strict approach to the provisions of NIAA 2002 Sch 3, the recent judgment in *Clue v Birmingham*[93] shows the tide shifting towards a recognition of the need for authorities to support children with their families in all cases save where the family's immigration application is abusive or hopeless.

6.48    The previous position was exemplified by *R (Kimani) v Lambeth LBC*,[94] where the Court of Appeal held that it was lawful for a local authority to refuse to accommodate a Kenyan woman and child under the Asylum Support (Interim Provisions) Regulations 1999[95] on the ground that she was excluded from support by virtue of NIAA 2002 Sch 3. It rejected the appellant's claims that the refusal

---

91  [2005] EWHC 2950 (Admin); this part of the judgment of Lloyd Jones J was not appealed to the Court of Appeal. Although Lloyd Jones J was concerned with the circumstances in which a local authority might be obliged to provide support under National Assistance Act 1948 s21, this aspect of his judgment was concerned with the construction of NIAA 2002 Sch 3 para 3, which applies equally to eligibility for CA 1989 s17 support.

92  Para 76.

93  [2010] EWCA Civ 460, [2010] 1 WLR 99.

94  [2003] EWCA Civ 1150, [2004] 1 WLR 272.

95  SI No 3056.

of support would violate her ECHR rights because it considered that she had the option of leaving the UK and returning to Kenya, even though she could not be required to do so while she had an appeal against removal pending. The court regarded an existing ECHR article 8 appeal against removal as 'clearly specious'[96] and concluded that in those circumstances, article 8 did not require Ms Kimani to be permitted to remain in the UK while her appeal against removal was considered.[97] The court contrasted her case with the appeal in *J v Enfield*,[98] in which the claimant had a viable case that her removal to Ghana would violate her article 3 rights because of the lack of treatment facilities for HIV/AIDS.[99]

6.49    *R (M) v Islington*[100] concerned a Guyanan national who had overstayed her visa by several years and in the meantime had married a British citizen and had a child by him. She applied for support from the local authority while she had a pending appeal to the Immigration Appeals Tribunal against the dismissal of her article 8 ECHR claim to remain in the UK. As noted above (para 6.22), the majority of the Court of Appeal concluded that the local authority was bound to provide her and her child with accommodation and support under the WWS Regs until the UKBA took steps to remove her from the UK, but Buxton LJ disagreed with their construction of the relevant guidance and gave detailed consideration of the position in respect of article 8 ECHR. He gave particular weight to the fact that M's child was a British citizen with an unfettered right to enter and reside in the UK,[101] and that the child's father, who had separated from M but retained contact with the child, was also a British citizen with a right of abode in the UK.[102] Buxton LJ considered that while the

96 Judgment at [49]; it also described the appeal as 'manifestly unsustainable' and rejected a submission that it should not prejudge the outcome of the appeal in the circumstances (para 40). Ms Kimani had originally unsuccessfully claimed asylum, and was now appealing against the refusal of a residence permit as the family member of an EEA national made on the grounds that her marriage was one of convenience, having since separated from her EEA national husband, who was not the father of her child. The court clearly viewed her immigration history unsympathetically and considered there was nothing to prevent her and her child returning to Kenya.

97 Judgment at [40], [49].

98 (2002) 5 CCLR 434.

99 Judgment at [47]–[48].

100 [2004] EWCA Civ 235.

101 Judgment at [23]–[29] and [46]. See also *ZH (Tanzania) v Secretary of State for the Home Department* [2011] UKSC 4, [2011] 2 WLR 48.

102 Judgment at [46].

WWS Regs 2002 did not give Islington the power either to pay for M's travel from the UK or to accommodate her for longer than about ten days,[103] the effect of article 8 ECHR might be that she was not excluded from support under CA 1989 s17 to the extent necessary to protect her convention rights. That might allow the local authority to pay for M's travel to return to Guyana, but before it could lawfully so conclude, it needed properly to assess the article 8 considerations, as well as whether the provision of travel tickets for M and her child to return to Guyana would meet its statutory duties to the child.[104]

6.50    In *R (Grant) v Lambeth LBC*,[105] the Court of Appeal held that a decision by a local authority to pay for travel for a family to return to Jamaica rather than continuing to provide accommodation and support in the UK was lawful, notwithstanding that Ms Grant, a Jamaican national, had a pending application for indefinite leave to remain on compassionate grounds. Ms Grant had overstayed her visa and had lived in the UK for 12 years by the time of the Court of Appeal hearing, and had a British citizen child, born in 2000, as well as two children born in Jamaica who had resided with her in the UK since 1998. The Court of Appeal rejected an argument that since the WWS Regs 2002 did not permit the local authority to make travel arrangements in such a case, it could not use its powers under LGA 2000 s2 to pay for the family to travel to Jamaica in order to avoid a breach of ECHR rights. The court considered that the local authority was entitled to reach the conclusion that the rights of Ms Grant and her children to respect for their family life under article 8 ECHR would be best protected by the family returning together to Jamaica.

6.51    The approach in *AW* to fresh asylum claims was applied by the High Court in an article 8 case in *R (Binomugisha) v Southwark LBC*,[106] in which a 19-year-old Ugandan sought support as a former relevant child under CA 1989 s23C (see para 7.16 below), pending consideration of his immigration application for further leave to remain. Andrew Nicol QC, sitting as a Deputy High Court Judge, held that the local authority had erred in reaching its own assessment of whether it would breach article 8 for the applicant to be returned to Uganda. He considered that the local authority 'should proceed on the assumption that the application will fail only if it is "manifestly

---

103  Judgment at [31]–[43].
104  Judgment at [45]–[49].
105  [2004] EWCA Civ 1711.
106  [2006] EWHC 2254 (Admin).

unfounded" ... It is not enough that they consider the application will fail or is not made out'.[107]

## The decision in *Clue*

6.52 The confusion created by these differing approaches was finally resolved by the Court of Appeal in *R (Clue) v Birmingham CC*.[108] *Clue* involved a Jamaican national who had come to the UK as a visitor in 2000, together with her eldest child, born in 1994. She had subsequently applied, unsuccessfully, for leave to remain as a student. She had three more children, born in 2004 and 2006, to a British father. In 2007, she applied for indefinite leave to remain on the basis that her eldest child had lived in the UK for more than seven years. At the relevant time, the UKBA had a policy under which it accepted that children who had spent seven years or more in the UK should not normally be uprooted ('the seven year rule').[109] In 2008, she sought assistance from the local authority. The local authority refused to provide assistance, on the grounds that Ms Clue and her children could return to Jamaica.

6.53 The Court of Appeal upheld the decision of Charles J to allow her claim for judicial review, but importantly did so for quite different reasons. The Court of Appeal held that when considering whether it was necessary to provide support to avoid a breach of a person's ECHR rights, the local authority was first required to consider whether the person could avoid destitution by recourse to other sources of support, and if not, whether there was anything to prevent the claimant returning to his or her country of origin.[110] If the only impediment was a practical one, the authority could simply provide the means of overcoming it, such as providing funds to pay for the journey.[111] The court considered that if no application for leave to remain had been made to the UKBA, the local authority was entitled to consider for itself whether the convention prevented the person from being expected to return to their country of origin.[112] However, where a person had made an application for further leave to remain to UKBA which expressly or implicitly raised ECHR grounds, the

107 Judgment at [53].
108 [2010] EWCA Civ 460, [2010] 1 WLR 99.
109 This policy was withdrawn in December 2008 on the basis that such cases could now be considered under article 8 ECHR.
110 Judgment at [55].
111 Judgment at [56].
112 Judgment at [59].

local authority should not enquire into the merits of that claim when deciding whether support was necessary to prevent a breach of a person's ECHR rights, beyond considering whether it was 'obviously hopeless or abusive'.[113]

6.54    The court distinguished both *Kimani* and *Grant*. *Kimani* was distinguished on the basis that it was concerned with family life, not private life, and that it was reasonable to expect Ms Kimani to return to Kenya to pursue her appeal from there. By contrast, on the evidence before it, Ms Clue and her children would have lost the right to pursue their application for indefinite leave to remain in the UK if they had returned to Jamaica.

6.55    *Grant* was rather more troubling because the Court of Appeal in that case had accepted that Ms Grant's application for indefinite leave to remain would lapse if she left the UK. However, it considered that she could 'renew' that application from abroad. In *Clue*, Dyson LJ explained the decision in *Grant* on the basis that Ms Grant's application for judicial review was not based on her ECHR rights or expressly on article 8 ECHR. Although Lambeth had argued that article 8 would not be breached by Ms Grant's removal from the UK, she had not advanced any claim that it would, and the court did not consider whether any interference would be proportionate.

6.56    Importantly, in *Clue* the court concluded that where it was established that a person who would otherwise be excluded from services under NIAA 2002 Sch 3 was destitute and had a pending application for leave to remain based expressly or implicitly on convention grounds (and which was not obviously hopeless or abusive), the financial resources of the local authority were irrelevant.[114] This is important because it means that where it is established that support is necessary to prevent a breach of ECHR rights, the local authority cannot rely on the type of considerations which persuaded the House of Lords in *R (G) v Barnet LBC* (see paras 6.32–6.34 above) that there was no duty to accommodate a family and their children together under CA 1989 s17(6) where they would otherwise be street homeless. This is obviously right and is consistent with the holding of Lloyd Jones J in *AW v Croydon* that where support is necessary to prevent a breach of ECHR rights, a local authority is under a duty to provide it.[115]

6.57    In the course of the *Clue* litigation, in which the SSHD was an interested party, the Director of the Case Resolution Directorate (CRD) at

113  Judgment at [66].
114  Judgment at [72].
115  See paras 6.42 and 6.46 above.

the UKBA accepted that it should prioritise applications for leave to remain made by families who were supported by local authorities, and should have regard to its duties under BCIA 2009 s55, in ensuring that timely decisions are made in cases involving children.[116] It is therefore obvious that the proper approach for any local authority asked to accommodate a family in a similar situation post-*Clue* is to provide the accommodation and put pressure on UKBA to make a speedy decision on the family's immigration application.

## Post-*Clue* process

6.58   In the light of *Clue*, it is now therefore clear that when considering applications for support under CA 1989 s17 by migrant children and their families who are excluded from mainstream benefits, the local authority must consider the following questions:

- But for the provisions of NIAA 2002 Sch 3, would the family be eligible for support? The answer to this question will almost always be positive as there is a low threshold for a child to be 'in need' (see chapter 4 at paras 4.10–4.13) and if a child is 'in need' services can be provided to any member of his or her family: CA 1989 s17(3).
- Absent the provision of support, would the family be destitute? In considering this question, the local authority will need to consider whether there are any other sources of support, such as family or friends or the possibility of work.
- If so, is there any impediment to the family returning to their country of origin?
- If the impediment is only a practical one, can the local authority remove it, for example, by providing funds for airfares?
- Has the family made an application for leave to remain which expressly or implicitly raises convention grounds?
- If so, is it obviously hopeless or abusive? If not, the local authority must provide support until a decision is made on the application by the UKBA.
- If no application has been made to the UKBA, the local authority is entitled to consider for itself whether article 8 is engaged, and it may take account of its financial resources when deciding whether an interference in the individual family's article 8 rights is justified and proportionate.[117]

116 Judgment at [84]–[85].
117 Judgment at [73].

6.59    Although *Clue* was concerned with the position of families who are ineligible for support under NIAA 2002 Sch 3 unless they can establish that support is necessary to prevent a breach of their ECHR rights, its basic principles will apply to families who are not excluded under Schedule 3. If such a family has a pending application for leave to remain based on ECHR grounds, and would otherwise be destitute, then the local authority should provide accommodation and support under CA 1989 s17 unless the application is obviously hopeless or abusive. To refuse to provide that support would be inconsistent with the local authority's duty, under HRA 1998 s6, to act compatibly with the ECHR.

6.60    The difference is that for families who are not excluded under NIAA 2002 Sch 3, there may also be other situations, not involving a potential breach of ECHR (or EU) rights, in which a local authority might need to exercise its power to provide accommodation to a family who is excluded from mainstream support. Such situations are likely to be less common, and the considerations which persuaded the House of Lords in *G v Barnet* to find that a general policy of refusing to accommodate families together was lawful are likely to carry more weight in circumstances such as these.

## Services to unaccompanied minors

6.61    Where a person who is – or claims to be – a child arrives in the UK without a parent or other appropriate adult carer (such as an adult sibling) they will often be in a particularly vulnerable position. The relevant local authority circular, LAC 2003(13) (as amended), recognises that such children are likely to be children 'in need' even when they are 16 or 17 years old as they lack any parental or other family support or guidance. They will almost certainly need accommodation under CA 1989 s20; see chapter 5. Chapter 3 discusses the question of age disputes, but once a child is accepted or found to be under 18, responsibility for the child's care and accommodation falls on the local authority in whose area the child is found.

6.62    Asylum support under Part VI of the IAA 1999 is not available for unaccompanied asylum-seeking children (UASCs). This is because the definition of an 'asylum-seeker' in IAA 1999 s94 applies only to a person who is 'not under 18'. UASCs must therefore turn to local authorities for accommodation and support. As noted above, children are not excluded from support under CA 1989 Part III by NIAA 2002 Sch 3 and in any event CA 1989 s20 is not amongst the excluded provisions.

6.63 The Department of Health Guidance *Children (Leaving Care Act) 2000: regulations and guidance* ('the Leaving Care Guidance', published in October 2001) emphasises that:

> Unaccompanied asylum-seeking children (UASC) are covered by the Children Act 1989 and the new provisions introduced by the Children (Leaving Care) Act in exactly the same way as other children in this country. However they will also have an immigration status – applying for asylum, acceptance as a refugee, granted exceptional leave to remain or refused leave to remain – which will need to be taken into account by councils providing services for them.[118]

## The immigration position

6.64 UKBA policy is not to remove unaccompanied children[119] from the UK unless it is satisfied that there are adequate reception arrangements for the children in the proposed destination country. This will normally require that the child is in contact with a parent or other suitable adult carer who is able to meet him or her on return and take responsibility for the child's care. However, in some circumstances the test may also be met where UKBA can show that the local social services provision in the receiving country is adequate and that the state in question has confirmed that the child will be received into its care. This is extremely rare, although the government has recently announced much-publicised plans to establish a reception centre for children in Kabul. It is for the UKBA to show that adequate reception arrangements have been made if a child challenges a decision to remove him under article 8 ECHR, and on appeal the First-tier Tribunal is bound to decide whether adequate reception arrangements have been made even where UKBA undertakes not to remove the child without making such arrangements.[120]

6.65 UKBA policy is to grant unaccompanied children who cannot be removed discretionary leave to remain until they are 17.5 years old, if they do not qualify for asylum or humanitarian protection.[121] There

---

118 Para 7.
119 UKBA defines an 'unaccompanied child' as a child who is in the UK without a parent or other adult who is by law or custom responsible for their care.
120 *CL (Vietnam) v SSHD* [2008] EWCA Civ 1558, [2009] 1 WLR 1873. Note the assumption that other EU member states will make adequate arrangements for the care of child asylum-seekers in *R (BT) v SSHD*, judgment 21 December 2010.
121 APU Notice 3/2007, 30 March 2007, para 6: 'For all decisions made on or after 1 April 2007 (where asylum/HP is being refused) DL must only be granted to 17.5 years.'

are no conditions attached to a grant of discretionary leave to remain, so such a child is entitled to have recourse to public funds and to take employment (if the child is old enough). A child wishing to remain beyond 18 will need to apply for further leave to remain before the expiry of his or her existing leave. If the child does so, then that leave is statutorily extended on the same conditions until the UKBA make a decision on the application and/or any appeal is finally determined.[122] This means that pending consideration of an application for further leave to remain (which can take months, if not years), the young person is entitled to work and to claim benefits.

## The position of UASC care leavers

6.66   If a UASC has current leave to remain when he or she turns 18, or has statutorily extended leave (pending an application for further leave or an appeal), then he or she will continue to be entitled to support in the same way as any other care leaver. If the UASC has accrued the qualifying period of looked after time, then he or she will be entitled to leaving care support in the same way as any other young person.[123]

6.67   Where a child's asylum application (or an appeal against refusal of that asylum application) is still outstanding when he or she reaches the age of 18, the child may apply for asylum support from the UKBA.[124] Paragraph 5.1 of UKBA Asylum Support Policy Bulletin 29 'Transition at age 18' ('the T18 Guidance') emphasises the importance of local authorities planning ahead to ensure that support is in place when such children turn 18, and UKBA expects local authorities to provide a letter setting out what support they have been providing and when that support will cease. The guidance, however, emphasises that a young person will only be eligible for asylum support if he or she meets the other qualifying criteria, which include being destitute, and UKBA will take into account support provided by a local authority under its leaving care duties in assessing whether the child is destitute.[125]

---

122  IA 1971 s3C. Note that a gap of even one day between the expiry of the previous grant of leave and the application for further leave to remain will deprive the child of the benefit of this provision.

123  See chapter 7 for a discussion of the duties owed to care leavers.

124  The guidance refers to 'NASS', the former National Asylum Support Service, part of the Immigration and Nationality Directorate of the Home Office, which has since been abolished. The functions of providing asylum support under both IAA 1999 s4 and Part 6 are now carried out by UKBA.

125  T18 Guidance, para 8.3.

6.68     This T18 Guidance and the Leaving Care Guidance clearly envisage that when a care leaver has a pending asylum application on turning 18, he or she will be eligible for asylum support and will become the financial responsibility of UKBA. As discussed below, the guidance also makes provision for care leavers who are eligible for asylum support to be accommodated by UKBA in the area of the local authority which had previously looked after them,[126] and for UKBA to reimburse some of the costs incurred by the local authority in providing accommodation and support.[127] However, in *R (O) v LB Barking & Dagenham and SSHD (The Children's Society Intervening)*,[128] the Court of Appeal held that in the case of a former relevant child entitled to support under the leaving care provisions who was also an asylum seeker or former asylum-seeker:

> ... since the powers under s. 95 (and s. 4) of the Immigration and Asylum Act 1999 are residual, and cannot be exercised if the asylum seeker (or failed asylum seeker) is entitled to accommodation under some other provision, a local authority is not entitled, when considering whether a former relevant child's welfare requires that he be accommodated by it, to take into account the possibility of support from NASS.[129]

6.69     The effect of this judgment is that such young people remain the responsibility of the local authority, and are unlikely to be eligible for asylum support because they will not be destitute.

6.70     This judgment does not, however, preclude consideration of the provisions of NIAA 2002 Sch 3. Support under CA 1989 s23C is excluded under paragraph 1 of Schedule 3 so a former relevant child who is ineligible for support by virtue of one of the paragraphs of Schedule 3 would need to show that support was necessary to avoid a breach of his or her ECHR or EU rights. In the case of a current asylum seeker, this will ordinarily be a straightforward matter since it would not be reasonable to expect a person to abandon his or her asylum claim to avoid destitution. In *O* itself, the local authority had conceded before the Administrative Court that his fresh claim for asylum was not manifestly unfounded so that he had established that the provision of accommodation was necessary to avoid a breach of

---

126 Asylum support is usually provided on a no-choice basis in dispersal areas throughout the UK. Ministers have agreed not to disperse former UASCs who qualify as former relevant children – see the T18 Guidance, para 6.3.

127 See para 6.72 below.

128 [2010] EWCA Civ 1101, (2010) 12 CCLR 591.

129 Para 40.

his ECHR rights. A former relevant child with leave to remain (including leave that is statutorily extended under IA 1971 s3C – see para 6.65 above) will not be caught by NIAA 2002 Sch 3.

6.71    The flowchart opposite sets out the type of support to which a former relevant child who is or has been an asylum-seeker is entitled and whether the local authority will receive any assistance from UKBA.

## UKBA support for local authorities

6.72    In recognition of the burden that is placed on local authorities to accommodate and support UASCs, the UKBA provides grant support to assist local authorities to meet their obligations to UASCs and former UASCs.[130] This comprises three separate programmes:

1) A grant to reimburse the costs of supporting UASCs.[131] There are exclusions from this grant, including children who arrived with a parent or carer and have subsequently become separated from them, and children who are nationals of another EEA state. The grant is payable for a period of 21 days for age disputed minors found to be over 18 following a prompt, *Merton*-compliant age assessment.[132]

2) Grant support of £150 per week, per care leaver where a local authority is supporting at least 25 care leavers. This support is only available where the care leaver in question was a UASC and either has existing leave to remain (including statutorily extended leave under IA 1971 s3C) or became appeal rights exhausted

130 IAA 1999 s110 gives the SSHD a wide power to reimburse local authorities for expenditure incurred in connection with asylum seekers, former asylum seekers and their dependants. In *R (Westminster City Council) v NASS* [2001] EWCA Civ 512, (2001) 33 HLR 83, Simon Brown LJ accepted the proposition that this power might be used to assist local authorities who were supporting infirm destitute asylum seekers under the National Assistance Act 1948 s21 (Court of Appeal judgment at [31] – the issue was not referred to in the opinions of the House of Lords). However, in practice, that power is only likely to be exercised in the cases set out in this section, relating to UASCs, or where the SSHD has used her powers under IAA 1999 ss99–101 to require local authorities to assist her in providing support for asylum seekers.

131 There are set maximum weekly levels of reimbursement. Grant conditions for 2010/11 are at www.ukba.homeoffice.gov.uk/sitecontent/documents/aboutus/ workingwithasylumseekers/local-authority-grants/uasc/grant-instructions. pdf?view=Binary.

132 For a discussion of what amounts to a *Merton*-compliant age assessment, see chapter 3.

# Figure 2

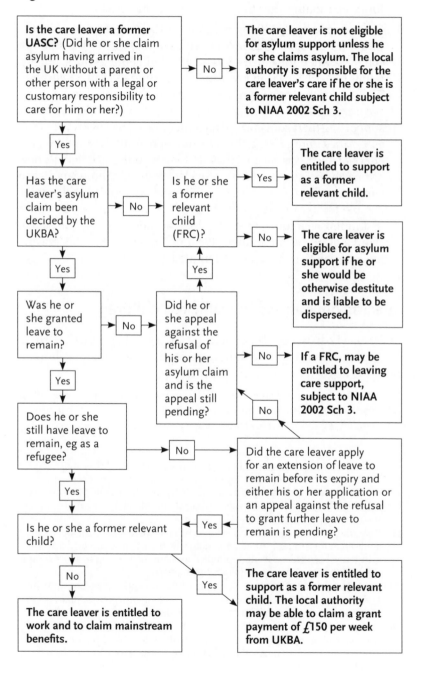

(ARE) after 1 April 2010, in which case the grant will be provided for three months after the care leaver became ARE.[133]

3) Grant support of £140 per week for UASCs whose asylum application (or an appeal against the refusal of asylum[134]) is still outstanding when they turn 18, who are eligible for asylum support under IAA 1999 s95, and who are also former relevant children.[135] The aim of this provision is to enable such young persons to be accommodated in the area of the local authority which has been supporting them and is an arrangement made by UKBA with local authorities under IAA 1999 s99. However, as discussed above, the effect of the decision in *SO* is that such young people will now ordinarily be entitled to be provided with accommodation and support under CA 1989 s23C as care leavers, and so will not be eligible for asylum support. It appears from the policy guidance that in those circumstances, the local authority will not be able to claim a grant payment under the T18 Guidance. For this reason, this possibility is not included in the flowchart.

## Specific obligations to trafficked children

6.73   Children who have been brought to the UK by traffickers are a particularly vulnerable group of children 'in need'. 'Trafficking' in human beings is defined in the Palermo Protocol[136] as:

> ... the recruitment, transportation, transfer, harbouring or receipt of persons, by means of the threat of or use of force or other forms of coercion, of abduction, of fraud, of deception, of the abuse of power or

---

133 These are the main grant conditions for 2010/11. The care leaver must also not be excluded by NIAA 2002 Sch 3. The full grant instructions are available at www.ukba.homeoffice.gov.uk/sitecontent/documents/aboutus/workingwithasylumseekers/local-authority-grants/leaving-care/grant-instructions.pdf?view=Binary.

134 Save where the former UASC also has existing leave to remain, or a pending application for further leave to remain, in which case he or she will have statutorily extended leave and be entitled to claim mainstream benefits and/or to work, and thus not eligible for asylum support.

135 See UKBA Asylum Support Policy Bulletin 29, 'Transition at age 18', available at www.ukba.homeoffice.gov.uk/sitecontent/documents/policyandlaw/asylumsupportbulletins/children/pb29?view=Binary.

136 Palermo Protocol to Prevent, Suppress and Punish Trafficking in Persons, Especially Women and Children, Supplementing the United Nations Convention Against Transnational Organised Crime (2000) (ratified by the UK on 6 February 2006).

of a position of vulnerability or of the giving or receiving of payments or benefits to achieve the consent of a person having control over another person, for the purpose of exploitation ...[137]

6.74 In the case of children, it is not necessary to show that the recruitment, transportation, transfer, harbouring or receipt occurred by any of the means set out, providing that it is for the purposes of exploitation.[138] It should also be noted that a person is to be treated as a victim of trafficking even if they have not yet been exploited, since it is the recruitment, transportation, transfer etc which constitutes trafficking if it is done *for the purpose* of exploitation. This definition was adopted in the Council of Europe Convention on Action Against Trafficking in Human Beings ('the Trafficking Convention').[139] Trafficking in human beings as defined in the Palermo Protocol and the Trafficking Convention engages the prohibition of slavery, servitude and forced or compulsory labour in article 4 ECHR.[140]

6.75 While the majority of trafficked children are likely to be migrants, British citizen children may also be victims of trafficking, and the definition of trafficking does not require movement across borders. Children may be trafficked within the UK and there is increasing evidence of girls in particular being internally trafficked for sexual exploitation.[141] However, it has been recognised that:

> Where children and young people have arrived in the UK as unaccompanied minors and especially when they have been trafficked from overseas, they are particularly vulnerable to being exploited and controlled. For example, they may be concerned about their immigration status if they contact the UK authorities, and they may believe that they or their families may be at risk if they resist the exploitation.[142]

6.76 Practice Guidance issued jointly by the Home Office and the then Department of Children, Schools and Families (DCSF) on *Safeguarding*

---

137 Art 3(a).
138 Art 3(c).
139 Ratified by the UK on 17 December 2008 and implemented from 1 April 2009. The definition in article 4 of the Trafficking Convention expressly mirrors that in the Palermo Protocol.
140 *Rantsev v Cyprus and Russia* (2010) 51 EHRR 1.
141 HM Government (issued by the Home Office and Department for Children, Schools and Families), *Safeguarding children who may have been trafficked* (2007), paras 3.22–3.24. See also London Safeguarding Children Board (LSCB), *London Safeguarding Trafficked Children Guidance* (LSCB guidance), February 2011, paras 5.3.7–5.3.9.
142 Department of Children, Schools and Families, *Working Together to Safeguard Children from Sexual Exploitation* (2009), para 6.54.

*children who may have been trafficked* ('the Trafficking Guidance')[143] emphasises that trafficking of children deprives them 'of their rights to health care and freedom from exploitation and abuse' and will normally expose children to significant risks of physical, emotional and psychological and sexual abuse and to neglect.[144] Because of these serious risks, concerns about trafficking of children will often raise child protection concerns necessitating use of the coercive powers in CA 1989, Parts IV and V, and the initiation of child protection enquiries under CA 1989 s 47. However, the position of child victims of trafficking and the need to identify potential victims is also plainly relevant to the duties and powers of local authorities under CA 1989 Part III and this is the focus of the following paragraphs.

## Identification of child victims of trafficking

6.77   Child victims of trafficking may be particularly difficult to identify. This is because:

- They may enter the UK accompanied by persons who claim to be or are their parents or legitimate guardians. Children 'are likely to be very loyal to their parents or caregivers'[145] and may thus be reluctant to disclose trafficking;

- At the point of entry they will often have been led to believe that they are coming to the UK for legitimate purposes such as study, or to improve their opportunities for the future;[146]

- They may travel on false documents describing them as adults;[147]

- They may not show any obvious signs of distress or imminent harm when first encountered;[148]

- A common tactic is for children to be registered with schools or to apply for asylum as unaccompanied minors and then to disappear;[149]

---

143   HM Government, 2008. This is non-statutory guidance, intended to supplement the statutory guidance, *Working Together to Safeguard Children*; see chapter 2 at 2.46–2.50.

144   Trafficking Guidance, paras 3.25 – 3.33.

145   UKBA Asylum Process Guidance, *Victims of Trafficking: Guidance for Frontline Staff* ('UKBA Guidance for Frontline Staff'), p8.

146   Trafficking Guidance, para 3.9, para 7.2.

147   Trafficking Guidance, para 3.10.

148   See for example para 3.25 of the Trafficking Guidance.

149   Trafficking Guidance, para 3.21. Note that a partnership project between the Home Office, DCSF, London Councils, the London Asylum Seekers

- Since they lack life experience, they may not realise that what they are being asked or forced to do by their exploiters is wrong.[150] As the London Safeguarding Children Board (LSCB) guidance notes, 'some children are unaware that they have been trafficked, while others may actively participate in hiding that they have been trafficked.'[151]; and

- Beliefs in voodoo or witchcraft are used to 'frighten children ... into thinking that if they tell anyone about the traffickers, they and their families will die ...'[152]

6.78    These difficulties mean that the role of inter-agency working is particularly crucial in identifying and protecting child victims of trafficking. This is underlined by the Trafficking Guidance, which also sets out a useful series of indicators that a child may have been trafficked to guide practitioners.[153] The Trafficking Guidance emphasises the particular role to be played by the UKBA,[154] which will often be the first agency to have contact with children who are victims of trafficking, and underlines the importance of good inter-agency relationships between other agencies concerned in the protection of children and UKBA.[155]

6.79    The UKBA Guidance for Frontline Staff for its part emphasises that:

> Where the victim is under the age of 18 years, officers should refer that child or young person to their local authority Children's Services. Children's Services are the primary service provider for safeguarding

Consortium, the Association of Directors of Children's Services and local authorities has established the 'National Register of Unaccompanied Children' which aims to record information about all unaccompanied asylum seeking children supported by local authorities in England. This should be used as a tool to identify when unaccompanied children have gone missing after claiming asylum.

150  UKBA Guidance for Frontline Staff, p13.

151  LSCB Guidance, para 5.3.9.

152  Trafficking Guidance, para 3.11. See also the Every Child Matters Guidance 'Safeguarding Children from Abuse linked to a belief in Spirit Possession' (2007).

153  Trafficking Guidance, paras 7.8–7.14.

154  The Guidance in fact refers to UKBA's predecessor, the Border and Immigration Agency (BIA), but the reference should be read as applying to UKBA.

155  Trafficking Guidance, paras 5.26–5.32. Note that the statutory guidance issued under the UK Borders Act 2007 has been replaced by the s55 Guidance, discussed above.

and responding to the needs of a child trafficking victim, regardless of their nationality or immigration status.[156]

6.80 In the case of children (and adults) who are subject to immigration control, the UKBA also acts as the 'Competent Authority' for the purpose of fulfilling the UK's obligations under the Trafficking Convention to identify victims of trafficking.[157] Any person who encounters a potential victim of trafficking should make a referral to UKBA[158] which will then investigate and take decisions as to whether, first, there are reasonable grounds to consider that the person is a victim of trafficking and, if so, reach a conclusive decision about whether on the balance of probabilities the person has been trafficked. In the case of children, UKBA's Guidance for Competent Authorities emphasises that where interviews are required as part of the identification process, children 'should, where possible, be interviewed by specialist trained child protection police or social work professionals'.[159]

## Immigration decisions in relation to trafficked children

6.81 Under the Trafficking Convention, the consequences of a decision that there are 'reasonable grounds' to consider that a child is a victim of trafficking, and/or of a conclusive decision that he or she is a victim of trafficking, include obligations to allow a period of recovery and reflection,[160] and to provide appropriate accommodation and support,

---

156 UKBA Asylum Process Guidance, Victims of Trafficking: guidance for competent authorities, p17.

157 Article 10(1) of the Trafficking Convention provides that: 'Each Party shall provide its competent authorities with persons who are trained and qualified in preventing and combating trafficking in human beings, in identifying and helping victims, including children, and shall ensure that the different authorities collaborate with each other as well as with relevant support organisations, so that victims can be identified in a procedure duly taking into account the special situation of women and child victims and, in appropriate cases, issued with residence permits under the conditions provided for in article 14 of the present Convention.' In other cases, the UK Human Trafficking Centre (UKHTC) acts as the CA.

158 Or the UKHTC if relevant.

159 Page 18.

160 Article 13 of the Trafficking Convention. In the UK this is provided by way of a grant of temporary admission or temporary release for 45 days. Temporary admission/release is a kind of tolerated status which permits a person liable to detention to reside in the community, subject to conditions of residence and reporting. The UKBA's Guidance indicates that reporting requirements for victims of trafficking during this period should be very light touch (p 28).

and medical, counselling and legal advice services.[161] UKBA has a policy of granting twelve months' leave to remain to accepted victims of trafficking who have agreed to co-operate with police enquiries.[162] Beyond this, however, the conclusive decision will not automatically lead to any grant of immigration status, and UKBA's Guidance for Competent Authorities requires it to process applications to remain in the UK by victims of trafficking in the same way as other asylum and non-asylum applications to remain.[163] The Trafficking Guidance however emphasises that:

> In many cases, and with advice from their lawyers, trafficked children apply to the [UKBA] for asylum or humanitarian protection. This is often because of the high risk they face of coming to harm if they are forced to return to their countries of origin. ... Among the factors to consider if the child is deported is the risk of him or her being re-trafficked with the possibility of further exploitation and abuse.[164]

6.82 The interplay between the Trafficking Convention, the ECHR and the return of trafficked children to other countries was considered by Charles J in *In re S (A Child) (Care Proceedings: Jurisdiction)*,[165] in the context of a return decision under the EU's Brussels II Regulation.[166] Charles J concluded that when considering the return of a child to another jurisdiction, the court and the local authority were bound to have regard to the ECHR and EU law obligations, which meant refraining from acts which would defeat the purpose of the Trafficking Convention. However, the ECHR, the Trafficking Convention and the Brussels Regulation had to be applied 'constructively and sensibly having regard to their overlapping and complementary terms and purposes'. The risk of re-trafficking and reprisals were part of the balancing exercise under the Regulation, but it could be assumed that the Romanian courts, which had jurisdiction under the Brussels II Regulation, would take the necessary measures to ensure that the child was protected as part of its assessment of the relevant welfare decisions.

---

161 Article 10(2) of the Trafficking Convention.
162 UKBA Guidance, p35.
163 See the Guidance for Frontline Staff at p25 which cross-refers to UKBA's main asylum process guidance on assessing claims. This includes in cases where the child's age is disputed, where UKBA will follow the procedure set out in its age disputes policy, discussed in Chapter 3.
164 Para 7.43.
165 [2008] EWHC 3013 (Fam), [2009] 2 FLR 550.
166 Regulation (EC) No 2201/2003 of 27 November 2003 concerning jurisdiction and the recognition and enforcement of judgments in matrimonial matters and the matters of parental responsibility.

## Support for trafficked children

6.83   The Trafficking Guidance was adopted in 2007[167] and is not statutory guidance, but is intended to set out best practice and to supplement the *Working together to safeguard children* statutory guidance (see chapter 2 at 2.46–2.50). It emphasises that any procedures developed to safeguard children who may have been trafficked must be consistent with the statutory guidance.[168] Local Safeguarding Children Boards are advised to:

> … consider whether they should have inter-agency strategies and protocols in place for the early identification and notification to the relevant agencies of potential trafficking victims. LSCBs should maintain close links with community groups and have a strategy in place for raising awareness within the local community of the possibility that children are trafficked and exploited, and how to raise a concern. This may include public awareness work.[169]

6.84   The Trafficking Guidance emphasises that:

- 'Local authorities have a general duty to safeguard and promote the welfare of all children in need in their area, regardless of their immigration status';[170]

- 'The nationality or immigration status of the child does not affect agencies' statutory responsibilities under the 1989 or 2004 Children Acts. These issues should be addressed in discussion with the [UKBA] only when the child's need for protection from harm has been addressed and should not hold up action to protect the child from harm' (emphasis in original).[171]

- 'Where a child has been referred to the local authority because of trafficking concerns children's social care should decide within 24 hours whether to undertake an initial assessment to determine whether the child is a child in need and, where appropriate, following a strategic discussion, initiate a section 47 enquiry'.[172] It also sets out flowcharts describing a process of assessment and child protection enquiries which reflects the standard process

---

167   That is, before the Trafficking Convention was ratified by the UK and before the UKBA was placed under the obligation to safeguard and promote the welfare of children in November 2009 by s. 55 of the UKBA 2007. It must be read with this in mind.

168   Trafficking Guidance, para 1.3.

169   Trafficking Guidance, para 4.2.

170   Trafficking Guidance, para 5.4.

171   Trafficking Guidance, para 7.6.

172   Trafficking Guidance, para 5.5.

which should follow any referral of a child who is or may be in need or at risk of significant harm;[173]

- 'All practitioners who come into contact with children and young people in their everyday work need to be able to recognise children who have been trafficked, and be competent to act to support and protect these children from harm';[174] and

- 'All agencies working with children who may have been trafficked into and within the UK should work together to safeguard and promote their welfare, providing the same standard of care that is available to any other child in the UK. This may be the crucial intervention which breaks the cycle of the child being vulnerable to continuing or further exploitation'.[175]

6.85     The Trafficking Guidance also sets out specific steps to be taken in cases where an assessment of needs and/or child protection enquiries are being conducted where the child is thought to be a victim of trafficking. These include:

- Requesting relevant information from equivalent agencies in the child's country of origin, or other countries in which the child has lived;[176]

- Checking documentation such as passports and visas to ensure that information provided correlates with the child's details and those of any person claiming to be the child's mother or father.[177] Immigration staff should be asked for advice in this process;[178]

- If it is decided that an interview should be conducted, 'standard social work practice should be followed', including that children should not be interviewed in the presence of carers.[179] Questions should focus on issues that are likely to reveal coached accounts or implausibilities in the child's personal history which might indicate trafficking;[180] and

- Ensuring that 'appropriately trained and CRB checked independent interpreters' are available.[181]

173  Trafficking Guidance, pp33–37.
174  Trafficking Guidance, para 7.5.
175  Trafficking Guidance, para 7.7.
176  Trafficking Guidance, para 7.24.
177  Trafficking Guidance, para 7.26.
178  Trafficking Guidance, para 7.27.
179  Trafficking Guidance, para 7.31.
180  Trafficking Guidance, paras 7.32–7.33.
181  Trafficking Guidance, para 7.39.

6.86    If a child who is or is believed to be a victim of trafficking is looked after by the local authority under CA 1989 s 20 (see chapter 5) then there are clearly particular obligations on the local authority to ensure that he or she is not exposed to further exploitation. The Trafficking Guidance emphasises the importance of ensuring that any needs assessment addresses 'the child's vulnerability to the continuing influence/control of his or her traffickers',[182] and sets out specific obligations to ensure that this risk is carefully managed:

- The care plan should include a risk assessment and contingency plans for if the child goes missing;[183]
- The location of the child should not be divulged to any enquirers until they have been interviewed by a social worker and their identity and relationship/connection with the child established, if necessary with the help of police and immigration services. Particular care should be taken with adults who claim to have a family connection to the child;[184] and
- Particular vigilance is required on the part of foster carers or residential workers to look out for indicators of risk, such as cars waiting outside the premises or telephone enquiries.[185]

6.87    Local authorities and other agencies do not only have duties towards those children who are known to be, or believed to be, victims of trafficking. The threshold is lower than this: if there are circumstances which give rise to a 'credible suspicion' that a child might have been a victim of trafficking, that is sufficient to trigger the positive obligations under art 4 ECHR to protect against, as well as investigate, trafficking.[186]

6.88    It should also be borne in mind that ascertaining the true age of a victim of trafficking is often difficult.[187] Child victims may not be known to be children. A child may have entered the country using documents which are fake, or may have been given documents belonging to another child, in order to make them appear older or younger. Children may be coerced to lie about their age by the adults trafficking and exploiting them. Accordingly, information

---

182  Para 7.57.
183  Para 7.58.
184  Paras 7.60–7.62.
185  Para 7.60.
186  *Rantsev v Cyprus and Russia* (2010) 51 EHRR 1 at [286].
187  This is recognised by UKBA's Guidance for Competent Authorities (p11) and its Guidance for Frontline Staff (p13).

about a child provided by an accompanying adult or carer may not be accurate; and even the child him- or herself may provide incorrect information.

6.89 It is unfortunate that the Trafficking Guidance is silent on this important issue, and does not emphasise the imperative on local authorities and other agencies to be alert to the child's true age. Where there is a question over the age of the young person, s/he should be treated as a child by the local authority; appropriate age assessment procedures should be undertaken;[188] and in the interim appropriate services and/or accommodation should be provided. Unlike the Trafficking Guidance, however, the February 2011 LSCB guidance (applicable only within London) does squarely address the important question of age of trafficking victims. It states that, when the age of the victim is uncertain and there are reasons to believe that s/he may be a child, then 's/he should be presumed to be a child and be provided with full protection as a child victim of trafficking',[189] and,

> Where there is concern that a child may have been trafficked and an age dispute arises, the child should be given the benefit of the doubt as to their age until his/her age is verified. This is in accordance with the Council of Europe Convention.[190]

## Conclusion

6.90 Migrant children should be treated as children first, migrants second. They are rarely responsible for, or even involved in, the decisions of the adults around them to move across international frontiers. That is so whether they move with their families, or are sent independently by parents who believe they are giving their child the chance of a better life. Their needs as children should be at the forefront of decision-making about their lives and their futures.

6.91 The impact of the new obligations on UKBA to have regard to the need to safeguard and promote the welfare of children and to treat the best interests of the child as a primary consideration in exercising its

---

188 UKBA's Guidance for Competent Authorities provides that cases of age dispute should be considered in line with UKBA's standard guidance on age disputes (p11). See further *R (A) v Croydon London Borough Council* [2009] UKSC 8, [2009] WLR (D) 342 and chapter 3.

189 LSCB guidance, para 9.5.

190 LSCB guidance, para 9.6. UKBA's Guidance for Competent Authorities also states that 'Cases where age cannot be established should continue to be given the benefit of the doubt and be treated as if they were children.' (p11)

immigration functions has already been established by the Supreme Court in *ZH (Tanzania) v Secretary of State for the Home Department*.[191] It is to be hoped that these requirements, together with a more generous interpretation of local authority duties towards migrant children and families in cases such as *Clue*[192] and *O v Barking and Dagenham*,[193] will lead to an improvement in the situation of migrant children and their families, and reduce their vulnerability.

191  [2011] UKSC 4. See para 6.6 above.
192  See paras 6.52–6.57 above.
193  See also para 6.68 above.

# Duties to children leaving care

## Key points

- Care leavers are a particularly vulnerable group, more prone to homelessness and unemployment than other young adults and having far worse educational outcomes than their peers.
- Leaving care should be a gradual process, not a one-off event.
- Abruptly or prematurely leaving care can cause serious difficulties for the child or young person.
- If a child is accommodated by a local authority ('looked after') for 13 weeks between the ages of 14 and 18, with at least one day being on or after the child's sixteenth birthday, he or she becomes entitled to a wide range of long-term support.
- Two of the most important requirements in relation to care leavers are (a) to appoint a personal adviser and (b) to prepare a pathway plan.
- This support continues until the age of at least 21.
- If the young person is in higher or further education, this support may continue until 24 or 25.
- Accommodation provided under Children Act 1989 s17 or the Housing Act 1996 does not count towards 'looked after' time.
- Key changes for care leavers are being introduced from April 2011.

## Introduction

7.1    For any child or young person, leaving home and starting to live independently is a key stage in their lives. Those who have spent part of their childhood in the care of local authorities ('looked after') are no different in this respect. However, there are some fundamental differences in their experiences. For example, young people who have been looked after for a substantial period are unlikely to have adequate financial, emotional or practical support from their families. Despite this, they are likely to move to independent living between the ages of 16 and 18, whereas the average age for the general population is 22.[1] Whilst many care leavers can and do go on to have successful lives, their chances of doing so are far worse than other young

---

1 'Me, survive, out there? New arrangements for young people in and leaving care', Department of Health (DoH), 1999.

people. Research has long demonstrated that this group of young people is particularly vulnerable – more likely to suffer homelessness, be imprisoned and be on benefits than others; and less likely than other young people to continue in education or to secure stable employment.[2] These difficulties may of course be in part due to the experiences which led to their entry into care in the first place.

7.2     These difficulties are now well recognised – and more than ten years have passed since the Children Act (CA) 1989 was amended by the Children (Leaving Care) Act (CLCA) 2000 to tackle them. However, outcomes for this vulnerable group remain poor and so the legislation has been reinforced with important amendments in force as of April 2011. This chapter outlines the statutory schemes, and explains the ongoing duties owed by children's services authorities to children or young people who are leaving their care.

# Background to the leaving care scheme

7.3     In 1999 an extensive consultation process took place concerning how to improve the life chances of those who had been in care or looked after for a substantial period of time as children. As we have seen in chapter 5, in addition to local authorities having formal parental responsibility for children under a Care Order or Interim Care Order, children may be 'looked after' by a local authority children's services department under CA 1989 s20, if they are children 'in need' who are homeless and require accommodation for any of the reasons set out in section 20(1) or (3).

7.4     Janet Rich, co-ordinator of National Care Leavers' Week, has described how, at the time of the 1999 consultation process, the amount of support provided by local authorities to children and young people when they left care was 'very patchy across the country'.[3] There were discretionary powers in place in the CA 1989 to provide help to care leavers, but they were rarely and inconsistently used. Research by the

---

2 'Me, survive, out there?', DoH, 1999, para 2.6; J Wade and J Dixon, 'Making a home, finding a job: investigating early housing and employment outcomes for young people leaving care' (2006) 11 *Child and family social work* 3, pp 199–208; P Mendes and B Moslehuddin, 'From dependence to interdependence: towards better outcomes for young people leaving state care' (2006) *Child abuse review*, vol 15, issue 2, pp110–126.

3 J Rich, 'Care leavers should not become yesterday's news', interview with epolitix.com, 27 October 2009, available at www.epolitix.com.

Department of Health and others showed that provision of support was uneven, with considerable variation in the services provided to young people even within individual local authorities, as well as between local authorities.[4] Many young care leavers received very little support from their 'corporate parent', the local authority; and often their time in care ended abruptly at the age of 16 or 17 (often on their 16th birthday, when they were transferred to adult services). This absence of support and inadequate transition planning undoubtedly contributed to the stark statistics cited in the 1999 consultation document:

- 75 per cent of young people leaving care had no educational qualifications;
- Up to 50 per cent of young people leaving care were unemployed; and
- 20 per cent experienced some form of homelessness within two years of leaving care.

7.5    The Department of Health's (DoH) consultation paper was poignantly entitled, 'Me, survive, out there?', a phrase taken from a poem written by a 15-year-old girl about her panic at the prospect of being cut loose from children's services on her 16th birthday.[5] The consultation paper recognised the difficulties faced by this group, criticised the 'increasing trend' by local authorities to discharge young people from care early, and considered how to put in place effective mechanisms to alter this situation. It also proposed what was later implemented as the 'leaving care' regime. As Baroness Hale later put it in *R (G) v Southwark LBC*[6] the general aim of the 'leaving care' duties which resulted from that consultation process is to 'provide a child or young person with the sort of parental guidance and support which most young people growing up in their own families can take for granted but which those who are separated or estranged from their families cannot'.[7]

---

4  N Biehal, J Clayden, M Stein and J Wade, *Moving on: young people and leaving care schemes*, HMSO, 1995; 'When leaving home is also leaving care: an inspection of services for young people leaving care', Social Services Inspectorate, DoH, 1997; B Broad, *Young people leaving care: life after the Children Act 1989*, Jessica Kingsley, London, 1998; J Wade and J Dixon, 'Making a home, finding a job: investigating early housing and employment outcomes for young people leaving care' (2006) 11 *Child and Family Social Work* 3, pp 199–208.

5  DoH, 1999.

6  [2009] UKHL 26, [2009] 1 WLR 1299.

7  [2009] UKHL 26, [2009] 1 WLR 1299 at [8].

7.6    In the foreword to the DoH consultation paper, Frank Dobson MP, then Secretary of State for Health, recognised that local authorities were 'corporate parents' to such young people, and described:

> Our determination to end the practice of forcing some children as young as 16 to leave care and fend for themselves. That's wrong. It shouldn't happen and it won't happen in future. Local authorities should look after young people of 16 and 17 and help them to develop the skills they need to look after themselves in the outside world. We have a special responsibility to young people who are in care. As their corporate parent we owe them a special duty ...

> I am determined that young people living in and leaving care will in the future get the same support, as far as possible, as other young people who are living at home and leaving home. This means a home to live or return to, a shoulder to cry on, encouragement with work or school or college, someone to take you out for a meal or out for a drink, someone to help you with a bit of cash when you need it, somewhere to get the washing done.[8]

7.7    Following the 1999 consultation process, parliament introduced the Children (Leaving Care) Act (CLCA) 2000, followed by detailed regulations (Children (Leaving Care) (England) Regulations (CLCE Regs) 2001)[9] and associated guidance. The Act, regulations and guidance together constitute the 'leaving care regime'.[10] Although criticised by some groups for not going far enough,[11] the new scheme established that 'corporate parents' (local authorities) have responsibility for children beyond their time in care, and mandated a certain level of support for care leavers until the age of at least 21, with more limited duties until the age of 24. Reflecting the stated aspirations in the 1999 consultation paper, the guidance makes clear from the outset that the support provided under the leaving care scheme 'should be, broadly, the support that a good parent might be expected to give'.[12]

7.8    Whilst the leaving care regime was a welcome and essential legal development, problems on the ground persisted. Many young people who should have benefitted from the scheme did not do so. Some local authorities failed to comply with their duties to young people

---

8  'Me, survive, out there?' DoH, 1999, p5.

9  SI No 2874. In Wales, the Children (Leaving Care) (Wales) (CLCW Regs) Regulations 2001 SI No 2189.

10 C(LC)A 2000 amends the CA 1989, and so the leaving care provisions are to be found in CA 1989 as amended.

11 Eg, the Care Leavers' Association.

12 *Children (Leaving Care) Act 2000 regulations and guidance*, DoH, 2001 (*'C(LC)A 2000 Guidance (2001)'*), chapter 4 para 3.

entitled to the benefit of it, despite the mandatory and clear nature of the statutory scheme, and despite a series of judgments from the Administrative Court, most notably the landmark case of *R (J) v Caerphilly CBC*[13] (see below at paras 7.40–7.41). In 2008, the court in *R (G) v Nottingham City Council and Nottingham University Hospitals NHS Trust*[14] described the 'catalogue of failings' towards a care leaver by the local authority in that case as 'depressing', given the decade that had passed since the 1999 consultation process, and the three years that had passed since the *Caerphilly* judgment.[15]

7.9     Critics of the scheme also focused upon difficulties in the transition process, with young people often transferred from children's services to the leaving care team abruptly, on a particular date, and without an understanding of the need for better transitional support. Detailed research in 2006 demonstrated that children and young people continued to be at sharply heightened risk of homelessness soon after leaving care; continued to have low educational attainment, with the majority leaving care without any qualifications; and that the majority failed to establish a stable pattern of education, training or work in the early years after leaving care[16] – precisely the problems which the 1999 consultation paper and 2000 legislation and guidance were intended to address.

7.10    A further consultation paper, issued in 2006, addressed a number of the deficiencies in the leaving care scheme.[17] This was followed by a 2007 white paper which focused on children in care, but also recommended some changes to the leaving care regime.[18] In November 2008 parliament passed the Children and Young Persons Act (CYPA) 2008. It further amends the CA 1989 by extending support for young people in and leaving care. The suite of guidance regarding care leavers was revised in October 2010 and will come into force in April 2011.

7.11    Regrettably, it remains the case that the life chances of care leavers are severely restricted, and that many of them receive inadequate support from their corporate parent, the local authority. Some groups of young care leavers are particularly vulnerable to poor outcomes (in

13  [2005] EWHC 586 (Admin), [2005] 2 FLR 860.
14  [2008] EWHC 400 (Admin), (2008) 11 CCLR 280.
15  [2008] EWHC 400 (Admin), (2008) 11 CCLR 280 at [39].
16  J Wade and J Dixon, 'Making a home, finding a job: investigating early housing and employment outcomes for young people leaving care' (2006) 11 *Child and Family Social Work* 3, pp199–208.
17  *Care matters: transforming the lives of children and young people in care*, Department for Education and Skills, October 2006, Cm 6932.
18  *Care matters: time for change*, Department for Education, June 2007, Cm 7137.

terms of homelessness, poverty and unemployment), including those with mental health problems or a history of persistent offending and disabled young people.[19] These groups are likely to need intensive remedial support from leaving care services to assist them. It is clear that key ingredients for success for care leavers are settled care, thorough transition planning and assessment and, crucially, delaying young people's transitions from care.[20] In the authors' view, the April 2011 changes go some way towards recognising these persistent problems, and enshrining the need for longer and better-supported transitions to adulthood for young care leavers within the legislation.

## Basic statutory scheme: the current leaving care regime

7.12    The CLCA 2000 and the CLCE Regs 2001[21] introduced both a full leaving care package, for children and young people who had been looked after for a substantial period of time, and some more limited support for those who had been looked after for a shorter period and did not qualify for the full scheme. Below we examine the full scheme, and then detail the more limited advice and assistance scheme. In Wales, there are separate regulations, also dating from 2001, which are to similar effect.[22] From April 2011 the CLCE Regs 2001 are amended by and supplemented with the Care Leavers (England) Regulations 2010 which are discussed below at paras 7.104–7.109.[23]

7.13    From the perspective of the young person, identifying precisely when they were 'looked after' is essential to determine the nature and extent of their eligibility for leaving care support. However, in many cases, the exact chronology of the dates the young person has spent 'looked after' by the local authority may be unclear. Often, it is necessary to issue urgent judicial review proceedings before this has been definitely clarified, although on the available information it appears the young person has been 'looked after' for a sufficient period to attract the full leaving care entitlements. In those circumstances, it is sensible to plead both that the claimant is entitled to the full

---

19  See, for example, *R (P) v Newham LBC* [2004] EWHC 2210 (Admin), [2005] 2 FCR 171.

20  J Wade and J Dixon (2006) 11 *Child and Family Social Work* 3, p200.

21  SI No 2874.

22  See *R (J) v Caerphilly CBC* [2005] EWHC 586 (Admin), [2005] 2 FLR 860.

23  SI No 2571.

leaving care package, and as a fall-back that he or she is in any event entitled to the more limited support afforded to 'qualifying' children (see below, paras 7.89–7.100). Disclosure of the claimant's housing file and social services file should be requested in order to obtain a full chronology of the relevant dates, which may assist in proving that the claimant is entitled to the full leaving care package.

7.14    CA 1989 (as amended) and CLCE Regs 2001 are underpinned by the Leaving Care (LC) Guidance.[24] As of 1 April 2011, the CLCE Regs 2001 and the LC Guidance are replaced by the Care Leavers (England) Regulations 2010 and the 'Transition Guidance',[25] discussed at paras 7.104–7.118 below. The LC Guidance and Transitional Guidance were issued under Local Authority Social Services Act 1970 s7. This provision requires local authorities in their social services functions to act under the general guidance of the secretary of state. As such, social services departments are bound to follow the guidance unless there is good reason not to.[26]

7.15    The LC Guidance states that 'it is designed to bring managers and practitioners an understanding of the principles behind the ... 2000 Act'. It is often relied upon and cited by the courts in leaving care cases. In relation to what it describes as 'the policy context', the LC Guidance states at para 1 that:

> The main purpose of the [CLCA 2000] is to improve the life chances of young people living and leaving local authority care. Its main aims are: to delay young people's discharge from care until they are prepared and ready to leave; to improve the assessment, preparation and planning for leaving care; to provide better personal support for young people after leaving care and to improve the financial arrangements for care leavers.

## The full leaving care scheme

7.16    The full scheme is set out in CA 1989 ss23A–23C and Sch 2, as amended by CLCA 2000 and CLCE Regs 2001. This provides for a three-stage scheme, with three broad categories of person to whom the full leaving care provisions apply:

1) an 'eligible child' (see paras 7.25–7.75 below) – this is a child of 16 or 17 who has been looked after for sufficient time to qualify

24    *Children (Leaving Care) Act 2000 regulations and guidance,* DoH, 2001.
25    The Children Act 1989 guidance and regulations, vol 3: planning transition to adulthood for care leavers, DfE, October 2010.
26    *R v Islington LBC, ex p Rixon* (1997–98) 1 CCLR 119, per Sedley J at 123 J–K. See para 2.8 above.

for the full leaving care package, and who remains a 'looked after' child (see chapter 5 at paras 5.76–5.96 above for definition of a 'looked after' child);

2) a 'relevant child' (see paras 7.76–7.81 below) – this is a child of 16 or 17 who has been looked after for sufficient time to qualify for the full leaving care package, but who is no longer looked after; and

3) a 'former relevant child' (see paras 7.82–7.88 below) – this is a young person aged 18 or over who has been an eligible or a relevant child and is entitled to the full leaving care package.

7.17 Underpinning each of these three categories is the duty detailed in CA 1989 Sch 2 para 19A (which appears under the heading 'preparation for ceasing to be looked after'):

> It is the duty of the local authority looking after a child to advise, assist and befriend him with a view to promoting his welfare when they have ceased to look after him.

7.18 A similar general duty to prepare young people for the time they are no longer cared for also applies to voluntary organisations (CA 1989 s61(1)(c)) and those providing children's homes (CA 1989 s64(1)(c)), although these bodies do not have the specific and detailed duties placed on responsible local authorities.

### Responsible local authority

7.19 Throughout this chapter, reference is made to the 'responsible local authority.' This is the last authority which looked after an 'eligible' or 'relevant' child or young person. That definition is now contained within the Care Leavers (England) Regulations 2010 reg 2(1), in force as of 1 April 2011. However, it also appears in the primary statute, in CA 1989 s23A(4). Under the leaving care scheme that local authority retains this responsibility for a care leaver wherever the young person may be living in England or Wales. According to the LC Guidance, the aim of this is twofold:

- First, to reinforce continuity of care. Research suggests that this, along with stability and the maintenance of family links, may contribute to positive outcomes for care leavers, especially in relation to their self esteem and sense of identity; and

- Second, to prevent disputes between local authorities over the issue of who is responsible for services.[27]

---

27 *C(LC)A 2000 Guidance* (2001), chapter 3 para 1.

7.20    If a young person moves to a different local authority, funding can be transferred by the responsible local authority to the local authority where the young person is living to enable them to provide leaving care services. A further example of where such outsourcing may be appropriate is given in the LC Guidance:

> Such arrangements are also available as a possible solution in cases where a young person's relationship with the responsible authority breaks down. Under such circumstances the authority will be able to discharge its duties through arrangements made with another authority, though it will still keep ultimate responsibility.[28]

7.21    In any outsourcing case, however, it is essential that support is provided whilst new arrangements are being made and, where necessary, the funding transferred. In difficult cases the guidance states that this may mean use of the second authority's emergency services.[29]

7.22    There are particular difficulties which arise for local authorities in supporting young people who live outside of their area. Since 2004 there has been in place a National Protocol on Inter-Authority Arrangements for Careleavers, with the current edition dating from 2006.[30] It is a voluntary, non-binding document, agreed between the then-Department for Education and Skills (DfES) Leaving Care Project Group and the Association of Directors of Social Services (ADSS) as a model for managing joint working arrangements between local authorities, where a care leaver who is the responsibility of one authority is residing in another authority. According to DfES and ADSS, it was intended to provide a floor, not a ceiling; they state from the outset of the protocol that it 'represents a minimum standard of joint working required of authorities to implement the Children (Leaving Care) Act'.[31]

7.23    The protocol states that each authority will provide a 'lead officer,' who will be a 'service manager with accountability for the authority's leaving care services, who can be contacted in the event of difficulty and who will try to resolve any concerns reported about the service offered to young people'. The National Care Advisory Service (NCAS) on behalf of DfE (previously DfES) maintains and updates the database of lead officers for every local authority in England.

---

28   *C(LC)A 2000 Guidance* (2001), chapter 3 para 2.
29   *C(LC)A 2000 Guidance* (2001), chapter 3 paras 3–4.
30   2nd edn, July 2006.
31   *National protocol on inter-authority arrangements for careleavers*, DfES and ADSS, 2nd edn, July 2006, p1, para 1.

7.24     NCAS produced a report in 2009 regarding how well the protocol was working. This raised a number of serious concerns. For
example, they concluded that there were particular difficulties arising for disabled young people and unaccompanied asylum seeking
young people who lived outside their authority. Worryingly, NCAS
found that provision of services was grossly uneven:

> The level of service provided by a non-responsible authority to care
> leavers living out of their own authority varied enormously from basic
> duty provision through to full leaving care service.[32]

## 'Eligible child'

7.25     CA 1989 Sch 2 para 19B places certain duties on local authorities in
relation to 'an eligible child whom they are looking after'. An eligible
child is a child aged 16 or 17 (para 19B(2)(a)) who has been looked
after by a local authority for a cumulative total of 13 weeks beginning
after the age of 14 and ending after the age of 16 (para 19B(2)(b) and
CLCE Regs 2001 reg 3), and who continues to be looked after.

7.26     Given the statutory definition, this of course means that an 'eligible child' of 16 or 17 will simultaneously have that status, with certain entitlements under the leaving care scheme, but will also remain
'looked after' or subject to a Care Order. Regulation 5(4) of the CLCE
Regs 2001 provides that none of the regulations shall prevent the
carrying out of any other assessment or review, such as, for example,
an assessment under CA 1989 s17, or a looked after child review.
The responsible local authority therefore has parallel duties to an eligible child of 16 or 17 – ongoing duties to him or her as a 'looked
after' child and a child 'in need', but also the additional duties which
arise under the leaving care scheme. They are not alternatives. However, the CA 1989 provides for streamlining of leaving care and other
assessments into a single process where practicable, 'so that the child
is not subject to a whole succession of overlapping assessments',[33]
For example, CA 1989 s23E(1A) provides that the Pathway Assessment may be carried out at the same time as an assessment carried
out under any other enactment.[34]

---

32  NCAS, *NCAS review of the inter authority protocol for care leavers* (2009) p1.

33  *C(LC)A 2000 Guidance* (2001), chapter 5 para 10.

34  See also CA 1989 Sch 2 para 3 which provides that an assessment carried out
    under CA 1989 s17 of a child 'in need' can be carried out at the same time as
    any other statutory assessment.

7.27    As noted above, central to advising and acting for 'looked after' children or care leavers will be establishing whether or not there has been a 13-week period for which the child has been looked after, as this triggers the full requirements of the leaving care scheme. The 13-week period can be made up of a single, continuous period of time, or a series of shorter periods. At least one day must be on or after the child's 16th birthday. Careful consideration of the child's housing and social services files will be required if this is in dispute.

7.28    Legal advisers must be alert to the possibility that some local authorities may attempt to evade their responsibilities by, for example, transferring a child to the housing department or housing authority on the eve of his or her 16th birthday (as being accommodated under the Housing Act 1996 does not constitute 'looked after' time),[35] or claiming that the 13-week mark has not been reached because the child was being accommodated under a voluntary arrangement with a relative or friend, and so was not looked after at this time. Such approaches are unlawful. The Supreme Court has made clear that local authorities cannot lawfully evade their responsibilities to eligible children by 'labelling' time which is, in truth, looked after time as something else: *R (G) v Southwark LBC*[36] (see also paras 5.105–5.107).

7.29    There is an exclusionary provision in the CLCE Regs 2001, regulation 3(2) and (3), which exclude from the definition of 'eligible child' certain children who have accumulated 13 weeks looked after time and would otherwise be entitled to the benefits of the full leaving care scheme. A child falls into this excluded group:

if he has been looked after by a local authority in circumstances where –
(a) the local authority has arranged to place him in a pre-planned series of short-term placements, none of which individually exceeds four weeks (even though they may amount in all to the prescribed period); and
(b) at the end of each such placement the child returns to the care of his parent, or a person who is not a parent but who has parental responsibility for him.

This exclusion is now repeated in the Care Leavers (England) Regulations 2010[37] reg 3(3), in force as of 1 April 2011.

7.30    This exclusion is intended to ensure that the full leaving care scheme does not apply to children (primarily disabled children) who

---

35   *R (L) v Nottinghamshire CC* [2007] EWHC 2364 (Admin), [2007] ACD 92.
36   [2009] UKHL 29, [2009] 1 WLR 1299.
37   SI No 2571.

are looked after by way of short breaks (still sometimes referred to as 'respite care'), but who remain the sole responsibility of their parents or other carers. This is because the leaving care scheme is designed to assist those who rely on the local authority in place of their family, and it is modelled on what good parents would normally be expected to provide for their children. Such support is not intended to apply to children looked after by way of regular, intermittent respite care. However, legal advisers must ensure that the regulation 3 exclusion is not used inappropriately, in order to evade statutory duties to other children.[38]

7.31    A local authority has the following five duties in relation to eligible children:

1) Duty to appoint a 'personal adviser' for the child (CA 1989 Sch 2 para 19C). The personal adviser's role is discussed below at paras 7.32–7.51.

2) Duty to prepare a 'written statement describing the manner in which the needs of each eligible ... child will be addressed' (CLCE Regs 2001 reg 5). This written statement must be made available to both the child and the child's personal adviser (CLCE Regs 2001 regs 5(3) and 7(5)). Its content is prescribed by the CLCE Regs 2001; see below at paras 7.52–7.53.

3) Duty to 'carry out an assessment of his needs with a view to determining what advice, assistance and support it would be appropriate for them to provide him ... (a) while they are looking after him; and (b) after they cease to look after him' (CA 1989 Sch 2 para 19B(4)). The timeframe for, content and process of this assessment are set out below at paras 7.54–7.68.

4) Duty to prepare a 'Pathway Plan' 'as soon as possible after the assessment' (CA 1989 Sch 2 para 19B(4); CLCE Regs 2001 reg 8 and Care Leavers (England) Regulations 2010 reg 6(1)). This is a crucial document for a care-leaver, and it should be a 'detailed operational plan' (*R (J) v Caerphilly CBC*[39]). It must include a number of matters mandated in the schedule to the CLCE Regs 2001. The importance and required content of the Pathway Plan is set out below at paras 7.69–7.75. A copy of the Pathway Plan must be provided to the child 'without delay' (CLCE Regs 2001 reg 6) or, under the new Care Leavers (England) Regulations 2010 reg 4(2): 'as soon as practicable'.

---

38  See further chapter 4 at paras 4.54–4.62 in relation to residential short breaks.
39  [2005] EWHC 586 (Admin), [2005] 2 FLR 860.

5) Duty to keep the Pathway Plan under regular review (CA 1989 Sch 2 para 19B(5)).

### (1) Personal adviser

7.32   The local authority has a mandatory duty to appoint a personal adviser for an eligible child (CA 1989 Sch 2 para 19C). The statutory scheme does not specify a precise date by which the personal adviser is to be appointed. Paragraph 19C merely provides that:

> A local authority shall arrange for each child whom they are looking after who is an eligible child for the purposes of paragraph 19B to have a personal adviser.

However, as the personal adviser has a crucial role to play in the next step of the process, the preparation of the Pathway Assessment (which must be completed within a three-month period, see below at para 7.55), it is apparent that he or she must be appointed promptly.

7.33   Munby J (as he then was) in *R (G) v Nottingham CC and Nottingham University Hospitals NHS Trust* considered the timing of the personal adviser's appointment given the absence of any explicit requirement in the scheme. He concluded that the appointment must be made 'forthwith' or as soon as reasonably practicable:

> Given that the duty is mandatory, and tied to the fact that the child in question 'is' an eligible child, it follows, in my judgment, that the duty to arrange for the appointment of a personal adviser arises the moment the child becomes an eligible child. No doubt the process of arranging the appointment of a personal adviser will take at least a few days, perhaps weeks. So the duty is, in my judgment, a duty to secure the appointment of the personal adviser forthwith – in the sense of as soon as reasonably practicable – once the child has become an eligible child. G became an eligible child on 2 August 2006, so her personal adviser should have been appointed as soon as practicable thereafter.[40]

7.34   The personal adviser performs a crucial role for the eligible child. The adviser is an advocate for the child, and the conduit between the child and the local authority. This is clear from CLCE Regs 2001 regs 7 and 12 and the LC Guidance; and this is confirmed in the new Care Leavers (England) Regualtions 2010 and accompanying transition guidance.[41]

7.35   Regulation 7 concerns the Pathway Assessment (see further below at paras 7.54–7.68). In preparing that assessment, the basis for

40  [2008] EWHC 400 (Admin), (2008) 11 CCLR 280 at [21].
41  *The Children Act 1989 Guidance & Regulations vol 3: Planning Transition and Adulthood for Care Leavers,* October 2010, in force from 1 April 2011.

the planning process for the young person's future, the responsible authority is obliged to 'seek and take into account the views' of the personal adviser (regulation 7(5)(g)).

7.36    Regulation 12, entitled 'Functions of personal advisers', details seven functions of that role:

(a) to provide advice (including practical advice) and support;
(b) where applicable, to participate in his assessment and the preparation of his pathway plan;
(c) to participate in reviews of the pathway plan;
(d) to liaise with the responsible authority in the implementation of the pathway plan;
(e) to co-ordinate the provision of services, and to take reasonable steps to ensure that he makes use of such services;
(f) to keep informed about his progress and wellbeing; and
(g) to keep a written record of contacts with him.

7.37    Regulations 7 and 12 are supplemented by chapter 6 of the LC Guidance. Paragraph 1 of that chapter highlights the importance and centrality of the personal adviser role to the leaving care scheme:

The Children (Leaving Care) Act requires the responsible authority to arrange for each eligible and relevant child to have a personal adviser and to continue the appointment for former relevant children. The appointment of a personal adviser is therefore a statutory requirement. This emphasises the importance of the role and reflects the belief that young people living in and leaving care should be able to identify someone as committed to their well being and development on a long term basis.

7.38    Paragraphs 3–9 of chapter 6 of the LC Guidance provide more detail concerning what is expected of the personal adviser given the functions set out in regulation 12 (see above, para 7.36). These paragraphs are detailed, clear and practical. For example, the requirement in regulation 12(e), 'to coordinate the provision of services, and to take reasonable steps to ensure that he makes use of such services', is dealt with as follows in the LC Guidance (para 7):

**12(2)(e) To co-ordinate the provision of services and to take reasonable steps to ensure that he [the child or young person] makes use of such services.**
The range of services required to meet the young person's needs will be identified in the pathway plan and agreed by those responsible for the services. The role of the personal adviser in this context is to act as a broker in securing the collaboration of other agencies and individuals; to ensure that services are provided at the right time; and to make other agencies and individuals aware of each other's contribution. Fully

engaging the young person in drawing up the pathway plan and in subsequent reviews will clearly assist the take up of services. The personal adviser may also have an important role in facilitating a young person's access by, for example, helping with travel arrangements and fares.

7.39   Given the nature of the role, it is apparent that the personal adviser must be independent of the local authority decision-makers, although the personal adviser can be an employee of the local authority. This is confirmed in paragraph 10 of the LC Guidance:

> **Budget-holding**
> In order to avoid setting up conflicts of interest, the personal adviser should not also be the budget-holder.

7.40   In *R (J) v Caerphilly CBC* Munby J (as he then was) confirmed the centrality of the role the personal adviser plays in the life of a young person preparing to leave care.[42] The case concerned the corresponding Welsh regulations, rather than the English regulations. However, Munby J has subsequently made clear that he considers the *Caerphilly* principles to be of equal relevance to England, stating in *R (G) v Nottingham CC and Nottingham University Hospitals NHS Trust* that, 'nothing turns' on the fact that the case concerned the Welsh regulations, 'for although they differ in detail their effect is the same.'[43]

7.41   In *Caerphilly*, Munby J undertook a detailed review of personal adviser's role, describing it as follows:

> It is not part of the personal adviser's functions to undertake the statutory assessment or the preparation of the pathway plan, nor should he do so. The Regulations, in my judgment, show that it is not permissible for him to do so. It is, in any event, undesirable that he should do so. Part of the personal adviser's role is, in a sense, to be the advocate or representative of the child in the course of the child's dealings with the local authority. As the Children Leaving Care Act Guidance puts it, the personal adviser plays a 'negotiating role on behalf of the child'. He is, in a sense, a 'go-between' between the child and the local authority. His vital role and function are apt to be compromised if he is, at one and the same time, both the author of the local authority's pathway plan and the person charged with important duties owed to the child in respect of its preparation and implementation.[44]

In that case the pathway plan had been prepared by the personal adviser, Mr S. The claimant, 'J', complained that in these circumstances

42  [2005] EWHC 586 (Admin), [2005] 2 FLR 860.
43  [2008] EWHC 400 (Admin), (2008) 11 CCLR 280 at [30].
44  [2005] EWHC 586 (Admin), [2005] 2 FLR 860 at [30].

the local authority had not in truth provided J with a personal adviser, for Mr S was in a position where his dual roles put him in a position of conflict, or at least ambiguity, and prevented him single-mindedly acting in his role as personal adviser. That function, it was argued, had been obscured and compromised. J was entitled to a personal adviser and sought a mandatory order to compel the local authority to provide one. Munby J found there to be 'compelling force in counsel's complaints',[45] and held:

> J is entitled to a personal adviser whose function is just that, and whose function is not obscured and compromised by the conflicts and ambiguities which, unfortunately, cloud Mr S's position. The present situation cannot continue and must be remedied.[46]

7.42    Although it is essential that the personal adviser is independent of the local authority, unfortunately, it is all too common to find that a pathway assessment and pathway plan have been prepared without the appointment of a personal adviser at all, or with the child's social worker, or another social worker from the same local authority, having been purportedly appointed to this role. In these circumstances, the local authority has acted unlawfully, and a fresh assessment will be required. Conversely, neither a pathway plan nor a review of such a plan can be completed by a personal adviser.[47]

7.43    The LC Guidance includes detailed material regarding the appointment, training and deployment of personal advisers. Much of this is common-sense, for example making clear to local authorities that, while there is 'no prescribed professional or occupational qualification for the post of personal adviser',

> ... given the level of knowledge and skill required, it is likely that many personal advisers will have qualifications and/or extensive experience in working with adolescents, for example as social workers, teachers or youth workers. Many specialist leaving care services both in the statutory and voluntary sector already have staff of this kind who are carrying out similar functions to those envisaged for the personal adviser and who have established effective, authoritative relationships with other agencies. It is anticipated that such services will provide an important source of suitable people. Councils may wish to contract with voluntary organisations for the provision of personal advisers.[48]

---

45  *R (G) v Nottingham CC* [2008] EWHC 400 (Admin) at [33].
46  *R (J) v Caerphilly CBC* [2005] EWHC 586 (Admin), [2005] 2 FLR 860 at [32].
47  *R (A) v Lambeth LBC* [2010] EWHC 1652 (Admin).
48  *C(LC)A 2000 Guidance* (2001), chapter 6 para 13.

And:

> Given the history and circumstances of many young people living in and leaving care, personal advisers will generally require high levels of knowledge and skill to work effectively with them. Personal attributes which engender trust and confidence in the adviser will also be very important, given that in many cases the contact between adviser and young person is likely to be close and may continue over many years.[49]

7.44   The LC Guidance also suggests that a network or team of personal advisers may be necessary in order for individuals properly to fulfil their roles to individual young people. This is because personal advisers need to be in a position to offer continuity of support; should be accessible throughout the day 'and at other times in the event of crisis in young people's lives'; and, crucially, a network allows there to be 'fall-back' support and cover arrangements when the personal adviser is absent.[50]

7.45   In order to ensure that appropriate appointments can be made, and that the young person's preferences can be taken into account, local authorities should ensure that they have a sufficiently wide range of advisers. The LC Guidance explicitly refers to the need to ensure that 'considerations of gender and ethnic origin' are taken into account in establishing an available pool of advisers,[51] but other matters, such as religion, will of course also be relevant.

7.46   An issue which sometimes arises in practice is whether an individual already involved in the child or young person's life – for example, a foster carer, residential key worker, or advocate provided by Voice (a national charity committed to empowering children and young people in public care) or another voluntary agency – may or should become his or her personal adviser. There is nothing preventing such a person becoming the personal adviser, and the LC Guidance makes clear that any such requests 'should always be considered seriously and the young person's wishes accommodated as far as possible', provided the local authority is satisfied that the person has the requisite abilities and availability.[52] However, the personal adviser role is intended to supplement rather than supplant existing sources of support; and there is no reason why a young person should not continue to derive support from an existing significant adult in their life, whilst also having a personal adviser. In these circumstances,

---

49   *C(LC)A 2000 Guidance* (2001), chapter 6 para 12.
50   *C(LC)A 2000 Guidance* (2001), chapter 6 para 15.
51   *C(LC)A 2000 Guidance* (2001), chapter 6 para 14.
52   *C(LC)A 2000 Guidance* (2001), chapter 6 para 14.

the other significant adult should still be involved in the pathway assessment and pathway planning process.[53]

7.47      In *R (Deeming) v Birmingham City Council* Elias J considered the appropriateness of the appointment of a particular personal adviser.[54] The claimant was a vulnerable 18-year-old care leaver with a chaotic history, and who had been previously diagnosed with Asperger syndrome, obsessive-compulsive disorder (OCD) and attention deficit hyperactivity disorder (ADHD). Although Birmingham was the responsible authority, the claimant was by now at college in Bromley, and the authority had made arrangements for a private, London-based care provider (London Care Solutions (LCS)) to carry out certain functions on its behalf, including regular contact with an outreach worker in London. The authority had appointed a Birmingham-based personal adviser, 150 miles away from the claimant, who necessarily had infrequent direct contact with him. In a highly fact-specific decision, Elias J concluded that, in the circumstances, the authority had not acted irrationally, illegally or improperly in this appointment. Although it was plain that there might be circumstances where it was extremely difficult for a personal adviser to be so far away from the young person, a lot would also depend upon the degree of support that the young person had locally and his or her views. Elias J considered that the claimant's 'significant degree' of Bromley-based support was very relevant here, particularly the LCS outreach worker;[55] he pointed to the LC Guidance's reference to contact having to take place at least every six months;[56] he referred to the claimant's wishes and right to privacy;[57] and he noted a phrase in the LC Guidance concerning the personal adviser being the main source of support for some young people, but for others being 'largely a peripheral figure in their lives'.[58] The fact-sensitive nature of this outcome is demonstrated by Elias J's warning note concerning the possibility of needing to revisit the appropriateness of the personal adviser in the event that the LCS support were to be withdrawn.[59]

7.48      At the time of drafting the LC Guidance in 2001, the Connexions service for young people had not yet been introduced. It had been announced by the government in February 2000, and its introduction

---

53   CLCE Regs 2001 reg 7(5)(h).
54   [2006] EWHC 3719 (Admin), [2006] All ER (D) 3.
55   Judgment at [24].
56   Judgment at [21].
57   Judgment at [22] and [24].
58   Judgment at [20].
59   Judgment at [25].

was shortly due to commence (it began on a phased basis from April 2001 onwards). The LC Guidance includes three specific paragraphs regarding the then new Connexions service and personal advisers, and strongly suggests that the Connexions adviser and the personal adviser should be one and the same person. It is stated that:

> This will be a universal service, available to all young people aged 13–19 in England who will have access to a personal adviser to support them in the transition from adolescence to adulthood and working life. Because of the close correspondence between the role of the personal adviser and that envisaged for the Connexions Service personal adviser, it would clearly prevent confusion and duplication if one person fulfilled both roles. It is expected, therefore, that the leaving care personal adviser will normally also act as the young person's Connexions adviser.[60]

7.49    It appears to the authors that these paragraphs may have been added to the LC Guidance as an afterthought, to take account of the pending Connexions scheme. Whatever their genesis, by appearing to recommend that the personal adviser role be subsumed with the universal Connexions adviser role available to any child or young person aged 13–19, this part of the LC Guidance undoubtedly jars with the overriding purpose of the leaving care scheme – to provide *additional* support to this particularly vulnerable group of young people. This section is also at odds with the LC Guidance's explicit recognition a number of paragraphs earlier that the personal adviser role is not intended to supplant existing support structures.

7.50    Under the new Transition Guidance, in force from April 2011, far more detail is given concerning the role of the personal adviser.[61] Much of the material simply replicates that in the existing LC Guidance, but there are important additional requirements. For example, the new guidance refers to the need for the personal adviser to 'possess a sound demonstrable understanding of human growth and development (in particular, being competent in understanding the insecurities faced by looked after children as they make their transition to adulthood)',[62] highlights the importance of a good 'working relationship' between the adviser and young person,[63] and

60  *C(LC)A 2000 Guidance* (2001), chapter 6 paras 16–18.
61  *The Children Act 1989 guidance and regulations, vol 3: planning transition to adulthood for care leavers,* October 2010, chapter 3.
62  *The Children Act 1989 guidance and regulations, vol 3: planning transition to adulthood for care leavers,* October 2010, chapter 3, para 3.21.
63  *The Children Act 1989 guidance and regulations, vol 3: planning transition to adulthood for care leavers,* October 2010, chapter 3, para 3.26.

gives practical examples of the types of support the adviser may be required to provide.[64] Further, the reference to Connexions advisers has, sensibly, been removed.

7.51 However, there are some worrying issues in this part of the new Transition Guidance. For example, reference is made to changing personal adviser at the age of 18, 'where young people have continued to have a qualified social worker as their personal adviser',[65] appearing to suggest that this role could be performed by a social worker from within the local authority. It is also unfortunate that the Transition Guidance has not drawn in more detail on the case-law over the past decade and has lost sight of the crucial role of a personal adviser – to represent independently the interests of the young care leaver.

### (2) Written statement

7.52 The responsible local authority also has a duty to prepare a 'written statement describing the manner in which the needs of each eligible ... child will be addressed' (CLCE Regs 2001 reg 5). This written statement must be made available to both the child and the child's personal adviser (CLCE Regs 2001 regs 5(3) and 7(5)). Its content is prescribed by the CLCE Regs 2001, in a non-exhaustive list set out in regulation 5(2). It must include, in particular, information about:

(a) the person responsible for the conduct and coordination of the assessment;
(b) the timetable for the assessment;
(c) who is to be consulted for the purposes of the assessment;
(d) the arrangements for recording the outcome of the assessment;
(e) the procedure for making representations in the event of a disagreement.

7.53 This is, in essence, a 'signposting' or planning document, which is a precursor to the preparation of the pathway assessment and pathway plan. The authority must make a copy of the statement available to the child and the persons specified in regulation 7(5), including the personal adviser (the full list of persons set out in regulation 7(5) can be found below at para 7.62). These people are those who are entitled to involvement in the pathway assessment process, so it stands to reason that they should be informed of the commencement of the process, the relevant timeframe, and other logistical arrangements.

---

64 *The Children Act 1989 guidance and regulations, vol 3: planning transition to adulthood for care leavers*, October 2010, chapter 3, para 3.28.
65 *The Children Act 1989 guidance and regulations, vol 3: planning transition to adulthood for care leavers*, October 2010, chapter 3, para 3.19.

Unfortunately, the new regulations, in force as of 1 April 2011, omit the requirement in the 2001 Regulations for a written statement. This is, in the authors' view, unfortunate, as it plays an important part in ensuring meaningful involvement of the child, personal adviser and others in the assessment and planning process.

### (3) Pathway assessment

7.54    Following the appointment of the personal adviser, and the production of the written statement, a 'pathway assessment' must be prepared. CA 1989 Sch 2 para 19B(4) places the local authority under a duty to 'carry out an assessment of his needs with a view to determining what advice, assistance and support it would be appropriate for them to provide him … (a) while they are looking after him; and (b) after they cease to look after him'. This assessment then forms the basis for preparing the pathway plan (see below at paras 7.69–7.75).

7.55    The assessment is to be completed 'in the case of an eligible child, not more than three months after the date on which he reaches the age of 16 or becomes an eligible child after that age' (CLCE Regs 2001 reg 7(2)(a) and Care Leavers (England) Regulations 2010 reg 5(2)(a)). This is a maximum timeframe – the pathway assessment must be completed within three months at most. While this may seem a relatively onerous requirement on a local authority, for the majority of eligible children the authority will have been aware of their pending status in advance. It is of course also significantly more than the 35 working days given to local authorities to complete a core assessment; see chapter 4 at para 4.27 above. If an authority knows that a young person whom it is looking after is about to become an eligible child at the age of 16, preparatory work can be undertaken ahead of that date, although the assessment cannot be finalised until after his or her 16th birthday.[66] In complying with the three-month timeframe, the local authority should ensure that there is minimal disruption to the young person, whilst maximising the young person's involvement. For example, in setting the timetable for the assessment the authority 'should bear in mind any considerations such as forthcoming exams, and take all reasonable steps to avoid disrupting the young person's preparation for them'.[67]

7.56    As with assessments under CA 1989 s17, involvement of the child or young person is a prerequisite to a meaningful assessment

---

66   *C(LC)A 2000 Guidance* (2001), chapter 5 para 6.
67   *C(LC)A 2000 Guidance* (2001), chapter 5 para 7.

process (see further chapter 4 at paras 4.27–4.28). This is recognised in regulation 6 of the 2001 Regulations, which provides that:

(1) The responsible authority in carrying out an assessment ... shall, unless it is not reasonably practicable–
  (a) seek and have regard to the views of the child or young person to whom it relates; and
  (b) take all reasonable steps to enable him to attend and partici-pate in any meetings at which his case is to be considered.
(2) The responsible authority shall without delay provide the child or young person with copies of–
  (a) the results of his assessment ... and shall ensure that the con-tents of each document are explained to him in accordance with his level of understanding unless it is not reasonably prac-ticable to do so.

These requirements are now repeated in reg 5 of the 2010 Regulations.

7.57    Regulation 6 was supplemented in this regard by the LC Guid-ance, which provides:

Regulation 6 specifies that the responsible authority should take all reasonable steps to make sure that it seeks out and takes account of the views and wishes of the young person for the assessment, the preparation of the pathway plan, and the review of the plan. Clearly, the further the young person can be involved in the process the more successful it will be. Where these processes involve meetings then the responsible authority should take reasonable steps to make sure that the young person can attend and take part. Such steps might include scheduling meetings at a time which is convenient for the young per-son, or, if he or she has to travel in order to attend, paying reasonable travel and subsistence costs.[68]

Similarly, the 2010 Regulations and Transition Guidance repeat and expand upon these requirements.

7.58    References to the need for adequate and meaningful involvement of the young person in the assessment process are also peppered throughout the LC Guidance. From the outset it is recognised that the leaving care regime follows relevant key principles of the prima-ry legislation, the CA 1989: 'taking into account the views of young people, consulting with them and keeping them informed'.[69]

---

68   *C(LC)A 2000 Guidance* (2001), chapter 5 para 5.
69   *C(LC)A 2000 Guidance* (2001), chapter 1 para 7. See also chapter 1 para 9(j) and chapter 4 para 4.

7.59    The LC Guidance recognises that the responsible authority will not be starting from a blank sheet when preparing the pathway assessment:

> As a looked-after child, an eligible child will already have had a needs assessment in order to formulate a Care Plan, and this should form the basis for the assessment required under the 2000 Act.[70]

Similarly, it is assumed that there will already be a care plan, 'which has been reviewed regularly and updated as part of the process for children who are looked after'.[71] This care plan should have been developed following assessment of the young person as a child 'in need' (see chapter 4 at paras 4.10–4.13), a condition precedent to the young person becoming a 'looked after' child.

7.60    The content of the pathway assessment and the considerations to be taken into account by the local authority in preparing it are prescribed by CLCE Regs 2001 reg 7(4). It provides that:

> In carrying out an assessment the responsible authority shall take account of the following considerations –
> (a) the child's health and development;
> (b) the child's need for education, training or employment;
> (c) the support available to the child from members of his family and other persons;
> (d) the child's financial needs;
> (e) the extent to which the child possesses the practical and other skills necessary for independent living; and
> (f) the child's needs for care, support and accommodation.

This is now repeated verbatim in reg 5(4)(a) of the 2010 Regulations.

7.61    Regulation 7(4) sets the minimum requirements in terms of areas to be covered in the assessment. This is not an exhaustive list of issues to be considered. Individual cases may need more specialist assessment in other areas such as disability, or the young person's sense of identity, self esteem or parenting skills.

7.62    When conducting the assessment, the local authority must both 'seek' and 'take into account' the views of a number of people, as well as the child or young person. A list of essential participants is set out in CLCE Regs 2001 reg 7(5):

> (a) the child's parents;
> (b) any person who is not a parent but has parental responsibility for the child;

---

70  *C(LC)A 2000 Guidance* (2001), chapter 5 para 1.
71  *C(LC)A 2000 Guidance* (2001), chapter 5 para 13.

(c) any person who on a day to day basis cares for, or provides accommodation for the child;

(d) any school or college attended by the child, or the local education authority for the area in which he lives;

(e) any independent visitor appointed for the child;

(f) any person providing health care or treatment to the child;

(g) the personal adviser appointed for the child; and

(h) any other person whose views the responsible authority, or the child consider may be relevant.

7.63    Each of these people should be proactively contacted by the local authority in order for their views to be ascertained ('seek'), and then those views should be given appropriate weight ('take into account'), 'unless it is not reasonably practicable to do so' (CLCE Regs 2001 reg 7(5)).

7.64    The LC Guidance requires that, in the case of a young person with particular communication or cognitive impairment needs, 'at least one person involved in the needs assessment' must have 'a clear understanding of how he expresses his wishes and feelings'.[72]

7.65    Regulation 7(5)(h) indicates the need – if reasonably practicable – to involve in the assessment process any person the child considers to be relevant. In addition, when deciding whom to involve under the other headings, the child's views should be taken into account. For example, the child may wish that a particular teacher (regulation 7(5)(d)) or GP (regulation 7(5)(f)) is involved, rather than a different school staff member or other medical professional. The LC Guidance indicates how the authority should respond to the child's wishes:

> When deciding who needs to be involved in the assessment, the responsible authority should make every effort to take account of the wishes of the young person. This does not amount to giving young people the right of veto, but if they have strong objections to parents taking part, for example, the authority should balance the desirability of involving them against the risk of alienating the young person and possibly losing his or her co-operation.[73]

7.66    Munby J (as he then was) in *R (G) v Nottingham CC and Nottingham University Hospitals NHS Trust* emphasised the true nature of the duty on the local authority in the assessment stage:

> It will be noted that the local authority's duty during the assessment is not merely to identify the child's needs – though that is presumably part of the process of assessing them – it is to 'assess' the child's

---

72  *C(LC)A 2000 Guidance* (2001), chapter 5 para 11.

73  *C(LC)A 2000 Guidance* (2001), chapter 5 para 12.

needs. 'Assessment' goes beyond mere identification of needs; it involves analysis and evaluation of the nature, extent and severity of the child's needs, a process which must go far enough to enable a pathway plan to be prepared setting out in sufficiently precise detail the 'manner in which' those needs are to be met.[74]

7.67    A lawful pathway assessment must therefore both identify and assess the child's needs, in preparation for the pathway planning process, and should put in place a clear and detailed timeframe. A series of cases have emphasised the level of detail and analysis mandated by the CLCE Regs 2001 and LC Guidance. Elias J in *R (Deeming) v Birmingham CC*,[75] for example, repeatedly referred to the 'specificity' required in a lawful pathway assessment regarding each particular area detailed in the regulations. There, the authority had essentially outsourced many of their functions to a private care provider, London Care Solutions (LCS). The authority argued that LCS would put in place the operational details, but this was rejected by Elias J:

> ... another difficulty that does exist ... is the lack of specificity in relation to what is being recommended. It is not identified who should carry out this programme or on what time scale ... I am told that it would be envisaged that this would be the kind of thing that LCS would do, but it does seem necessary to identify that LCS would be responsible for that, and for them to agree to that, and for there to be a specific timetable.[76]

7.68    There is detailed and helpful discussion in the *Deeming* case regarding two issues of great practical concern in leaving care cases: financial arrangements for care leavers, and contingency planning. As regards financial arrangements, Elias J accepted (at paras 34–36) the claimant's submission that the income supplied through the benefit system 'should be the minimum standard and should not be seen as the norm and that what is required is a package which meets the needs of the particular individual', and held that if the person's assessed needs demonstrate that further money is required, the authority must provide it. In practice, unfortunately, many pathway assessments simply refer to the available standard benefits rather than conducting a true assessment of the person's financial needs. Second, Elias J highlighted the importance of full contingency planning for vulnerable young people such as this claimant:

---

74  [2008] EWHC 400 (Admin), (2008) 11 CCLR 280 at [36].
75  [2006] EWHC 3719 (Admin), [2006] All ER (D) 3.
76  [2006] EWHC 3719 (Admin), [2006] All ER (D) 3 at [33].

Again, there is some consideration of certain contingencies that might arise. They include, for example, the claimant not maintaining his tenancy, or if he fails to make contact, if he leaves school without any qualifications, and so forth, but Mr Wise says that is unsatisfactory in a number of respects. In particular, it seems to me there is again a legitimate concern in this area. An important issue for somebody in the claimant's situation is what is to happen if he faces an emotional crisis, perhaps a breakdown of a relationship or some other event in his life? Who should he go to in those circumstances? Who is to take responsibility for dealing with that?[77]

## (4) Pathway plan

7.69    The responsible local authority also has a duty to prepare a 'pathway plan' for an eligible child (CA 1989 Sch 2 para 19B(4); and CLCE Regs 2001 reg 8). There is no explicit timeframe in the scheme for the preparation of a pathway plan. Instead, the duty is to prepare a pathway plan 'as soon as possible after the assessment' (CA 1989 Sch 2 para 19B(4); and CLCE Regs 2001 reg 8). For eligible children – ie children who are entitled to a leaving care package but who continue to be looked after – the pathway plan will be produced before they leave care, allowing for a detailed plan to be put in place for their gradual transition from care to independence. This is recognised in the LC Guidance, which describes how, 'well before a young person leaves care, a continuing care plan should be formulated with him or her'.[78]

7.70    Throughout the pathway planning process the authority must seek and have regard to the child's views (CLCE Regs 2001 reg 6(1)(a)), and take all reasonable steps to enable the child to attend and participate in any meetings at which his or her case is to be considered (reg 6(1)(b)). As with the written statement and pathway assessment, once prepared, a copy of the pathway plan must be provided to the child 'without delay', and its content must be appropriately explained to the child in accordance with his or her level of understanding (reg 6(2)).

7.71    The content of the pathway plan is mandated by regulation 8 and the Schedule to the CLCE Regs 2001. Regulation 8 provides:

(1) A pathway plan prepared under paragraph 19B of Schedule 2 to ... the Act, must be prepared as soon as possible after the assessment and must include, in particular, the matters referred to in the Schedule.

---

77  [2006] EWHC 3719 (Admin), [2006] All ER (D) 3 at [37].
78  *C(LC)A 2000 Guidance* (2001), chapter 4 para 4.

(2) The pathway plan must, in relation to each of the matters referred to in the Schedule, set out–
   (a) the manner in which the responsible authority proposes to meet the needs of the child; and
   (b) the date by which, and by whom, any action required to implement any aspect of the plan will be carried out.
(3) The pathway plan must be recorded in writing.

7.72   The schedule then details the matters which must be dealt with in the pathway plan, setting out nine specific issues which must be covered in any lawful pathway plan:

1. The nature and level of contact and personal support to be provided, and by whom, to the child or young person.
2. Details of the accommodation the child or young person is to occupy.
3. A detailed plan for the education or training of the child or young person.
4. How the responsible authority will assist the child or young person in relation to employment or other purposeful activity or occupation.
5. The support to be provided to enable the child or young person to develop and sustain appropriate family and social relationships.
6. A programme to develop the practical and other skills necessary for the child or young person to live independently.
7. The financial support to be provided to the child or young person, in particular where it is to be provided to meet his accommodation and maintenance needs.
8. The health needs, including any mental health needs, of the child or young person, and how they are to be met.
9. Contingency plans for action to be taken by the responsible authority should the pathway plan for any reason cease to be effective.

7.73   The High Court in a series of cases has emphasised the rigour and detail required of a local authority embarking upon a pathway assessment and the subsequent pathway plan under the leaving care provisions. Although *R (AB and SB) v Nottingham CC* concerned a CA 1989 s17 assessment, the words of Richards J have been oft-cited subsequently in relation to the requirements of pathway assessments and pathway plans. He held that at the end of the assessment process, what is needed is a document from which 'it should be possible to see what help and support the child and family need and which agencies might be best placed to give that help'.[79] He struck down the assessment in that case, stating:

79 [2001] EWHC Admin 235, (2001) 4 CCLR 294 at [20]. See also chapter 2 at para 2.32.

It was essentially a descriptive document rather than an assessment, and in any event sufficient detail was still lacking both as regards the assessment itself and as regards the care plan and service provision. There was no clear identification of needs, or what was to be done about them, by whom and by when.[80]

7.74 These words were approved and echoed by Munby J in *R (J) v Caerphilly CBC*, who considered that 'those last few words' of Richards J 'helpfully encapsulate the essence of what is needed of a pathway plan if it is to meet the requirements of the Regulations'. He went on to describe how what is needed is a detailed operational plan:

> To repeat, because the point is so important, and a clear statement of what is required may assist not merely this but other local authorities: A pathway plan must clearly identify the child's needs, and what is to be done about them, by whom and by when. Or, if another aphorism would help, a pathway plan must spell out who does what, where and when.[81]

7.75 Preparation of the pathway assessment and the pathway plan should be very different processes, resulting in very different documents. They have different purposes. They should also be undertaken at two distinct stages, to allow for the pathway assessment to be considered and for there to then be input into the planning process. This much is clear from the statutory scheme. However, unfortunately it is often the case in practice that the pathway assessment and pathway plan are prepared simultaneously, or there is no separate pathway assessment produced at all. This is clearly impermissible under the statutory scheme.

### 'Relevant child'

7.76 The next category of person entitled to the benefit of the full leaving care package is a 'relevant child', as defined in CA 1989 s23A. A relevant child is a 16- or 17-year-old who is not being looked after by a local authority but was, before last ceasing to be looked after, an eligible child under CA 1989 Sch 2 para 19B. In other words, a relevant child is a child who is no longer being looked after, but who has already accumulated sufficient looked after time to qualify for the full leaving care package (13 weeks between the ages of 14 and 18, including at least one day on or after his or her 16th birthday).

7.77 The CLCE Regs 2001 both expand and contract the definition in CA 1989 s23A:

---

80 [2001] EWHC Admin 235, (2001) 4 CCLR 294 at [43].
81 [2005] EWHC 586 (Admin), (2005) 8 CCLR 255 at [45].

1) Expansion of definition: Regulation 4(1) and (2) detail an additional category of relevant children. A child falls within this expanded category if the child is aged 16 or 17, is not subject to a care order, and at the time of his or her 16th birthday was detained or admitted to hospital, having been looked after by a local authority for a 13-week period since the age of 14. 'Detained' means detained in a remand centre, a Young Offenders Institution or a secure training centre, 'or any other institution pursuant to an order of a court' (CLCE Regs 2001 reg 4(4)(a)), and 'hospital' means either any health service hospital or a registered establishment within the meaning of the Mental Health Act 1983 (reg 4(b)). This expanded definition is repeated in reg 3 of the Care leavers (England) Regulations 2010 ('the 2010 Regulations'), in force from 1 April 2011.

2) Contraction of definition:
   • The CLCE Regs 2001 exclude from the definition of 'relevant child' any child who has accumulated 13 weeks only through 'a pre-planned series of short-term placements, none of which individually exceeded four weeks, where at the end of each such placement the child returned to the care of his parent, or a person who is not a parent but who has parental responsibility for him'. In other words, short-break ('respite care') arrangements cannot suffice to make a child 'eligible'.[82] This restriction is repeated in 2010 Regulations reg 3.
   • The CLCE Regs 2001 also stipulate that a child who returns home successfully should cease to be a relevant child. This means that the child must have been settled for at least six months with a person falling within CA 1989 s22C(3) – that is, with a parent or other person with parental responsibility, or who had a residence order in place prior to the child becoming looked after ('a family placement').[83] However, if the placement breaks down and the child ceases to live there, the child's status reverts to what it would have been had he or she not returned home – ie the child is to be treated as a relevant child.[84] This restriction is also repeated in 2010 Regulations reg 3.
   • However, children excluded from the full leaving care package by these provisions will nevertheless be entitled to the more limited 'qualifying child' provisions (see below at paras 7.89–7.100).

82  CLCE Regs 2001 reg 4(3).
83  CLCE Regs 2001 reg 4(5).
84  CLCE Regs 2001 reg 4(7).

7.78    The responsible local authority has the following duties to a 'relevant child':

1) Duty to appoint a personal adviser if they have not already done so (CA 1989 s23B(2)). The functions and responsibilities of the personal adviser are detailed above at paras 7.32–7.51.

2) Duty to prepare a written statement 'describing the manner in which the needs of each ... relevant child will be assessed' in accordance with the requirements of CLCE Regs 2001 reg 5. The process and content of this statement are set out above at paras 7.52–7.53.

3) Duty to 'carry out an assessment of his needs with a view to determining what advice, assistance and support it would be appropriate to provide' if they have not already done so (CA 1989 s23B(3)(a)). Pathway assessments are addressed above at paras 7.54–7.68.

4) Duty to prepare a pathway plan for the child if they have not already done so (CA 1989 s23B(3)(b)). Pathway plans are addressed above at paras 7.69–7.75.

5) Duty to keep the pathway plan under regular review (CA 1989 s23E(1D)).

6) Duty to 'safeguard and promote the child's welfare' under CA 1989 s23B(8):

> The responsible local authority shall safeguard and promote the child's welfare and, unless they are satisfied that his welfare does not require it, support him by –
> (a) maintaining him;
> (b) providing him with or maintaining him in suitable accommodation; and
> (c) providing support of such other descriptions as may be prescribed.

7.79    The first five duties listed above merely repeat the duties owed to eligible children. However, the sixth and final duty, to 'safeguard and promote the child's welfare', is new. It does not appear in the statute or the regulations in relation to eligible children, as they will of course still be looked after by the local authority and so this additional duty is not required.[85]

7.80    The duty is supplemented by CLCE Regs 2001 reg 11. It provides that for the purposes of CA 1989 s23B(8)(c), the responsible local

---

85  See chapter 5 at paras 5.80–5.81 for the equivalent duty owed to 'looked after' children under CA 1989 s22.

authority must provide assistance, which may be in cash, in order to meet the child's needs in relation to education, training or employment as provided for in his or her pathway plan. The LC Guidance anxiously points out, however, that:

> The intention here is not that the local authority should take on all the costs associated with the young person's education, training or employment but that it stands ready to assist with those expenses which cannot be met through other means. Relevant young people will be eligible for Education Maintenance Allowances (where these are payable) in the same way that other young people on low incomes are eligible; and they should also apply if necessary for college access funds.[86]

7.81   With the recent abolition of the Educational Maintenance Allowance, and increased university tuition fees, the residual CA 1989 s23B(8)(c) duty may take on more significance for relevant children in future.

### 'Former relevant child'

7.82   Section 23C of the CA 1989 is entitled 'Continuing functions in respect of former relevant children'. A 'former relevant child' is 'a person who has been a relevant child for the purposes of section 23A (and would be one if he or she were under 18) and in relation to whom they were the last responsible authority' (section 23C(1)(a)). The continuing duties set out in section 23C subsist until the individual reaches the age of 21 unless his or her pathway plan sets out a programme of education or training which extends beyond his or her 21st birthday, in which case the category extends beyond that date.

7.83   There are three clusters of duties in relation to a former relevant child: contact (section 23C(2)); continuity (section 23C(3)); and assistance (section 23C(4)).

### Contact duties

7.84   CA 1989 s23C(2) provides that (emphasis added):

> (2) It is the duty of the local authority to take reasonable steps–
> (a) to keep in touch with a former relevant child *whether he is within their area or not*; and
> (b) if they lose touch with him, to re-establish contact.

---

86   *C(LC)A 2000 Guidance* (2001), chapter 7 para 20.

### Continuity duties

7.85    CA 1989 s23C(3) provides that:

It is the duty of the local authority–
(i) to continue to appointment of a personal advisor for a former relevant child; and
(ii) to continue to keep his pathway plan under regular review.

7.86    Unlike CA 1989 s23B, concerning the 'relevant child', section 23C does not include fall-back provisions in the event that there has been no appointment of a personal adviser, and/or no pathway plan has yet been put in place. This is because the status of a 'former relevant child' is derivative only: one cannot become a 'former relevant child' without first being either an eligible child or a relevant child, and the appointment of a personal adviser and the creation and regular review of a pathway plan are mandatory for these categories. The statute thus assumes that the former relevant child will already have such an adviser and such a plan in place, and it mandates the local authority to continue the appointment of the adviser and regular review of the pathway plan. The LC Guidance also makes this assumption (chapter 8). If the previous duties have not been complied with, then undoubtedly a personal adviser must be appointed and a pathway assessment and a pathway plan completed for a former relevant child.

### Assistance duties

7.87    Section 23C(4) provides (emphasis added):

It is the duty of the local authority to give a former relevant child –
(a) assistance of the kind referred to in s. 24B(1), to the extent that his welfare requires it;
(b) assistance of the kind referred to in s. 24B(2), to the extent that his welfare and his educational or training needs require it;
(c) *other assistance, to the extent that his welfare requires it.*

7.88    In the recent case of *R (O) v Barking and Dagenham LBC and SSHD, Children's Society intervening* the Court of Appeal held that CA 1989 s23C(4)(c) amounts to a statutory duty to accommodate a 'former relevant child' when the child's welfare requires it.[87] Thus, the leaving care regime may entitle a care leaver aged 18 or over to accommodation in circumstances where it would not otherwise be available to him or her, for example if he or she is considered to be intentionally homeless, or is otherwise disentitled to accommodation under

---

87  [2010] EWCA Civ 1101.

the Housing Acts (for example, by reason of his or her immigration status). Section 23C(4)(c) may also require the local authority to accommodate a young person if accommodation is otherwise available but it does not meet his or her welfare needs.

## Persons qualifying for advice and assistance

7.89   Many children and young people who spend time in care will not accumulate the requisite period of 13 weeks spent as a 'looked after' child to qualify for the full leaving care package. However, they may nevertheless qualify for a more limited form of 'advice and assistance' from the responsible local authority, sometimes referred to as 'aftercare'. The LC Guidance recognises that this group will also be in need of support and assistance:

> Councils will be most concerned about leaving care in the case of relevant and former relevant children. However they should also bear in mind the needs of those care leavers who do not qualify for the new arrangements but who will nonetheless qualify for advice and assistance under section 24(1). These young people too may be vulnerable and require good quality services from the council in order to safeguard and promote their welfare.[88]

7.90   CA 1989 s24 defines 'persons qualifying for advice and assistance'. A person may qualify in one of two ways:

1) If the person is aged between 16 and 21, and either is the subject of a special guardianship order (if aged 16 or 17), or was the subject of such an order when he or she reached 18 (section 24(1A)), and was looked after by a local authority immediately prior to the making of that order. There is no stipulated minimum period of looked-after time.

2) Or, if the person is aged between 16 and 21, and at any time when aged 16 or 17 was (but is no longer) looked after, accommodated or fostered (section 24(1B)).

7.91   'Looked after, accommodated or fostered' is defined further as follows (CA 1989 s24(2)):

> 'looked after, accommodated or fostered' means –
> (a) looked after by a local authority;
> (b) accommodated by or on behalf of a voluntary organisation;
> (c) accommodated in a private children's home;

---

88  *C(LC)A 2000 Guidance* (2001), chapter 4 para 1.

(d) accommodated for a consecutive period of at least three months–
    (i) by any [Local Health Board], Special Health Authority [or Primary Care Trust or by a local authority in the exercise of education functions], or
    (ii) in any care home or independent hospital or in any accommodation provided by a National Health Service trust [or an NHS foundation trust]; or
(e) privately fostered.

7.92    A young person will qualify for advice and assistance pursuant to section 24(2)(d) even if the three-month period began before he or she reached the age of 16.

7.93    CA 1989 s24(5) sets out which local authority is responsible for providing services under sections 24A and 24B to a qualifying young person. In the case of a young person formerly looked after by a local authority, the relevant authority is the one which last looked after him or her. In the case of someone qualifying for advice and assistance under any of the other provisions at section 24(2), the relevant authority is the one in whose area the person has asked for help.[89]

7.94    If a young person qualifies under CA 1989 s24, a number of consequences flow. First, a contact duty is owed: the authority which last looked after him or her must take 'such steps as they think appropriate to contact him at such times as they think appropriate' with a view to discharging their statutory functions (CA 1989 s24(4)). The specific duties are then detailed in sections 24A (advice and assistance) and 24B (employment, education and training).

### Advice and assistance

7.95    Although the young person qualifies by virtue of CA 1989 s24, the authority must also be satisfied that the conditions stipulated in section 24A(2) are met. These conditions are twofold:

a) the young person needs help of a kind that the authority can give under sections 24A or 24B;[90] and
b) if the young person was not being looked after by a local athority, the authority is satisfied that the person who was looking after the young person does not have the necessary facilities for advising or befriending him or her.[91]

---

89  *C(LC)A 2000 Guidance* (2001), chapter 7 para 25.
90  CA 1989 s24A(2)(a).
91  CA 1989 s24A(2)(b).

7.96    If these conditions are satisfied, and the young person was previously looked after by the local authority or a voluntary organisation, the authority *must* 'advise and befriend' him or her. This is a mandatory requirement. However, if the young person falls within section 24 for other reasons (for example, due to a private fostering arrangement, or time spent in hospital) the authority *may* 'advise and befriend' him or her.

7.97    If the authority is either under a duty, or empowered, to advise and befriend a person, 'they may also give him assistance' (CA 1989 s24A(4)). This is a weak provision, as it is permissive rather than mandatory. However, as with all powers the authority must give proper consideration as to whether its exercise is necessary in a particular case and must reach its decision rationally, reasonably and fairly. The assistance may be in kind and, in exceptional circumstances, it may be in the form of cash[92] or accommodation.[93]

### Employment, education and training

7.98    CA 1989 s24B provides that the relevant local authority may give assistance to a qualifying person 'by contributing to expenses incurred by him in living near the place where he is, or will be, employed or seeking employment' (section 24B(1)). This may be done through direct contributions, or making a grant.

7.99    The upper age limit of 21 is extended to 24 if the person is in 'full-time further or higher education' and requires accommodation during a vacation because the term-time accommodation is not available (such as a student flat on campus). In these circumstances, the local authority shall give the person assistance by providing him or her with suitable vacation accommodation,[94] or paying him or her enough to secure such accommodation himself or herself.[95]

7.100   The upper age limit of 24 has been extended to 25 by section 23(2) of the Children and Young Persons Act 2008, although this has yet to come into force.

92  CA 1989 s24A(5)(b).
93  CA 1989 s24A(5)(a).
94  CA 1989 s24B(5)(a).
95  CA 1989 s24B(5)(b).

# Housing for care leavers

7.101 One of the central problems facing young care leavers is potential homelessness, or lack of suitable and stable accommodation. The LC Guidance, while focusing on the lead role of social services departments, includes guidance concerning the role of the housing department (in unitary authorities) or housing authorities. Chapter 3 of the LC Guidance deals with this at paras 22–27. It indicates that the welfare of

> ... these young people [falling within the leaving care regime] are clearly likely to be at serious risk without the provision of suitable accommodation ... The Secretary of State considers that, with very few exceptions, most care leavers are likely to be significantly disadvantaged as a result of their age and circumstance, and he would normally expect authorities to find that such applicants are vulnerable and hence in priority need of accommodation.

7.102 This has since been confirmed by the Homelessness (Priority Need for Accommodation) (England) Order 2002,[96] which provides that care leavers aged 18, 19 or 20 will be in 'priority need' for the purposes of the Housing Act 1996. Both the LC Guidance and the *Homelessness Code of Guidance 2006* emphasise the importance of inter-agency working and advance planning for this group of vulnerable young people.

7.103 The LC Guidance also reminds authorities of their power to provide accommodation for young people aged 16 to 20 in their area if this is necessary to safeguard or promote their welfare (CA 1989 s20(5)).

# Children and Young Persons Act 2008

7.104 The Children and Young Persons Act 2008 amended the law concerning care leavers in a number of respects. In October 2008 the Secretary of State for Education made the Care Leavers (England) Regulations (CL Regs) 2010,[97] also in force as of 1 April 2011. New guidance has also been introduced with effect from April 2011.

7.105 The CL Regs 2010 amend and supplement the previous CLCE Regs 2001 and maintain the three-stage system for the full leaving care scheme – eligible child, relevant child and former relevant child.

96 SI No 2051.
97 SI No 2571.

The CL Regs 2010 largely replicate the requirements of the CLCE
Regs 2001 verbatim.

7.106    The new guidance includes a detailed volume entitled, 'Planning
transition to adulthood for care leavers', referred to below as the
Transition Guidance. This is fuller and clearer than its predecessor.

7.107    Under the new scheme, there are three key practical changes for
care leavers:

1) introduction of a higher education bursary for former relevant
   children (CA 1989 s23C(5A));
2) personal adviser, pathway assessment and pathway plan for
   former relevant children up to the age of 25 who take up a programme of education or training (CA 1989 s23CA);
3) role of the independent reviewing officer (IRO) in ensuring that
   children of 16 or 17 do not prematurely or inappropriately leave
   care.

## Higher education bursary

7.108    CA 1989 s23C(5A) provides for a bursary for care leavers going on
to higher education. Provision was made for this in the Children Act
1989 (Higher Education Bursary) (England) Regulations 2009, which
were made on 21 August 2009, and came into force the next day.[98]

7.109    By regulation 1(2), the regulations apply to a former relevant child
who is pursuing a course of higher education started on or after
1 September 2008. 'Higher education' in CA 1989 s23C(5A) means a
course of higher education that is of at least two academic years' duration and is designated by or under regulations made under Teaching and Higher Education Act 1998 s22(1). The amount payable is
£2,000.

## Personal adviser, pathway assessment and pathway plan to 25

7.110    CA 1989 s23CA extends provisions concerning former relevant children to an upper limit of age 25 in the case of a person who 'has informed the responsible local authority that he is pursuing, or wishes
to pursue, a programme of education or training'. Unlike the definition of 'course of higher education,' there is no specific definition
given for 'programme of education or training'. The Transition Guidance makes clear that the phrase should be interpreted broadly:

98 SI No 2274.

For example, this might include options such as: completion of a basic skills course, so that the young person has the numeracy and literacy skills needed to compete in the jobs market; take up of a course of further education; take up of a university place; support to enable the young person to complete a recognised postgraduate qualification; or participation in vocational training and apprenticeships.[99]

7.111    In such circumstances, there will be a duty to appoint a personal adviser, conduct an assessment of his or her related needs, and prepare a pathway plan. The Transition Guidance states that:

> The re-instated pathway plan must have a specific focus on the support that the individual care leaver will need to be able to meet the education or training goals agreed with their responsible authority.[100]

7.112    By virtue of CA 1989 s23CA(5), a former relevant child falling within this section is entitled to the same form of support available to qualifying persons under CA 1989 s24B – assistance through contributing to expenses, or making a grant.

7.113    Under the Transition Guidance, each local authority is required to develop 'its own specific policy setting out the support that it is prepared to offer to this group of care leavers.'[101] When in force, it would seem sensible for advisers to request sight of the local policy as a matter of course when engaging in pre-action correspondence in respect of an individual care leaver.

## Independent reviewing officer

7.114    A central issue for looked after children has been premature or abrupt moves from care to independence. A particular problem has been the persisting incorrect assumption by some that at 16 or 17 a child who has accumulated 13 weeks and falls within the leaving care regime should no longer be looked after, and should instead become the responsibility of the leaving care team, or adult services.

7.115    The government, during parliamentary debates on the Children and Young Persons Bill, indicated that looked-after 16- or 17-year-olds should generally continue to be looked after until the age of 18. This is a view with which the authors agree. The then-Minister Sarah

---

99  *The Children Act 1989 guidance and regulations, vol 3: planning transition to adulthood for care leavers*, October 2010, para 3.49.

100 *The Children Act 1989 guidance and regulations, vol 3: planning transition to adulthood for care leavers*, October 2010, para 3.53.

101 *The Children Act 1989 guidance and regulations, vol 3: planning transition to adulthood for care leavers*, October 2010, para 3.50.

McCarthy-Fry MP, during the third reading of the bill in the House of Commons, emphasised this point, stating:

> In future, there will be a presumption that children will continue to be looked after up to the age of 18 and that there will rarely be good reasons for a local authority to cease looking after a child before he or she turns 18. Therefore, it is Government policy that relevant children will become a residual category of children.[102]

7.116   However, the proposed, and accepted, response to this identified problem was to rely on the use of independent reviewing officers (IROs) to review individual children's cases. Ms McCarthy-Fry MP considered that a review process by IROs,

> will stop the current poor practice in local authorities that means that a child is placed in independent living arrangements without review and/or is automatically deemed to have left care at the same time. That poor practice is a misunderstanding of the current legislative framework. Clause 9 of the Bill, regulation-making powers and the revised Children Act statutory guidance, give us a review mechanism to correct that. So, in future, there may still be a small number of cases where a review of the young person's case endorses the social worker's assessment that the young person's welfare would be promoted by the young person leaving care because he or she is ready and wants to take on the challenge of living more independently.[103]

7.117   Concerningly, the assumption appears to be that a move to more 'independent' living will necessarily take a child outside the care system, whereas of course independent or semi-independent living may still be provided under CA 1989 s20.

7.118   In any event, CA 1989 ss25A–25C now provide for the appointment of IROs, and outline their review functions. It remains to be seen whether this will reduce the number of 16- and 17-year-olds discharged from care.

## Conclusion

7.119   Care leavers have long suffered great disadvantages compared to their peers. Since 1999, substantial progress has been made in introducing and developing a legal framework to protect care leavers and

---

102 Third reading debate, Children and Young Persons Bill, *Hansard*, House of Commons, 8 October 2008, col 343.
103 Third reading debate, Children and Young Persons Bill, *Hansard*, House of Commons, 8 October 2008, col 343.

to ensure that their life chances are maximised. Unfortunately, however, those protections are not always realised in practice. The central difficulties identified in 1999 – high risk of homelessness, poor employment and education prospects – still persist, more than a decade after the CA 1989 was amended by the CLCA 2000 to tackle them.

7.120    Leaving care should be a gradual process, not a one-off, abrupt event. The April 2011 changes to the system recognise that, and emphasise the importance of a smooth transition from care to independence. It is to be hoped that these legislative changes translate into improved outcomes for this very vulnerable group of young people.

# APPENDICES

*continued*

# Resources

## General

The Children Act 1989 Guidance and Regulations, Volume 2: Care Planning, Placement and Case Review, HM Government (March 2010)
http://education.gov.uk/publications/eOrderingDownload/DCSF-00185-2010.pdf

United Nations Convention on the Rights of the Child
http://www2.ohchr.org/english/law/crc.htm

Charter of Fundamental Rights of the European Union
www.europarl.europa.eu/charter/pdf/text_en.pdf

UN Convention on the Rights of Persons with Disabilities
www.un.org/disabilities/convention/conventionfull.shtml

Optional Protocol to the Convention on the Rights of Persons with Disabilities
www.un.org/disabilities/default.asp?id=311

## Chapter 1: Introduction

*The Protection of Children in England: A Progress Report*, The Lord Laming (March 2009)
www.education.gov.uk/publications//eOrderingDownload/HC-330.pdf

## Chapter 2: Legal fundamentals

*Statutory Guidance on Making Arrangements to Safeguard and Promote the Welfare of Children under section 11 of the Children Act 2004*, Department for Education and Skills (April 2007)
www.education.gov.uk/publications/eOrderingDownload/DFES-0036-2007.pdf

*Working Together to Safeguard Children: A guide to inter-agency working to safeguard and promote the welfare of children*, Department for Children, Schools and Families (March 2010)
www.education.gov.uk/publications/eOrderingDownload/00305-2010DOM-EN-v3.pdf

*Safeguarding Disabled Children – Practice Guidance,* Department for
Children, Schools and Families (July 2009)
www.education.gov.uk/publications//eOrderingDownload/00374-2009
DOM-EN.pdf

## Chapter 3: Age disputes
*Practice Guidelines for Age Assessment of Young Unaccompanied Asylum
Seekers*
www.childrenslegalcentre.com/Resources/CLC/Documents/PDF%20NZ/
Practice%20Guidelines%20only.pdf

*Assessing Age,* UKBA
www.ukba.homeoffice.gov.uk/sitecontent/documents/policyandlaw/
asylumprocessguidance/specialcases/guidance/assessing-age?view=Binary

## Chapter 4: Services for children in need
*Framework for the Assessment of Children in Need and their Families,*
Department of Health, Department for Education and Employment and
Home Office (April 2000)
www.dh.gov.uk/prod_consum_dh/groups/dh_digitalassets/@dh/@en/
documents/digitalasset/dh_4014430.pdf

*Framework for the Assessment of Children in Need and their Families,* National
Assembly for Wales and Home Office (March 2001)
http://wales.gov.uk/docs/caecd/publications/110323frameworken.pdf

*Prioritising need in the context of Putting People First: A whole system
approach to eligibility for social care, England 2010,* Department of Health
(February 2010)
www.dh.gov.uk/prod_consum_dh/groups/dh_digitalassets/@dh/@en/@
ps/documents/digitalasset/dh_113155.pdf

*Guidance on direct payments for community care, services for carers and
children's services: England 2009,* Department of Health (September 2009)
www.dh.gov.uk/prod_consum_dh/groups/dh_digitalassets/@dh/@en/@
ps/documents/digitalasset/dh_121131.pdf

*Short Breaks: Statutory guidance on how to safeguard and promote the welfare
of disabled children using short breaks,* Department for Children, Schools and
Families (April 2010)
http://education.gov.uk/publications/eOrderingDownload/short%20breaks
%20statutory%20guidance%20march%202010.pdf

## Chapter 5: Duties and powers to accommodate
*LAC (2003)13: Guidance on accommodating children in need and their
families,* Department of Health (June 2003)

www.dh.gov.uk/prod_consum_dh/groups/dh_digitalassets/@dh/@en/
documents/digitalasset/dh_4012756.pdf

*Homelessness Code of Guidance for Local Authorities,* Department for
Communities and Local Government (July 2006)
www.communities.gov.uk/documents/housing/pdf/152056.pdf

*Provision of Accommodation for 16 and 17 year old young people who may be
homeless and/or require accommodation,* Department for Children, Schools
and Families and Department for Communities and Local Government
(April 2010)
http://education.gov.uk/publications/Standard/publicationDetail/page1/
dcsf-15005-2010

*Sufficiency: Statutory guidance on securing sufficient accommodation for
looked after children,* Department for Children, Schools and Families (March
2010)
http://education.gov.uk/publications/eOrderingDownload/DCSF-00186-
2010.pdf

## Chapter 6: Services for migrant children
*Every Child Matters: Change for Children, Statutory Guidance to the UK
Border Agency on making arrangements to safeguard and promote the welfare
of children,* UKBA and Department for Children, Schools and Families
(November 2009)
www.ukba.homeoffice.gov.uk/sitecontent/documents/policyandlaw/
legislation/bci-act1/change-for-children.pdf?view=Binary

*UKBA Asylum Support Policy Bulletin 29: Transition at age 18* (February
2004)
www.ukba.homeoffice.gov.uk/sitecontent/documents/policyandlaw/
asylumsupportbulletins/children/pb29?view=Binary

*Safeguarding children who may have been trafficked,* HM Government, 2008
www.education.gov.uk/publications//eOrderingDownload/DCSF_
Child%20Trafficking.pdf

## Chapter 7: Leaving care
*Children (Leaving Care) Act 2000 Regulations and Guidance,* Department of
Health (October 2001)
www.dh.gov.uk/prod_consum_dh/groups/dh_digitalassets/@dh/@en/
documents/digitalasset/dh_4058600.pdf

*National Standards on Youth Justice Services,* Ministry of Justice and
Department for Children, Schools and Families (2010)
www.yjb.gov.uk/publications/Scripts/prodView.asp?idproduct=466&eP=

*Safeguarding Children and Young People who may be affected by Gang Activity*, Department for Children, Schools and Families and Home Office (2010)
www.wlscb.org.uk/dcsf-00064-2011.pdf

*The Children Act 1989 Guidance and Regulations Volume 3: Planning Transition to Adulthood for Care Leavers*, Department for Education (October 2010)
http://education.gov.uk/publications/eOrderingDownload/DfE-00554-2010.pdf

*IRO Handbook: Statutory guidance for independent reviewing officers and local authorities on their functions in relation to case management and review for looked after children*, Department for Children, Schools and Families (March 2010)
http://education.gov.uk/publications/eOrderingDownload/DCSF-00184-2010.pdf

*The Children Act 1989 Guidance and Regulations: Local authority responsibilities towards former looked after children in custody (Statutory guidance to the Visits to Former Looked After Children in Detention (England) Regulations 2010)*, Department of Education (November 2010)
http://media.education.gov.uk/assets/files/pdf/l/local%20authority%20responsibilities%20towards%20former%20looked%20after%20children%20in%20custody.pdf

# Primary legislation[1]

# CHILDREN ACT 1989

## Part III: Local Authority Support for Children and Families

### *Provision of services for children and their families*

#### Provision of services for children in need, their families and others

17 (1) It shall be the general duty of every local authority (in addition to the other duties imposed on them by this Part)–

  (a) to safeguard and promote the welfare of children within their area who are in need; and

  (b) so far as is consistent with that duty, to promote the upbringing of such children by their families,

by providing a range and level of services appropriate to those children's needs.

  (2) For the purpose principally of facilitating the discharge of their general duty under this section, every local authority shall have the specific duties and powers set out in Part I of Schedule 2.

  (3) Any service provided by an authority in the exercise of functions conferred on them by this section may be provided for the family of a particular child in need or for any member of his family, if it is provided with a view to safeguarding or promoting the child's welfare.

  (4) The appropriate national authority may by order amend any provision of Part I of Schedule 2 or add any further duty or power to those for the time being mentioned there.

  (4A) Before determining what (if any) services to provide for a particular child in need in the exercise of functions conferred on them by this section, a local authority shall, so far as is reasonably practicable and consistent with the child's welfare–

  (a) ascertain the child's wishes and feelings regarding the provision of those services; and

  (b) give due consideration (having regard to his age and understanding) to such wishes and feelings of the child as they have been able to ascertain.

  (5) Every local authority–

  (a) shall facilitate the provision by others (including in particular voluntary organisations) of services which it is a function of the authority to provide by virtue of this section, or section 18, 20, 22A to 22C, 23B to 23D, 24A or 24B; and

  (b) may make such arrangements as they see fit for any person to act on their behalf in the provision of any such service.

  (6) The services provided by a local authority in the exercise of functions conferred on them by this section may include providing accommodation and giving assistance in kind or in cash.

  (7) Assistance may be unconditional or subject to conditions as to the repayment of the assistance or of its value (in whole or in part).

  (8) Before giving any assistance or imposing any conditions, a local authority shall have regard to the means of the child concerned and of each of his parents.

  (9) No person shall be liable to make any repayment of assistance or of its value at any time when he is in receipt [of income support under Part VII of the

Social Security Contributions and Benefits Act 1992],[2] of any element of child tax credit other than the family element, of working tax credit, of an income-based jobseeker's allowance or of an income-related employment and support allowance.

(10) For the purposes of this Part a child shall be taken to be in need if–

    (a) he is unlikely to achieve or maintain, or to have the opportunity of achieving or maintaining, a reasonable standard of health or development without the provision for him of services by a local authority under this Part;

    (b) his health or development is likely to be significantly impaired, or further impaired, without the provision for him of such services; or

    (c) he is disabled,

and 'family', in relation to such a child, includes any person who has parental responsibility for the child and any other person with whom he has been living.

(11) For the purposes of this Part, a child is disabled if he is blind, deaf or dumb or suffers from mental disorder of any kind or is substantially and permanently handicapped by illness, injury or congenital deformity or such other disability as may be prescribed; and in this Part–

'development' means physical, intellectual, emotional, social or behavioural development; and

'health' means physical or mental health.

(12) The Treasury may by regulations prescribe circumstances in which a person is to be treated for the purposes of this Part (or for such of those purposes as are prescribed) as in receipt of any element of child tax credit other than the family element or of working tax credit.

### Direct payments

17A(1) The appropriate national authority may by regulations make provision for and in connection with requiring or authorising the responsible authority in the case of a person of a prescribed description who falls within subsection (2) to make, with that person's consent, such payments to him as they may determine in accordance with the regulations in respect of his securing the provision of the service mentioned in that subsection.

  (2) A person falls within this subsection if he is–

    (a) a person with parental responsibility for a disabled child,

    (b) a disabled person with parental responsibility for a child, or

    (c) a disabled child aged 16 or 17,

and a local authority ('the responsible authority') have decided for the purposes of section 17 that the child's needs (or, if he is such a disabled child, his needs) call for the provision by them of a service in exercise of functions conferred on them under that section.

  (3) Subsections (3) to (5) and (7) of section 57 of the 2001 Act shall apply, with any necessary modifications, in relation to regulations under this section as they apply in relation to regulations under that section.

---

2  Words in square brackets repealed by the Welfare Reform Act (WRA) 2009 ss9(3)(b), 58(1), Sch 7 Pt 1. Not yet in force.

*(3A)* *The modifications mentioned in subsection (3) include, in particular, the omission of the provisions inserted into section 57 of the 2001 Act by the Health and Social Care Act 2008.*[3]

(4) Regulations under this section shall provide that, where payments are made under the regulations to a person falling within subsection (5)–

   (a) the payments shall be made at the rate mentioned in subsection (4)(a) of section 57 of the 2001 Act (as applied by subsection (3)); and

   (b) subsection (4)(b) of that section shall not apply.

(5) A person falls within this subsection if he is–

   (a) a person falling within subsection (2)(a) or (b) and the child in question is aged 16 or 17, or

   (b) a person who is in receipt [of income support. . . under Part 7 of the Social Security Contributions and Benefits Act 1992][4] , of any element of child tax credit other than the family element, of working tax credit, of an income-based jobseeker's allowance or of an income-related employment and support allowance.

(6) In this section–

'the 2001 Act' means the Health and Social Care Act 2001;

'disabled' in relation to an adult has the same meaning as that given by section 17(11) in relation to a child;

'prescribed' means specified in or determined in accordance with regulations under this section (and has the same meaning in the provisions of the 2001 Act mentioned in subsection (3) as they apply by virtue of that subsection).

### Vouchers for persons with parental responsibility for disabled children

17B(1) The [Secretary of State] *appropriate national authority*[5] may by regulations make provision for the issue by a local authority of vouchers to a person with parental responsibility for a disabled child.

(2) 'Voucher' means a document whereby, if the local authority agrees with the person with parental responsibility that it would help him care for the child if the person with parental responsibility had a break from caring, that person may secure the temporary provision of services for the child under section 17.

(3) The regulations may, in particular, provide–

   (a) for the value of a voucher to be expressed in terms of money, or of the delivery of a service for a period of time, or both;

   (b) for the person who supplies a service against a voucher, or for the arrangement under which it is supplied, to be approved by the local authority;

   (c) for a maximum period during which a service (or a service of a prescribed description) can be provided against a voucher.

---

3  Inserted by the Health and Social Care Act (HSCA) 2008 s160, Sch 14 para 1. Not yet in force.

4  Words in square brackets repealed by WRA 2009 ss9(3)(b), 58(1), Sch 7 Pt 1. Not yet in force.

5  Words in square brackets repealed and words in italics inserted by CYPA 2008 s39 and Sch 3. Not yet in force. Amendment will come into force on the same day as the Carers and Disabled Children Act 2000 s7(1) comes into force in relation to Wales.

**Day care for pre-school and other children**

18 (1) Every local authority shall provide such day care for children in need within their area who are–
(a) aged five or under; and
(b) not yet attending schools,
as is appropriate.

(2) A local authority in Wales may provide day care for children within their area who satisfy the conditions mentioned in subsection (1)(a) and (b) even though they are not in need.

(3) A local authority may provide facilities (including training, advice, guidance and counselling) for those–
(a) caring for children in day care; or
(b) who at any time accompany such children while they are in day care.

(4) In this section 'day care' means any form of care or supervised activity provided for children during the day (whether or not it is provided on a regular basis).

(5) Every local authority shall provide for children in need within their area who are attending any school such care or supervised activities as is appropriate–
(a) outside school hours; or
(b) during school holidays.

(6) A local authority in Wales may provide such care or supervised activities for children within their area who are attending any school even though those children are not in need.

(7) In this section 'supervised activity' means an activity supervised by a responsible person.

19    [Repealed.]

## Provision of accommodation for children

**Provision of accommodation for children: general**

20 (1) Every local authority shall provide accommodation for any child in need within their area who appears to them to require accommodation as a result of–
(a) there being no person who has parental responsibility for him;
(b) his being lost or having been abandoned; or
(c) the person who has been caring for him being prevented (whether or not permanently, and for whatever reason) from providing him with suitable accommodation or care.

(2) Where a local authority provide accommodation under subsection (1) for a child who is ordinarily resident in the area of another local authority, that other local authority may take over the provision of accommodation for the child within–
(a) three months of being notified in writing that the child is being provided with accommodation; or
(b) such other longer period as may be prescribed.

(3) Every local authority shall provide accommodation for any child in need within their area who has reached the age of sixteen and whose welfare the authority consider is likely to be seriously prejudiced if they do not provide him with accommodation.

(4) A local authority may provide accommodation for any child within their area (even though a person who has parental responsibility for him is able to

provide him with accommodation) if they consider that to do so would safe-guard or promote the child's welfare.

(5) A local authority may provide accommodation for any person who has reached the age of sixteen but is under twenty-one in any community home which takes children who have reached the age of sixteen if they consider that to do so would safeguard or promote his welfare.

(6) Before providing accommodation under this section, a local authority shall, so far as is reasonably practicable and consistent with the child's welfare–

(a) ascertain the child's wishes and feelings regarding the provision of accommodation; and

(b) give due consideration (having regard to his age and understanding) to such wishes and feelings of the child as they have been able to ascertain.

(7) A local authority may not provide accommodation under this section for any child if any person who–

(a) has parental responsibility for him; and

(b) is willing and able to–

(i) provide accommodation for him; or

(ii) arrange for accommodation to be provided for him,

objects.

(8) Any person who has parental responsibility for a child may at any time remove the child from accommodation provided by or on behalf of the local authority under this section.

(9) Subsections (7) and (8) do not apply while any person–

(a)   in whose favour a residence order is in force with respect to the child;

. . .

(aa) who is a special guardian of the child; or

(b)   who has care of the child by virtue of an order made in the exercise of the High Court's inherent jurisdiction with respect to children,

agrees to the child being looked after in accommodation provided by or on behalf of the local authority.

(10) Where there is more than one such person as is mentioned in subsection (9), all of them must agree.

(11) Subsections (7) and (8) do not apply where a child who has reached the age of sixteen agrees to being provided with accommodation under this section.

### Provision for accommodation for children in police protection or detention or on remand, etc

21 (1) Every local authority shall make provision for the reception and accommodation of children who are removed or kept away from home under Part V.

(2) Every local authority shall receive, and provide accommodation for, children–

(a) in police protection whom they are requested to receive under section 46(3)(f);

(b) whom they are requested to receive under section 38(6) of the Police and Criminal Evidence Act 1984;

(c) who are–

(i)   on remand *(within the meaning of the section)*[6] under section 23(1) of the Children and Young Persons Act 1969;

---

6   Words in italics inserted by the Criminal Justice and Public Order Act (CJPOA) 1994 s172(2). Not yet in force.

(ia) remanded to accommodation provided by or on behalf of a local authority by virtue of paragraph 4 of Schedule 1 or paragraph 6 of Schedule 8 to the Powers of Criminal Courts (Sentencing) Act 2000 (breach etc of referral orders and reparation orders);

(ii) remanded to accommodation provided by or on behalf of a local authority by virtue of paragraph 21 of Schedule 2 to the Criminal Justice and Immigration Act 2008 (breach etc of youth rehabilitation orders);

(iia) remanded to accommodation provided by or on behalf of a local authority by virtue of paragraph 10 of the Schedule to the Street Offences Act 1959 (breach of orders under section 1(2A) of that Act);

(iii) the subject of a youth rehabilitation order imposing a local authority residence requirement or a youth rehabilitation order with fostering,

and with respect to whom they are the designated authority.

(2A) In subsection (2)(c)(iii), the following terms have the same meanings as in Part 1 of the Criminal Justice and Immigration Act 2008 (see section 7 of that Act)–

'local authority residence requirement';

'youth rehabilitation order';

'youth rehabilitation order with fostering'.

(3) Where a child has been–

(a) removed under Part V; or

(b) detained under section 38 of the Police and Criminal Evidence Act 1984,

and he is not being provided with accommodation by a local authority or in a hospital vested in the Secretary of State, the Welsh Ministers or a Primary Care Trust, or otherwise made available pursuant to arrangements made by a Local Health Board or a Primary Care Trust, any reasonable expenses of accommodating him shall be recoverable from the local authority in whose area he is ordinarily resident.

## Duties of local authorities in relation to children looked after by them

### General duty of local authority in relation to children looked after by them

22 (1) In this Act, any reference to a child who is looked after by a local authority is a reference to a child who is–

(a) in their care; or

(b) provided with accommodation by the authority in the exercise of any functions (in particular those under this Act) which are social services functions within the meaning of the Local Authority Social Services Act 1970, apart from functions under sections 17, 23B and 24B.

(2) In subsection (1) 'accommodation' means accommodation which is provided for a continuous period of more than 24 hours.

(3) It shall be the duty of a local authority looking after any child–

(a) to safeguard and promote his welfare; and

(b) to make such use of services available for children cared for by their own parents as appears to the authority reasonable in his case.

(3A) The duty of a local authority under subsection (3)(a) to safeguard and promote the welfare of a child looked after by them includes in particular a duty to promote the child's educational achievement.

(4) Before making any decision with respect to a child whom they are looking after, or proposing to look after, a local authority shall, so far as is reasonably practicable, ascertain the wishes and feelings of–
  (a) the child;
  (b) his parents;
  (c) any person who is not a parent of his but who has parental responsibility for him; and
  (d) any other person whose wishes and feelings the authority consider to be relevant,
regarding the matter to be decided.

(5) In making any such decision a local authority shall give due consideration–
  (a) having regard to his age and understanding, to such wishes and feelings of the child as they have been able to ascertain;
  (b) to such wishes and feelings of any person mentioned in subsection (4)(b) to (d) as they have been able to ascertain; and
  (c) to the child's religious persuasion, racial origin and cultural and linguistic background.

(6) If it appears to a local authority that it is necessary, for the purpose of protecting members of the public from serious injury, to exercise their powers with respect to a child whom they are looking after in a manner which may not be consistent with their duties under this section, they may do so.

(7) If the appropriate national authority considers it necessary, for the purpose of protecting members of the public from serious injury, to give directions to a local authority with respect to the exercise of their powers with respect to a child whom they are looking after, the appropriate national authority may give such directions to the local authority.

(8) Where any such directions are given to an authority they shall comply with them even though doing so is inconsistent with their duties under this section.

### Provision of accommodation for children in care

22A   When a child is in the care of a local authority, it is their duty to provide the child with accommodation.

### Maintenance of looked after children

22B   It is the duty of a local authority to maintain a child they are looking after in other respects apart from the provision of accommodation.

### Ways in which looked after children are to be accommodated and maintained

22C (1)This section applies where a local authority are looking after a child ('C').

(2) The local authority must make arrangements for C to live with a person who falls within subsection (3) (but subject to subsection (4)).

(3) A person ('P') falls within this subsection if–
  (a) P is a parent of C;
  (b) P is not a parent of C but has parental responsibility for C; or

(c) in a case where C is in the care of the local authority and there was a residence order in force with respect to C immediately before the care order was made, P was a person in whose favour the residence order was made.

(4) Subsection (2) does not require the local authority to make arrangements of the kind mentioned in that subsection if doing so–
(a) would not be consistent with C's welfare; or
(b) would not be reasonably practicable.

(5) If the local authority are unable to make arrangements under subsection (2), they must place C in the placement which is, in their opinion, the most appropriate placement available.

(6) In subsection (5) 'placement' means–
(a) placement with an individual who is a relative, friend or other person connected with C and who is also a local authority foster parent;
(b) placement with a local authority foster parent who does not fall within paragraph (a);
(c) placement in a children's home in respect of which a person is registered under Part 2 of the Care Standards Act 2000; or
(d) subject to section 22D, placement in accordance with other arrangements which comply with any regulations made for the purposes of this section.

(7) In determining the most appropriate placement for C, the local authority must, subject to the other provisions of this Part (in particular, to their duties under section 22)–
(a) give preference to a placement falling within paragraph (a) of subsection (6) over placements falling within the other paragraphs of that subsection;
(b) comply, so far as is reasonably practicable in all the circumstances of C's case, with the requirements of subsection (8); and
(c) comply with subsection (9) unless that is not reasonably practicable.

(8) The local authority must ensure that the placement is such that–
(a) it allows C to live near C's home;
(b) it does not disrupt C's education or training;
(c) if C has a sibling for whom the local authority are also providing accommodation, it enables C and the sibling to live together;
(d) if C is disabled, the accommodation provided is suitable to C's particular needs.

(9) The placement must be such that C is provided with accommodation within the local authority's area.

(10) The local authority may determine–
(a) the terms of any arrangements they make under subsection (2) in relation to C (including terms as to payment); and
(b) the terms on which they place C with a local authority foster parent (including terms as to payment but subject to any order made under section 49 of the Children Act 2004).

(11) The appropriate national authority may make regulations for, and in connection with, the purposes of this section.

(12) In this Act 'local authority foster parent' means a person who is approved as a local authority foster parent in accordance with regulations made by virtue of paragraph 12F of Schedule 2.

### Review of child's case before making alternative arrangements for accommodation

22D(1) Where a local authority are providing accommodation for a child ('C') other than by arrangements under section 22C(6)(d), they must not make such arrangements for C unless they have decided to do so in consequence of a review of C's case carried out in accordance with regulations made under section 26.

(2) But subsection (1) does not prevent a local authority making arrangements for C under section 22C(6)(d) if they are satisfied that in order to safeguard C's welfare it is necessary–

(a) to make such arrangements; and

(b) to do so as a matter of urgency.

### Children's homes provided by appropriate national authority

22E   Where a local authority place a child they are looking after in a children's home provided, equipped and maintained by an appropriate national authority under section 82(5), they must do so on such terms as that national authority may from time to time determine.

### Regulations as to children looked after by local authorities

22F   Part 2 of Schedule 2 has effect for the purposes of making further provision as to children looked after by local authorities and in particular as to the regulations which may be made under section 22C(11).

### General duty of local authority to secure sufficient accommodation for looked after children

22G(1) It is the general duty of a local authority to take steps that secure, so far as reasonably practicable, the outcome in subsection (2).

(2) The outcome is that the local authority are able to provide the children mentioned in subsection (3) with accommodation that–

(a) is within the authority's area; and

(b) meets the needs of those children.

(3) The children referred to in subsection (2) are those–

(a) that the local authority are looking after,

(b) in respect of whom the authority are unable to make arrangements under section 22C(2), and

(c) whose circumstances are such that it would be consistent with their welfare for them to be provided with accommodation that is in the authority's area.

(4) In taking steps to secure the outcome in subsection (2), the local authority must have regard to the benefit of having–

(a) a number of accommodation providers in their area that is, in their opinion, sufficient to secure that outcome; and

(b) a range of accommodation in their area capable of meeting different needs that is, in their opinion, sufficient to secure that outcome.

(5) In this section 'accommodation providers' means–

local authority foster parents; and

children's homes in respect of which a person is registered under Part 2 of the Care Standards Act 2000.

## *Visiting*

### Duty of local authority to ensure visits to, and contact with, looked after children and others

23ZA(1)This section applies to–

    (a) a child looked after by a local authority;

    (b) a child who was looked after by a local authority but who has ceased to be looked after by them as a result of prescribed circumstances.

(2) It is the duty of the local authority–

    (a) to ensure that a person to whom this section applies is visited by a representative of the authority ('a representative');

    (b) to arrange for appropriate advice, support and assistance to be available to a person to whom this section applies who seeks it from them.

(3) The duties imposed by subsection (2)–

    (a) are to be discharged in accordance with any regulations made for the purposes of this section by the appropriate national authority;

    (b) are subject to any requirement imposed by or under an enactment applicable to the place in which the person to whom this section applies is accommodated.

(4) Regulations under this section for the purposes of subsection (3)(a) may make provision about–

    (a) the frequency of visits;

    (b) circumstances in which a person to whom this section applies must be visited by a representative; and

    (c) the functions of a representative.

(5) In choosing a representative a local authority must satisfy themselves that the person chosen has the necessary skills and experience to perform the functions of a representative.

### Independent visitors for children looked after by a local authority

23ZB(1)A local authority looking after a child must appoint an independent person to be the child's visitor if–

    (a) the child falls within a description prescribed in regulations made by the appropriate national authority; or

    (b) in any other case, it appears to them that it would be in the child's interests to do so.

(2) A person appointed under this section must visit, befriend and advise the child.

(3) A person appointed under this section is entitled to recover from the appointing authority any reasonable expenses incurred by that person for the purposes of that person's functions under this section.

(4) A person's appointment as a visitor in pursuance of this section comes to an end if–

    (a) the child ceases to be looked after by the local authority;

    (b) the person resigns the appointment by giving notice in writing to the appointing authority; or

    (c) the authority give him notice in writing that they have terminated it.

(5) The ending of such an appointment does not affect any duty under this section to make a further appointment.

(6) Where a local authority propose to appoint a visitor for a child under this section, the appointment shall not be made if–
  (a) the child objects to it; and
  (b) the authority are satisfied that the child has sufficient understanding to make an informed decision.

(7) Where a visitor has been appointed for a child under this section, the local authority shall terminate the appointment if–
  (a) the child objects to its continuing; and
  (b) the authority are satisfied that the child has sufficient understanding to make an informed decision.

(8) If the local authority give effect to a child's objection under subsection (6) or (7) and the objection is to having anyone as the child's visitor, the authority does not have to propose to appoint another person under subsection (1) until the objection is withdrawn.

(9) The appropriate national authority may make regulations as to the circumstances in which a person is to be regarded for the purposes of this section as independent of the appointing authority.

### Advice and assistance for certain children and young persons

### The responsible authority and relevant children

23A(1) The responsible local authority shall have the functions set out in section 23B in respect of a relevant child.

(2) In subsection (1) 'relevant child' means (subject to subsection (3)) a child who–
  (a) is not being looked after by any local authority;
  (b) was, before last ceasing to be looked after, an eligible child for the purposes of paragraph 19B of Schedule 2; and
  (c) is aged sixteen or seventeen.

(3) The appropriate national authority may prescribe–
  (a) additional categories of relevant children; and
  (b) categories of children who are not to be relevant children despite falling within subsection (2).

(4) In subsection (1) the 'responsible local authority' is the one which last looked after the child.

(5) If under subsection (3)(a) the appropriate national authority prescribes a category of relevant children which includes children who do not fall within subsection (2)(b) (for example, because they were being looked after by a local authority in Scotland), the appropriate national authority may in the regulations also provide for which local authority is to be the responsible local authority for those children.

### Additional functions of the responsible authority in respect of relevant children

23B(1) It is the duty of each local authority to take reasonable steps to keep in touch with a relevant child for whom they are the responsible authority, whether he is within their area or not.

(2) It is the duty of each local authority to appoint a personal adviser for each relevant child (if they have not already done so under paragraph 19C of Schedule 2).

(3) It is the duty of each local authority, in relation to any relevant child who does not already have a pathway plan prepared for the purposes of paragraph 19B of Schedule 2–

(a) to carry out an assessment of his needs with a view to determining what advice, assistance and support it would be appropriate for them to provide him under this Part; and

(b) to prepare a pathway plan for him.

(4) [Repealed.]

(5) [Repealed.]

(6) [Repealed.]

(7) [Repealed.]

(8) The responsible local authority shall safeguard and promote the child's welfare and, unless they are satisfied that his welfare does not require it, support him by–

(a) maintaining him;

(b) providing him with or maintaining him in suitable accommodation; and

(c) providing support of such other descriptions as may be prescribed.

(9) Support under subsection (8) may be in cash.

(10) The appropriate national authority may by regulations make provision about the meaning of 'suitable accommodation' and in particular about the suitability of landlords or other providers of accommodation.

(11) If the local authority have lost touch with a relevant child, despite taking reasonable steps to keep in touch, they must without delay–

(a) consider how to re-establish contact; and

(b) take reasonable steps to do so,

and while the child is still a relevant child must continue to take such steps until they succeed.

(12) Subsections (7) to (9) of section 17 apply in relation to support given under this section as they apply in relation to assistance given under that section.

(13) Subsections (4) and (5) of section 22 apply in relation to any decision by a local authority for the purposes of this section as they apply in relation to the decisions referred to in that section.

### Continuing functions in respect of former relevant children

23C(1) Each local authority shall have the duties provided for in this section towards–

(a) a person who has been a relevant child for the purposes of section 23A (and would be one if he were under eighteen), and in relation to whom they were the last responsible authority; and

(b) a person who was being looked after by them when he attained the age of eighteen, and immediately before ceasing to be looked after was an eligible child,

and in this section such a person is referred to as a 'former relevant child'.

(2) It is the duty of the local authority to take reasonable steps–

(a) to keep in touch with a former relevant child whether he is within their area or not; and

(b) if they lose touch with him, to re-establish contact.

(3) It is the duty of the local authority–

(a) to continue the appointment of a personal adviser for a former relevant child; and

(b) to continue to keep his pathway plan under regular review.

(4) It is the duty of the local authority to give a former relevant child–

    (a) assistance of the kind referred to in section 24B(1), to the extent that his welfare requires it;

    (b) assistance of the kind referred to in section 24B(2), to the extent that his welfare and his educational or training needs require it;

    (c) other assistance, to the extent that his welfare requires it.

(5) The assistance given under subsection (4)(c) may be in kind or, in exceptional circumstances, in cash.

(5A) It is the duty of the local authority to pay the relevant amount to a former relevant child who pursues higher education in accordance with a pathway plan prepared for that person.

(5B) The appropriate national authority may by regulations–

    (a) prescribe the relevant amount for the purposes of subsection (5A);

    (b) prescribe the meaning of 'higher education' for those purposes;

    (c) make provision as to the payment of the relevant amount;

    (d) make provision as to the circumstances in which the relevant amount (or any part of it) may be recovered by the local authority from a former relevant child to whom a payment has been made.

(5C) The duty set out in subsection (5A) is without prejudice to that set out in subsection (4)(b).

(6) Subject to subsection (7), the duties set out in subsections (2), (3) and (4) subsist until the former relevant child reaches the age of twenty-one.

(7) If the former relevant child's pathway plan sets out a programme of education or training which extends beyond his twenty-first birthday–

    (a) the duty set out in subsection (4)(b) continues to subsist for so long as the former relevant child continues to pursue that programme; and

    (b) the duties set out in subsections (2) and (3) continue to subsist concurrently with that duty.

(8) For the purposes of subsection (7)(a) there shall be disregarded any interruption in a former relevant child's pursuance of a programme of education or training if the local authority are satisfied that he will resume it as soon as is reasonably practicable.

(9) Section 24B(5) applies in relation to a person being given assistance under subsection (4)(b) or who is in receipt of a payment under subsection (5A) as it applies in relation to a person to whom section 24B(3) applies.

(10) Subsections (7) to (9) of section 17 apply in relation to assistance given under this section as they apply in relation to assistance given under that section.

### Further assistance to pursue education or training[7]

23CA(1) This section applies to a person if–

    (a) he is under the age of twenty-five or of such lesser age as may be prescribed by the appropriate national authority;

    (b) he is a former relevant child (within the meaning of section 23C) towards whom the duties imposed by subsections (2), (3) and (4) of that section no longer subsist; and

---

7  This section does not extend to Scotland: see s108(11).

(c) he has informed the responsible local authority that he is pursuing, or wishes to pursue, a programme of education or training.

(2) It is the duty of the responsible local authority to appoint a personal adviser for a person to whom this section applies.

(3) It is the duty of the responsible local authority–
   (a) to carry out an assessment of the needs of a person to whom this section applies with a view to determining what assistance (if any) it would be appropriate for them to provide to him under this section; and
   (b) to prepare a pathway plan for him.

(4) It is the duty of the responsible local authority to give assistance of a kind referred to subsection (5) to a person to whom this section applies to the extent that his educational or training needs require it.

(5) The kinds of assistance are–
   (a) contributing to expenses incurred by him in living near the place where he is, or will be, receiving education or training; or
   (b) making a grant to enable him to meet expenses connected with his education and training.

(6) If a person to whom this section applies pursues a programme of education or training in accordance with the pathway plan prepared for him, the duties of the local authority under this section (and under any provision applicable to the pathway plan prepared under this section for that person) subsist for as long as he continues to pursue that programme.

(7) For the purposes of subsection (6), the local authority may disregard any interruption in the person's pursuance of a programme of education or training if they are satisfied that he will resume it as soon as is reasonably practicable.

(8) Subsections (7) to (9) of section 17 apply to assistance given to a person under this section as they apply to assistance given to or in respect of a child under that section, but with the omission in subsection (8) of the words 'and of each of his parents'.

(9) Subsection (5) of section 24B applies to a person to whom this section applies as it applies to a person to whom subsection (3) of that section applies.

(10) Nothing in this section affects the duty imposed by subsection (5A) of section 23C to the extent that it subsists in relation to a person to whom this section applies; but the duty to make a payment under that subsection may be taken into account in the assessment of the person's needs under subsection (3)(a).

(11) In this section 'the responsible local authority' means, in relation to a person to whom this section applies, the local authority which had the duties provided for in section 23C towards him.

## *Personal advisers and pathway plans*

### Personal advisers

23D (1) The appropriate national authority may by regulations require local authorities to appoint a personal adviser for children or young persons of a prescribed description who have reached the age of sixteen but not the age of twenty-five who are not–
   (a) children who are relevant children for the purposes of section 23A;
   (b) the young persons referred to in section 23C; or
   (c) the children referred to in paragraph 19C of Schedule 2; or
   (d) persons to whom section 23CA applies.

(2) Personal advisers appointed under or by virtue of this Part shall (in addition to any other functions) have such functions as the appropriate national authority prescribes.

### Pathway plans

23E (1) In this Part, a reference to a 'pathway plan' is to a plan setting out–
   (a) in the case of a plan prepared under paragraph 19B of Schedule 2–
      (i) the advice, assistance and support which the local authority intend to provide a child under this Part, both while they are looking after him and later; and
      (ii) when they might cease to look after him; and
   (b) in the case of a plan prepared under section 23B or 23CA, the advice, assistance and support which the local authority intend to provide under this Part,
   and dealing with such other matters (if any) as may be prescribed.
 (1A) A local authority may carry out an assessment under section 23B(3) or 23CA(3) of a person's needs at the same time as any assessment of his needs is made under–
   (a) the Chronically Sick and Disabled Persons Act 1970;
   (b) Part 4 of the Education Act 1996 (in the case of an assessment under section 23B(3));
   (c) the Disabled Persons (Services, Consultation and Representation) Act 1986; or
   (d) any other enactment.
 (1B) The appropriate national authority may by regulations make provision as to assessments for the purposes of section 23B(3) or 23CA.
 (1C) Regulations under subsection (1B) may in particular make provision about–
   (a) who is to be consulted in relation to an assessment;
   (b) the way in which an assessment is to be carried out, by whom and when;
   (c) the recording of the results of an assessment;
   (d) the considerations to which a local authority are to have regard in carrying out an assessment.
 (1D) A local authority shall keep each pathway plan prepared by them under section 23B or 23CA under review.
   (2) The appropriate national authority may by regulations make provision about pathway plans and their review.

### Persons qualifying for advice and assistance

24 (1) In this Part 'a person qualifying for advice and assistance' means a person to whom subsection (1A) or (1B) applies.
 (1A) This subsection applies to a person–
   (a) who has reached the age of sixteen but not the age of twenty-one;
   (b) with respect to whom a special guardianship order is in force (or, if he has reached the age of eighteen, was in force when he reached that age); and
   (c) who was, immediately before the making of that order, looked after by a local authority.
 (1B) This subsection applies to a person to whom subsection (1A) does not apply, and who–
   (a) is under twenty-one; and

(b) at any time after reaching the age of sixteen but while still a child was, but is no longer, looked after, accommodated or fostered.

(2) In subsection (1B)(b), 'looked after, accommodated or fostered' means–
  (a) looked after by a local authority;
  (b) accommodated by or on behalf of a voluntary organisation;
  (c) accommodated in a private children's home;
  (d) accommodated for a consecutive period of at least three months–
    (i) by any Local Health Board, Special Health Authority or Primary Care Trust or by a local authority in the exercise of education functions, or
    (ii) in any care home or independent hospital or in any accommodation provided by a National Health Service trust or an NHS foundation trust; or
  (e) privately fostered.

(3) Subsection (2)(d) applies even if the period of three months mentioned there began before the child reached the age of sixteen.

(4) In the case of a person qualifying for advice and assistance by virtue of subsection (2)(a), it is the duty of the local authority which last looked after him to take such steps as they think appropriate to contact him at such times as they think appropriate with a view to discharging their functions under sections 24A and 24B.

(5) In each of sections 24A and 24B, the local authority under the duty or having the power mentioned there ('the relevant authority') is–
  (za) in the case of a person to whom subsection (1A) applies, a local authority determined in accordance with regulations made by the appropriate national authority;
  (a) in the case of a person qualifying for advice and assistance by virtue of subsection (2)(a), the local authority which last looked after him; or
  (b) in the case of any other person qualifying for advice and assistance, the local authority within whose area the person is (if he has asked for help of a kind which can be given under section 24A or 24B).

**Advice and assistance**

24A (1) The relevant authority shall consider whether the conditions in subsection (2) are satisfied in relation to a person qualifying for advice and assistance.

(2) The conditions are that–
  (a) he needs help of a kind which they can give under this section or section 24B; and
  (b) in the case of a person to whom section 24(1A) applies, or to whom section 24(1B) applies and who was not being looked after by any local authority, they are satisfied that the person by whom he was being looked after does not have the necessary facilities for advising or befriending him.

(3) If the conditions are satisfied–
  (a) they shall advise and befriend him if he is a person to whom section 24(1A) applies, or he is a person to whom section 24(1B) applies and he was being looked after by a local authority or was accommodated by or on behalf of a voluntary organisation; and
  (b) in any other case they may do so.

(4) Where as a result of this section a local authority are under a duty, or are empowered, to advise and befriend a person, they may also give him assistance.

(5) The assistance may be in kind and, in exceptional circumstances, assistance may be given–
  (a) by providing accommodation, if in the circumstances assistance may not be given in respect of the accommodation under section 24B, or
  (b) in cash.
(6) Subsections (7) to (9) of section 17 apply in relation to assistance given under this section or section 24B as they apply in relation to assistance given under that section.

### Employment, education and training
24B (1) The relevant local authority may give assistance to any person who qualifies for advice and assistance by virtue of section 24(1A) or section 24(2)(a) by contributing to expenses incurred by him in living near the place where he is, or will be, employed or seeking employment.
  (2) The relevant local authority may give assistance to a person to whom subsection (3) applies by–
  (a) contributing to expenses incurred by the person in question in living near the place where he is, or will be, receiving education or training; or
  (b) making a grant to enable him to meet expenses connected with his education or training.
  (3) This subsection applies to any person who–
  (a) is under twenty-five; and
  (b) qualifies for advice and assistance by virtue of section 24(1A) or section 24(2)(a), or would have done so if he were under twenty-one.
  (4) Where a local authority are assisting a person under subsection (2) they may disregard any interruption in his attendance on the course if he resumes it as soon as is reasonably practicable.
  (5) Where the local authority are satisfied that a person to whom subsection (3) applies who is in full-time further or higher education needs accommodation during a vacation because his term-time accommodation is not available to him then, they shall give him assistance by–
  (a) providing him with suitable accommodation during the vacation; or
  (b) paying him enough to enable him to secure such accommodation himself.
  (6) The appropriate national authority may prescribe the meaning of 'full-time', 'further education', 'higher education' and 'vacation' for the purposes of subsection (5).

### Information
24C(1) Where it appears to a local authority that a person–
  (a) with whom they are under a duty to keep in touch under section 23B, 23C or 24; or
  (b) whom they have been advising and befriending under section 24A; or
  (c) to whom they have been giving assistance under section 24B,
  proposes to live, or is living, in the area of another local authority, they must inform that other authority.
  (2) Where a child who is accommodated–
  (a) by a voluntary organisation or in a private children's home;
  (b) by any Local Health Board, Special Health Authority or Primary Care Trust or by a local authority in the exercise of education functions; or

(c) in any care home or independent hospital or any accommodation provided by a National Health Service trust or an NHS foundation trust,

ceases to be so accommodated, after reaching the age of sixteen, the organisation, authority or (as the case may be) person carrying on the home shall inform the local authority within whose area the child proposes to live.

(3) Subsection (2) only applies, by virtue of paragraph (b) or (c), if the accommodation has been provided for a consecutive period of at least three months.

(4) In a case where a child was accommodated by a local authority in the exercise of education functions, subsection (2) applies only if the local authority who accommodated the child are different from the local authority within whose area the child proposes to live.

### Representations: sections 23A to 24B

24D (1)Every local authority shall establish a procedure for considering representations (including complaints) made to them by–

(a) a relevant child for the purposes of section 23A or a young person falling within section 23C;

(b) a person qualifying for advice and assistance; or

(c) a person falling within section 24B(2),

about the discharge of their functions under this Part in relation to him.

(1A) Regulations may be made by the appropriate national authority imposing time limits on the making of representations under subsection (1).

(2) In considering representations under subsection (1), a local authority shall comply with regulations (if any) made by the appropriate national authority for the purposes of this subsection.

## *Secure accommodation*

### Use of accommodation for restricting liberty[8]

25 (1) Subject to the following provisions of this section, a child who is being looked after by a local authority may not be placed, and, if placed, may not be kept, in accommodation provided for the purpose of restricting liberty ('secure accommodation') unless it appears–

(a) that–

(i) he has a history of absconding and is likely to abscond from any other description of accommodation; and

(ii) if he absconds, he is likely to suffer significant harm; or

(b) that if he is kept in any other description of accommodation he is likely to injure himself or other persons.

(2) The appropriate national authority may by regulations–

(a) specify a maximum period–

(i) beyond which a child may not be kept in secure accommodation without the authority of the court; and

(ii) for which the court may authorise a child to be kept in secure accommodation;

(b) empower the court from time to time to authorise a child to be kept in secure accommodation for such further period as the regulations may specify; and

---

8 Subss (1)–(7), (9) do not extend to Scotland.

(c) provide that applications to the court under this section shall be made only by local authorities.

(3) It shall be the duty of a court hearing an application under this section to determine whether any relevant criteria for keeping a child in secure accommodation are satisfied in his case.

(4) If a court determines that any such criteria are satisfied, it shall make an order authorising the child to be kept in secure accommodation and specifying the maximum period for which he may be so kept.

(5) On any adjournment of the hearing of an application under this section, a court may make an interim order permitting the child to be kept during the period of the adjournment in secure accommodation.

(6) No court shall exercise the powers conferred by this section in respect of a child who is not legally represented in that court unless, having been informed of his right to apply for representation funded by the Legal Services Commission as part of the Community Legal Service or Criminal Defence Service and having had the opportunity to do so, he refused or failed to apply.

(7) The appropriate national authority may by regulations provide that–
   (a) this section shall or shall not apply to any description of children specified in the regulations;
   (b) this section shall have effect in relation to children of a description specified in the regulations subject to such modifications as may be so specified;
   (c) such other provisions as may be so specified shall have effect for the purpose of determining whether a child of a description specified in the regulations may be placed or kept in secure accommodation.

(8) The giving of an authorisation under this section shall not prejudice any power of any court in England and Wales or Scotland to give directions relating to the child to whom the authorisation relates.

(9) This section is subject to section 20(8).

## Independent reviewing officers

### Appointment of independent reviewing officer

25A(1) If a local authority are looking after a child, they must appoint an individual as the independent reviewing officer for that child's case.

(2) The initial appointment under subsection (1) must be made before the child's case is first reviewed in accordance with regulations made under section 26.

(3) If a vacancy arises in respect of a child's case, the local authority must make another appointment under subsection (1) as soon as is practicable.

(4) An appointee must be of a description prescribed in regulations made by the appropriate national authority.

### Functions of the independent reviewing officer

25B (1) The independent reviewing officer must–
   (a) monitor the performance by the local authority of their functions in relation to the child's case;
   (b) participate, in accordance with regulations made by the appropriate national authority, in any review of the child's case;
   (c) ensure that any ascertained wishes and feelings of the child concerning the case are given due consideration by the local authority;

(d) perform any other function which is prescribed in regulations made by the appropriate national authority.

(2) An independent reviewing officer's functions must be performed–
   (a) in such manner (if any) as may be prescribed in regulations made by the appropriate national authority; and
   (b) having regard to such guidance as that authority may issue in relation to the discharge of those functions.

(3) If the independent reviewing officer considers it appropriate to do so, the child's case may be referred by that officer to–
   (a) an officer of the Children and Family Court Advisory and Support Service; or
   (b) a Welsh family proceedings officer.

(4) If the independent reviewing officer is not an officer of the local authority, it is the duty of the authority–
   (a) to co-operate with that individual; and
   (b) to take all such reasonable steps as that individual may require of them to enable that individual's functions under this section to be performed satisfactorily.

### Referred cases

25C(1) In relation to children whose cases are referred to officers under section 25B(3), the Lord Chancellor may by regulations–
   (a) extend any functions of the officers in respect of family proceedings (within the meaning of section 12 of the Criminal Justice and Court Services Act 2000) to other proceedings;
   (b) require any functions of the officers to be performed in the manner prescribed by the regulations.

(2) The power to make regulations in this section is exercisable in relation to functions of Welsh family proceedings officers only with the consent of the Welsh Ministers.

### *Supplemental*

### Review of cases and inquiries into representations

26 (1) The appropriate national authority may make regulations requiring the case of each child who is being looked after by a local authority to be reviewed in accordance with the provisions of the regulations.

(2) The regulations may, in particular, make provision–
   (a) as to the manner in which each case is to be reviewed;
   (b) as to the considerations to which the local authority are to have regard in reviewing each case;
   (c) as to the time when each case is first to be reviewed and the frequency of subsequent reviews;
   (d) requiring the authority, before conducting any review, to seek the views of–
      (i) the child;
      (ii) his parents;
      (iii) any person who is not a parent of his but who has parental responsibility for him; and

     (iv) any other person whose views the authority consider to be relevant, including, in particular, the views of those persons in relation to any particular matter which is to be considered in the course of the review;

    (e) requiring the authority, in the case of a child who is in their care–

      (i) to keep the section 31A plan for the child under review and, if they are of the opinion that some change is required, to revise the plan, or make a new plan, accordingly,

      (ii) to consider, whether an application should be made to discharge the care order;

    (f) requiring the authority, in the case of a child in accommodation provided by the authority–

      (i) if there is no plan for the future care of the child, to prepare one,

      (ii) if there is such a plan for the child, to keep it under review and, if they are of the opinion that some change is required, to revise the plan or make a new plan, accordingly,

      (iii) to consider, whether the accommodation accords with the requirements of this Part;

    (g) requiring the authority to inform the child, so far as is reasonably practicable, of any steps he may take under this Act;

    (h) requiring the authority to make arrangements, including arrangements with such other bodies providing services as it considers appropriate, to implement any decision which they propose to make in the course, or as a result, of the review;

    (i) requiring the authority to notify details of the result of the review and of any decision taken by them in consequence of the review to–

      (i) the child;

      (ii) his parents;

      (iii) any person who is not a parent of his but who has parental responsibility for him; and

      (iv) any other person whom they consider ought to be notified;

    (j) requiring the authority to monitor the arrangements which they have made with a view to ensuring that they comply with the regulations;

    (k) [Repealed.]

(2A) [Repealed.]

(2B) [Repealed.]

(2C) [Repealed.]

(2D) [Repealed.]

   (3) Every local authority shall establish a procedure for considering any representations (including any complaint) made to them by–

    (a) any child who is being looked after by them or who is not being looked after by them but is in need;

    (b) a parent of his;

    (c) any person who is not a parent of his but who has parental responsibility for him;

    (d) any local authority foster parent;

    (e) such other person as the authority consider has a sufficient interest in the child's welfare to warrant his representations being considered by them,

about the discharge by the authority of any of their qualifying functions in relation to the child.

(3A) The following are qualifying functions for the purposes of subsection (3)–
  (a) functions under this Part,
  (b) such functions under Part 4 or 5 as are specified by the appropriate national authority in regulations.
(3B) The duty under subsection (3) extends to representations (including complaints) made to the authority by–
  (a) any person mentioned in section 3(1) of the Adoption and Children Act 2002 (persons for whose needs provision is made by the Adoption Service) and any other person to whom arrangements for the provision of adoption support services (within the meaning of that Act) extend,
  (b) such other person as the authority consider has sufficient interest in a child who is or may be adopted to warrant his representations being considered by them,
  about the discharge by the authority of such functions under the Adoption and Children Act 2002 as are specified by the appropriate national authority in regulations.
(3C) The duty under subsection (3) extends to any representations (including complaints) which are made to the authority by–
  (a) a child with respect to whom a special guardianship order is in force,
  (b) a special guardian or a parent of such a child,
  (c) any other person the authority consider has a sufficient interest in the welfare of such a child to warrant his representations being considered by them, or
  (d) any person who has applied for an assessment under section 14F(3) or (4),
  about the discharge by the authority of such functions under section 14F as may be specified by the appropriate national authority in regulations.
 (4) The procedure shall ensure that at least one person who is not a member or officer of the authority takes part in–
  (a) the consideration; and
  (b) any discussions which are held by the authority about the action (if any) to be taken in relation to the child in the light of the consideration,
  but this subsection is subject to subsection (5A).
(4A) Regulations may be made by the appropriate national authority imposing time limits on the making of representations under this section.
 (5) In carrying out any consideration of representations under this section a local authority shall comply with any regulations made by the appropriate national authority for the purpose of regulating the procedure to be followed.
(5A) Regulations under subsection (5) may provide that subsection (4) does not apply in relation to any consideration or discussion which takes place as part of a procedure for which provision is made by the regulations for the purpose of resolving informally the matters raised in the representations.
 (6) The appropriate national authority may make regulations requiring local authorities to monitor the arrangements that they have made with a view to ensuring that they comply with any regulations made for the purposes of subsection (5).
 (7) Where any representation has been considered under the procedure established by a local authority under this section, the authority shall–
  (a) have due regard to the findings of those considering the representation; and

(b) take such steps as are reasonably practicable to notify (in writing)–
   (i) the person making the representation;
   (ii) the child (if the authority consider that he has sufficient understanding); and
   (iii) such other persons (if any) as appear to the authority to be likely to be affected,
   of the authority's decision in the matter and their reasons for taking that decision and of any action which they have taken, or propose to take.
(8) Every local authority shall give such publicity to their procedure for considering representations under this section as they consider appropriate.

26ZA  [Repealed.]

### Representations: further consideration (Wales)

26ZB(1) The Welsh Ministers may by regulations make provision for the further consideration of representations which have been considered by a local authority in Wales under section 24D or section 26.
(2) The regulations may in particular make provision–
   (a) for the further consideration of a representation by an independent panel established under the regulations;
   (b) about the procedure to be followed on the further consideration of a representation;
   (c) for the making of recommendations about the action to be taken as the result of a representation;
   (d) about the making of reports about a representation;
   (e) about the action to be taken by the local authority concerned as a result of the further consideration of a representation;
   (f) for a representation to be referred back to the local authority concerned for reconsideration by the authority.
(3) The regulations may require–
   (a) the making of a payment, in relation to the further consideration of a representation under this section, by any local authority in respect of whose functions the representation is made;
   (b) any such payment to be–
      (i) made to such person or body as may be specified in the regulations;
      (ii) of such amount as may be specified in, or calculated or determined under, the regulations; and
   (c) for an independent panel to review the amount chargeable under paragraph (a) in any particular case and, if the panel thinks fit, to substitute a lesser amount.
(4) The regulations may also–
   (a) provide for different parts or aspects of a representation to be treated differently;
   (b) require the production of information or documents in order to enable a representation to be properly considered;
   (c) authorise the disclosure of information or documents relevant to a representation to a person or body who is further considering a representation under the regulations;
   and any such disclosure may be authorised notwithstanding any rule of common law that would otherwise prohibit or restrict the disclosure.

### Advocacy services

26A(1) Every local authority shall make arrangements for the provision of assistance to–

    (a) persons who make or intend to make representations under section 24D; and

    (b) children who make or intend to make representations under section 26.

  (2) The assistance provided under the arrangements shall include assistance by way of representation.

 (2A) The duty under subsection (1) includes a duty to make arrangements for the provision of assistance where representations under section 24D or 26 are further considered under section 26ZB.

  (3) The arrangements–

    (a) shall secure that a person may not provide assistance if he is a person who is prevented from doing so by regulations made by the appropriate national authority; and

    (b) shall comply with any other provision made by the regulations in relation to the arrangements.

  (4) The appropriate national authority may make regulations requiring local authorities to monitor the steps that they have taken with a view to ensuring that they comply with regulations made for the purposes of subsection (3).

  (5) Every local authority shall give such publicity to their arrangements for the provision of assistance under this section as they consider appropriate.

### Co-operation between authorities

27 (1) Where it appears to a local authority that any authority mentioned in subsection (3) could, by taking any specified action, help in the exercise of any of their functions under this Part, they may request the help of that other authority, specifying the action in question.

  (2) An authority whose help is so requested shall comply with the request if it is compatible with their own statutory or other duties and obligations and does not unduly prejudice the discharge of any of their functions.

  (3) The authorities are–

    (a) any local authority;

    (b) [Repealed.]

    (c) any local housing authority;

    (d) any Local Health Board, Special Health Authority, Primary Care Trust, National Health Service trust or NHS foundation trust; and

    (e) any person authorised by the appropriate national authority for the purposes of this section.

  (4) [Repealed.]

28    [Repealed.]

### Recoupment of cost of providing services etc

29 (1) Where a local authority provide any service under section 17 or 18, other than advice, guidance or counselling, they may recover from a person specified in subsection (4) such charge for the service as they consider reasonable.

  (2) Where the authority are satisfied that that person's means are insufficient for it to be reasonably practicable for him to pay the charge, they shall not require him to pay more than he can reasonably be expected to pay.

(3) No person shall be liable to pay any charge under subsection (1) for a service provided under section 17 or section 18(1) or (5) at any time when he is in receipt [of income support under Part VII of the Social Security Contributions and Benefits Act 1992],⁹ of any element of child tax credit other than the family element, of working tax credit, of an income-based jobseeker's allowance or of an income-related employment and support allowance.

(3A) No person shall be liable to pay any charge under subsection (1) for a service provided under section 18(2) or (6) at any time when he is in receipt [of income support under Part VII of the Social Security Contributions and Benefits Act 1992],¹⁰ of an income-based jobseeker's allowance or of an income-related employment and support allowance.

(3B) No person shall be liable to pay any charge under subsection (1) for a service provided under section 18(2) or (6) at any time when–
    (a) he is in receipt of guarantee state pension credit under section 1(3)(a) of the State Pension Credit Act 2002, or
    (b) he is a member of a couple (within the meaning of that Act) the other member of which is in receipt of guarantee state pension credit.

(4) The persons are–
    (a) where the service is provided for a child under sixteen, each of his parents;
    (b) where it is provided for a child who has reached the age of sixteen, the child himself; and
    (c) where it is provided for a member of the child's family, that member.

(5) Any charge under subsection (1) may, without prejudice to any other method of recovery, be recovered summarily as a civil debt.

(6) Part III of Schedule 2 makes provision in connection with contributions towards the maintenance of children who are being looked after by local authorities and consists of the re-enactment with modifications of provisions in Part V of the Child Care Act 1980.

(7) Where a local authority provide any accommodation under section 20(1) for a child who was (immediately before they began to look after him) ordinarily resident within the area of another local authority, they may recover from that other authority any reasonable expenses incurred by them in providing the accommodation and maintaining him.

(8) Where a local authority provide accommodation under section 21(1) or (2)(a) or (b) for a child who is ordinarily resident within the area of another local authority and they are not maintaining him in–
    (a) a community home provided by them;
    (b) a controlled community home; or
    (c) a hospital vested in the Secretary of State, the Welsh Ministers or a Primary Care Trust, or any other hospital made available pursuant to arrangements made by a Strategic Health Authority, a Local Health Board or a Primary Care Trust,
they may recover from that other authority any reasonable expenses incurred by them in providing the accommodation and maintaining him.

---

9 Words in square brackets repealed by WRA 2009 ss9, 61(3), (4). Not yet in force.
10 Words in square brackets repealed by WRA 2009 ss9, 61(3), (4). Not yet in force.

(9) Except where subsection (10) applies, where a local authority comply with any request under section 27(2) in relation to a child or other person who is not ordinarily resident within their area, they may recover from the local authority in whose area the child or person is ordinarily resident any reasonable expenses incurred by them in respect of that person.

(10) Where a local authority ('authority A') comply with any request under section 27(2) from another local authority ('authority B') in relation to a child or other person–

    (a) whose responsible authority is authority B for the purposes of section 23B or 23C; or

    (b) whom authority B are advising or befriending or to whom they are giving assistance by virtue of section 24(5)(a),

authority A may recover from authority B any reasonable expenses incurred by them in respect of that person.

### Miscellaneous

**30** (1) Nothing in this Part shall affect any duty imposed on a local authority by or under any other enactment.

(2) Any question arising under section 20(2), 21(3) or 29(7) to (9) as to the ordinary residence of a child shall be determined by agreement between the local authorities concerned or, in default of agreement, by the determining authority.

(2A) For the purposes of subsection (2) 'the determining authority' is–

    (a) in a case where all the local authorities concerned are in Wales, the Welsh Ministers;

    (b) in any other case, the Secretary of State.

(2B) In a case where–

    (a) the determining authority is the Secretary of State, and

    (b) one or more of the local authorities concerned are in Wales,

the Secretary of State must consult the Welsh Ministers before making a determination for the purposes of subsection (2).

(3) [Repealed.]

(4) The appropriate national authority may make regulations for determining, as respects any education functions specified in the regulations, whether a child who is being looked after by a local authority is to be treated, for purposes so specified, as a child of parents of sufficient resources or as a child of parents without resources.

### Meaning of appropriate national authority

**30A** In this Part 'the appropriate national authority' means–

    (a) in relation to England, the Secretary of State; and

    (b) in relation to Wales, the Welsh Ministers.

. . .

### Local authority's duty to investigate

**47** (1) Where a local authority–

    (a) are informed that a child who lives, or is found, in their area–

        (i) is the subject of an emergency protection order; or

        (ii) is in police protection;

        (iii) [Repealed.]

(b) have reasonable cause to suspect that a child who lives, or is found, in their area is suffering, or is likely to suffer, significant harm,

the authority shall make, or cause to be made, such enquiries as they consider necessary to enable them to decide whether they should take any action to safeguard or promote the child's welfare.

(2) Where a local authority have obtained an emergency protection order with respect to a child, they shall make, or cause to be made, such enquiries as they consider necessary to enable them to decide what action they should take to safeguard or promote the child's welfare.

(3) The enquiries shall, in particular, be directed towards establishing–

    (a) whether the authority should make any application to the court, or exercise any of their other powers under this Act or section 11 of the Crime and Disorder Act 1998 (child safety orders), with respect to the child;

    (b) whether, in the case of a child–

        (i) with respect to whom an emergency protection order has been made; and

        (ii) who is not in accommodation provided by or on behalf of the authority, it would be in the child's best interests (while an emergency protection order remains in force) for him to be in such accommodation; and

    (c) whether, in the case of a child who has been taken into police protection, it would be in the child's best interests for the authority to ask for an application to be made under section 46(7).

(4) Where enquiries are being made under subsection (1) with respect to a child, the local authority concerned shall (with a view to enabling them to determine what action, if any, to take with respect to him) take such steps as are reasonably practicable–

    (a) to obtain access to him; or

    (b) to ensure that access to him is obtained, on their behalf, by a person authorised by them for the purpose,

unless they are satisfied that they already have sufficient information with respect to him.

(5) Where, as a result of any such enquiries, it appears to the authority that there are matters connected with the child's education which should be investigated, they shall consult the local authority (as defined in section 579(1) of the Education 1996), if different, specified in subsection (5ZA).

(5ZA) The local authority referred to in subsection (5) is–

    (a) the local authority who–

        (i) maintain any school at which the child is a pupil, or

        (ii) make arrangements for the provision of education for the child otherwise than at school pursuant to section 19 of the Education Act 1996, or

    (b) in a case where the child is a pupil at a school which is not maintained by a local authority, the local authority in whose area the school is situated.

(5A) For the purposes of making a determination under this section as to the action to be taken with respect to a child, a local authority shall, so far as is reasonably practicable and consistent with the child's welfare–

    (a) ascertain the child's wishes and feelings regarding the action to be taken with respect to him; and

    (b) give due consideration (having regard to his age and understanding) to such wishes and feelings of the child as they have been able to ascertain.

(6) Where, in the course of enquiries made under this section–
  (a) any officer of the local authority concerned; or
  (b) any person authorised by the authority to act on their behalf in connection with those enquiries–
      (i)  is refused access to the child concerned; or
      (ii) is denied information as to his whereabouts,
  the authority shall apply for an emergency protection order, a child assessment order, a care order or a supervision order with respect to the child unless they are satisfied that his welfare can be satisfactorily safeguarded without their doing so.

(7) If, on the conclusion of any enquiries or review made under this section, the authority decide not to apply for an emergency protection order, a child assessment order, a care order or a supervision order they shall–
  (a) consider whether it would be appropriate to review the case at a later date; and
  (b) if they decide that it would be, determine the date on which that review is to begin.

(8) Where, as a result of complying with this section, a local authority conclude that they should take action to safeguard or promote the child's welfare they shall take that action (so far as it is both within their power and reasonably practicable for them to do so).

(9) Where a local authority are conducting enquiries under this section, it shall be the duty of any person mentioned in subsection (11) to assist them with those enquiries (in particular by providing relevant information and advice) if called upon by the authority to do so.

(10) Subsection (9) does not oblige any person to assist a local authority where doing so would be unreasonable in all the circumstances of the case.

(11) The persons are–
  (a) any local authority;
  (b) [Repealed.]
  (c) any local housing authority;
  (d) any Local Health Board, Special Health Authority, Primary Care Trust, National Health Service trust or NHS foundation trust; and
  (e) any person authorised by the Secretary of State for the purposes of this section.

(12) Where a local authority are making enquiries under this section with respect to a child who appears to them to be ordinarily resident within the area of another authority, they shall consult that other authority, who may undertake the necessary enquiries in their place.

. . .

## SCHEDULE 2

## LOCAL AUTHORITY SUPPORT FOR CHILDREN AND FAMILIES

### Sections 17, 23, 29

### Part I: Provision of services for families

### *Identification of children in need and provision of information*

1 (1) Every local authority shall take reasonable steps to identify the extent to which there are children in need within their area.

  (2) Every local authority shall–

  (a) publish information–

  (i) about services provided by them under sections 17, 18, 20, 23B to 23D, 24A and 24B; and

  (ii) where they consider it appropriate, about the provision by others (including, in particular, voluntary organisations) of services which the authority have power to provide under those sections; and

  (b) take such steps as are reasonably practicable to ensure that those who might benefit from the services receive the information relevant to them.

1A [Repealed.]

### *Maintenance of a register of disabled children*

2 (1) Every local authority shall open and maintain a register of disabled children within their area.

  (2) The register may be kept by means of a computer.

### *Assessment of children's needs*

3     Where it appears to a local authority that a child within their area is in need, the authority may assess his needs for the purposes of this Act at the same time as any assessment of his needs is made under–

  (a) the Chronically Sick and Disabled Persons Act 1970;

  (b) Part IV of the Education Act 1996;

  (c) the Disabled Persons (Services, Consultation and Representation) Act 1986; or

  (d) any other enactment.

### *Prevention of neglect and abuse*

4 (1) Every local authority shall take reasonable steps, through the provision of services under Part III of this Act, to prevent children within their area suffering ill-treatment or neglect.

  (2) Where a local authority believe that a child who is at any time within their area–

  (a) is likely to suffer harm; but

  (b) lives or proposes to live in the area of another local authority they shall inform that other local authority.

  (3) When informing that other local authority they shall specify–

  (a) the harm that they believe he is likely to suffer; and

  (b) (if they can) where the child lives or proposes to live.

## *Provision of accommodation in order to protect child*

5 (1) Where–

(a) it appears to a local authority that a child who is living on particular premises is suffering, or is likely to suffer, ill treatment at the hands of another person who is living on those premises; and

(b) that other person proposes to move from the premises,

the authority may assist that other person to obtain alternative accommodation.

(2) Assistance given under this paragraph may be in cash.

(3) Subsections (7) to (9) of section 17 shall apply in relation to assistance given under this paragraph as they apply in relation to assistance given under that section.

## *Provision for disabled children*

6 (1) Every local authority shall provide services designed–

(a) to minimise the effect on disabled children within their area of their disabilities; and

(b) to give such children the opportunity to lead lives which are as normal as possible; and

(c) to assist individuals who provide care for such children to continue to do so, or to do so more effectively, by giving them breaks from caring.

(2) The duty imposed by sub-paragraph (1)(c) shall be performed in accordance with regulations made by the appropriate national authority.

## *Provision to reduce need for care proceedings etc*

7   Every local authority shall take reasonable steps designed–

(a) to reduce the need to bring–

(i) proceedings for care or supervision orders with respect to children within their area;

(ii) criminal proceedings against such children;

(iii) any family or other proceedings with respect to such children which might lead to them being placed in the authority's care; or

(iv) proceedings under the inherent jurisdiction of the High Court with respect to children;

(b) to encourage children within their area not to commit criminal offences; and

(c) to avoid the need for children within their area to be placed in secure accommodation.

## *Provision for children living with their families*

8   Every local authority shall make such provision as they consider appropriate for the following services to be available with respect to children in need within their area while they are living with their families–

(a) advice, guidance and counselling;

(b) occupational, social, cultural, or recreational activities;

(c) home help (which may include laundry facilities);

(d) facilities for, or assistance with, travelling to and from home for the purpose of taking advantage of any other service provided under this Act or of any similar service;

(e) assistance to enable the child concerned and his family to have a holiday.

## Provision for accommodated children

8A(1) Every local authority shall make provision for such services as they consider appropriate to be available with respect to accommodated children.

(2) 'Accommodated children' are those children in respect of whose accommodation the local authority have been notified under section 85 or 86.

(3) The services shall be provided with a view to promoting contact between each accommodated child and that child's family.

(4) The services may, in particular, include–
  (a) advice, guidance and counselling;
  (b) services necessary to enable the child to visit, or to be visited by, members of the family;
  (c) assistance to enable the child and members of the family to have a holiday together.

(5) Nothing in this paragraph affects the duty imposed by paragraph 10.

## Family centres

9 (1) Every local authority shall provide such family centres as they consider appropriate in relation to children within their area.

(2) 'Family centre' means a centre at which any of the persons mentioned in sub-paragraph (3) may–
  (a) attend for occupational, social, cultural or recreational activities;
  (b) attend for advice, guidance or counselling; or
  (c) be provided with accommodation while he is receiving advice, guidance or counselling.

(3) The persons are–
  (a) a child;
  (b) his parents;
  (c) any person who is not a parent of his but who has parental responsibility for him;
  (d) any other person who is looking after him.

## Maintenance of the family home

10   Every local authority shall take such steps as are reasonably practicable, where any child within their area who is in need and whom they are not looking after is living apart from his family–
  (a) to enable him to live with his family; or
  (b) to promote contact between him and his family,
if, in their opinion, it is necessary to do so in order to safeguard or promote his welfare.

## Duty to consider racial groups to which children in need belong

11   Every local authority shall, in making any arrangements–
  (a) for the provision of day care within their area; or
  (b) designed to encourage persons to act as local authority foster parents,
have regard to the different racial groups to which children within their area who are in need belong.

## Part II: Children looked after by local authorities

### *Regulations as to conditions under which child in care is allowed to live with parent, etc*

12A Regulations under section 22C may, in particular, impose requirements on a local authority as to–

(a) the making of any decision by a local authority to allow a child in their care to live with any person falling within section 22C(3) (including requirements as to those who must be consulted before the decision is made and those who must be notified when it has been made);

(b) the supervision or medical examination of the child concerned;

(c) the removal of the child, in such circumstances as may be prescribed, from the care of the person with whom the child has been allowed to live;

(d) the records to be kept by local authorities.

### *Regulations as to placements of a kind specified in section 22C(6)(d)*

12B Regulations under section 22C as to placements of the kind specified in section 22C(6)(d) may, in particular, make provision as to–

(a) the persons to be notified of any proposed arrangements;

(b) the opportunities such persons are to have to make representations in relation to the arrangements proposed;

(c) the persons to be notified of any proposed changes in arrangements;

(d) the records to be kept by local authorities;

(e) the supervision by local authorities of any arrangements made.

### *Placements out of area*

12C Regulations under section 22C may, in particular, impose requirements which a local authority must comply with–

(a) before a child looked after by them is provided with accommodation at a place outside the area of the authority; or

(b) if the child's welfare requires the immediate provision of such accommodation, within such period of the accommodation being provided as may be prescribed.

### *Avoidance of disruption in education*

12D(1) Regulations under section 22C may, in particular, impose requirements which a local authority must comply with before making any decision concerning a child's placement if he is in the fourth key stage.

(2) A child is 'in the fourth key stage' if he is a pupil in the fourth key stage for the purposes of Part 6 or 7 of the Education 2002 (see section 82 and 103 of that Act).

### *Regulations as to placing of children with local authority foster parents*

12E Regulations under section 22C may, in particular, make provision–

(a) with regard to the welfare of children placed with local authority foster parents;

(b) as to the arrangements to be made by local authorities in connection with the health and education of such children;

(c) as to the records to be kept by local authorities;

(d) for securing that where possible the local authority foster parent with whom a child is to be placed is–
   (i) of the same religious persuasion as the child; or
   (ii) gives an undertaking that the child will be brought up in that religious persuasion;

(e) for securing the children placed with local authority foster parents, and the premises in which they are accommodated, will be supervised and inspected by a local authority and that the children will be removed from those premises if their welfare appears to require it.

**12F**(1) Regulations under section 22C may, in particular, also make provision–

(a) for securing that a child is not placed with a local authority foster parent unless that person is for the time being approved as a local authority foster parent by such local authority as may be prescribed;

(b) establishing a procedure under which any person in respect of whom a qualifying determination has been made may apply to the appropriate national authority for a review of that determination by a panel constituted by that national authority.

(2) A determination is a qualifying determination if–

(a) it relates to the issue of whether a person should be approved, or should continue to be approved, as a local authority foster parent; and

(b) it is of a prescribed description.

(3) Regulations made by virtue of sub-paragraph (1)(b) may include provision as to–

(a) the duties and powers of a panel;

(b) the administration and procedures of a panel;

(c) the appointment of members of a panel (including the number, or any limit on the number, of members who may be appointed and any conditions for appointment);

(d) the payment of fees to members of a panel;

(e) the duties of any person in connection with a review conducted under the regulations;

(f) the monitoring of any such reviews.

(4) Regulations made by virtue of sub-paragraph (3)(e) may impose a duty to pay to the appropriate national authority such sum as that national authority may determine; but such a duty may not be imposed upon a person who has applied for a review of a qualifying determination.

(5) The appropriate national authority must secure that, taking one financial year with another, the aggregate of the sums which become payable to it under regulations made by virtue of sub-paragraph (4) does not exceed the cost to it of performing its independent review functions.

(6) The appropriate national authority may make an arrangement with an organisation under which independent review functions are performed by the organisation on the national authority's behalf.

(7) If the appropriate national authority makes such an arrangement with an organisation, the organisation is to perform its functions under the arrangement in accordance with any general or special directions given by that national authority.

(8) The arrangement may include provision for payments to be made to the organisation by the appropriate national authority.

(9) Payments made by the appropriate national authority in accordance with such provision shall be taken into account in determining (for the purpose of sub-paragraph (5)) the cost to that national authority of performing its independent review functions.

(10) Where the Welsh Ministers are the appropriate national authority, sub-paragraphs (6) and (8) also apply as if references to an organisation included references to the Secretary of State.

(11) In this paragraph–

'financial year' means a period of twelve months ending with 31st March;

'independent review function' means a function conferred or imposed on a national authority by regulations made by virtue of sub-paragraph (1)(b);

'organisation' includes a public body and a private or voluntary organisation.

**12G** Regulations under section 22C may, in particular, also make provision as to the circumstances in which local authorities may make arrangements for duties imposed on them by the regulations to be discharged on their behalf.

### Promotion and maintenance of contact between child and family

**15** (1) Where a child is being looked after by a local authority, the authority shall, unless it is not reasonably practicable or consistent with his welfare, endeavour to promote contact between the child and–

(a) his parents;

(b) any person who is not a parent of his but who has parental responsibility for him; and

(c) any relative, friend or other person connected with him.

(2) Where a child is being looked after by a local authority–

(a) the authority shall take such steps as are reasonably practicable to secure that–

(i) his parents; and

(ii) any person who is not a parent of his but who has parental responsibility for him,

are kept informed of where he is being accommodated; and

(b) every such person shall secure that the authority are kept informed of his or her address.

(3) Where a local authority ('the receiving authority') take over the provision of accommodation for a child from another local authority ('the transferring authority') under section 20(2)–

(a) the receiving authority shall (where reasonably practicable) inform–

(i) the child's parents; and

(ii) any person who is not a parent of his but who has parental responsibility for him;

(b) sub-paragraph (2)(a) shall apply to the transferring authority, as well as the receiving authority, until at least one such person has been informed of the change; and

(c) sub-paragraph (2)(b) shall not require any person to inform the receiving authority of his address until he has been so informed.

(4) Nothing in this paragraph requires a local authority to inform any person of the whereabouts of a child if–

(a) the child is in the care of the authority; and

(b) the authority has reasonable cause to believe that informing the person would prejudice the child's welfare.

(5) Any person who fails (without reasonable excuse) to comply with sub-paragraph (2)(b) shall be guilty of an offence and liable on summary conviction to a fine not exceeding level 2 on the standard scale.

(6) It shall be a defence in any proceedings under sub-paragraph (5) to prove that the defendant was residing at the same address as another person who was the child's parent or had parental responsibility for the child and had reasonable cause to believe that the other person had informed the appropriate authority that both of them were residing at that address.

### Visits to or by children: expenses

**16** (1) This paragraph applies where–
(a) a child is being looked after by a local authority; and
(b) the conditions mentioned in sub-paragraph (3) are satisfied.

(2) The authority may–
(a) make payments to–
  (i) a parent of the child;
  (ii) any person who is not a parent of his but who has parental responsibility for him; or
  (iii) any relative, friend or other person connected with him,
  in respect of travelling, subsistence or other expenses incurred by that person in visiting the child; or
(b) make payments to the child, or to any person on his behalf, in respect of travelling, subsistence or other expenses incurred by or on behalf of the child in his visiting–
  (i) a parent of his;
  (ii) any person who is not a parent of his but who has parental responsibility for him; or
  (iii) any relative, friend or other person connected with him.

(3) The conditions are that–
(a) it appears to the authority that the visit in question could not otherwise be made without undue financial hardship; and
(b) the circumstances warrant the making of the payments.

**17**    [Repealed.]

### Power to guarantee apprenticeship deeds etc

**18** (1) While a child is being looked after by a local authority, or is a person qualifying for advice and assistance, the authority may undertake any obligation by way of guarantee under any deed of apprenticeship or articles of clerkship which he enters into.

(2) Where a local authority have undertaken any such obligation under any deed or articles they may at any time (whether or not they are still looking after the person concerned) undertake the like obligation under any supplemental deed or articles.

### Arrangements to assist children to live abroad

**19** (1) A local authority may only arrange for, or assist in arranging for, any child in their care to live outside England and Wales with the approval of the court.

(2) A local authority may, with the approval of every person who has parental responsibility for the child arrange for, or assist in arranging for, any other child looked after by them to live outside England and Wales.

(3) The court shall not give its approval under sub-paragraph (1) unless it is satisfied that–

(a) living outside England and Wales would be in the child's best interests;

(b) suitable arrangements have been, or will be, made for his reception and welfare in the country in which he will live;

(c) the child has consented to living in that country; and

(d) every person who has parental responsibility for the child has consented to his living in that country.

(4) Where the court is satisfied that the child does not have sufficient understanding to give or withhold his consent, it may disregard sub-paragraph (3)(c) and give its approval if the child is to live in the country concerned with a parent, guardian, special guardian, or other suitable person.

(5) Where a person whose consent is required by sub-paragraph (3)(d) fails to give his consent, the court may disregard that provision and give its approval if it is satisfied that that person–

(a) cannot be found;

(b) is incapable of consenting; or

(c) is withholding his consent unreasonably.

(6) Section 85 of the Adoption and Children Act 2002 (which imposes restrictions on taking children out of the United Kingdom) shall not apply in the case of any child who is to live outside England and Wales with the approval of the court given under this paragraph.

(7) Where a court decides to give its approval under this paragraph it may order that its decision is not to have effect during the appeal period.

(8) In sub-paragraph (7) 'the appeal period' means–

(a) where an appeal is made against the decision, the period between the making of the decision and the determination of the appeal; and

(b) otherwise, the period during which an appeal may be made against the decision.

(9) This paragraph does not apply to a local authority placing a child for adoption with prospective adopters.

### *Preparation for ceasing to be looked after*

19A It is the duty of the local authority looking after a child to advise, assist and befriend him with a view to promoting his welfare when they have ceased to look after him.

19B(1) A local authority shall have the following additional functions in relation to an eligible child whom they are looking after.

(2) In sub-paragraph (1) 'eligible child' means, subject to sub-paragraph (3), a child who–

(a) is aged sixteen or seventeen; and

(b) has been looked after by a local authority for a prescribed period, or periods amounting in all to a prescribed period, which began after he reached a prescribed age and ended after he reached the age of sixteen.

(3) The appropriate national authority may prescribe–

(a) additional categories of eligible children; and

(b) categories of children who are not to be eligible children despite falling within sub-paragraph (2).

(4) For each eligible child, the local authority shall carry out an assessment of his needs with a view to determining what advice, assistance and support it would be appropriate for them to provide him under this Act–

(a) while they are still looking after him; and

(b) after they cease to look after him,

and shall then prepare a pathway plan for him.

(5) The local authority shall keep the pathway plan under regular review.

(6) Any such review may be carried out at the same time as a review of the child's case carried out by virtue of section 26.

(7) The appropriate national authority may by regulations make provision as to assessments for the purposes of sub-paragraph (4).

(8) The regulations may in particular provide for the matters set out in section 23B(6).

### Personal advisers

19C   A local authority shall arrange for each child whom they are looking after who is an eligible child for the purposes of paragraph 19B to have a personal adviser.

### Death of children being looked after by local authorities

20 (1) If a child who is being looked after by a local authority dies, the authority–

(a) shall notify the appropriate national authority and (in the case of a local authority in England) Her Majesty's Chief Inspector of Education, Children's Services and Skills;

(b) shall, so far as is reasonably practicable, notify the child's parents and every person who is not a parent of his but who has parental responsibility for him;

(c) may, with the consent (so far as it is reasonably practicable to obtain it) of every person who has parental responsibility for the child, arrange for the child's body to be buried or cremated; and

(d) may, if the conditions mentioned in sub-paragraph (2) are satisfied, make payments to any person who has parental responsibility for the child, or any relative, friend or other person connected with the child, in respect of travelling, subsistence or other expenses incurred by that person in attending the child's funeral.

(2) The conditions are that–

(a) it appears to the authority that the person concerned could not otherwise attend the child's funeral without undue financial hardship; and

(b) that the circumstances warrant the making of the payments.

(3) Sub-paragraph (1) does not authorise cremation where it does not accord with the practice of the child's religious persuasion.

(4) Where a local authority have exercised their power under sub-paragraph (1)(c) with respect to a child who was under sixteen when he died, they may recover from any parent of the child any expenses incurred by them.

(5) Any sums so recoverable shall, without prejudice to any other method of recovery, be recoverable summarily as a civil debt.

(6) Nothing in this paragraph affects any enactment regulating or authorising the burial, cremation or anatomical examination of the body of a deceased person.

## Part III: Contributions towards maintenance of children looked after by local authorities

### *Liability to contribute*

**21** (1) Where a local authority are looking after a child (other than in the cases mentioned in sub-paragraph (7)) they shall consider whether they should recover contributions towards the child's maintenance from any person liable to contribute ('a contributor').

(2) An authority may only recover contributions from a contributor if they consider it reasonable to do so.

(3) The persons liable to contribute are–
(a) where the child is under sixteen, each of his parents;
(b) where he has reached the age of sixteen, the child himself.

(4) A parent is not liable to contribute during any period when he is in receipt of income support under Part VII of the Social Security Contributions and Benefits Act 1992[11] , of any element of child tax credit other than the family element, of working tax credit, of an income-based jobseeker's allowance or of an income-related employment and support allowance.

(5) A person is not liable to contribute towards the maintenance of a child in the care of a local authority in respect of any period during which the child is living with, under arrangements made by the authority in accordance with section 22C, a parent of his.

(6) A contributor is not obliged to make any contribution towards a child's maintenance except as agreed or determined in accordance with this Part of this Schedule.

(7) The cases are where the child is looked after by a local authority under–
(a) section 21;
(b) an interim care order;
(c) section 92 of the Powers of Criminal Courts (Sentencing) Act 2000.

### *Agreed contributions*

**22** (1) Contributions towards a child's maintenance may only be recovered if the local authority have served a notice ('a contribution notice') on the contributor specifying–
(a) the weekly sum which they consider that he should contribute; and
(b) arrangements for payment.

(2) The contribution notice must be in writing and dated.

(3) Arrangements for payment shall, in particular, include–
(a) the date on which liability to contribute begins (which must not be earlier than the date of the notice);
(b) the date on which liability under the notice will end (if the child has not before that date ceased to be looked after by the authority); and
(c) the date on which the first payment is to be made.

(4) The authority may specify in a contribution notice a weekly sum which is a standard contribution determined by them for all children looked after by them.

(5) The authority may not specify in a contribution notice a weekly sum greater than that which they consider–

---

11  Repealed by WRA 2009 ss9, 61(3), (4). Not yet in force.

(a) they would normally be prepared to pay if they had placed a similar child with local authority foster parents; and

(b) it is reasonably practicable for the contributor to pay (having regard to his means).

(6) An authority may at any time withdraw a contribution notice (without prejudice to their power to serve another).

(7) Where the authority and the contributor agree–

(a) the sum which the contributor is to contribute; and

(b) arrangements for payment,

(whether as specified in the contribution notice or otherwise) and the contributor notifies the authority in writing that he so agrees, the authority may recover summarily as a civil debt any contribution which is overdue and unpaid.

(8) A contributor may, by serving a notice in writing on the authority, withdraw his agreement in relation to any period of liability falling after the date of service of the notice.

(9) Sub-paragraph (7) is without prejudice to any other method of recovery.

### Contribution orders

23 (1) Where a contributor has been served with a contribution notice and has–

(a) failed to reach any agreement with the local authority as mentioned in paragraph 22(7) within the period of one month beginning with the day on which the contribution notice was served; or

(b) served a notice under paragraph 22(8) withdrawing his agreement,

the authority may apply to the court for an order under this paragraph.

(2) On such an application the court may make an order ('a contribution order') requiring the contributor to contribute a weekly sum towards the child's maintenance in accordance with arrangements for payment specified by the court.

(3) A contribution order–

(a) shall not specify a weekly sum greater than that specified in the contribution notice; and

(b) shall be made with due regard to the contributor's means.

(4) A contribution order shall not–

(a) take effect before the date specified in the contribution notice; or

(b) have effect while the contributor is not liable to contribute (by virtue of paragraph 21); or

(c) remain in force after the child has ceased to be looked after by the authority who obtained the order.

(5) An authority may not apply to the court under sub-paragraph (1) in relation to a contribution notice which they have withdrawn.

(6) Where–

(a) a contribution order is in force;

(b) the authority serve another contribution notice; and

(c) the contributor and the authority reach an agreement under paragraph 22(7) in respect of that other contribution notice,

the effect of the agreement shall be to discharge the order from the date on which it is agreed that the agreement shall take effect.

(7) Where an agreement is reached under sub-paragraph (6) the authority shall notify the court–

(a) of the agreement; and

(b) of the date on which it took effect.

(8) A contribution order may be varied or revoked on the application of the contributor or the authority.

(9) In proceedings for the variation of a contribution order, the authority shall specify–

(a) the weekly sum which, having regard to paragraph 22, they propose that the contributor should contribute under the order as varied; and

(b) the proposed arrangements for payment.

(10) Where a contribution order is varied, the order–

(a) shall not specify a weekly sum greater than that specified by the authority in the proceedings for variation; and

(b) shall be made with due regard to the contributor's means.

(11) An appeal shall lie in accordance with rules of court from any order made under this paragraph.

### Enforcement of contribution orders etc

24 (1) A contribution order made by a magistrates' court shall be enforceable as a magistrates' court maintenance order (within the meaning of section 150(1) of the Magistrates' Courts Act 1980).

(2) Where a contributor has agreed, or has been ordered, to make contributions to a local authority, any other local authority within whose area the contributor is for the time being living may–

(a) at the request of the local authority who served the contributions notice; and

(b) subject to agreement as to any sum to be deducted in respect of services rendered,

collect from the contributor any contributions due on behalf of the authority who served the notice.

(3) In sub-paragraph (2) the reference to any other local authority includes a reference to–

(a) a local authority within the meaning of section 1(2) of the Social Work (Scotland) Act 1968; and

(b) a Health and Social Services Board established under Article 16 of the Health and Personal Social Services (Northern Ireland) Order 1972.

(4) The power to collect sums under sub-paragraph (2) includes the power to–

(a) receive and give a discharge for any contributions due; and

(b) (if necessary) enforce payment of any contributions,

even though those contributions may have fallen due at a time when the contributor was living elsewhere.

(5) Any contribution collected under sub-paragraph (2) shall be paid (subject to any agreed deduction) to the local authority who served the contribution notice.

(6) In any proceedings under this paragraph, a document which purports to be–

(a) a copy of an order made by a court under or by virtue of paragraph 23; and

(b) certified as a true copy by the designated officer for the court,

shall be evidence of the order.

(7) In any proceedings under this paragraph, a certificate which–

(a) purports to be signed by the clerk or some other duly authorised officer of the local authority who obtained the contribution order; and

(b) states that any sum due to the authority under the order is overdue and unpaid,

shall be evidence that the sum is overdue and unpaid.

### Regulations

25   The appropriate national authority may make regulations–
   (a) as to the considerations which a local authority must take into account in deciding–
      (i)  whether it is reasonable to recover contributions; and
      (ii) what the arrangements for payment should be;
   (b) as to the procedures a local authority must follow in reaching agreements with–
      (i)  contributors (under paragraphs 22 and 23); and
      (ii) any other local authority (under paragraph 23).

# CHILDREN ACT 2004

## Co-operation to improve well-being

**10** (1) Each local authority in England must make arrangements to promote co-operation between–

(a) the authority;

(b) each of the authority's relevant partners; and

(c) such other persons or bodies as the authority consider appropriate, being persons or bodies of any nature who exercise functions or are engaged in activities in relation to children in the authority's area.

(2) The arrangements are to be made with a view to improving the well-being of children in the authority's area so far as relating to–

(a) physical and mental health and emotional well-being;

(b) protection from harm and neglect;

(c) education, training and recreation;

(d) the contribution made by them to society;

(e) social and economic well-being.

(3) In making arrangements under this section a local authority in England must have regard to the importance of parents and other persons caring for children in improving the well-being of children.

(4) For the purposes of this section each of the following is a relevant partner of a local authority in England–

(a) where the authority is a county council for an area for which there is also a district council, the district council;

(b) the police authority and the chief officer of police for a police area any part of which falls within the area of the local authority;

(c) a local probation board for an area any part of which falls within the area of the authority;

(ca) the Secretary of State in relation to his functions under sections 2 and 3 of the Offender Management Act 2007, so far as they are exercisable in relation to England;

(cb) any provider of probation services that is required by arrangements under section 3(2) of the Offender Management Act 2007 to act as a relevant partner of the authority;

(d) a youth offending team for an area any part of which falls within the area of the authority;

(e) a Strategic Health Authority and Primary Care Trust for an area any part of which falls within the area of the authority;

(f) a person providing services in pursuance of section 68 of the Education and Skills Act 2008 in any part of the area of the authority;

(fa) the governing body of a maintained school that is maintained by the authority;

(fb) the proprietor of a school approved by the Secretary of State under section 342 of the Education Act 1996 and situated in the authority's area;

(fc) the proprietor of a city technology college, city college for the technology of the arts or Academy situated in the authority's area;

(fd) the governing body of an institution within the further education sector the main site of which is situated in the authority's area;

(fe)  the Secretary of State, in relation to the Secretary of State's functions under section 2 of the Employment and Training Act 1973;

(g)  [Repealed.]

(5)  The relevant partners of a local authority in England must co-operate with the authority in the making of arrangements under this section.

(5A) For the purposes of arrangements under this section a relevant person or body may–

(a)  provide staff, goods, services, accommodation or other resources to another relevant person or body;

(b)  make contributions to a fund out of which relevant payments may be made.

(6)  [Repealed.]

(7)  [Repealed.]

(8)  A local authority in England and each of their relevant partners must in exercising their functions under this section have regard to any guidance given to them for the purpose by the Secretary of State.

(9)  Arrangements under this section may include arrangements relating to–

(a)  persons aged 18 and 19;

(b)  persons over the age of 19 who are receiving services under sections 23C to 24D of the Children Act 1989;

(c)  persons over the age of 19 but under the age of 25 who have a learning difficulty, within the meaning of section 15ZA(6) and (7) of the Education Act 1996, and are receiving services under section 15ZA of the Education Act 1996 or section 66, 86 or 87 of the Apprenticeships, Skills, Children and Learning Act 2009.

(10) In deciding for the purposes of subsection (4)(fd) whether the main site of an institution within the further education sector is situated within the area of a local authority, the authority and the governing body of the institution must have regard to any guidance given to them by the Secretary of State.

(11) In this section–

'governing body', in relation to an institution within the further education sector, has the meaning given by section 90 of the Further and Higher Education Act 1992;

'institution within the further education sector' has the meaning given by section 4(3) of the Education Act 1996;

'maintained school' has the meaning given by section 39(1) of the Education Act 2002;

'proprietor', in relation to a city technology college, city college for the technology of the arts, Academy or other school, means the person or body of persons responsible for its management;

'relevant payment', in relation to a fund, means a payment in respect of expenditure incurred, by a relevant person or body contributing to the fund, in the exercise of its functions;

'relevant person or body' means–

(a)  a local authority in England;

(b)  a relevant partner of a local authority in England.

### Arrangements to safeguard and promote welfare

**11** (1) This section applies to each of the following–

(a) a local authority in England;

(b) a district council which is not such an authority;

(c) a Strategic Health Authority;

(d) a Special Health Authority, so far as exercising functions in relation to England, designated by order made by the Secretary of State for the purposes of this section;

(e) a Primary Care Trust;

(f) an NHS trust all or most of whose hospitals, establishments and facilities are situated in England;

(g) an NHS foundation trust;

(h) the police authority and chief officer of police for a police area in England;

(i) the British Transport Police Authority, so far as exercising functions in relation to England;

(j) a local probation board for an area in England;

(ja) the Secretary of State in relation to his functions under sections 2 and 3 of the Offender Management Act 2007, so far as they are exercisable in relation to England;

(k) a youth offending team for an area in England;

(l) the governor of a prison or secure training centre in England (or, in the case of a contracted out prison or secure training centre, its director);

(m) any person to the extent that he is providing services in pursuance of section 74 of the Education and Skills Act 2008.

(2) Each person and body to whom this section applies must make arrangements for ensuring that–

(a) their functions are discharged having regard to the need to safeguard and promote the welfare of children; and

(b) any services provided by another person pursuant to arrangements made by the person or body in the discharge of their functions are provided having regard to that need.

(3) In the case of a local authority in England, the reference in subsection (2) to functions of the authority does not include functions to which section 175 of the Education Act 2002 applies.

(4) Each person and body to whom this section applies must in discharging their duty under this section have regard to any guidance given to them for the purpose by the Secretary of State.

# CHILDCARE ACT 2006

## Part 1: General Functions of Local Authority: England

### *Improvement of young children's well-being*

#### General duties of local authority in relation to well-being of young children

1 (1) An English local authority must–
   (a) improve the well-being of young children in their area, and
   (b) reduce inequalities between young children in their area in relation to the matters mentioned in subsection (2).

   (2) In this Act 'well-being', in relation to children, means their well-being so far as relating to–
   (a) physical and mental health and emotional well-being;
   (b) protection from harm and neglect;
   (c) education, training and recreation;
   (d) the contribution made by them to society;
   (e) social and economic well-being.

   (3) The Secretary of State may, in accordance with regulations, set targets for–
   (a) the improvement of the well-being of young children in the area of an English local authority;
   (b) the reduction of inequalities between young children in the area of an English local authority in relation to the matters mentioned in subsection (2).

   (4) In exercising their functions, an English local authority must act in the manner that is best calculated to secure that any targets set under subsection (3) (so far as relating to the area of the local authority) are met.

   (5) In performing their duties under this section, an English local authority must have regard to any guidance given from time to time by the Secretary of State.

#### Meaning of 'early childhood services' for purposes of section 3

2 (1) In section 3 'early childhood services', in relation to an English local authority, means–
   (a) early years provision;
   (b) the social services functions of the local authority, so far as relating to young children, parents or prospective parents;
   (c) health services relating to young children, parents or prospective parents;
   (d) the provision, under arrangements made under section 2 of the Employment and Training Act 1973, of assistance to parents or prospective parents;
   (e) the service provided by the local authority under section 12 (duty to provide information and assistance) so far as relating to parents or prospective parents.

   (2) In this section–
   'parent' means a parent of a young child, and includes any individual who–
   (a) has parental responsibility for a young child, or
   (b) has care of a young child;
   'prospective parent' means a pregnant woman or any other person who is likely to become, or is planning to become, a parent;
   'social services functions', in relation to a local authority, has the same meaning as in the Local Authority Social Services Act 1970.

### Specific duties of local authority in relation to early childhood services

3 (1) For the purpose of their general duty under section 1(1), an English local authority have the further duties imposed by subsections (2) and (3).

(2) The authority must make arrangements to secure that early childhood services in their area are provided in an integrated manner which is calculated to–

    (a) facilitate access to those services, and

    (b) maximise the benefit of those services to parents, prospective parents and young children.

(3) The authority must take steps–

    (a) to identify parents or prospective parents in the authority's area who would otherwise be unlikely to take advantage of early childhood services that may be of benefit to them and their young children, and

    (b) to encourage those parents or prospective parents to take advantage of those services.

(4) An English local authority must take all reasonable steps to encourage and facilitate the involvement in the making and implementation of arrangements under this section of–

    (a) parents and prospective parents in their area,

    (b) early years providers in their area, including those in the private and voluntary sectors, and

    (c) other persons engaged in activities which may improve the well-being of young children in their area.

(4A) In deciding what arrangements to make under this section, an English local authority must in particular have regard to–

    (a) the quantity and quality of early childhood services that are provided, or that the authority expect to be provided, in their area, and

    (b) where in that area those services are provided or are expected to be provided.

(5) In discharging their duties under this section, an English local authority must have regard to such information about the views of young children as is available to the local authority and appears to them to be relevant to the discharge of those duties.

(6) In discharging their duties under this section, an English local authority must have regard to any guidance given from time to time by the Secretary of State.

(7) In this section–

'early years provider' has the same meaning as in Part 3;

'parent' and 'prospective parent' have the same meaning as in section 2.

### Duty of local authority and relevant partners to work together

4 (1) For the purposes of this section each of the following is a relevant partner of an English local authority–

    (a) a Strategic Health Authority or Primary Care Trust for an area any part of which falls within the area of the local authority;

    (b) the Secretary of State, in relation to his functions under section 2 of the Employment and Training Act 1973.

(2) An English local authority must make arrangements to work with each of the authority's relevant partners in the performance by the authority of their duties under sections 1 and 3.

(3) Each of the relevant partners of an English local authority must work with the authority and with the other relevant partners in the making of the arrangements.

(4) An English local authority and each of their relevant partners may for the purposes of arrangements under this section–
   (a) provide staff, goods, services, accommodation or other resources;
   (b) establish and maintain a pooled fund.

(5) For the purposes of subsection (4) a pooled fund is a fund–
   (a) which is made up of contributions by the authority and the relevant partner or partners concerned, and
   (b) out of which payments may be made towards expenditure incurred in the discharge of functions of the authority and functions of the relevant partner or partners.

(6) An English local authority and each of their relevant partners falling within subsection (1)(a) must, in exercising their functions under this section, have regard to any guidance given from time to time by the Secretary of State.

### Power to amend sections 2 and 4

5   The Secretary of State may by order–
   (a) amend the definition of 'early childhood services' in section 2(1), and
   (b) in connection with any amendment of that definition, make such other amendments of section 2 or 4 as appear to him to be necessary or expedient.

## *Children's centres*

### Arrangements for provision of children's centres

5A(1) Arrangements made by an English local authority under section 3(2) must, so far as is reasonably practicable, include arrangements for sufficient provision of children's centres to meet local need.

(2) 'Local need' is the need of parents, prospective parents and young children in the authority's area.

(3) In determining what provision of children's centres is sufficient to meet local need, an authority may have regard to any children's centres–
   (a) that are provided outside the authority's area, or
   (b) that the authority expect to be provided outside their area.

(4) For the purposes of this Part and Part 3A a 'children's centre' is a place, or a group of places–
   (a) which is managed by or on behalf of, or under arrangements made with, an English local authority, with a view to securing that early childhood services in their area are made available in an integrated manner,
   (b) through which each of the early childhood services is made available, and
   (c) at which activities for young children are provided, whether by way of early years provision or otherwise.

(5) For the purposes of this section, a service is made available–
   (a) by providing the service, or
   (b) by providing advice and assistance to parents and prospective parents on gaining access to the service.

(6) Guidance given under section 3(6) in respect of arrangements made under section 3(2) by virtue of subsection (1) of this section may, in particular, relate to–

(a) circumstances in which any early childhood services should be made available through children's centres as mentioned in subsection (5)(a);

(b) circumstances in which any early childhood services should be made available through children's centres as mentioned in subsection (5)(b).

(7) A children's centre provided by virtue of arrangements made by an English local authority under section 3(2) is to be known as a Sure Start Children's Centre.

### Children's centres: staffing, organisation and operation

5B(1) Regulations may make provision about the staffing, organisation and operation of children's centres.

(2) The regulations may in particular–

(a) require English local authorities to secure that children's centres have governing bodies;

(b) impose obligations and confer powers on any such governing bodies.

### Children's centres: advisory boards

5C(1) This section applies where arrangements made by an English local authority under section 3(2) include arrangements for the provision of one or more children's centres.

(2) The authority must make arrangements to secure that each of the children's centres is within the remit of an advisory board.

(3) A children's centre is within the remit of an advisory board if it is specified in relation to the board by the responsible authority.

(4) An advisory board must provide advice and assistance for the purpose of ensuring the effective operation of the children's centres within its remit.

(5) An advisory board must include persons representing the interests of–

(a) each children's centre within its remit;

(b) the responsible authority;

(c) parents or prospective parents in the responsible authority's area.

(6) An advisory board may also include persons representing the interests of any other persons or bodies that the responsible authority think appropriate.

(7) In exercising their functions under this section, an English local authority must have regard to any guidance given from time to time by the Secretary of State.

(8) The guidance may in particular relate to–

(a) the membership of advisory boards;

(b) the organisation and operation of advisory boards.

(9) The 'responsible authority', in relation to an advisory board in respect of which arrangements have been made under subsection (2), is the authority that made the arrangements.

### Children's centres: consultation

5D(1) An English local authority must secure that such consultation as they think appropriate is carried out–

(a) before making arrangements under section 3(2) for the provision of a children's centre;

(b) before any significant change is made in the services provided through a relevant children's centre;

(c) before anything is done that would result in a relevant children's centre ceasing to be a children's centre.

(2) In discharging their duty under this section, an English local authority must have regard to any guidance given from time to time by the Secretary of State.

(3) For the purposes of this section a change in the manner in which, or the location at which, services are provided is to be treated as a change in the services.

(4) A 'relevant children's centre', in relation to an authority, is a children's centre provided by virtue of arrangements made by the authority under section 3(2).

**Duty to consider providing services through a children's centre**

5E (1) This section applies where arrangements made by an English local authority under section 3(2) include arrangements for the provision of one or more children's centres.

(2) The authority must consider whether each of the early childhood services to be provided by them should be provided through any of those children's centres.

(3) Each relevant partner of the authority must consider whether each of the early childhood services to be provided by it in the authority's area should be provided through any of those children's centres.

(4) In discharging their duties under this section, the authority and each relevant partner must take into account whether providing a service through any of the children's centres in question would–
   (a) facilitate access to it, or
   (b) maximise its benefit to parents, prospective parents and young children.

(5) In discharging their duties under this section, an English local authority and each of their relevant partners must have regard to any guidance given from time to time by the Secretary of State.

(6) For the purposes of this section, early childhood services are provided by a person or body if they are provided on behalf of, or under arrangements made with, that person or body.

(7) For the avoidance of doubt, nothing in this section is to be taken as preventing an English local authority or any of their relevant partners from providing early childhood services otherwise than through a children's centre.

**Children's centres: transitional provision**

5F (1) This section applies if immediately before the commencement date an English local authority has made arrangements for the provision of a children's centre.

(2) To the extent that this would not otherwise be the case, the arrangements are to be treated for the purposes of this Part and Part 3A as made under section 3(2).

(3) 'The commencement date' is the day on which section 198 of the Apprenticeships, Skills, Children and Learning Act 2009 comes into force.

**Children's centres: interpretation**

5G    In sections 5A to 5F–
   'children's centre' has the meaning given by section 5A(4);
   'early childhood services' has the same meaning as in section 3;
   'parent' and 'prospective parent' have the same meaning as in section 2;
   'relevant partner' has the same meaning as in section 4.

## *Provision of childcare*

### Duty to secure sufficient childcare for working parents

**6** (1) An English local authority must secure, so far as is reasonably practicable, that the provision of childcare (whether or not by them) is sufficient to meet the requirements of parents in their area who require childcare in order to enable them–

 (a) to take up, or remain in, work, or

 (b) to undertake education or training which could reasonably be expected to assist them to obtain work.

 (2) In determining for the purposes of subsection (1) whether the provision of childcare is sufficient to meet those requirements, a local authority–

 (a) must have regard to the needs of parents in their area for–

 (i) the provision of childcare in respect of which the child care element of working tax credit is payable, and

 (ii) the provision of childcare which is suitable for disabled children, and

 (b) may have regard to any childcare which they expect to be available outside their area.

 (3) In discharging their duty under subsection (1), a local authority must have regard to any guidance given from time to time by the Secretary of State.

 (4) The Secretary of State may by order amend subsection (2) (and subsection (6) so far as relating to that subsection) so as to modify the matters to which a local authority must or may have regard in determining whether the provision of childcare is sufficient.

 (5) Except in relation to a disabled child, this section does not apply in relation to childcare for a child on or after the 1st September next following the date on which he attains the age of 14.

 (6) In this section–

 'child care element', in relation to working tax credit, is to be read in accordance with section 12 of the Tax Credits Act 2002;

 'disabled child' means a child who has a disability for the purposes of the Equality Act 2010;

 'parent' includes any individual who–

 (a) has parental responsibility for a child, or

 (b) has care of a child.

### Duty to secure prescribed early years provision free of charge

**7** (1) An English local authority must secure that early years provision of a prescribed description is available free of charge for such periods as may be prescribed for each young child in their area who–

 (a) has attained such age as may be prescribed, but

 (b) is under compulsory school age.

 (2) In discharging their duty under subsection (1), a local authority must have regard to any guidance given from time to time by the Secretary of State.

. . .

### *Interpretation*

#### Meaning of childcare

**18** (1) This section applies for the purposes of this Part and Part 3.

(2) 'Childcare' means any form of care for a child and, subject to subsection (3), care includes–

(a) education for a child, and

(b) any other supervised activity for a child.

(3) 'Childcare' does not include–

(a) education (or any other supervised activity) provided by a school during school hours for a registered pupil who is not a young child, or

(b) any form of health care for a child.

(4) 'Childcare' does not include care provided for a child by–

(a) a parent or step-parent of the child;

(b) a person with parental responsibility for the child;

(c) a relative of the child;

(d) a person who is a local authority foster parent in relation to the child;

(e) a person who is a foster parent with whom the child has been placed by a voluntary organisation;

(f) a person who fosters the child privately.

(5) 'Childcare' does not include care provided for a child if the care–

(a) is provided in any of the following establishments as part of the establishment's activities–

(i) a children's home in respect of which a person is registered under Part 2 of the Care Standards Act 2000,

(ii) a care home,

(iii) a hospital in which the child is a patient,

(iv) a residential family centre, and

(b) is so provided by the person carrying on the establishment or a person employed to work at the establishment.

(6) The reference in subsection (5)(b) to a person who is employed includes a reference to a person who is employed under a contract for services.

(7) 'Childcare' does not include care provided for a child who is detained in–

(a) a young offender institution, or

(b) a secure training centre.

(8) In this section–

(a) 'local authority foster parent', 'to foster a child privately' and 'voluntary organisation' have the same meaning as in the Children Act 1989;

(b) 'care home', 'children's home' and 'residential family centre' have the same meaning as in the Care Standards Act 2000;

(ba) 'hospital' has the meaning given by section 275 of the National Health Service Act 2006.

(c) 'relative', in relation to a child, means a grandparent, aunt, uncle, brother or sister, whether of the full blood or half blood or by marriage or civil partnership.

#### Meaning of 'young child'

**19**   For the purposes of this Part and Part 3, a child is a 'young child' during the period–

(a) beginning with his birth, and

(b) ending immediately before the 1st September next following the date on which he attains the age of five.

**Meaning of 'early years provision'**

20    In this Part 'early years provision' means the provision of childcare for a young child.

## CHRONICALLY SICK AND DISABLED PERSONS ACT 1970

### Provision of welfare services

2 (1) Where a local authority having functions under section 29 of the National Assistance Act 1948 are satisfied in the case of any person to whom that section applies who is ordinarily resident in their area that it is necessary in order to meet the needs of that person for that authority to make arrangements for all or any of the following matters, namely–

(a) the provision of practical assistance for that person in his home;

(b) the provision for that person of, or assistance to that person in obtaining, wireless, television, library or similar recreational facilities;

(c) the provision for that person of lectures, games, outings or other recreational facilities outside his home or assistance to that person in taking advantage of educational facilities available to him;

(d) the provision for that person of facilities for, or assistance in, travelling to and from his home for the purpose of participating in any services provided under arrangements made by the authority under the said section 29 or, with the approval of the authority, in any services provided otherwise than as aforesaid which are similar to services which could be provided under such arrangements;

(e) the provision of assistance for that person in arranging for the carrying out of any works of adaptation in his home or the provision of any additional facilities designed to secure his greater safety, comfort or convenience;

(f) facilitating the taking of holidays by that person, whether at holiday homes or otherwise and whether provided under arrangements made by the authority or otherwise;

(g) the provision of meals for that person whether in his home or elsewhere;

(h) the provision for that person of, or assistance to that person in obtaining, a telephone and any special equipment necessary to enable him to use a telephone,

then, subject to the provisions of section 7(1) of the Local Authority Social Services Act 1970 (which requires local authorities in the exercise of certain functions, including functions under the said section 29, to act under the general guidance of the Secretary of State) and to the provisions of section 7A of that Act (which requires local authorities to exercise their social services functions in accordance with directions given by the Secretary of State it shall be the duty of that authority to make those arrangements in exercise of their functions under the said section 29.

(1A) Subsections (3) to (5) of section 32 of the National Assistance Act 1948 (which relate to the determination of any question arising under Part 3 of that Act as to a person's ordinary residence) apply in relation to any question arising under this section as to a person's ordinary residence as they apply in relation to such a question arising under Part 3 of that Act.

(2) [Repealed.]

. . .

### Application of Act to authorities having functions under the Children Act 1989

28A This Act applies with respect to disabled children in relation to whom a local authority have functions under Part III of the Children Act 1989 as it applies in relation to persons to whom section 29 of the National Assistance Act 1948 applies.

# BORDERS, CITIZENSHIP AND IMMIGRATION ACT 2009
## *Children*
### Duty regarding the welfare of children

55 (1) The Secretary of State must make arrangements for ensuring that–
    (a) the functions mentioned in subsection (2) are discharged having regard to the need to safeguard and promote the welfare of children who are in the United Kingdom, and
    (b) any services provided by another person pursuant to arrangements which are made by the Secretary of State and relate to the discharge of a function mentioned in subsection (2) are provided having regard to that need.

(2) The functions referred to in subsection (1) are–
    (a) any function of the Secretary of State in relation to immigration, asylum or nationality;
    (b) any function conferred by or by virtue of the Immigration Acts on an immigration officer;
    (c) any general customs function of the Secretary of State;
    (d) any customs function conferred on a designated customs official.

(3) A person exercising any of those functions must, in exercising the function, have regard to any guidance given to the person by the Secretary of State for the purpose of subsection (1).

(4) The Director of Border Revenue must make arrangements for ensuring that–
    (a) the Director's functions are discharged having regard to the need to safeguard and promote the welfare of children who are in the United Kingdom, and
    (b) any services provided by another person pursuant to arrangements made by the Director in the discharge of such a function are provided having regard to that need.

(5) A person exercising a function of the Director of Border Revenue must, in exercising the function, have regard to any guidance given to the person by the Secretary of State for the purpose of subsection (4).

(6) In this section–
    'children' means persons who are under the age of 18;
    'customs function', 'designated customs official' and 'general customs function' have the meanings given by Part 1.

(7) A reference in an enactment (other than this Act) to the Immigration Acts includes a reference to this section.

(8) Section 21 of the UK Borders Act 2007 (children) ceases to have effect.

# Secondary legislation[1]

## CHILDREN (LEAVING CARE) (ENGLAND) REGULATIONS 2001 SI NO 2874

### Citation, commencement and extent

1 (1) These Regulations may be cited as the Children (Leaving Care) (England) Regulations 2001 and shall come into force on 1st October 2001.

(2) These Regulations extend to England only.

### Interpretation

2 (1) In these Regulations, unless the context otherwise requires–

'the Act' means the Children Act 1989;

'placement' means the provision of accommodation and maintenance by a local authority for a child they are looking after by any of the means specified in section 23(2)(a) to (d) or (f) of the Act;

'responsible authority'–

(a) in relation to an eligible child, means the local authority looking after him; and

(b) in relation to a relevant child or a former relevant child, has the meaning given to it by section 23A(4) of the Act.

(2) In these Regulations, a reference–

(a) to a numbered regulation or Schedule is to the regulation in, or Schedule to, these Regulations bearing that number;

(b) in a regulation or Schedule to a numbered paragraph, is to the paragraph in that regulation or Schedule bearing that number.

### Eligible children

3 (1) For the purposes of paragraph 19B(2)(b) of Schedule 2 to the Act, the prescribed period is 13 weeks and the prescribed age is 14.

(2) A child falling within paragraph (3) is not an eligible child despite falling within paragraph 19B(2) of Schedule 2 to the Act.

(3) A child falls within this paragraph if he has been looked after by a local authority in circumstances where–

(a) the local authority has arranged to place him in a pre-planned series of short-term placements, none of which individually exceeds four weeks (even though they may amount in all to the prescribed period); and

(b) at the end of each such placement the child returns to the care of his parent, or a person who is not a parent but who has parental responsibility for him.

### Relevant children

4 (1) For the purposes of section 23A(3), children falling within paragraph (2) are an additional category of relevant children.

(2) Subject to paragraph (3) a child falls within this paragraph if–

(a) he is aged 16 or 17;

(b) he is not subject to a care order; and

(c) at the time when he attained the age of 16 he was detained or in hospital and immediately before he was detained or admitted to hospital he had been looked after by a local authority for a period or periods amounting in all to at least 13 weeks, which began after he reached the age of 14.

(3) In calculating the period of 13 weeks referred to in paragraph (2)(c), no account is to be taken of any period in which the child was looked after by a

local authority in any of a pre-planned series of short-term placements, none of which individually exceeded four weeks, where at the end of each such placement the child returned to the care of his parent, or a person who is not a parent but who has parental responsibility for him.

(4) For the purposes of this regulation–

    (a) 'detained' means detained in a remand centre, a young offenders institution or a secure training centre, or any other institution pursuant to an order of a court; and

    (b) 'hospital' means–

        (i) any health service hospital within the meaning of the National Health Service Act 1977; or

        (ii) a registered establishment within the meaning of section 34(1) of the Mental Health Act 1983.

(5) Subject to paragraph (7), any child who has lived with a person falling within section 23(4) of the Act ('a family placement') for a continuous period of six months or more is not to be a relevant child despite falling within section 23A(2) of the Act.

(6) Paragraph (5) applies whether the period of six months commences before or after a child ceases to be looked after by a local authority.

(7) Where a family placement within the meaning of paragraph (5) breaks down and the child ceases to live with the person concerned, the child is to be treated as a relevant child.

## Assessments and pathway plans–general

5 (1) The responsible authority must prepare a written statement describing the manner in which the needs of each eligible and relevant child will be assessed.

(2) The written statement must include, in relation to each child whose needs are to be assessed, information about, in particular–

    (a) the person responsible for the conduct and co-ordination of the assessment;

    (b) the timetable for the assessment;

    (c) who is to be consulted for the purposes of the assessment;

    (d) the arrangements for recording the outcome of the assessment;

    (e) the procedure for making representations in the event of a disagreement.

(3) The responsible authority must make a copy of the statement available to the child and the persons specified in regulation 7(5).

(4) Nothing in these Regulations shall prevent the carrying out of any assessment or review under these Regulations at the same time as any assessment, review or consideration under any other enactment.

## Involvement of the child or young person

6 (1) The responsible authority in carrying out an assessment and in preparing or reviewing a pathway plan shall, unless it is not reasonably practicable–

    (a) seek and have regard to the views of the child or young person to whom it relates; and

    (b) take all reasonable steps to enable him to attend and participate in any meetings at which his case is to be considered.

(2) The responsible authority shall without delay provide the child or young person with copies of–

(a)  the results of his assessment,

(b)  his pathway plan, and

(c)  each review of his pathway plan,

and shall ensure that the contents of each document are explained to him in accordance with his level of understanding unless it is not reasonably practicable to do so.

## Assessment of needs

7 (1)  The responsible authority shall assess the needs of each eligible child, and each relevant child who does not already have a pathway plan, in accordance with these Regulations.

(2)  The assessment is to be completed–

(a)  in the case of an eligible child, not more than three months after the date on which he reaches the age of 16 or becomes an eligible child after that age; and

(b)  in the case of a relevant child who does not already have a pathway plan, not more than three months after the date on which he becomes a relevant child.

(3)  Each responsible authority shall ensure that a written record is kept of–

(a)  the information obtained in the course of an assessment;

(b)  the deliberations at any meeting held in connection with any aspect of an assessment; and

(c)  the results of the assessment.

(4)  In carrying out an assessment the responsible authority shall take account of the following considerations–

(a)  the child's health and development;

(b)  the child's need for education, training or employment;

(c)  the support available to the child from members of his family and other persons;

(d)  the child's financial needs;

(e)  the extent to which the child possesses the practical and other skills necessary for independent living; and

(f)  the child's needs for care, support and accommodation.

(5)  The responsible authority shall, unless it is not reasonably practicable to do so, seek and take into account the views of–

(a)  the child's parents;

(b)  any person who is not a parent but has parental responsibility for the child;

(c)  any person who on a day to day basis cares for, or provides accommodation for the child;

(d)  any school or college attended by the child, or the local education authority for the area in which he lives;

(e)  any independent visitor appointed for the child;

(f)  any person providing health care or treatment to the child;

(g)  the personal adviser appointed for the child; and

(h)  any other person whose views the responsible authority, or the child consider may be relevant.

## Pathway plans

8  (1)  A pathway plan prepared under paragraph 19B of Schedule 2 to, or section 23B of, the Act, must be prepared as soon as possible after the assessment and must include, in particular, the matters referred to in the Schedule.

(2) The pathway plan must, in relation to each of the matters referred to in the Schedule, set out–
  (a) the manner in which the responsible authority proposes to meet the needs of the child; and
  (b) the date by which, and by whom, any action required to implement any aspect of the plan will be carried out.
(3) The pathway plan must be recorded in writing.

### Review of pathway plans

9 (1) The responsible authority shall review the pathway plan of each eligible, relevant and former relevant child in accordance with this regulation.
(2) The responsible authority shall arrange a review–
  (a) if requested to do so by the child or young person;
  (b) if it, or the personal adviser considers a review necessary; and
  (c) in any other case, at intervals of not more than six months.
(3) In carrying out a review, the responsible authority shall, to the extent it considers it appropriate to do so, seek and take account of the views of the persons mentioned in regulation 7(5).
(4) The responsible authority conducting a review must consider–
  (a) in the case of an eligible or relevant child, whether, in relation to each of the matters set out in the Schedule, any change to the pathway plan is necessary; and
  (b) in the case of a former relevant child, whether in relation to the matters set out in paragraphs 1, 3 and 4 of the Schedule, any change to the pathway plan is necessary.
(5) The results of the review must be recorded in writing.

### Retention and confidentiality of records

10 (1) Records relating to assessments, pathway plans and their review shall be retained by the responsible authority until the seventy-fifth anniversary of the date of birth of the child or young person to whom they relate, or if the child dies before attaining the age of 18, for a period of fifteen years beginning with the date of his death.
(2) The requirement in paragraph (1) may be complied with by retaining the original written records or copies of them, or by keeping all or part of the information contained in them in some other accessible form such as a computer record.
(3) The records mentioned in paragraph (1) must be kept securely and may not be disclosed to any person except in accordance with–
  (a) any provision of, or made under, or by virtue of, a statute under which access to such records is authorised; or
  (b) any court order authorising access to such records.

### Support and accommodation

11 (1) For the purposes of section 23B(8)(c) (support for relevant children), the responsible local authority must provide assistance in order to meet the child's needs in relation to education, training or employment as provided for in his pathway plan.
(2) For the purposes of section 23B(10), 'suitable accommodation' means accommodation–

(a) which so far as reasonably practicable is suitable for the child in the light of his needs, including his health needs and any needs arising from any disability;

(b) in respect of which the responsible authority has satisfied itself as to the character and suitability of the landlord or other provider; and

(c) in respect of which the responsible authority has so far as reasonably practicable taken into account the child's–

   (i)  wishes and feelings; and

   (ii) education, training or employment needs.

(3) For the purposes of section 24B(5) (provision of vacation accommodation)–

(a) 'higher education' means education provided by means of a course of a description referred to in regulations made under section 22 of the Teaching and Higher Education Act 1998;

(b) 'further education' has the same meaning as in the Education Act 1996 save that for the purposes of this regulation it only includes further education which is provided on a full-time residential basis.

### Functions of personal advisers

12 A personal adviser shall have the following functions in relation to an eligible or a relevant child or a young person who is a former relevant child–

(a) to provide advice (including practical advice) and support;

(b) where applicable, to participate in his assessment and the preparation of his pathway plan;

(c) to participate in reviews of the pathway plan;

(d) to liaise with the responsible authority in the implementation of the pathway plan;

(e) to co-ordinate the provision of services, and to take reasonable steps to ensure that he makes use of such services;

(f) to keep informed about his progress and wellbeing; and

(g) to keep a written record of contacts with him.

13 [Repealed.]

### Transitional provision

14 Where a child who becomes a former relevant child on or before 1st January 2002 does not already have a pathway plan, the local authority shall (as the circumstances require) assess his needs and prepare a pathway plan for him in accordance with these regulations as if he were (as the case may be) still an eligible child or a relevant child.

## SCHEDULE: MATTERS TO BE DEALT WITH IN THE PATHWAY PLAN AND REVIEW

1   The nature and level of contact and personal support to be provided, and by whom, to the child or young person.

2   Details of the accommodation the child or young person is to occupy.

3   A detailed plan for the education or training of the child or young person.

4   How the responsible authority will assist the child or young person in relation to employment or other purposeful activity or occupation.

5   The support to be provided to enable the child or young person to develop and sustain appropriate family and social relationships.

6   A programme to develop the practical and other skills necessary for the child or young person to live independently.

7   The financial support to be provided to the child or young person, in particular where it is to be provided to meet his accommodation and maintenance needs.

8   The health needs, including any mental health needs, of the child or young person, and how they are to be met.

9   Contingency plans for action to be taken by the responsible authority should the pathway plan for any reason cease to be effective.

# CARE LEAVERS (ENGLAND) REGULATIONS 2010 SI NO 2571

## Part 1: General

### Citation, commencement and application

1 (1) These Regulations may be cited as the Care Leavers (England) Regulations 2010 and come into force on 1st April 2011.

(2) These Regulations apply in relation to England only.

### Interpretation

2 (1) In these Regulations–

'the 1989 Act' means the Children Act 1989;

'personal adviser' means the person appointed–

    (i)   under paragraph 19C of Schedule 2 to the 1989 Act for an eligible child,

    (ii)  under section 23B(2) for a relevant child, or

    (iii) under section 23CA(2) for a former relevant child;

'placement' has the meaning given in section 22C(6);

'relevant child' has the meaning given in section 23A(2) and regulation 3; and

'responsible authority' means the local authority that last looked after the child.

(2) In these Regulations, save as otherwise appears, any reference to a numbered section is a reference to that section in the 1989 Act.

### Relevant children

3 (1) For the purposes of section 23A(3), children falling within paragraph (2) are an additional category of relevant children.

(2) Subject to paragraph (3), a child falls within this paragraph if–

    (a)  the child is aged 16 or 17,

    (b)  the child is not subject to a care order, and

    (c)  on attaining the age of 16 the child was detained, or in hospital, and immediately before being detained or admitted to hospital had been looked after by a local authority for a period or periods amounting in total to at least 13 weeks, which began after the child attained the age of 14.

(3) In calculating the period of 13 weeks referred to in paragraph (2)(b), no account is to be taken of any period in which the child was looked after by a local authority in the course of a pre-planned series of short-term placements, none of which individually exceeded four weeks, where at the end of each such placement the child returned to the care of their parent, or a person who is not a parent but who has parental responsibility for them.

(4) For the purposes of this regulation–

    (a)  'detained' means detained in a remand centre, a young offender institution or a secure training centre, or any other institution pursuant to an order of a court, and

    (b)  'hospital' has the meaning given in section 275(1) of the National Health Service Act 2006.

(5) Subject to paragraph (6), a child who has lived for a continuous period of six months or more (whether that period commenced before or after they ceased to be looked after) with–

(a) their parent,

(b) someone who is not their parent but who has parental responsibility for them, or

(c) where they were in care and there was a residence order in force immediately before the care order was made, a person in whose favour the residence order was made,

is not a relevant child despite falling within section 23A(2).

(6) Where living arrangements described in paragraph (5) break down and the child ceases to live with the person concerned, the child is a relevant child.

## Part 2: Assessments of Need and Pathway Plans

### Involvement of relevant child or former relevant child

4 (1) In carrying out an assessment of needs under regulation 5, and in preparing or reviewing a pathway plan under regulation 6 or 7, the responsible authority must, unless it is not reasonably practicable–

(a) seek and have regard to the views of the relevant or former relevant child to whom the assessment or pathway plan relates, and

(b) take all reasonable steps to enable the relevant or former relevant child to attend and participate in any meetings at which their case is to be considered.

(2) The responsible authority must as soon as practicable provide the relevant or former relevant child with copies of–

(a) the results of the assessment,

(b) the pathway plan,

(c) each review of the pathway plan

and must ensure that the contents of each document are explained to the relevant or former relevant child having regard to their level of understanding, unless it is not reasonably practicable to do so.

(3) The responsible authority must ensure that a written record is kept of the views obtained under paragraph (1)(a).

### Assessment of needs

5 (1) The responsible authority must assess the needs of each relevant child who does not already have a pathway plan, and each former relevant child falling within section 23CA (further assistance to pursue education or training), in accordance with this regulation.

(2) The assessment of needs must be completed–

(a) in the case of a relevant child who does not already have a pathway plan, not more than three months after the date on which the child becomes a relevant child, and

(b) in the case of a former relevant child falling within section 23CA, not more than three months after the date on which the responsible authority are informed, in accordance with section 23CA(1)(c), that the former relevant child is pursuing, or wishes to pursue, a programme of education or training.

(3) The responsible authority must ensure that a written record is kept of–

(a) the identity of the persons whose views have been sought for the purpose of carrying out the assessment,

(b) the information obtained in the course of the assessment,

(c) the deliberations at any meeting held in connection with any aspect of the assessment, and

(d) the results of the assessment.

(4) In carrying out an assessment of the needs of a relevant child who does not already have a pathway plan, the responsible authority must–

    (a) take into account–

        (i)    the child's health and development,

        (ii)   the child's needs for education, training or employment,

        (iii)  the support available to the child from members of the child's family and other persons,

        (iv)  the child's financial needs,

        (v)   the extent to which the child possesses the practical and other skills necessary for independent living, and

        (vi)  the child's needs for care, support and accommodation, and

    (b) unless it is not reasonably practicable or appropriate to do so, seek and take into account the views of–

        (i)    the child's parents,

        (ii)   any person who is not the child's parent but has parental responsibility for the child,

        (iii)  any person who on a day to day basis cares for, or provides accommodation for the child,

        (iv)  any school or institution within the further education sector attended by the child,

        (v)   the local authority for the area in which the child lives where that is different from the responsible authority,

        (vi)  the designated teacher at the school where the child is a registered pupil,

        (vii) any person providing health care or treatment to the child,

        (viii) any person by whom assistance by way of representation is provided to the child by virtue of arrangements made by the responsible authority under section 26A(*advocacy services*),

        (ix)  the personal adviser, and

        (x)   any other person whose views the responsible authority, or the child, consider may be relevant.

(5) In carrying out an assessment of the needs of a former relevant child falling within section 23CA, the responsible authority must–

    (a) take into account–

        (i)   the former relevant child's needs for education, training or employment, and

        (ii)  any other considerations the responsible authority consider relevant, and

    (b) unless it is not reasonably practicable to do so, seek and take into account the views of–

        (i)   the personal adviser, and

        (ii)  any other person whose views the responsible authority, or the former relevant child consider may be relevant.

(6) In this regulation–

    (a) 'institution within the further education sector' has the meaning given in section 91(3) of the Further and Higher Education Act 1992,

(b) 'registered pupil' has the meaning given in section 434(5) of the Education Act 1996, and

(c) 'school' has the meaning given in section 4 of the Education Act 1996.

## Pathway plans

6 (1) A pathway plan prepared under section 23B(3) (relevant children) or 23CA(3) must be prepared as soon as possible after the assessment of needs referred to in regulation 5 is completed.

(2) The pathway plan must include, in particular–

(a) in the case of a plan prepared under section 23B(3), the matters referred to in Schedule 1, and

(b) in the case of a plan prepared under section 23CA, the matters referred to in paragraphs 1 to 4 of Schedule 1.

(3) The pathway plan must, in relation to each of the matters included in it by virtue of paragraph (2), set out–

(a) the manner in which the responsible authority propose to meet the needs of the relevant or former relevant child, and

(b) the date by which, and by whom, any action required to implement any aspect of the pathway plan will be carried out.

(4) The pathway plan must be recorded in writing.

## Review of pathway plans

7 (1) The responsible authority must review the pathway plan of each relevant and former relevant child in accordance with this regulation.

(2) The responsible authority must arrange a review–

(a) if requested to do so by the relevant or former relevant child,

(b) if the responsible authority, or the personal adviser, consider a review necessary, and

(c) in any event, at intervals of not more that six months.

(3) If the responsible authority provide the relevant child or former relevant child with accommodation under section 23B or section 24B, the responsible authority must also–

(a) arrange a review as soon as is practicable after the end of a period of 28 days beginning on the day on which the accommodation is first provided, and

(b) on completing a review under sub-paragraph (a), determine at what intervals (not exceeding three months) subsequent reviews will be carried out.

(4) In carrying out a review the responsible authority must–

(a) to the extent it considers it appropriate to do so, seek and take account of the views of the persons mentioned in regulation 5(4)(b) or, as the case may be, regulation 5(5)(b), and

(b) consider whether, in relation to each of the matters set out in the pathway plan, any change is necessary.

(5) The results of the review and any change to the pathway plan must be recorded in writing.

## Part 3: Personal Advisers

## Functions of personal advisers

8 (1) A personal adviser has the following functions in relation to the relevant child or former relevant child for whom they are appointed–

(a)  to provide advice (including practical advice) and support,
(b)  where applicable, to participate in the assessment and the preparation of the pathway plan,
(c)  to participate in reviews of the pathway plan,
(d)  to liaise with the responsible authority in the implementation of the pathway plan,
(e)  to co-ordinate the provision of services, and to take reasonable steps to ensure that the child makes use of such services and that they are appropriate to the child's needs,
(f)  to remain informed about the relevant child's or former relevant child's progress and wellbeing, and
(g)  to keep a written record of contacts with, and of services provided to, the relevant or former relevant child.

(2)  In addition, where accommodation is provided to a relevant child or former relevant child by the responsible authority under section 23B or section 24B, the personal adviser must visit the relevant child or former relevant child at that accommodation–
(a)  within 7 days of the accommodation first being provided,
(b)  subsequently, before the pathway plan is reviewed under regulation 7(3), and
(c)  at subsequent intervals of not more than two months.

## Part 4: Miscellaneous

### Support and accommodation

9 (1)  For the purposes of section 23B(8)(c) (other support for relevant children), the responsible authority must provide assistance in order to meet the relevant child's needs in relation to education, training or employment as provided for in the pathway plan.

(2)  For the purposes of section 23B(10), 'suitable accommodation' means accommodation–
(a)  which so far as reasonably practicable is suitable for the relevant child in the light of their needs, including any health needs and any needs arising from any disability,
(b)  in respect of which the responsible authority have satisfied themselves as to the character and suitability of the landlord or other provider, and
(c)  in respect of which the responsible authority have, so far as reasonably practicable, taken into account the relevant child's–
(i)  wishes and feelings, and
(ii)  education, training or employment needs.

(3)  In determining for the purposes of paragraph (2)(a) whether accommodation is suitable for a relevant child, the responsible authority must have regard to the matters set out in Schedule 2.

(4)  For the purposes of section 24B(5) (provision of vacation accommodation)–
(a)  'higher education' means education provided by means of a course of a description referred to in regulations made under section 22 of the Teaching and Higher Education Act 1998, and
(b)  'further education' has the same meaning as in section 2(3) and (5) of the Education Act 1996 save that for the purposes of this regulation it only includes further education which is provided on a full-time residential basis.

### Records

10 (1) The responsible authority must establish and maintain a written case record for each relevant child and former relevant child ('the case record').

(2) The case record must include the written records required by virtue of regulation 4(3), and regulation 5(3)(a) to (c), and the following records ('relevant records')–

(a) any assessment of needs,

(b) any pathway plan,

(c) any review of a pathway plan.

(3) Relevant records must be retained by the responsible authority until the seventy-fifth anniversary of the date of birth of the relevant or former relevant child to whom they relate or, if the child dies before attaining the age of 18, for a period of fifteen years beginning with the date of death.

(4) The requirement in paragraph (1) may be complied with by retaining the original written records or copies of them, or by keeping all or part of the information contained in them in some other accessible form such as a computer record.

(5) Relevant records must be kept securely and may not be disclosed to any person except in accordance with–

(a) any provision of, or made under or by virtue of, a statute under which access to such records is authorised, or

(b) any court order authorising access to such records.

### Revocation of Regulations

11 The Children (Leaving Care) (England) Regulations 2001 are revoked.

### SCHEDULE 1: Matters to be Dealt with in the Pathway Plan and Review

#### Regulation 6

1 The nature and level of contact and personal support to be provided, and by whom, to the child or young person.

2 A detailed plan for the education or training of the child or young person.

3 How the responsible authority will assist the child or young person in relation to employment or other purposeful activity or occupation.

4 Contingency plans for action to be taken by the responsible authority should the pathway plan for any reason cease to be effective.

5 Details of the accommodation the child or young person is to occupy (including an assessment of its suitability in the light of the child's or young person's needs, and details of the considerations taken into account in assessing that suitability).

6 The support to be provided to enable the child or young person to develop and sustain appropriate family and social relationships.

7 A programme to develop the practical and other skills necessary for the child or young person to live independently.

8 The financial support to be provided to the child or young person, in particular where it is to be provided to meet accommodation and maintenance needs.

9 The health needs, including any mental health needs, of the child or young person, and how they are to be met.

**10** Details of the arrangements made by the authority to meet the child's needs in relation to identity with particular regard to their religious persuasion, racial origin and cultural and linguistic background.

### SCHEDULE 2: Matters to be Considered in Determining the Suitability of Accommodation

**Regulation 9**

**1**   In respect of the accommodation, the–
  (a) facilities and services provided,
  (b) state of repair,
  (c) safety,
  (d) location,
  (e) support,
  (f) tenancy status, and
  (g) the financial commitments involved for the relevant child and their affordability.
**2**   In respect of the relevant child, their–
  (a) views about the accommodation,
  (b) understanding of their rights and responsibilities in relation to the accommodation, and
  (c) understanding of funding arrangements.

## CARE PLANNING, PLACEMENT AND CASE REVIEW (ENGLAND) REGULATIONS 2010 SI NO 959

### Part 1: General

**Citation and commencement**

1 (1) These Regulations may be cited as the Care Planning, Placement and Case Review (England) Regulations 2010 and come into force on 1st April 2011.

  (2) These Regulations apply in relation to England only.

**Interpretation**

2 (1) In these Regulations–

'the 1989 Act' means the Children Act 1989;

'the 2002 Regulations' means the Fostering Services Regulations 2002;

'appropriate person' means–

  (a) P, where C is to live, or lives, with P;

  (b) F, where C is to be placed, or is placed, with F;

  (c) where C is to be placed, or is placed, in a children's home, the person who is registered under Part 2 of the Care Standards Act 2000 in respect of that home; or

  (d) where C is to be placed, or is placed, in accordance with other arrangements under section 22C(6)(d), the person who will be responsible for C at the accommodation;

'area authority' means the local authority for the area in which C is placed, or is to be placed, where this is different from the responsible authority;

'C' means a child who is looked after by the responsible authority;

'care plan' means the plan for the future care of C prepared in accordance with Part 2;

'case record' has the meaning given in regulation 49;

'connected person' has the meaning given in regulation 24;

'director of children's services' means the officer of the responsible authority appointed for the purposes of section 18 of the Children Act 2004;

'F' means a person who is approved as a local authority foster parent and with whom it is proposed to place C or, as the case may be, with whom C is placed;

'fostering service provider' has the meaning given in regulation 2(1) of the 2002 Regulations;

'full assessment process' has the meaning given in regulation 24(2)(c);

'health plan' has the meaning given in regulation 5(b)(i);

'independent visitor' means the independent person appointed to be C's visitor under section 23ZB;

'IRO' means the independent reviewing officer appointed for C's case under section 25A(1);

'nominated officer' means a senior officer of the responsible authority nominated in writing by the director of children's services for the purposes of these Regulations;

'P' means–

  (a) a person who is C's parent;

  (b) a person who is not C's parent but who has parental responsibility for C; or

(c) where C is in the care of the responsible authority and there was a residence order in force with respect to C immediately before the care order was made, a person in whose favour the residence order was made;

'pathway plan' has the meaning given in section 23E(1)(a);

'personal adviser' means the personal adviser arranged for C under paragraph 19C of Schedule 2 to the 1989 Act;

'personal education plan' has the meaning given in regulation 5(b)(ii);

'placement' means–

(i) arrangements made by the responsible authority for C to live with P in accordance with section 22C(2), where C is in the care of the responsible authority, or

(ii) arrangements made by the responsible authority to provide for C's accommodation and maintenance by any of the means specified in section 22C(6);

'placement plan' has the meaning given in regulation 9(1)(a);

'R' means the representative of the responsible authority who is appointed to visit C in accordance with arrangements made by them under section 23ZA;

'responsible authority' means the local authority that looks after C;

'special educational needs' and 'special educational provision' have the meanings given in section 312 of the Education Act 1996;

'temporary approval' has the meaning given in regulation 24(1); and

'working day' means any day other than–

(a) a Saturday or a Sunday,

(b) Christmas day or Good Friday, or

(c) a bank holiday in England and Wales under the Banking and Financial Dealings Act 1971.

(2) In these Regulations any reference to any document or other record includes any such document or record that is kept or provided in a readily accessible form and includes copies of original documents and electronic methods of recording information.

(3) Save as otherwise appears–

(a) any reference in these Regulations to a numbered section is a reference to that section in the 1989 Act; and

(b) any reference in these Regulations to a numbered regulation, Part or Schedule is a reference to that regulation, Part or Schedule in these Regulations.

3   These Regulations do not apply in relation to any child who is looked after by a local authority and who has been placed for adoption under the Adoption and Children Act 2002.

## Part 2: Arrangements for Looking After a Child

### Care planning

4 (1) Where C is not in the care of the responsible authority and a care plan for C has not already been prepared, the responsible authority must assess C's needs for services to achieve or maintain a reasonable standard of health or development, and prepare such a plan.

(2) Except in the case of a child to whom section 31A (care orders: care plans) applies, or where paragraph (6) applies, the care plan must be prepared before

C is first placed by the responsible authority or, if it is not practicable to do so, within ten working days of the start of the first placement.

(3) When assessing C's needs under paragraph (1), the responsible authority must consider whether C's placement meets the requirements of Part 3 of the 1989 Act.

(4) Unless paragraph (5) applies, the care plan should, so far as is reasonably practicable, be agreed by the responsible authority with–

    (a) any parent of C's and any person who is not C's parent but who has parental responsibility for C, or

    (b) if there is no such person, the person who was caring for C immediately before the responsible authority arranged a placement for C.

(5) Where C is aged 16 or over and agrees to be provided with accommodation under section 20, the care plan should be agreed with C by the responsible authority.

(6) Where C was first placed by the responsible authority before 1st April 2011, the care plan must be prepared as soon as reasonably practicable.

### Preparation and content of the care plan

5   The care plan must include a record of the following information–

    (a) the long term plan for C's upbringing ('the plan for permanence'),

    (b) the arrangements made by the responsible authority to meet C's needs in relation to–

        (i) health, including the information set out in paragraph 1 of Schedule 1 ('the health plan'),

        (ii) education and training, including, so far as reasonably practicable, the information set out in paragraph 2 of Schedule 1 ('the personal education plan'),

        (iii) emotional and behavioural development,

        (iv) identity, with particular regard to C's religious persuasion, racial origin and cultural and linguistic background,

        (v) family and social relationships and in particular the information set out in paragraph 3 of Schedule 1,

        (vi) social presentation, and

        (vii) self-care skills,

    (c) except in a case where C is in the care of the responsible authority but is not provided with accommodation by them by any of the means specified in section 22C, the placement plan,

    (d) the name of the IRO, and

    (e) details of the wishes and feelings of the persons listed in section 22(4) about the arrangements referred to in sub-paragraph (b) and the placement plan that have been ascertained and considered in accordance with section 22(4) and (5) and the wishes and feelings of those persons in relation to any change, or proposed change, to the care plan.

6 (1) The responsible authority must keep C's care plan under review in accordance with Part 6 and, if they are of the opinion some change is required, they must revise the care plan or prepare a new care plan accordingly.

(2) Save as otherwise provided in these Regulations, the responsible authority must not make any significant change to the care plan unless the proposed change has first been considered at a review of C's case.

(3) Subject to paragraph (4), the responsible authority must give a copy of the care plan–
   (a) to C, unless it would not be appropriate to do so having regard to C's age and understanding,
   (b) to P,
   (c) to the IRO,
   (d) where C is to be placed, or is placed, with F, to the fostering service provider that approved F in accordance with the 2002 Regulations,
   (e) where C is to be placed, or is placed, in a children's home, to the person who is registered under Part 2 of the Care Standards Act 2000 in respect of that home, and
   (f) where C is to be placed, or is placed, in accordance with other arrangements under section 22C(6)(d), to the person who will be responsible for C at the accommodation.
(4) The responsible authority may decide not to give a copy of the care plan, or a full copy of the care plan, to P if to do so would put C at risk of significant harm.

### Health care

7 (1) Before C is first placed by them or, if that is not reasonably practicable, before the first review of C's case, the responsible authority must make arrangements for a registered medical practitioner to–
   (a) carry out an assessment of C's state of health, and
   (b) provide a written report of the assessment, addressing the matters specified in paragraph 1 of Schedule 1,
   as soon as reasonably practicable.
(2) Paragraph (1) does not apply if, within a period of three months immediately preceding the placement, an assessment of C's state of health has been carried out and the responsible authority has obtained a written report that meets the requirements of that paragraph.
(3) The responsible authority must make arrangements for a registered medical practitioner or a registered nurse or registered midwife acting under the supervision of a registered medical practitioner to review C's state of health and provide a written report of each review, addressing the matters specified in paragraph 1 of Schedule 1–
   (a) at least once in every period of six months before C's fifth birthday, and
   (b) at least once in every period of 12 months after C's fifth birthday.
(4) Paragraphs (1) and (3) do not apply if C refuses consent to the assessment, being of sufficient age and understanding to do so.
(5) The responsible authority must take all reasonable steps to ensure that C is provided with appropriate health care services, in accordance with the health plan, including–
   (a) medical and dental care and treatment, and
   (b) advice and guidance on health, personal care and health promotion issues.

### Contact with a child in care

8 (1) This regulation applies if C is in the care of the responsible authority and they have decided under section 34(6) (refusal of contact as a matter of urgency) to refuse to allow contact that would otherwise be required by virtue of

section 34(1) or an order under section 34 (parental contact etc with children in care).

(2) The responsible authority must immediately give written notification to the following persons of the information specified in paragraph (3) ('the specified information')–

    (a) C, unless it would not be appropriate to do so having regard to C's age and understanding,

    (b) P,

    (c) where, immediately before the care order was made, a person had care of C by virtue of an order made in exercise of the High Court's inherent jurisdiction with respect to children, that person,

    (d) any other person whose wishes and feelings the responsible authority consider to be relevant, and

    (e) the IRO.

(3) The specified information is–

    (a) the responsible authority's decision,

    (b) the date of the decision,

    (c) the reasons for the decision,

    (d) the duration of the decision (if applicable), and

    (e) remedies available in case of dissatisfaction.

(4) The responsible authority may depart from the terms of any order made under section 34 by agreement with the person in relation to whom the order is made, provided that–

    (a) C, being of sufficient age and understanding, also agrees, and

    (b) written notification of the specified information is given within five working days to the persons listed in paragraph (2).

(5) Where the responsible authority has decided to vary or suspend any arrangements made (otherwise than under an order under section 34) with a view to affording any person contact with C, the responsible authority must immediately give written notification containing the specified information to the persons listed in paragraph (2).

(6) The responsible authority must record any decision made under this regulation in C's care plan.

## Part 3: Placements–General Provisions

### Placement plan

9 (1) Subject to paragraphs (2) and (4), before making arrangements in accordance with section 22C for C's placement, the responsible authority must–

    (a) prepare a plan for the placement ('the placement plan') which–

        (i) sets out how the placement will contribute to meeting C's needs, and

        (ii) includes all the matters specified in Schedule 2 as are applicable, having regard to the type of the placement, and

    (b) ensure that–

        (i) C's wishes and feelings have been ascertained and given due consideration, and

        (ii) the IRO has been informed.

(2) If it is not reasonably practicable to prepare the placement plan before making the placement, the placement plan must be prepared within five working days of the start of the placement.

(3) The placement plan must be agreed with, and signed by, the appropriate person.

(4) Where the arrangements for C's placement were made before 1st April 2011, the responsible authority must prepare the placement plan as soon as reasonably practicable.

### Avoidance of disruption in education

10 (1) Subject to paragraphs (2) and (3), if C is a registered pupil at a school in the fourth key stage, a decision to make any change to C's placement that would have the effect of disrupting the arrangements made for C's education must not be put into effect until it has been approved by a nominated officer.

(2) Before approving a decision under paragraph (1), the nominated officer must be satisfied that–

(a) the requirements of regulation 9(1)(b)(i) have been complied with,

(b) the educational provision made for C at the placement will promote C's educational achievement and is consistent with C's personal education plan,

(c) the designated teacher at the school has been consulted, and

(d) the IRO has been consulted.

(3) Paragraph (1) does not apply in any case where–

(a) the responsible authority terminates C's placement in accordance with regulation 14(3), or

(b) it is necessary for any other reason to change C's placement in an emergency,

and in such a case the responsible authority must make appropriate arrangements to promote C's educational achievement as soon as reasonably practicable.

(4) In any case not falling within paragraph (1), but where the responsible authority propose making any change to C's placement that would have the effect of disrupting the arrangements made for C's education or training, the responsible authority must ensure that other arrangements are made for C's education or training that meet C's needs and are consistent with C's personal education plan.

(5) In this regulation–

(a) 'registered pupil' has the meaning given in section 20(7) of the Children and Young Persons Act 2008, and

(b) 'school' has the meaning given in section 4 of the Education Act 1996.

### Placement out of area

### Placement decision

11 (1) Subject to paragraphs (3) and (4), a decision to place C outside the area of the responsible authority (including a placement outside England) must not be put into effect until it has been approved by a nominated officer.

(2) Before approving a decision under paragraph (1), the nominated officer must be satisfied that–

(a) the requirements of regulation 9(1)(b)(i) have been complied with,

(b) the placement is the most appropriate placement available for C and consistent with C's care plan,

(c) C's relatives have been consulted, where appropriate,

(d) the area authority have been notified, and

(e) the IRO has been consulted.

(3) In the case of a placement made in an emergency, paragraph (2) does not apply and before approving a decision under paragraph (1) the nominated officer must–

(a) be satisfied that regulation 9(1)(b)(i) and the requirements of sub-paragraph (2)(b) have been complied with, and

(b) take steps to ensure that regulation 9(1)(b)(ii) and the requirements set out in sub-paragraphs (2)(c) and (d) are complied with by the responsible authority within five working days of approval of the decision under paragraph (1).

(4) Paragraphs (1) and (2) do not apply to a decision to place C outside the area of the responsible authority with–

(a) F who is a connected person, or

(b) F who is approved as a local authority foster parent by the responsible authority.

## Placements outside England and Wales

**12** (1) This regulation applies if–

(a) C is in the care of the responsible authority, and

(b) the responsible authority make arrangements to place C outside England and Wales in accordance with the provisions of paragraph 19 of Schedule 2 to the 1989 Act (placement of a child in care outside England and Wales).

(2) The responsible authority must take steps to ensure that, so far as is reasonably practicable, requirements corresponding with the requirements which would have applied under these Regulations had C been placed in England, are complied with.

(3) The responsible authority must include in the care plan details of the arrangements made by the responsible authority to supervise C's placement.

## Notification of placement

**13** (1) Subject to paragraph (3), the responsible authority must give written notification to the persons listed in paragraph (2) of the arrangements for C's placement before the placement is made or, if the placement is made in an emergency, within five working days of the start of the placement, unless it is not reasonably practicable to do so.

(2) The persons referred to in paragraph (1) are–

(a) C, unless it would not be appropriate to do so having regard to C's age and understanding,

(b) P,

(c) if C is in the care of the responsible authority, any person who is allowed contact with C under section 34(1) and any person who has contact with C by virtue of an order under section 34,

(d) if C is looked after but is not in the care of the responsible authority, any person who has contact with C pursuant to an order made under section 8 (residence, contact and other orders with respect to children),

(e) any person who was caring for C immediately before the arrangements were made,

(f) the Primary Care Trust (or in the case of a child living or to be placed in Wales, the local health board) for the area in which C is living and, if different, for the area in which C is to be placed,

(g) C's registered medical practitioner and, where applicable, the registered medical practitioner with whom C is to be registered during the placement,

(h) any educational institution attended by, or person providing education or training for, C, and

(i) the IRO.

(3) The responsible authority may decide not to give notification to any of the persons listed in sub-paragraphs (b) to (e) if to do so would put C at risk of significant harm.

### Termination of placement by the responsible authority

14 (1) Subject to paragraphs (3) and (5), the responsible authority may only terminate C's placement following a review of C's case in accordance with Part 6.

(2) Subject to paragraphs (3) and (4), before terminating C's placement, the responsible authority must–

(a) make other arrangements for C's accommodation, in accordance with section 22C,

(b) inform the IRO,

(c) so far as is reasonably practicable, give written notification of their intention to terminate the placement to–

(i) all the persons to whom notification of the placement was given under regulation 13,

(ii) the person with whom C is placed,

(iii) where C is placed in the area of another local authority, that authority.

(3) Where there is an immediate risk of significant harm to C, or to protect others from serious injury, the responsible authority must terminate C's placement, and in those circumstances–

(a) paragraph (1) does not apply, and

(b) they must comply with paragraph (2)(a) and (b) as soon as reasonably practicable.

(4) If it is not reasonably practicable to notify any person in accordance with paragraph (2)(c), then the responsible authority must give written notification to that person, within ten working days of the date on which the placement is terminated, of the fact that the placement has been terminated.

(5) This regulation does not apply where C's placement is terminated under regulation 19(c), regulation 23(2) or regulation 25(6), nor where section 22D (review of child's case before making alternative arrangements for accommodation) applies.

## Part 4: Provision for Different Types of Placement

### Chapter 1: Placement of a Child in Care with P

#### Application

15 (1) This Chapter applies if C is in the care of the responsible authority and they, acting in accordance with section 22C(2), propose to place C with P.

(2) Nothing in this Chapter requires the responsible authority to remove C from P's care if C is living with P before a placement decision is made about C.

### Effect of contact order

16 The responsible authority must not place C with P if to do so would be incompatible with any order made by the court under section 34.

### Assessment of P's suitability to care for a child

17 Before deciding to place C with P, the responsible authority must–
  (a) assess the suitability of P to care for C, including the suitability of–
    (i) the proposed accommodation, and
    (ii) all other persons aged 18 and over who are members of the household in which it is proposed that C will live,
  (b) take into account all the matters set out in Schedule 3 in making their assessment,
  (c) consider whether, in all the circumstances and taking into account the services to be provided by the responsible authority, the placement will safeguard and promote C's welfare and meet C's needs set out in the care plan, and
  (d) review C's case in accordance with Part 6.

### Decision to place a child with P

18 (1) The decision to place C with P must not be put into effect until it has been approved by a nominated officer, and the responsible authority have prepared a placement plan for C.
  (2) Before approving a decision under paragraph (1), the nominated officer must be satisfied that–
    (a) the requirements of regulation 9(1)(b)(i) have been complied with,
    (b) the requirements of regulation 17 have been complied with,
    (c) the placement will safeguard and promote C's welfare, and
    (d) the IRO has been consulted.

### Circumstances in which a child may be placed with P before assessment completed

19 Where the nominated officer considers it to be necessary and consistent with C's welfare, the responsible authority may place C with P before their assessment under regulation 17 ('the assessment') is completed provided that they–
  (a) arrange for P to be interviewed in order to obtain as much of the information specified in Schedule 3 about P and the other persons living in P's household who are aged 18 and over as can be readily ascertained at that interview,
  (b) ensure that the assessment and the review of C's case are completed in accordance with regulation 17 within ten working days of C being placed with P, and
  (c) ensure that a decision in accordance with regulation 18 is made and approved within ten working days after the assessment is completed, and–
    (i) if the decision is to confirm the placement, review the placement plan and, if appropriate amend it, and
    (ii) if the decision is not to confirm the placement, terminate the placement.

**Support for P**

20 Where C is placed, or is to be placed, with P, the responsible authority must provide such services and support to P as appear to them to be necessary to safeguard and promote C's welfare and must record details of such services and support in C's care plan.

## Chapter 2: Placement with Local Authority Foster Parents

**Interpretation**

21 (1) In this Chapter 'registered person' has the same meaning as in the 2002 Regulations.

(2) Where C is placed jointly with two persons each of whom is approved as a local authority foster parent, any reference in these Regulations to a local authority foster parent is to be interpreted as referring equally to both such persons and any requirement to be satisfied by or relating to a particular local authority foster parent must be satisfied by, or treated as relating to, both of them.

**Conditions to be complied with before placing a child with a local authority foster parent**

22 (1) This regulation applies where the responsible authority propose to place C with F.

(2) The responsible authority may only place C with F if–

(a) F is approved by–

(i) the responsible authority, or

(ii) provided that the conditions specified in paragraph (3) are also satisfied, another fostering service provider,

(b) the terms of F's approval are consistent with the proposed placement, and

(c) F has entered into a foster care agreement either with the responsible authority or with another fostering service provider in accordance with regulation 28(5)(b) of the 2002 Regulations.

(3) The conditions referred to in paragraph (2)(a)(ii) are that–

(a) the fostering service provider by whom F is approved consents to the proposed placement, and

(b) where any other local authority currently have a child placed with F, that local authority consents to the proposed placement.

**Emergency placement with a local authority foster parent**

23 (1) Where it is necessary to place C in an emergency, the responsible authority may place C with any local authority foster parent who has been approved in accordance with the 2002 Regulations, even if the terms of that approval are not consistent with the placement, provided that the placement is for no longer than six working days.

(2) When the period of six working days referred to in paragraph (1) expires, the responsible authority must terminate the placement unless the terms of that person's approval have been amended to be consistent with the placement.

**Temporary approval of relative, friend or other person connected with C**

24 (1) Where the responsible authority is satisfied that–

(a) the most appropriate placement for C is with a connected person, notwithstanding that the connected person is not approved as a local authority foster parent, and

(b) it is necessary for C to be placed with the connected person before the connected person's suitability to be a local authority foster parent has been assessed in accordance with the 2002 Regulations,

they may approve that person as a local authority foster parent for a temporary period not exceeding 16 weeks ('temporary approval') provided that they first comply with the requirements of paragraph (2).

(2) Before making a placement under paragraph (1), the responsible authority must—

   (a) assess the suitability of the connected person to care for C, including the suitability of—
      (i) the proposed accommodation, and
      (ii) all other persons aged 18 and over who are members of the household in which it is proposed that C will live,
      taking into account all the matters set out in Schedule 4,

   (b) consider whether, in all the circumstances and taking into account the services to be provided by the responsible authority, the proposed arrangements will safeguard and promote C's welfare and meet C's needs set out in the care plan, and

   (c) make immediate arrangements for the suitability of the connected person to be a local authority foster parent to be assessed in accordance with the 2002 Regulations ('the full assessment process') before the temporary approval expires.

(3) In this regulation 'connected person' means a relative, friend or other person connected with C.

### Expiry of temporary approval

25 (1) Subject to paragraph (4), the responsible authority may extend the temporary approval of a connected person if—

   (a) it is likely to expire before the full assessment process is completed, or

   (b) the connected person, having undergone the full assessment process, is not approved and seeks a review of the decision in accordance with Regulations made under paragraph 12F(1)(b) of Schedule 2 to the 1989 Act.

(2) In a case falling within paragraph (1)(a), the responsible authority may extend the temporary approval once for a further period of up to eight weeks.

(3) In a case falling within paragraph (1)(b), the responsible authority may extend the temporary approval until the outcome of the review is known.

(4) Before deciding whether to extend the temporary approval in the circumstances set out in paragraph (1), the responsible authority must first—

   (a) consider whether placement with the connected person is still the most appropriate placement available,

   (b) seek the views of the fostering panel established by the fostering service provider in accordance with the 2002 Regulations, and

   (c) inform the IRO.

(5) A decision to extend temporary approval must be approved by a nominated officer.

(6) If the period of temporary approval and of any extension to that period expires and the connected person has not been approved as a local authority foster parent in accordance with the 2002 Regulations, the responsible authority must terminate the placement after first making other arrangements for C's accommodation.

### Independent fostering agencies–discharge of responsible authority functions

26 (1) A responsible authority may make arrangements in accordance with this regulation for the duties imposed on it as responsible authority by regulation 14(3) and regulation 22 to be discharged on their behalf by a registered person.

(2) No arrangements may be made under this regulation unless the responsible authority has entered into a written agreement with the registered person which includes the information set out in paragraph 1 of Schedule 5, and where the responsible authority proposes to make an arrangement under this regulation in relation to a particular child, the written agreement must also include the matters set out in paragraph 2 of Schedule 5.

(3) The responsible authority must report to the Chief Inspector of Education, Children's Services and Skills any concerns they may have about the services provided by a registered person.

## Chapter 3: Other Arrangements

### General duties of the responsible authority when placing a child in other arrangements

27   Before placing C in accommodation in an unregulated setting under section 22C(6)(d), the responsible authority must–

(a) be satisfied that the accommodation is suitable for C, having regard to the matters set out in Schedule 6,

(b) unless it is not reasonably practicable, arrange for C to visit the accommodation, and

(c) inform the IRO.

### Part 5: Visits by the Responsible Authority's Representative etc

### Frequency of visits

28 (1) As part of their arrangements for supervising C's welfare, the responsible authority must ensure that their representative ('R') visits C in accordance with this regulation, wherever C is living.

(2) Subject to paragraphs (3) to (6), the responsible authority must ensure that R visits C–

(a) within one week of the start of any placement,

(b) at intervals of not more than six weeks for the first year of any placement, and

(c) thereafter–

(i) where the placement is intended to last until C is aged 18, at intervals of not more than three months,

(ii) and in any other case, at intervals of not more than six weeks.

(3) Where regulation 19 applies, the responsible authority must ensure that R visits C–

(a) at least once a week until the first review carried out in accordance with Part 6, and

(b) thereafter at intervals of not more than six weeks.

(4) Where regulation 24 applies, or where an interim care order has been made in relation to C under section 38 (interim orders) and C is living with P, the responsible authority must ensure that R visits C–

(a) at least once a week until the first review carried out in accordance with Part 6, and

(b) thereafter at intervals of not more than four weeks.

(5) Where a care order has been made in relation to C under section 31 (care and supervision orders) and C is living with P, the responsible authority must ensure that R visits C–

(a) within one week of the making of the care order, and

(b) thereafter at intervals of not more than six weeks.

(6) Where C is in the care of the responsible authority but another person is responsible for the arrangements under which C is living for the time being ('C's living arrangements'), the responsible authority must ensure that R visits C–

(a) within one week of the start of C's living arrangements and within one week of any change to C's living arrangements,

(b) at intervals of not more that six weeks for the first year thereafter, and

(c) at intervals of not more than three months in any subsequent year.

(7) In addition to visits in accordance with paragraphs (2) to (6), the responsible authority must ensure that R visits C–

(a) whenever reasonably requested to do so by–

    (i)   C,

    (ii)  where paragraphs (2), (3) or (4) apply, the appropriate person, or

    (iii) where paragraph (5) applies, the person responsible for C's living arrangements,

(b) within one week of first receiving notification under section 30A of the Care Standards Act 2000 (notification of matters relating to persons carrying on or managing certain establishments or agencies), where the children's home in which C is placed for the time being is referred to in that notification.

## Conduct of visits

29   On each visit, R must speak to C in private unless–

(a) C, being of sufficient age and understanding to do so, refuses,

(b) R considers it inappropriate to do so, having regard to C's age and understanding, or

(c) R is unable to do so.

## Consequences of visits

30   Where, as the result of a visit carried out in accordance with this Part, R's assessment is that C's welfare is not adequately safeguarded and promoted by the placement, the responsible authority must review C's case in accordance with Part 6.

## Advice, support and assistance for the child

31   When making arrangements in accordance with section 23ZA(2)(b) for advice, support and assistance to be available to C between R's visits, the responsible authority must ensure that–

(a) the arrangements–

    (i)  are appropriate having regard to C's age and understanding, and

    (ii) give due consideration to C's religious persuasion, racial origin, cultural and linguistic background and to any disability C may have, and

(b) so far as is reasonably practicable having regard to C's age and understanding, C knows how to seek appropriate advice, support and assistance from them.

## Part 6: Reviews of the Child's Case

### General duty of the responsible authority to review the child's case

32 (1) The responsible authority must review C's case in accordance with this Part.

(2) The responsible authority must not make any significant change to C's care plan unless the proposed change has first been considered at a review of C's case, unless this is not reasonably practicable.

(3) Nothing in this Part prevents any review of C's case being carried out at the same time as any other review assessment or consideration of C's case under any other provision.

### Timing of reviews

33 (1) The responsible authority must first review C's case within 20 working days of the date on which C becomes looked after.

(2) The second review must be carried out not more than three months after the first, and subsequent reviews must be carried out at intervals of not more than six months.

(3) The responsible authority must carry out a review before the time specified in paragraph (1) or (2) if–

(a) the IRO so requests,

(b) regulation 30 applies,

(c) C is provided with accommodation under section 21(2)(b) or (c) and a review would not otherwise occur before C ceases to be so provided with accommodation,

(d) C is in the care of the responsible authority and is detained in a secure training centre or a young offenders institution, and a review would not otherwise occur before C ceases to be so detained, or

(e) C is looked after but is not in the care of the responsible authority and

(i) the responsible authority propose to cease to provide accommodation for C, and

(ii) accommodation will not subsequently be provided for C by C's parents (or one of them) or any person who is not C's parent but who has parental responsibility for C.

## *Conduct of reviews*

### Local authority's policy on reviews

34 (1) The responsible authority must prepare and implement a written policy regarding the manner in which they will review cases in accordance with this Part.

(2) The responsible authority must provide a copy of their policy to–

(a) C, unless it would not be appropriate to do so having regard to C's age and understanding,

(b) C's parents, or any person who is not C's parent but who has parental responsibility for C, and

(c) any other person whose views the responsible authority consider to be relevant.

### Considerations to which the responsible authority must have regard

35  The considerations to which the responsible authority must have regard in reviewing each case are set out in Schedule 7.

### The role of the IRO

36 (1) The IRO must–

(a) so far as reasonably practicable, attend any meeting held as part of the review ('the review meeting') and, if attending the review meeting, chair it,

(b) speak to C in private about the matters to be considered at the review unless C, being of sufficient understanding to do so, refuses or the IRO considers it inappropriate having regard to C's age and understanding,

(c) ensure that, so far as reasonably practicable, the wishes and feelings of C's parents, or any person who is not C's parent but who has parental responsibility for C, have been ascertained and taken into account, and

(d) ensure that the review is conducted in accordance with this Part and in particular–

(i) that the persons responsible for implementing any decision taken in consequence of the review are identified, and

(ii) that any failure to review the case in accordance with this Part or to take proper steps to implement decisions taken in consequence of the review are brought to the attention of an officer at an appropriate level of seniority within the responsible authority.

(2) The IRO may, if not satisfied that sufficient information has been provided by the responsible authority to enable proper consideration of any of the matters in Schedule 7, adjourn the review meeting once for not more than 20 working days, and no proposal considered in the course of the review may be implemented until the review has been completed.

### Arrangements for implementing decisions arising out of reviews

37  The responsible authority must–

(a) make arrangements to implement decisions made in the course, or as a result, of the review, and

(b) inform the IRO of any significant failure to make such arrangements, or any significant change of circumstances occurring after the review that affects those arrangements.

### Records of reviews

38  The responsible authority must ensure that a written record of the review is prepared, and that the information obtained in the course of the review, details of proceedings at the review meeting, and any decisions made in the course, or as a result, of the review are included in C's case record.

### Part 7: Arrangements Made by the Responsible Authority for Ceasing to Look After a Child

### Arrangements for ceasing to look after a child who is not an eligible child

39  In any case where–

(a) C is not in the care of the responsible authority and is not an eligible child, and

(b) C's circumstances have changed such that the responsible authority are likely to cease to provide C with accommodation

the care plan must include details of the advice, assistance and support that the responsible authority intend to provide for C when C ceases to be looked after by them.

## Eligible children

### Meaning of eligible child

40 (1) For the purposes of paragraph 19B(2)(b) of Schedule 2 to the 1989 Act (*meaning of eligible child*), the prescribed period is 13 weeks and the prescribed age is 14.

(2) For the purposes of paragraph 19B(3)(b) of that Schedule, if C is a child to whom regulation 48 applies, C is not an eligible child despite falling within paragraph 19B(2) of that Schedule.

### General duties

41   If C is an eligible child, the responsible authority must–

(a) assess C's needs in accordance with regulation 42, and

(b) prepare C's pathway plan, in accordance with regulation 43.

### Assessment of needs

42 (1) The responsible authority must complete the assessment of C's needs in accordance with paragraph 19B(4) of Schedule 2 to the 1989 Act not more than three months after the date on which C reaches the age of 16 or becomes an eligible child after that age.

(2) In carrying out their assessment of C's likely needs when C ceases to be looked after, the responsible authority must take account of the following considerations–

(a) C's state of health (including physical, emotional and mental health) and development,

(b) C's continuing need for education, training or employment,

(c) the support that will be available to C from C's parents and other connected persons,

(d) C's actual and anticipated financial resources and capacity to manage personal finances independently,

(e) the extent to which C possesses the practical and other skills necessary for independent living,

(f) C's need for continuing care, support and accommodation,

(g) the wishes and feelings of–

(i) C,

(ii) any parent of C's and any person who is not C's parent but who has parental responsibility for C,

(iii) the appropriate person,

(h) the views of–

(i) any person or educational institution that provides C with education or training and, if C has a statement of special educational needs, the local authority who maintain the statement (if different),

(ii) the IRO,

(iii) any person providing health (whether physical, emotional or mental health) or dental care or treatment to C,

    (iv)  the personal adviser appointed for C, and

    (v)  any other person whose views the responsible authority, or C, consider may be relevant.

### The pathway plan

**43** (1) The pathway plan must be prepared as soon as possible after the assessment of C's needs and must include, in particular–

    (a)  C's care plan, and

    (b)  the information referred to in Schedule 8.

  (2) The pathway plan must, in relation to each of the matters referred to in paragraphs 2 to 10 of Schedule 8, set out–

    (a)  the manner in which the responsible authority propose to meet C's needs, and

    (b)  the date by which, and by whom, any action required to implement any aspect of the plan will be carried out.

### Functions of the personal adviser

**44**    The personal adviser's functions in relation to C are to–

    (a)  provide advice (including practical advice) and support,

    (b)  participate in reviews of C's case carried out under Part 6,

    (c)  liaise with the responsible authority in the implementation of the pathway plan,

    (d)  co-ordinate the provision of services and take reasonable steps to ensure C makes use of such services,

    (e)  remain informed about C's progress and wellbeing, and

    (f)  maintain a written record of their contacts with C.

## Part 8: Independent Reviewing Officers and Independent Visitors

### Additional functions of independent reviewing officers

**45** (1) The IRO must ensure that, having regard to C's age and understanding, C has been informed by the responsible authority of the steps C may take under the 1989 Act and in particular, where appropriate, of–

    (a)  C's rights to apply, with leave, for a section 8 order (residence, contact and other orders with respect to children) and, where C is in the care of the responsible authority, to apply for the discharge of the care order, and

    (b)  the availability of the procedure established by them under section 26(3) for considering any representations (including complaints) C may wish to make about the discharge by the responsible authority of their functions, including the availability of assistance to make such representations under section 26A (advocacy services).

  (2) If C wishes to take legal proceedings under the 1989 Act, the IRO must–

    (a)  establish whether an appropriate adult is able and willing to assist C to obtain legal advice or bring proceedings on C's behalf, and

    (b)  if there is no such person, assist C to obtain such advice.

  (3) In the following circumstances the IRO must consider whether it would be appropriate to refer C's case to an officer of the Children and Family Court Advisory and Support Service–

    (a)  in the opinion of the IRO, the responsible authority have failed in any significant respect to–

      (i)  prepare C's care plan in accordance with these Regulations,

(ii) review C's case in accordance with these Regulations, or effectively implement any decision taken in consequence of a review,

or are otherwise in breach of their duties to C in any material respect, and

(b) having drawn the failure or breach to the attention of persons at an appropriate level of seniority within the responsible authority, it has not been addressed to the satisfaction of the IRO within a reasonable period of time.

(4) When consulted by the responsible authority about any matter concerning C, or when informed of any matter relating to C in accordance with these Regulations, the IRO must–

(a) ensure that the responsible authority have ascertained and, subject to C's age and understanding, given due consideration to, C's wishes and feelings concerning the matter in question, and

(b) consider whether to request a review of C's case.

### Qualifications and experience of independent reviewing officers

46 (1) The IRO must be registered as a social worker in a register maintained by the General Social Care Council or by the Care Council for Wales under section 56 of the Care Standards Act 2000, or in a corresponding register maintained under the law of Scotland or Northern Ireland.

(2) The IRO must have sufficient relevant social work experience with children and families to perform the functions of an independent reviewing officer set out in section 25B(1) and under these Regulations in an independent manner and having regard to C's best interests.

(3) The responsible authority must not appoint any of the following as the IRO–

(a) a person involved in preparing C's care plan or the management of C's case,

(b) R,

(c) C's personal adviser,

(d) a person with management responsibilities in relation to a person mentioned in sub-paragraphs (a) to (c), or

(e) a person with control over the resources allocated to the case.

### Independent visitors

47   A person appointed by the responsible authority as an independent visitor under section 23ZB(1) is to be regarded as independent of that authority where the person appointed is not connected with the responsible authority by virtue of being–

(a) a member of the responsible authority or any of their committees or subcommittees, whether elected or co-opted,

(b) an officer of the responsible authority employed in relation to the exercise of the functions referred to in section 18(2) of the Children Act 2004, or

(c) a spouse, civil partner or other person (whether of different sex or the same sex) living in the same household as the partner of a person falling within sub-paragraph (a) or (b).

## Part 9: Miscellaneous

### Application of these Regulations with modifications to short breaks

48 (1) In the circumstances set out in paragraph (2) these Regulations apply with the modifications set out in paragraph (3).

(2) The circumstances are that–
  (a) C is not in the care of the responsible authority,
  (b) the responsible authority have arranged to place C in a series of short-term placements with the same person or in the same accommodation ('short breaks'), and
  (c) the arrangement is such that–
    (i)   no single placement is intended to last for longer than 17 days,
    (ii)  at the end of each such placement, C returns to the care of C's parent or a person who is not C's parent but who has parental responsibility for C, and
    (iii) the short breaks do not exceed 75 days in total in any period of 12 months.
(3) The modifications are that–
  (a) regulations 5 and 9 do not apply, but instead the care plan must set out the arrangements made to meet C's needs with particular regard to–
    (i)   C's health and emotional and behavioural development, in particular in relation to any disability C may have,
    (ii)  promoting contact between C and C's parents and any other person who is not C's parent but who has parental responsibility for C, during any period when C is placed,
    (iii) C's leisure interests, and
    (iv)  promoting C's educational achievement,
    and must include the name and address of C's registered medical practitioner, and the information set out in paragraph 3 of Schedule 2, where appropriate,
  (b) regulations 7, 13 and 49(2)(b) do not apply,
  (c) regulation 28(2) does not apply, but instead the responsible authority must ensure that R visits C on days when C is in fact placed, at regular intervals to be agreed with the IRO and C's parents (or any person who is not C's parent but who has parental responsibility for C) and recorded in the care plan before the start of the first placement, and in any event–
    (i)  the first visit must take place within three months of the start of the first placement, or as soon as practicable thereafter, and
    (ii) subsequent visits must take place at intervals of not more than six months, for as long as the short breaks continue,
  (d) regulation 33 does not apply, but instead–
    (i)  the responsible authority must first review C's case within three months of the start of the first placement, and
    (ii) the second and subsequent reviews must be carried out at intervals of not more than six months.

### Records

### Establishment of records

49 (1) The responsible authority must establish and maintain a written case record for C ('C's case record'), if one is not already in existence.
  (2) The case record must include–
    (a) C's care plan, including any changes made to the care plan and any subsequent plans,
    (b) reports obtained under regulation 7,

(c) any other document created or considered as part of any assessment of C's needs, or of any review of C's case,

(d) any court order relating to C,

(e) details of any arrangements that have been made by the responsible authority with any other local authority or with an independent fostering agency under regulation 26 and Schedule 5, or with a provider of social work services, under which any of the responsible authority's functions in relation to C are discharged by that local authority or independent fostering agency or provider of social work services.

## HOMELESSNESS (PRIORITY NEED FOR ACCOMMODATION) (ENGLAND) ORDER 2002 SI NO 2051

### Citation, commencement and interpretation

1 (1) This Order may be cited as the Homelessness (Priority Need for Accommodation) (England) Order 2002 and shall come into force on the day after the day on which it is made.

(2) This Order extends to England only.

(3) In this Order–

'looked after, accommodated or fostered' has the meaning given by section 24(2) of the Children Act 1989; and

'relevant student' means a person to whom section 24B(3) of that Act applies–

(a) who is in full-time further or higher education; and

(b) whose term-time accommodation is not available to him during a vacation.

### Priority need for accommodation

2 The descriptions of person specified in the following articles have a priority need for accommodation for the purposes of Part 7 of the Housing Act 1996.

### Children aged 16 or 17

3 (1) A person (other than a person to whom paragraph (2) below applies) aged sixteen or seventeen who is not a relevant child for the purposes of section 23A of the Children Act 1989.

(2) This paragraph applies to a person to whom a local authority owe a duty to provide accommodation under section 20 of that Act (provision of accommodation for children in need).

### Young people under 21

4 (1) A person (other than a relevant student) who–

(a) is under twenty-one; and

(b) at any time after reaching the age of sixteen, but while still under eighteen, was, but is no longer, looked after, accommodated or fostered.

### Vulnerability: institutional backgrounds

5 (1) A person (other than a relevant student) who has reached the age of twenty-one and who is vulnerable as a result of having been looked after, accommodated or fostered.

(2) A person who is vulnerable as a result of having been a member of Her Majesty's regular naval, military or air forces.

(3) A person who is vulnerable as a result of–

(a) having served a custodial sentence (within the meaning of section 76 of the Powers of Criminal Courts (Sentencing) Act 2000);

(b) having been committed for contempt of court or any other kindred offence;

(c) having been remanded in custody (within the meaning of paragraph (b), (c) or (d) of section 88(1) of that Act).

### Vulnerability: fleeing violence or threats of violence

6 A person who is vulnerable as a result of ceasing to occupy accommodation by reason of violence from another person or threats of violence from another person which are likely to be carried out.

# International conventions

## UN CONVENTION ON THE RIGHTS OF THE CHILD (EXTRACTS)

### PART I

### Article 1

For the purposes of the present Convention, a child means every human being below the age of eighteen years unless under the law applicable to the child, majority is attained earlier.

### Article 2

1. States Parties shall respect and ensure the rights set forth in the present Convention to each child within their jurisdiction without discrimination of any kind, irrespective of the child's or his or her parent's or legal guardian's race, colour, sex, language, religion, political or other opinion, national, ethnic or social origin, property, disability, birth or other status.
2. States Parties shall take all appropriate measures to ensure that the child is protected against all forms of discrimination or punishment on the basis of the status, activities, expressed opinions, or beliefs of the child's parents, legal guardians, or family members.

### Article 3

1. In all actions concerning children, whether undertaken by public or private social welfare institutions, courts of law, administrative authorities or legislative bodies, the best interests of the child shall be a primary consideration.
2. States Parties undertake to ensure the child such protection and care as is necessary for his or her well-being, taking into account the rights and duties of his or her parents, legal guardians, or other individuals legally responsible for him or her, and, to this end, shall take all appropriate legislative and administrative measures.
3. States Parties shall ensure that the institutions, services and facilities responsible for the care or protection of children shall conform with the standards established by competent authorities, particularly in the areas of safety, health, in the number and suitability of their staff, as well as competent supervision.

### Article 4

States Parties shall undertake all appropriate legislative, administrative, and other measures for the implementation of the rights recognized in the present Convention. With regard to economic, social and cultural rights, States Parties shall undertake such measures to the maximum extent of their 361 available resources and, where needed, within the framework of international co-operation.

. . .

## Article 9

1. States Parties shall ensure that a child shall not be separated from his or her parents against their will, except when competent authorities subject to judicial review determine, in accordance with applicable law and procedures, that such separation is necessary for the best interests of the child. Such determination may be necessary in a particular case such as one involving abuse or neglect of the child by the parents, or one where the parents are living separately and a decision must be made as to the child's place of residence.
2. In any proceedings pursuant to paragraph 1 of the present article, all interested parties shall be given an opportunity to participate in the proceedings and make their views known.
3. States Parties shall respect the right of the child who is separated from one or both parents to maintain personal relations and direct contact with both parents on a regular basis, except if it is contrary to the child's best interests.
4. Where such separation results from any action initiated by a State Party, such as the detention, imprisonment, exile, deportation or death (including death arising from any cause while the person is in the custody of the State) of one or both parents or of the child, that State Party shall, upon request, provide the parents, the child or, if appropriate, another member of the family with the essential information concerning the whereabouts of the absent member(s) of the family unless the provision of the information would be detrimental to the well-being of the child. States Parties shall further ensure that the submission of such a request shall of itself entail no adverse consequences for the person(s) concerned.

. . .

## Article 12

1. States Parties shall assure to the child who is capable of forming his or her own views the right to express those views freely in all matters affecting the child, the views of the child being given due weight in accordance with the age and maturity of the child.
2. For this purpose, the child shall in particular be provided the opportunity to be heard in any judicial and administrative proceedings affecting the child, either directly, or through a representative or an appropriate body, in a manner consistent with the procedural rules of national law.

. . .

## Article 18

1. States Parties shall use their best efforts to ensure recognition of the principle that both parents have common responsibilities for the upbringing and development of the child. Parents or, as the case may be, legal guardians, have the primary responsibility for the upbringing and development of the child. The best interests of the child will be their basic concern.

2. For the purpose of guaranteeing and promoting the rights set forth in the present Convention, States Parties shall render appropriate assistance to parents and legal guardians in the performance of their child-rearing responsibilities and shall ensure the development of institutions, facilities and services for the care of children.

3. States Parties shall take all appropriate measures to ensure that children of working parents have the right to benefit from child-care services and facilities for which they are eligible.

## Article 19

1. States Parties shall take all appropriate legislative, administrative, social and educational measures to protect the child from all forms of physical or mental violence, injury or abuse, neglect or negligent treatment, maltreatment or exploitation, including sexual abuse, while in the care of parent(s), legal guardian(s) or any other person who has the care of the child.

2. Such protective measures should, as appropriate, include effective procedures for the establishment of social programmes to provide necessary support for the child and for those who have the care of the child, as well as for other forms of prevention and for identification, reporting, referral, investigation, treatment and follow-up of instances of child maltreatment described heretofore, and, as appropriate, for judicial involvement.

. . .

## Article 22

1. States Parties shall take appropriate measures to ensure that a child who is seeking refugee status or who is considered a refugee in accordance with applicable international or domestic law and procedures shall, whether unaccompanied or accompanied by his or her parents or by any other person, receive appropriate protection and humanitarian assistance in the enjoyment of applicable rights set forth in the present Convention and in other international human rights or humanitarian instruments to which the said States are Parties.

2. For this purpose, States Parties shall provide, as they consider appropriate, co-operation in any efforts by the United Nations and other competent intergovernmental organizations or non-governmental organizations co-operating with the United Nations to protect and assist such a child and to trace the parents or other members of the family of any refugee child in order to obtain information necessary for reunification with his or her family. In cases where no parents or other members of the family can be found, the child shall be accorded the same protection as any other child permanently or temporarily deprived of his or her family environment for any reason , as set forth in the present Convention.

## Article 23

1. States Parties recognize that a mentally or physically disabled child should enjoy a full and decent life, in conditions which ensure dignity, promote self-reliance and facilitate the child's active participation in the community.

2. States Parties recognize the right of the disabled child to special care and shall encourage and ensure the extension, subject to available resources, to the

eligible child and those responsible for his or her care, of assistance for which application is made and which is appropriate to the child's condition and to the circumstances of the parents or others caring for the child.

3. Recognizing the special needs of a disabled child, assistance extended in accordance with paragraph 2 of the present article shall be provided free of charge, whenever possible, taking into account the financial resources of the parents or others caring for the child, and shall be designed to ensure that the disabled child has effective access to and receives education, training, health care services, rehabilitation services, preparation for employment and recreation opportunities in a manner conducive to the child's achieving the fullest possible social integration and individual development, including his or her cultural and spiritual development

4. States Parties shall promote, in the spirit of international cooperation, the exchange of appropriate information in the field of preventive health care and of medical, psychological and functional treatment of disabled children, including dissemination of and access to information concerning methods of rehabilitation, education and vocational services, with the aim of enabling States Parties to improve their capabilities and skills and to widen their experience in these areas. In this regard, particular account shall be taken of the needs of developing countries.

## Article 24

1. States Parties recognize the right of the child to the enjoyment of the highest attainable standard of health and to facilities for the treatment of illness and rehabilitation of health. States Parties shall strive to ensure that no child is deprived of his or her right of access to such health care services.

2. States Parties shall pursue full implementation of this right and, in particular, shall take appropriate measures:
   (a) To diminish infant and child mortality;
   (b) To ensure the provision of necessary medical assistance and health care to all children with emphasis on the development of primary health care;
   (c) To combat disease and malnutrition, including within the framework of primary health care, through, inter alia, the application of readily available technology and through the provision of adequate nutritious foods and clean drinking-water, taking into consideration the dangers and risks of environmental pollution;
   (d) To ensure appropriate pre-natal and post-natal health care for mothers;
   (e) To ensure that all segments of society, in particular parents and children, are informed, have access to education and are supported in the use of basic knowledge of child health and nutrition, the advantages of breastfeeding, hygiene and environmental sanitation and the prevention of accidents;
   (f) To develop preventive health care, guidance for parents and family planning education and services.

3. States Parties shall take all effective and appropriate measures with a view to abolishing traditional practices prejudicial to the health of children.

4. States Parties undertake to promote and encourage international co-operation with a view to achieving progressively the full realization of the right recognized in the present article. In this regard, particular account shall be taken of the needs of developing countries.

## Article 25
States Parties recognize the right of a child who has been placed by the competent authorities for the purposes of care, protection or treatment of his or her physical or mental health, to a periodic review of the treatment provided to the child and all other circumstances relevant to his or her placement.

. . .

## Article 27
1. States Parties recognize the right of every child to a standard of living adequate for the child's physical, mental, spiritual, moral and social development.
2. The parent(s) or others responsible for the child have the primary responsibility to secure, within their abilities and financial capacities, the conditions of living necessary for the child's development.
3. States Parties, in accordance with national conditions and within their means, shall take appropriate measures to assist parents and others responsible for the child to implement this right and shall in case of need provide material assistance and support programmes, particularly with regard to nutrition, clothing and housing.
4. States Parties shall take all appropriate measures to secure the recovery of maintenance for the child from the parents or other persons having financial responsibility for the child, both within the State Party and from abroad. In particular, where the person having financial responsibility for the child lives in a State different from that of the child, States Parties shall promote the accession to international agreements or the conclusion of such agreements, as well as the making of other appropriate arrangements.

## Article 28
1. States Parties recognize the right of the child to education, and with a view to achieving this right progressively and on the basis of equal opportunity, they shall, in particular:
   (a) Make primary education compulsory and available free to all;
   (b) Encourage the development of different forms of secondary education, including general and vocational education, make them available and accessible to every child, and take appropriate measures such as the introduction of free education and offering financial assistance in case of need;
   (c) Make higher education accessible to all on the basis of capacity by every appropriate means;
   (d) Make educational and vocational information and guidance available and accessible to all children;
   (e) Take measures to encourage regular attendance at schools and the reduction of drop-out rates.
2. States Parties shall take all appropriate measures to ensure that school discipline is administered in a manner consistent with the child's human dignity and in conformity with the present Convention.
3. States Parties shall promote and encourage international cooperation in matters relating to education, in particular with a view to contributing to the elimination of ignorance and illiteracy throughout the world and facilitating access to scientific and technical knowledge and modern teaching methods.

In this regard, particular account shall be taken of the needs of developing countries.

## Article 29

1. States Parties agree that the education of the child shall be directed to:
   (a) The development of the child's personality, talents and mental and physical abilities to their fullest potential;
   (b) The development of respect for human rights and fundamental freedoms, and for the principles enshrined in the Charter of the United Nations;
   (c) The development of respect for the child's parents, his or her own cultural identity, language and values, for the national values of the country in which the child is living, the country from which he or she may originate, and for civilizations different from his or her own;
   (d) The preparation of the child for responsible life in a free society, in the spirit of understanding, peace, tolerance, equality of sexes, and friendship among all peoples, ethnic, national and religious groups and persons of indigenous origin;
   (e) The development of respect for the natural environment.
2. No part of the present article or article 28 shall be construed so as to interfere with the liberty of individuals and bodies to establish and direct educational institutions, subject always to the observance of the principle set forth in paragraph 1 of the present article and to the requirements that the education given in such institutions shall conform to such minimum standards as may be laid down by the State.

. . .

## Article 31

1. States Parties recognize the right of the child to rest and leisure, to engage in play and recreational activities appropriate to the age of the child and to participate freely in cultural life and the arts.
2. States Parties shall respect and promote the right of the child to participate fully in cultural and artistic life and shall encourage the provision of appropriate and equal opportunities for cultural, artistic, recreational and leisure activity.

. . .

## Article 34

States Parties undertake to protect the child from all forms of sexual exploitation and sexual abuse. For these purposes, States Parties shall in particular take all appropriate national, bilateral and multilateral measures to prevent:
   (a) The inducement or coercion of a child to engage in any unlawful sexual activity;
   (b) The exploitative use of children in prostitution or other unlawful sexual practices;
   (c) The exploitative use of children in pornographic performances and materials.

. . .

**Article 40**

1. States Parties recognize the right of every child alleged as, accused of, or recognized as having infringed the penal law to be treated in a manner consistent with the promotion of the child's sense of dignity and worth, which reinforces the child's respect for the human rights and fundamental freedoms of others and which takes into account the child's age and the desirability of promoting the child's reintegration and the child's assuming a constructive role in society.

2. To this end, and having regard to the relevant provisions of international instruments, States Parties shall, in particular, ensure that:

    (a) No child shall be alleged as, be accused of, or recognized as having infringed the penal law by reason of acts or omissions that were not prohibited by national or international law at the time they were committed;

    (b) Every child alleged as or accused of having infringed the penal law has at least the following guarantees:

        (i)   To be presumed innocent until proven guilty according to law;

        (ii)  To be informed promptly and directly of the charges against him or her, and, if appropriate, through his or her parents or legal guardians, and to have legal or other appropriate assistance in the preparation and presentation of his or her defence;

        (iii) To have the matter determined without delay by a competent, independent and impartial authority or judicial body in a fair hearing according to law, in the presence of legal or other appropriate assistance and, unless it is considered not to be in the best interest of the child, in particular, taking into account his or her age or situation, his or her parents or legal guardians;

        (iv)  Not to be compelled to give testimony or to confess guilt; to examine or have examined adverse witnesses and to obtain the participation and examination of witnesses on his or her behalf under conditions of equality;

        (v)   If considered to have infringed the penal law, to have this decision and any measures imposed in consequence thereof reviewed by a higher competent, independent and impartial authority or judicial body according to law;

        (vi)  To have the free assistance of an interpreter if the child cannot understand or speak the language used;

        (vii) To have his or her privacy fully respected at all stages of the proceedings.

3. States Parties shall seek to promote the establishment of laws, procedures, authorities and institutions specifically applicable to children alleged as, accused of, or recognized as having infringed the penal law, and, in particular:

    (a) The establishment of a minimum age below which children shall be presumed not to have the capacity to infringe the penal law;

    (b) Whenever appropriate and desirable, measures for dealing with such children without resorting to judicial proceedings, providing that human rights and legal safeguards are fully respected.

4. A variety of dispositions, such as care, guidance and supervision orders; counselling; probation; foster care; education and vocational training programmes and other alternatives to institutional care shall be available to ensure that

children are dealt with in a manner appropriate to their well-being and proportionate both to their circumstances and the offence.

. . .

## PART II

### Article 42
States Parties undertake to make the principles and provisions of the Convention widely known, by appropriate and active means, to adults and children alike.

# Guidance

### Framework for the Assessment of Children in Need and their Families, Department of Health, 2000, chapters 3 and 4[1]

# 3 The Process of Assessing Children in Need

## Process of Assessment and Timing

3.1   Assessment is the first stage in helping a vulnerable child and his or her family, its purpose being 'to contribute to the understanding necessary for appropriate planning' (Compton and Galaway, 1989) and action. Assessment has several phases which overlap and lead into planning, action and review:

- clarification of source of referral and reason;

- acquisition of information;

- exploring facts and feelings;

- giving meaning to the situation which distinguishes the child and family's understanding and feelings from those of the professionals;

- reaching an understanding of what is happening, problems, strengths and difficulties, and the impact on the child (with the family wherever possible);

- drawing up an analysis of the needs of the child and parenting capacity within their family and community context as a basis for formulating a plan.

3.2   Prior to social services departments becoming involved with a child and family, a number of other agencies and community based groups may have had contact with the family. For some children, assessments will have already been carried out for purposes other than determining whether they are a child in need. In particular, health and education will have undertaken routine assessments as part of monitoring children's developmental progress. The familiarity of other agencies with the Assessment Framework will assist when making a referral to a social services department or contributing to an assessment of a child in need, thereby facilitating a common understanding of the child's needs within their family context.

3.3   The response from social services departments to an initial contact or a referral requesting help is critically important. At that point the foundation is laid for future work with the child or family. Children and families may have contact with social services staff in a wide range of settings. These may be as diverse as a family or day centre, a social services area office, an accident and emergency, adult or paediatric unit in a hospital, an education setting, an adolescent drop-in service or specialist services for adults. Not all staff in these settings will be professionals or qualified in work with children and families. This will apply particularly to those who work predominantly

---

with adults. Whoever has first contact with a child or family member, however, has a vital role in influencing the course of future work. It is quite clear from research that the quality of the early or initial contact affects later working relationships with professionals. Furthermore, recording of information about the initial contact or referral contributes to the first phase of assessment. It is essential, therefore, that all staff responding to families or to referrers are familiar with the principles which underpin the Assessment Framework and are aware of the importance of the information collected and recorded at this stage.

3.4  For unqualified or inexperienced staff, the NSPCC chart *Referrals Involving A Child* (Cleaver *et al*, 1998) may act as a useful aide memoire to ensure that important information, which will assist later decision making, is not overlooked. It should not be treated as a check list but, used alongside local agency referral forms, it can serve as a reminder of:

- issues which may need to be covered in a response to the referrer;

- matters raised by the referrer that should be recorded.

The chart is included in Appendix C.

3.5  Arrangements for managing the reception of initial contacts or referrals vary widely according to local circumstances. It is important that social services for adults are aware of their responsibilities to children of adults who have parenting responsibilities and ensure that an initial assessment takes place to ascertain whether the children are children in need under s17 of the Children Act 1989 (Department of Health, forthcoming, a).

3.6  It is important also that each social services department has structures and systems in place to ensure an effective, accessible and speedy response to children and families. Some local authorities are developing innovative approaches to referrals and initial assessment. These include local telephone help lines, help desks, multi-agency information and advice centres and drop-in services. An example of this is the help desk service established in a rural county below (Figure 3). When there are such arrangements, it becomes imperative that reception staff are carefully selected and

**FEATURES:**

- one accessible, responsive point of contact in a district for child and family referrals.

- staffed by a team of specially selected and trained unqualified referral and information co-ordinators, administrative reception staff, qualified social workers (to undertake assessments of children whose welfare may need safeguarding and promoting) and a team manager.

- priority to provide a safe short term service at the front end through:
  - advice and advocacy eg. welfare benefits
  - information
  - help eg. by signposting
  - referral taking by telephone and personal interview
  - initial and core assessments of children in need
  - direct access to practical services

Figure 3  **Helpdesk for Children's Services in a Rural County**

trained for their tasks. Reception staff will also need the support of qualified practitioners and managers to ensure that situations of serious or immediate concern about a child receive prompt and expert professional attention.

3.7    Time, as discussed in Chapter 1, is critical in a child's life. A timely response to responding to a child's needs means that the process of assessment cannot continue unchecked over a prolonged period without an analysis being made of what is happening and what action is needed, however difficult or complex the child's circumstances. Prior to the publication of the Government's Objectives for children's social services (Department of Health, 1999e), no timescales had been set for completing assessments of children in need, although there had been timescales for action to be taken to protect children where there were concerns that a child was suffering or likely to suffer significant harm. This has now been remedied and timescales have been specified in the objectives for children's social services.

3.8    There is an expectation that **within one working day** of a referral being received or new information coming to or from within a social services department about an open case, there will be a decision about what response is required. A referral is defined as a request for services to be provided by the social services department. The response may include no action, but that is itself a decision and should be made promptly and recorded. The referrer should be informed of the decision and its rationale, as well as the parents or caregivers and the child, if appropriate.

3.9    A decision to gather more information constitutes an initial assessment. An initial assessment is defined as a brief assessment of each child referred to social services with a request for services to be provided. This should be undertaken **within a maximum of 7 working days** but could be very brief depending on the child's circumstances. It should address the dimensions of the Assessment Framework, determining whether the child is in need, the nature of any services required, from where and within what timescales, and whether a further, more detailed core assessment should be undertaken. An initial assessment is deemed to have commenced at the point of referral to the social services department or when new information on an open case indicates an initial assessment should be repeated. All staff responding to referrals and undertaking initial assessments should address the dimensions which constitute the Assessment Framework. There is more detailed discussion about the contribution of respective agencies in Chapter 5.

3.10    Depending on the child's circumstances, an initial assessment may include some or all of the following:

- interviews with child and family members, as appropriate;
- involvement of other agencies in gathering and providing information, as appropriate;
- consultation with supervisor/manager;
- record of initial analysis;
- decisions on further action/no action;
- record of decisions/rationale with family/agencies;
- informing other agencies of the decisions;

- statement to the family of decisions made and, if a child is in need, the plan for providing support.

As part of any initial assessment, the child should be seen. This includes observation and talking with the child in an age appropriate manner. This is further discussed in paragraphs 3.41 to 3.43.

3.11 **A core assessment** is defined as an in-depth assessment which addresses the central or most important aspects of the needs of a child and the capacity of his or her parents or caregivers to respond appropriately to these needs within the wider family and community context. While this assessment is led by social services, it will invariably involve other agencies or independent professionals, who will either provide information they hold about the child or parents, contribute specialist knowledge or advice to social services or undertake specialist assessments. Specific assessments of the child and/or family members may have already been undertaken prior to referral to the social services department. The findings from these should inform this assessment. At the conclusion of this phase of assessment, there should be an analysis of the findings which will provide an understanding of the child's circumstances and inform planning, case objectives and the nature of service provision. The timescale for completion of the core assessment is a **maximum of 35 working days**. A core assessment is deemed to have commenced at the point the initial assessment ended, or a strategy discussion decided to initiate enquiries under s47, or new information obtained on an open case indicates a core assessment should be undertaken. Where specialist assessments have been commissioned by social services from other agencies or independent professionals, it is recognised that they will not necessarily be completed within the 35 working day period. Appropriate services should be provided whilst awaiting the completion of the specialist assessment.

3.12 The Department of Health has published an **Initial Assessment Record**, which has been developed for all staff to record salient information about a child's needs, the parents' capacity and the family's circumstances, to assist in determining the social services' response and whether a core assessment should be considered. This record is consistent with the **Core Assessment Record**. These have been developed to assist in assessing the child's developmental needs in an age appropriate manner for the following age bands: 0–2 years, 3–4 years, 5–9 years, 10–14 years and 15 and upwards. These age bands are the same as those used in **Looking After Children Assessment and Action Records** (Department of Health, 1995b). The initial and core assessment recording forms have been designed to assist in the analysis of a child and family's circumstances (Department of Health and Cleaver, 2000) and in the development and reviewing of a plan of action.

3.13 At the conclusion of either an initial or core assessment, the parent(s) and child, if appropriate, should be informed in writing, and/or in another more appropriate medium, of the decisions made and be offered the opportunity to record their views, disagreements and to ask for corrections to recorded information. Agencies and individuals involved in the assessment should also be informed of the decisions, with reasons for these made clear. This sharing of information is important to assist agencies' own practice in their work with the child and family. Local authorities are required by section 26 of the Children Act 1989 to establish complaints procedures, and children and parents should be provided with information about these. Parents

Figure 4  **Maximum Timescales for Analysing the Needs of Child and Parenting Capacity**

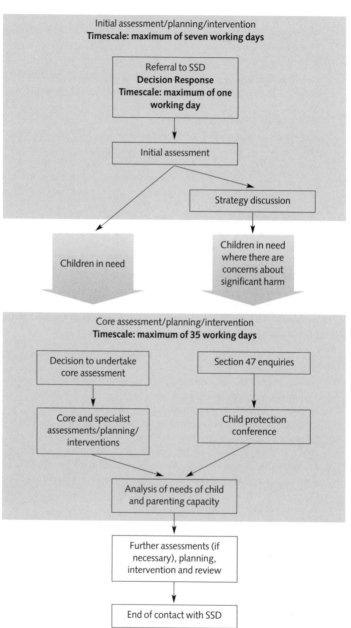

who have a complaint about a particular agency's services should take it up with the agency concerned.

3.14   The **maximum timescales** for completing an analysis of the needs of children and the parenting capacity to respond to those needs are represented in Figure 4. The needs of some children, in particular those who require emergency intervention, may mean that the initial assessment stage is brief. It may also be brief where the needs of the child can be determined in a period of less than seven working days. The same considerations apply to the minimum and maximum timescales for the core assessment.

## S47 and Core Assessment

3.15   At any stage, should there be suspicions or allegations about child maltreatment and concern that the child may be or is likely to suffer significant harm, there must be strategy discussions and inter-agency action in accordance with the guidance in *Working Together to Safeguard Children* (1999). Assessment of what is happening to a child in these circumstances is not a separate or different activity but continues the same process, although the pace and scope of assessment may well have changed (see paragraphs 5.33 to 5.38 in *Working Together to Safeguard Children* (1999)). A key part of the assessment will be to establish whether there is reasonable cause to suspect that this child is suffering or is likely to suffer significant harm and whether any emergency action is required to secure the safety of the child.

3.15   The way in which the initial and core assessments have been integrated into the processes for children who are considered to be, or likely to be suffering significant harm are set out in Figure 5. This flow chart concerning individual cases is reproduced from *Working Together to Safeguard Children* (1999, p.116).

3.16   As indicated in paragraphs 5.39 to 5.41 of *Working Together to Safeguard Children* (1999) sometimes it will be appropriate to undertake an investigative interview of a child who may have been a victim to a crime or a witness, with a view to gathering evidence for criminal proceedings. These interviews should take account of information known from any previous assessments. A child should never be interviewed in the presence of an alleged or suspected perpetrator of abuse, or somebody who may be colluding with a perpetrator. The guidance (which is currently being revised) in the *Memorandum of Good Practice on video recorded interviews for child witnesses for criminal proceedings* (Home Office and Department of Health, 1992) should be followed for all video-recorded investigative interviews with children.

3.17   All such interviews with children should be conducted by those with specialist training and experience in interviewing children. Additional specialist help may be necessary if the child's first language is not English; the child appears to have a degree of psychiatric disturbance but is deemed competent; the child has an impairment; or where interviewers do not have adequate knowledge and understanding of the child's racial, religious or cultural background. Consideration should also be given to the gender of interviewers particularly in cases of alleged sexual abuse.

3.18   Following the publication of *Speaking Up For Justice* (Home Office, 1998), the report of the Working Group on Vulnerable or Intimidated Witnesses, Part II of the Youth

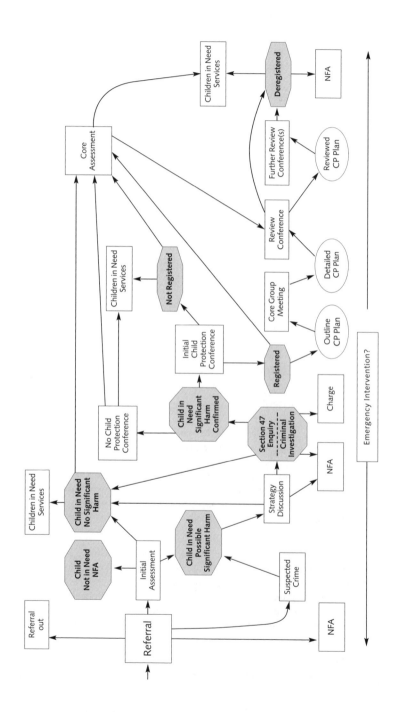

Justice and Criminal Evidence Act 1999 extends the range of measures available to assist child witnesses.

The Act provides different levels of protection for three groups of child witnesses according to the nature of assistance each group is considered to need. These are:

- All children in need of special protection – because they are giving evidence in a case that involves a sexual and/or violent offence – will give video-recorded evidence-in-chief unless this would not be in the interests of justice.

- Children under 17 who are giving evidence in a case involving violence, neglect, abduction or false imprisonment will be cross-examined via a live link at the trial.

- When facilities are available, children under 17 who are giving evidence in a sexual offence case will be cross-examined at a video-recorded pre-trial hearing unless the child informs the court that he would prefer to be cross-examined at trial (on live link or in court).

There is a presumption that all children who are giving evidence in cases involving other offences will give evidence-in-chief by means of a video recording, and will be cross-examined on live link at the trial.

3.19  The Act also provides a range of other measures to assist child witnesses including:

- assistance with communication;

- the use of an intermediary to assist with the questioning;

- screening the witness from the accused in court;

- the removal by judges of their wigs and gowns;

- clearing the public gallery in sexual offence cases.

The majority of these measures will be available to the Crown Court and youth courts by the end of 2000.

## Use of Assessments in Family Proceedings

3.20  It may be appropriate to use evidence gathered during the assessment process for family proceedings. This may arise where an assessment has been completed **before** the commencing of proceedings or because it is necessary to undertake an assessment **during** the proceedings. The following paragraphs set out some issues around the interface between the assessment processes and reporting in writing in family proceedings.

3.21  The term **family proceedings** is one that is defined statutorily in section 8 of the Children Act 1989. It includes all public law applications (care, adoption, emergency protection, contact) and a large range of private law matters concerning divorce and separation, including those within applications under section 8 for contact, residence, specific issue and prohibited steps.

## Care Applications and Assessment

3.22  In court proceedings involving the local authority, such as an application for a care or supervision order, the local authority's main evidence will be set out by way of one or more formal statements. These include the relevant history and the facts to support the **threshold criteria** (ie. significant harm) for an order under section 31. Information concerning the **welfare checklist** (section 1(3)) to which the court must have regard will also be included in the application.

3.23 Before making any order, the court must also consider the **no order principle** (section 1(5)). The court will look to the detail of the local authority's care plan for evidence as to how the care order, if made, would be implemented. Guidance about the structure and contents of care plans was issued in 1999 (*Care Plans and Care Proceedings under the Children Act 1989* LAC (99(29)).

3.24 Evidence arising from assessments may be used within the proceedings in one or more of the following ways by providing evidence:

- in support of the threshold criteria;

- around issues in the welfare checklist;

- about the rationale for the overall aim of the care plan or specific details within it (such as contact arrangements).

## Disclosure

3.25 In family proceedings, documents produced by parties are normally shared among all parties – typically, the local authority, the parents and the guardian ad litem. It should be remembered that an assessment undertaken for the purpose of the proceedings will generate information for the **court** and this cannot, save exceptionally with the court's agreement, be withheld in full or in part because aspects may be unfavourable to one of the parties.

3.26 Assessments may be commissioned before the commencement of court proceedings or where such proceedings have not been anticipated. Where such an assessment includes information, opinions and recommendations from professionals not employed by the local authority (such as specialists in child and adolescent mental health), those persons should be advised that their contribution may be used in family proceedings.

3.27 Appendix D sets out a number of practice issues to be considered when using information gathered during assessment for family proceedings.

## Court Sanctioned Assessments

3.28 A range of assessments may be made without legal restriction in respect of a child who is **not** the subject of care or related court applications.

3.29 Section 38(6) provides that where the Court makes an interim care order or interim supervision order it may give such directions (if any) as it considers appropriate with regard to the medical or psychiatric examination or other assessment of the child. By subsection (7) a direction may be to the effect that there is to be **no** such examination or assessment **unless** the Court directs otherwise.

3.30 Rule 18 of the Family Proceedings Courts (Children Act 1989) Rules 1991 provides that no person may without leave of the Justice's Clerk or the Court cause the child to be medically or psychiatrically examined, or otherwise assessed, for the purpose of the preparation of expert evidence for use in the proceedings. (See also paragraphs 3.61 to 3.62 in *An Introduction to the Children Act 1989* (1989) which deal with assessments in the context of care proceedings.) There are corresponding Rules for the County and High Court. Where care proceedings are underway, the nature and scope of any specialist assessment to be commissioned should be discussed in advance with legal advisers. Legal advisers will also help ensure that the implications of relevant case law, Practice Directions, Human Rights Act 1998, European Court of Human Rights judgments and other authoritative guidance are brought to the attention of those preparing assessments and subsequent reports for courts.

## Oral Evidence

3.31   The assessment provides the basis for formal written evidence for use in the proceedings. However, it may be necessary for the professional(s) undertaking the assessment to give additional evidence orally. In family proceedings, there is less emphasis on restrictions such as hearsay and generally the proceedings are considered to be less adversarial than non-family cases. The key worker should liaise closely with the local authority legal department in anticipating those issues likely to be raised.

## Working with Children and Families

3.32   Gathering information and making sense of a family's situation are key phases in the process of assessment. It is not possible to do this without the knowledge and involvement of the family. It requires direct work with children and with family members, explaining what is happening, why an assessment is being undertaken, what will be the process and what is likely to be the outcome. Gaining the family's co-operation and commitment to the work is crucially important. Families often have a number of fears and anxieties about approaching social services departments for help or about being referred to them by other agencies. Parents are fearful, for instance, that they will be perceived as failing in some way (Cleaver and Freeman, 1995; Aldgate and Bradley, 1999). They are also very clear about what they value from the professionals they meet, even in the most difficult circumstances. In particular, parents ask for clear explanations, openness and honesty, and to be treated with respect and dignity. Children's needs for explanations of what is happening may sometimes be overlooked. They should be informed clearly and sensitively even when they do not communicate through speech and where professionals may be unclear how much of what is being said is understood. They do not want to be kept in the dark or patronised. Studies have found that 'children are particularly sensitive to professionals who treat them personally, with care, and above all respect' (Jones and Ramchandani, 1999). It is especially important to help children handle uncertainty while plans are being formulated.

3.33   Different ways of providing explanations to families have been developed, some in written form accompanying the use of local authority records or materials for gathering information, which are shared with family members. An example of one such approach developed by a local authority is included above (Figure 6). Other local authorities have produced leaflets for families or use materials published by specialist

Figure 6   **Explaining Assessment to Family Members: An Example Accompanying a Written Record**

**What is an assessment?**

- Either you, or someone else on your behalf, has asked the social services departments for help with some difficulty you are having which affects your child (or children).

- Before we can help you, we need to know more about you and your family. This will involve collecting information, talking this through with you and agreeing what might be done. We call this an assessment.

**Why is an assessment being carried out?**

- Through making an assessment of your situation, it should be possible to see what help and support you and your family might need, and who could best give that help.

- Information will be gathered and written down. Although social workers and other professionals will normally take the lead in completing the assessment, this should always be done in a way which helps you to have your say, and encourages you to take part.

- Any information you give to us will be held in confidence within the social services department. If there is a need to discuss this information with anyone else, we will normally ask for your permission. The only exception to this is if information comes to light which, in the social worker's view, may indicate a serious threat to the welfare of your child. If this is the case, you will be told what your rights are in this new situation.

**What will happen?**

- Completing an assessment usually means the social worker will meet with you and members of your family a number of times.

- When children are old enough to take part in the assessment, the social worker will encourage and help them to do so.

- The assessment will take into consideration your ethnic and cultural background. If required, help will be provided in your first language.

- When other people are already helping you and your family, it is likely the social worker will talk to them too. We shall discuss this with you.

- If you do not agree with what the social worker says in the assessment, there will be an opportunity for you to record your point of view on the assessment record.

- The purpose of assessment is to draw up a plan of action to address the needs of your child (or children) and how you might need help to respond to these. You will be given a copy of the plan.

**What will be expected of you?**

- We know that almost all parents want to do their best for their children, and completing the assessment will help the social workers recognise the strengths you and your family have, as well as your difficulties.

- We can help you best if you tell us about what you do well in your family and your difficulties. We will keep you informed about what we are doing and thinking.

- An assessment is an important part of our working with you. In a very small number of cases, there are serious concerns about a child's safety. Making sure the child is safe will be our first concern. Please ask your social worker to explain this to you. You have a right to know.

**What can you expect of us?**

- We will listen carefully to what you have to say, offer advice and, if necessary, support to help you bring up your children and resolve your difficulties.
- We know that with a little help most families can sort out their own problems, and our aim is to help you do that.
- We will try our best to offer you any services you need as soon as possible. But there are often many more people needing services than there are services to give. This means that sometimes although everyone is agreed that you need a service, it might not be available at the time. If this happens we will always look to find an alternative, but we cannot guarantee to provide a particular service.

groups such as Family Rights Group, NSPCC or Who Cares? Trust. Key to the use of written materials is that they must be accompanied by direct communication and involvement by practitioners with family members and that repeated explanations may be necessary.

3.34    The issues of working with children and families where there are concerns that a child is being maltreated are explored in *The Challenge of Partnership in Child Protection* (Department of Health, 1995a). That publication provides detailed practice guidance about how to work with families throughout the process of enquiries being made and action taken to protect a child. It warns that 'those under the stress associated with allegations of child abuse may drift away from a working method which is sensitive to families' needs and which encourages their participation in the process' (p.46).

3.35    There will be situations where family members do not wish to work co-operatively with statutory agencies. This may be for a variety of reasons; they are too afraid or they believe they or their child have no problem or they are generally hostile to public welfare agencies. They may be resistant because of the nature of their own difficulties, such as psychiatric illness or problems of alcohol and drug misuse, or because of allegations being made against them. Whatever the reasons for their resistance, the door to co-operation should be kept open. At the very least, family members should be informed of what is happening and how they could participate more fully. Ways should be explored to engage some family members in the assessment process. The experience of research and practice confirms that, even after initial difficulties, the prospect of working in partnership with one or more family members may not be lost for ever, and that to do so will have long term beneficial outcomes for the child and family. The desirability of working with family members, however, must not override the importance of ensuring that children are safe.

3.36    Where there is resistance, 'a determination not to be overwhelmed, distracted or immobilised by the parents' initial response is essential' (Department of Health, 1995a). However, in a small number of instances, resistance to co-operation by a parent is accompanied by overtly aggressive, abusive or threatening behaviour or by more subtle underlying menace. Staff may be aware of the threat and in response either avoid family contact or unwisely place themselves in situations of danger (Cleaver *et al*, 1998). It is in these circumstances that access to available, skilled, expert supervision is essential so that the nature of the threat can be understood, the implications for the child and other family members identified and strategies found for maintaining work with the family. These may include co-working with experienced staff within or across agencies, changing times and venue for meetings with the family and other measures. Concerns about such matters should always be taken seriously and acted upon. It may be necessary to involve the expertise of professionals from a number of agencies to arrive at an understanding of the risks a particular individual may pose to the safety of staff, as well as to family members.

## Planning Assessment

3.37 Gathering information requires careful planning. However difficult the circumstances, the **purpose** of assessing the particular child and the family should always be kept in mind and the impact of the process on the child and family considered. It has to be remembered that:

- the aim is to clarify and identity the needs of the child;

- the process of assessment should be helpful and as unintrusive to the child and family as possible;

- families do not want to be subjected to repeated assessments by different agencies;

- if, during the assessment, the child's safety is or becomes a concern, it must be secured before proceeding with the assessment.

3.38 It is essential, therefore, that the process of assessment should be carefully planned, whatever the pressure to begin work. 'Preparation, process and outcome are inextricably linked' (Adcock, 2000). This planning should take place in discussion with the child and family members unless to do so would place the child at increased risk of significant harm (*Working Together to Safeguard Children*, 1999, paragraph 5.6). As part of the preparation, key questions should be considered:

- Who will undertake the assessment and what resources will be needed?

- Who in the family will be included and how will they be involved (remembering absent or live-out family members, wider family and others significant to the child)?

- In what groupings will the child and family members be seen and in what order?

- Are there communication issues? If so, what are the specific communication needs and how will they be met?

- What methods of collecting information will be used? Which questionnaires and scales will be used?

- What information is already available?

- What other sources of knowledge about the child and family are available and how will other agencies and professionals who know the family be informed and involved? How will family members consent be gained?

- Where will assessment take place?

- What will be the timescale?

- How will information be recorded?

- How will it be analysed and who will be involved?

3.39   The nature of concerns about a child's needs will determine how the process is carried out and the extent of detail collected. The greater the concern, the greater the need for specificity, for use of specialist knowledge and judgement in the process and, therefore, the need for careful co-ordination and management of work with the family and other agencies. The more complex or difficult the child's situation, the more important it will be that multiple sources of information are used. These may include:

- **Direct work with the child** through shared activities, interviews, questionnaires, scales and play, which are age and culturally appropriate to the child's age, development and culture.

- **Direct work with the parents** through interviews with one or more parental members; parental discussions; taking parental histories; using scales, questionnaires and other resources to gain a shared view of parental issues and parental functioning.

- **Direct work with the family** through interviews with the family in appropriate groupings of family members; taking family histories; using scales, questionnaires and other resources to gain a shared view of family issues and family functioning.

- **Direct work with the child and current caregivers**, if the child is not living with parents.

- **Observation** of the child alone and of the child/parent(s)/caregiver(s) interaction. Consideration should be given to doing this in the home, in school (both classroom and play areas) and with friends as well as family members.

- **Other sources of knowledge**, including those who have known the child over time, such as the midwife, health visitor, general practitioner, nursery staff or school teachers, and others who know the family such as staff from voluntary agencies, housing departments and adult health and social services. Other professionals may have become involved with the child or other children in the family for a specific purpose, for example educational psychologists, speech therapists, youth offending team members. Police and probation may also be important sources of information where there are concerns about a child or family members' safety.

- **Other information held on files and records and from previous assessments.** These should always be carefully checked as far as possible.

- **Specialist assessments** from a range of professionals may be commissioned to provide specific understanding about an aspect of the child's development, parental strengths and difficulties or the family's functioning. The timing of these and their particular contribution to the analysis of the child's needs and the plan of intervention will require careful consideration.

3.40   As a general principle, any records of assessments, plans or reports should be routinely shared with family members and children as appropriate, in addition to being shared with relevant professionals. These may require explanation and re-explanation to family members. Copies of assessments and plans, in their first language, should be given to family members wherever possible. Care should be taken to ensure that the meaning and implications of assessments are understood by the child and family members, as far as is possible.

## Communicating with Children

3.41   In responding to a request for help or a referral, the importance of working with family members has been emphasised. However, if the process of assessment is to be child centred, an understanding of what is happening to the child cannot only be gained from information contributed by family members or other professionals who know the child. Direct work with children is an essential part of assessment, as well as recognising their rights to be involved and consulted about matters which affect their lives. This applies to all children, including disabled children. Communicating with some disabled children requires more preparation, sometimes more time and on occasions specialist expertise, and consultation with those closest to the child. For example, for children with communication difficulties it may be necessary to use alternatives to speech such as signs, symbols, facial expression, eye pointing, objects of reference or drawing. Communicating with a child with very complex difficulties may benefit from help of a third party who knows the child well and is familiar with the child's communication methods (see Chapter 3 in Department of Health, 2000a). Children whose first language is not English should have the opportunity to speak to a professional in their first language, wherever possible. It is particularly important at turning points in their lives that 'children are enabled to express their wishes and feelings; make sense of their circumstances and contribute to decisions that affect them' (NSPCC *et al*, 1997).

3.42   It is essential that a child's safety is addressed, if appropriate, during the course of undertaking direct work with him or her. There are five critical components in direct work with children: seeing, observing, talking, doing and engaging:

- **Seeing children:** an assessment cannot be made without seeing the child, however young and whatever the circumstances. The more complex or unclear a situation or the greater the level of concern, the more important it will be to see the child regularly and to take note of appearance, physical condition, emotional wellbeing, behaviour and any changes which are occurring.

- **Observing children:** the child's responses and interactions in different situations should be carefully observed wherever possible, alone, with siblings, with parents and/or caregivers or in school or other settings. Children may hide or suppress their feelings in situations which are difficult or unsafe for them, so it is important that general conclusions are not reached from only limited observations.

- **Engaging children:** this involves developing a relationship with children so that they can be enabled to express their thoughts, concerns and opinions as part of the process of helping them make real choices, in a way that is age and developmentally appropriate. Children should clearly understand the parameters within which they can exercise choice. In offering children such options, adults must not abdicate their responsibilities for taking decisions about a child's welfare.

- **Talking to children:** although this may seem an obvious part of communicating with children, it is clear from research that this is often not done at all or not done well. It requires time, skill, confidence and careful preparation by practitioners. Issues of geographical distance, culture, language or communication needs because of impairments may require specific consideration before deciding how best to communicate with the child. Children themselves are particularly sensitive to how and when professionals talk to them and consult them. Their views must be sought before key meetings. Again, a range of opportunities for talking to children may be needed, appropriate to the child's circumstances, age and stage of development, which may include talking to the child on their own, in a family meeting or accompanied by or with the assistance of a trusted person.

- **Activities with children:** undertaking activities with children can have a number of purposes and beneficial effects. It is important that they are activities which the child understands and enjoys, in which trust with the worker can develop and which give the child an experience of safety. They can allow positive interaction between the worker and the child to grow and enable the professional to gain a better understanding of the child's responses and needs.

3.43 Children have been asked what they consider to be good professional practice. They value social workers who:

- **Listen** – carefully and without trivialising or being dismissive of the issues raised;
- are **available and accessible** – regular and predictable contact;
- are **non-judgemental and non-directive** – accepting, explaining and suggesting options and choices;
- have a sense of **humour** – it helps to build a rapport;
- are **straight-talking** – with realism and reliability; no 'false promises';
- can be **trusted** – maintain **confidentiality** and consult with children before taking matters forward.

Butler and Williamson (1994) reproduced from *Turning Points: A Resource Pack for Communicating with Children*. Introduction. pp. 1–2. (1997)

3.44 The exercise of professional judgement will be important in deciding when and how to communicate with children during the assessment process and how to interpret their communication in the context of the circumstances. Consideration should be given as to how children are informed and involved at each stage of the process, so that they have the opportunity to agree what the key issues are, what they would like to happen and to discuss what is possible and not possible. 'Children need to trust that they will be understood as individuals in their own right; usually they will want reassurance about what their parent/carer will be told about what they say' (Brandon, 1999).

3.45 Consideration of when and how to involve specific professionals with expertise and experience in assessing children's development will also be important throughout the assessment process. Professionals in a variety of child welfare agencies may be able to assist social services staff through discussion or advice based on their understanding and interpretation of information and views gathered from children. There may, however, be aspects of children's development and behaviour which require specialist assessment, either by joint work or referral to specific agencies. For example, assessing the strength of a child's attachment to a parent in circumstances of maltreatment or the educational potential of a school leaver who is living rough on the streets and seeking help. Children will require careful and straightforward explanations about why new professionals are being involved.

## Consent and Confidentiality

3.46   When a family approaches social services for help or is referred, the family is generally the first and most important source of information about the child and the family's circumstances. However, in establishing whether this is a child in need and how best those needs may be met, it is likely to be important to gather information from a number of professionals who have contact with and knowledge of the child and family.

3.47   Personal information about children and families held by professionals and agencies is subject to a legal duty of confidence and should not normally be disclosed without the consent of the subject. However, the law permits the disclosure of confidential information if it is necessary to safeguard a child or children in the public interest: that is, the public interest in child protection may override the public interest in maintaining confidentiality. Disclosure should be justifiable in each case, according to the particular facts of the case, and legal advice should be sought in cases of doubt.

3.48   Children are entitled to the same duty of confidence as adults, provided that, in the case of those under 16 years of age, they have the ability to understand the choices and their consequences relating to any treatment. In exceptional circumstances, it may be believed that a child seeking advice, for example on sexual matters, is being exploited or abused. In such cases, confidentiality may be breached, following discussion with the child.

3.49   All agencies working with children and families should make their policies about sharing personal information available to users of their services and other agencies. This includes ensuring that such information is accessible and appropriate to children and families. Individual professionals should always make sure their agency's policies are known to the family with whom they are working. There will be variations in policy between agencies in accordance with their roles and responsibilities. Personal information about a child and family should always be respected but, in order to achieve good outcomes for the child, it may be appropriate to share it between professionals and teams within the same agency. Sensitive and careful judgements are required in the child's best interests.

3.50   In obtaining consent to seek information from other parties or to disclose information about the child or other individuals under the Data Protection Act 1998 it is important that explanations include:

- clarity about the purpose of approaching other individuals or agencies;
- reasons for disclosure of any information, for example about the referral or details about the child or family members;
- details of the individuals or agencies being contacted;
- what information will be sought or shared;
- why the information is important;
- what it is hoped to achieve.

3.51   The **Data Protection Act 1998** allows for disclosure without the consent of the subject in certain conditions, including for the purposes of the prevention or detection of crime, or the apprehension or prosecution of offenders, and where failure to disclose would be likely to prejudice those objectives in a particular case.

3.52 Article 8 of the **European Convention on Human Rights** states that:

(1) Everyone has the right to respect for his private and family life, his home and his correspondence.

(2) There shall be no interference by a public authority with the exercise of this right except such as in accordance with the law and is necessary in a democratic society in the interests of national security, public safety or the economic wellbeing of the country, for the prevention of disorder or crime, for the protection of health or morals, or for the protection of the rights and freedoms of others.

3.53 Disclosure of information without consent might give rise to an issue under Article 8. Disclosure of information to safeguard children will usually be for the protection of health or morals, for the protection of the rights and freedoms of others, and for the prevention of disorder or crime. Disclosure should be appropriate for the purpose and only to the extent necessary to achieve that purpose.

3.54 Obtaining consent and respecting confidentiality may not always be straightforward, particularly in situations of family conflict or dispute, or where a number of parental figures including absent parents are involved or where there are allegations of abuse about which enquiries are being made. The consent of any one parent acting alone, rather than all those with parental responsibility, is required to disclose information about a child (section 2(7) of the Children Act 1989).

3.55 Where there are concerns that a child may be suffering or is likely to suffer significant harm, it is essential that professionals and other people share information for it is often 'only when information from a number of sources has been shared and is then put together that it becomes clear that a child is at risk of or is suffering harm' (*Working Together to Safeguard Children*, 1999, paragraph 7.27). Unless to do so would place the child or children at increased risk of significant harm the nature of the child protection concerns should be explained to family members and to children, where appropriate, and their consent to contact other agencies sought. This requires careful explanation in plain language. It may be helpful to have written as well as verbal explanations (an example of this is the statement for family members on pages 39 and 40). For some families under stress or coping in difficult circumstances, explanations may need to be repeated several times. In all cases where the police are involved the decision about when to inform the parents will have a bearing on the conduct of police investigations and should inform part of the strategy discussion.

3.56 In any potential conflict between the responsibilities of professionals towards children and towards other family members, the needs of the child must come first. Where there are concerns that a child is or may be at risk of suffering significant harm, the overriding principle must be to safeguard the child. In such cases, when it is considered that a child may be in danger or that a crime is being or has been committed, the duty of confidence can be overridden. However, it will be important that the respective duties and powers of different agencies are clearly understood by all parties.

3.57 These matters are fully discussed in paragraphs 7.27 to 7.46 of *Working Together to*

*Safeguard Children* (1999) in the context of the legal framework and professional guidelines for different agencies. In this publication, Appendix E reproduces an abridged version of the Data Protection Registrar's checklist for setting up information sharing arrangements.

## Assessment of Children in Special Circumstances

3.58 Some of the children referred for help because of the nature of their problems or circumstances, will require particular care and attention during assessment. These are children who may become lost to the statutory agencies, whose wellbeing or need for immediate services may be overlooked and for whom subsequent planning and intervention may be less than satisfactory. This may be for a number of reasons including the following:

- They are **children in transition**. For example, their families may be moving from one geographical location to another; they may be moving schools, leaving school or leaving care, or moving into young adulthood and into the remit of adult rather than children's services. They may be disabled young people and their families, moving from child to adult services (Morris, 1999). They may be part of a travelling community or in families based periodically overseas, such as the armed forces.

- They are **children in hospital** for long periods of time. Under section 85 of the Children Act 1989 the social services department has a duty to assess the welfare of a child in hospital for longer than three months consecutively. This assessment is to ascertain whether the child's welfare is being adequately safeguarded and promoted and whether the child and their family require services.

- They (or their parents) have specific **communication needs**, for example they do not use English as a first language, or they do not communicate through speech.

- They (or their families, including siblings) have **a long history of contact with social services** and other child welfare agencies. Their circumstances may be chaotic; files numerous; many staff may have been involved; they may not currently have an allocated worker. Any of these circumstances may result in the need for assessment or reassessment at this point in time not being recognised.

- They are children whose problems or those of their parents are **not sufficiently serious to receive services** under social services priorities. These children's health or development may not be considered to be being impaired, but an analysis of the risk factors and stressors in their lives would suggest they are likely to suffer impairment in the future. What is required is recognition of the interaction of child and/or parental problems on a child's health and development and the cumulative effect of such problems over time. For example, a mother with a mild learning disability may not reach the criteria for help from an adult services team and her child's standard of care may not be sufficiently poor to meet the criteria for children's services intervention. However, the failure to recognise the need for early intervention to provide support to the child and family on a planned basis from both children's and adult's services may result in the child's current and future development being impaired.

- They are **children and young people involved in the use of drugs** where the level and nature of their drug use is unknown to their parents and/or any professionals to whom they are known, for example, teachers, although their general health or behaviour may be a cause for concern. These children may be fearful of asking for help from statutory agencies and may be more receptive to approaches from voluntary agencies or specialist drug services.

- They are young people about whom there are concerns that they are becoming or might be **involved in prostitution**. Draft government *Guidance on Children Involved in Prostitution,* issued for consultation in December 1998, sets out an inter-agency approach to helping this group of young people. The emphasis is on both preventing these vulnerable children from becoming involved in prostitution and safeguarding and promoting the welfare of those who are being abused through prostitution. These situations may require careful assessment of the young person's needs and consideration of how best to help him or her.

- They are children **separated from their country of origin** who are without the care and protection of their parents or legal guardian, often referred to as **unaccompanied asylum seeking children**. Their status, age and circumstances may all be uncertain, in addition to their having experienced or witnessed traumatic events, and they may be suffering the most extreme forms of loss. The situations in which they are accommodated, albeit on a temporary basis, may be less than adequate, for example, where an 18 year old Eritrean young woman is caring for her 10 year old brother in bed and breakfast accommodation for homeless people. There is a helpful *Statement of Good Practice* (Separated Children in Europe Programme, 1999) which provides a straightforward account of the policies and practice required to act to protect the rights of such children.

- They are **children of asylum seeking families** who may have extensive unmet needs while the focus of activity is on resolving the adults' asylum applications, accommodation or other pressing issues.

- They have **a parent in prison**. It is estimated that 125,000 children have a parent in prison at any one time (Ramsden, 1998). In 1997, approximately 8,000 women were received into the prison system (either untried and/or following custodial sentences). A survey by the Home Office (Caddle and Crisp, 1997) suggests that over 60% have children under the age of 18 and over half the women have had their first or only child as teenagers. At the very least, children in these circumstances experience disruptions in their care, but for some the consequences are much more severe and long lasting. Furthermore, social services departments may be asked by the Prison Service to contribute to assessments when there are children involved (See paragraph 5.82).

3.59 There are common features which apply to the assessment of children in all these and other similar situations:

- they require a high degree of co-operation and co-ordination between staff in different agencies, in planning or preparing for assessments, in undertaking and completing them;

- extra care must be taken to ensure that there is an holistic view of the child and that the child does not become lost between the agencies involved and their different systems and procedures;

- as most children are registered with a GP, this route could be used for locating lost children and obtaining information about their past histories;

- particular attention should be given to health and education assessments of these children. The older the child, the more these may be overlooked or found difficult to arrange;

- consideration must be given to the means by which information will be analysed and action planned, how the outcome of assessment is communicated and to whom;

- responsibility for action and providing services must be clearly identified and recorded, with specific timescales;

- overall responsibility for ensuring the welfare of the child in need must be clearly allocated.

3.60   It is significant that, where adolescents are the subject of assessment, studies emphasise the importance of staff finding time to engage in direct work with young people and getting to know them well, although it may be difficult sometimes 'to get below the surface' (Sinclair *et al*, 1995). Sadly, such studies reveal that all too often assessments with older children fail to be completed, especially where specialist professional assessments are required. Even greater efforts are necessary to co-ordinate and achieve co-operation from all parties in these situations.

## Assessing the Needs of Young Carers

3.61   A group of children whose needs are increasingly more clearly recognised are young carers for example those who assume important caring responsibilities for parents and siblings. Some children care for parents who are disabled, physically or mentally ill, others for parents dependent on alcohol or involved in drug misuse. For further information and guidance refer to the *Carers (Recognition and Services) Act 1995: Policy Guidance and Practice Guide* (Department of Health, 1996a) and *Young Carers: Making a Start* (Department of Health, 1998a).

3.62   An assessment of family circumstances is essential. Young carers should not be expected to carry inappropriate levels of caring which have an adverse impact on their development and life chances. It should not be assumed that children should take on similar levels of caring responsibilities as adults. Services should be provided to parents to enhance their ability to fulfil their parenting responsibilities. There may be differences of view between children and parents about appropriate levels of care. Such differences may be out in the open or concealed. The resolution of such tensions will require good quality joint work between adult and children's social services as well as co-operation from schools and health care workers. This work should include direct work with the young carer to understand his or her perspective and opinions. The young person who is a primary carer of his or her parent or sibling may have a good understanding of the family's functioning and needs which should be incorporated into the assessment.

3.63   Young carers can receive help from both local and health authorities. Where a child is providing a substantial amount of care on a regular basis for a parent, the child will be entitled to an assessment of their ability to care under section 1(1) of the *Carers (Recognition and Services) Act 1995* and the local authority must take that assessment into account in deciding what community care services to provide for the parent. Many young carers are not aware that they can ask for such an assessment. In addition, consideration must be given as to whether a young carer is a child in need under the Children Act 1989. The central issue is whether a child's welfare or development might suffer if support is not provided to the child or family. As part of the *National Strategy for Carers* (1999a), local authorities should take steps to identify children with additional family burdens. Services should be provided to promote the health and development of young carers while not undermining the parent.

## The Assessment Framework and Children Looked After

3.64 The Assessment Framework has been designed to assess children's needs across the same developmental dimensions as the Looking After Children materials (Parker (eds), 1991; Department of Health, 1995b). This will enable the Looking After Children system to be revised during 1999–2001 in a way which will result in an integrated model for assessing and providing services to the wider group of children in need and their families than looked after children. Most children who come into contact with social services departments do not enter the care system. However, should a child need to be looked after, congruence in the system will ensure that good quality baseline information is available about the child's developmental and wider needs at the point of entry to the looked after system. This will support improved assessment of the child's needs which will enable better placement matching in foster and residential care. The parenting capacity domain within the Assessment Framework can also be used with foster carers in assessing suitability for a particular child. It will also inform the provision of services to children and birth and foster families during the care episode. When children return home, or are placed with a permanent substitute family, using the same Assessment Framework will ensure continuity of planning to secure the best outcomes for the child.

3.65 The parenting capacity dimensions in the Assessment Framework will be particularly useful for evaluating improvements in parenting capacities as part of any decision making processes and, where appropriate, a reunification programme. This information will also be important in planning and managing contact. Once baseline information on parenting capacity has been collected during the core assessment, it will be possible to identify key areas for change and target social work and other resources more effectively whilst the child is looked after and reunification plans are being implemented. It should also enable social workers to decide when family reunification will not be possible and an alternative placement is required.

## Children Being Placed for Adoption

3.66 In circumstances where there are children for whom adoption is planned, the Assessment Framework may be used as part of the assessment of the capacities of potential adopters, matching children with approved adopters, and planning what kinds of services a child and adopting parents might benefit from post placement and post adoption. These services might include help to understand any specific needs the child has and how best to respond to them. Some needs may require time limited interventions whereas others may exist on a continuing basis. The medical adviser to the social services department has a critical role to play in offering advice and information from the point at which a child is being considered for adoption and throughout the adoption process. A holistic approach to the consideration of what are likely to be complex needs of the child requires good inter-disciplinary co-operation and co-ordination.

## Children Leaving Care

3.67   Where children leave care and live independently of their families, family links often remain very important. Research has pointed to the considerable potential of working in partnership with the child and their family during this transition period (Marsh and Peel, 1999).

3.68   The Children (Leaving Care) Bill which has been introduced in the 1999/2000 Parliamentary Session will, subject to Royal Assent, provide for every looked after child to have a personal adviser and a pathway plan by their sixteenth birthday. The pathway plan will be informed by an assessment of need based on the Assessment Framework and will, in effect, extend existing assessment and planning requirements to cover the child's transition to adulthood. The plan will be subject to regular review irrespective of whether the child remains looked after or has left care and the Bill provides for the continuation of the plan and contact by the personal adviser until the young person reaches the age of 21 and, where supported in higher education and training, up to the age of 24.

# 4 Analysis, Judgement and Decision Making

Treatment itself is intimately bound up with assessment, relying on it as a house relies on its foundation. Consequently, assessment continues throughout the treatment process, despite a change in focus during its course (Jones, 1997).

4.1 The Guidance has emphasised that assessment is not an end in itself but a process which will lead to an improvement in the wellbeing or outcomes for a child or young person. The conclusion of an assessment should result in:

- an analysis of the needs of the child and the parenting capacity to respond appropriately to those needs within their family context;

- identification of whether and, if so, where intervention will be required to secure the wellbeing of the child or young person;

- a realistic plan of action (including services to be provided), detailing who has responsibility for action, a timetable and a process for review.

4.2 Generally, all these phases of the assessment process should be undertaken in partnership with the child and key family members, and with their agreement. This includes finalising the plan of action. There may be exceptions when there are concerns that a child is suffering or may be suffering significant harm.

4.3 In many approaches or referrals to social services departments, families are clear about their problems but may not be sure where to turn or how to obtain services. With advice and information, they are able to take appropriate action. This action may be all that is required by a social services department. Where there is a question about whether a child is in need and therefore services are necessary an assessment is required. For some families, the process of assessment is in itself a therapeutic intervention. Being able to look at problems in a constructive manner with a professional who is willing to listen and who helps family members to reflect on what is happening, is enough to help them find solutions. During the assessment process, it may emerge that families will best be helped by agencies other than social services. Armed with this information, families may wish to seek solutions themselves; others may wish to have help in gaining access to other agencies or practical services.

4.4 A significant proportion of families who seek help from social services are unable to resolve stresses or problems solely from within their own emotional or practical resources or from their own support network. It is for these families that assessment may be important in order to identify the nature of their children's needs and, simultaneously, may be the first stage in a longer process of positive intervention. Ultimately, careful judgements must be made about balancing the needs of children and parents.

4.5   In most situations, meeting children's needs will almost always involve responding also to the needs of family members. The two are closely connected and it is rarely possible to promote the welfare of children without promoting the welfare of significant adults in their lives. In some cases, meeting the children's needs may mean giving others either parenting responsibility or legal parental responsibility for the child, either for short periods or on a longer term basis. Where consideration is being given to meeting parents' needs, as part of the plan of intervention, this must be because it is in the best interests of the child and will assist in securing better outcomes for the child. Parents may also require help in their own right as adults who have specific needs.

## Analysis

4.6   In Chapter 3 it was emphasised that gathering information is a crucial phase in the assessment process, which requires careful planning about how best to undertake it. Information may be gathered from a variety of sources, using methods which will be determined by the purpose of the assessment and the particular circumstances of each child and family (see paragraph 3.38). Some of the information may have been gathered through the use of questionnaires and scales, such as those published in the accompanying materials (Department of Health, Cox and Bentovim, 2000). The **Home Inventory** (Caldwell and Bradley, 1984) and the **Assessment of Family Competence, Strengths and Difficulties** (Bentovim and Bingley Miller, forthcoming), due for publication later in 2000 will also provide important information about the child's world and family functioning respectively.

4.7   The information should be organised according to the dimensions of the Assessment Framework as a necessary beginning to the next phase of analysis. Information should be summarised under each of the three domains ie. children's developmental needs, parents' or caregivers' capacities to respond, and wider family and environmental factors. The Department of Health has developed assessment recording forms to assist practitioners and their managers in this phase of work (Department of Health and Cleaver, 2000).

4.8   In organising the information, there may be different perspectives to be explored, recorded and taken into account, for example, the child may have a different understanding and interpretation of what is happening from that of either parent or of a professional. These differences are important when developing an understanding of the child's needs within the family context. Different family members may attach different meanings to the same information, for example, the significance of past family history or events. The same information may vary in its salience for different family members, for example, the impact of a bereavement in a family. Sometimes these differences in perception can lead to conflicts in the family or between family members and professionals. In reaching a shared understanding of what is happening in a family, it is important to keep the focus on the needs of the child. This enables family members and professionals to agree a plan of action, even in the context of some differences or tensions, that will address the identified needs of the child with the aim of improving outcomes for the child.

4.9 By this point, there should be clear summaries which identify from the information gathered the child's developmental needs, parenting capacity and family and environmental factors. In each of these domains, both strengths and difficulties should be identified. Children's needs do not exist in a vacuum (Jones, 2000) and, therefore, the inter-relationships between the child, family and environment must be understood. Some factors will work positively to support children's growing up while others will militate against or undermine their healthy development. In weighing up the impact that various factors have on a child, it has to be borne in mind that not all factors will have equal significance and the cumulative effect of some relatively minor factors may be considerable. Thus the analysis of a child's needs is a complex activity drawing on knowledge from research and practice combined with an understanding of the child's needs within his or her family.

4.10 The elements of parenting capacity can be described, and minimum parenting standards or requirements assessed by the practitioner and related to their child. However, it is not possible to ascribe numerical values to each element because parenting capabilities and behaviours are complex and subject to influences from within and outside the family (Jones, 2000). Parenting capacity can only be understood within the overall context in which children are being brought up. The analysis should identify the family and environmental factors which have an impact on the different aspects of the child's development and on the parent(s) capacity in order to explore the relationship between the three domains (Department of Health and Cleaver, 2000). At some points in time judgements may be made (based on the analysis of their parental functioning) that the parent is unable to respond to their child's needs.

4.11 To summarise the analysis stage:

- A child's needs must be based on knowledge of what would be expected of this child's development;

- Parenting capacity should draw on knowledge about what would be reasonable to expect of parental care given to a similar child;

- Family and environmental factors should draw on knowledge about the impact these will have on both parenting capacity and directly on a child's development.

## Judgements

4.12 Professionals will be drawing on their respective knowledge bases to inform the judgements they come to about a child's circumstances, whether the child is in need and whether their health and development is likely to be impaired without the provision of services. For some children, decisions will also have been made about whether they are suffering or are likely to suffer significant harm. The knowledge base will include information about the factors which are intrinsic to all children such as temperament, genetic make-up and race, and other factors which may be intrinsic to some children, such as physical or sensory impairments.

4.13    Critical to an understanding of what is happening to a child is the knowledge of the way in which children need to achieve certain tasks at particular ages and stages of development. Bentovim (1998) summarises current views on child development which 'emphasise that what matters for development is that the various systems – biological and psychological – should be well integrated. Development is about progression, change and re-organisation throughout life' (p.66). This normal pattern of development may not be achieved for some children either because of unavoidable factors such as impairments or because they are suffering significant harm (Bentovim, 1998).

4.14    There is a considerable literature to assist professionals when making a judgement about a parent's capacity and assessing what is a reasonable standard of care (Jones, 2000; Cleaver *et al*, 1999) 'even though research cannot provide the kind of numerical accuracy which is often sought' (Jones, 2000).

4.15    Critical at this phase will be judgements about a number of key issues (Jones, 1998):

- determining what has been happening and whether this is a child in need or is suffering significant harm;

- understanding the child and family context sufficiently to be able to secure the child's wellbeing or safety;

- assessing the likelihood of change;

    and later

- reviewing whether such change is being achieved.

4.16    It is important to identify strengths in the child's family system and to use these areas as the basis on which the child's development can be promoted. The more complex the family's problems, the more these will involve sophisticated inter-disciplinary and inter-agency co-operation in order to reach judgements about these issues. Stevenson (1998) provides a cautionary note in such circumstances. 'The families themselves may seem overwhelmed to the point of powerlessness, so the workers may experience similar feelings' (p.18). The reflective process for professionals working with children and families may be stressful, particularly in difficult circumstances. Some children's lives are such that profound, sensitive judgements may be required. This could include judgements about medical treatment in life threatening situations; judgements about whether to separate a child from his or her parents or caregivers; judgements about whether to place children with permanent substitute families. However, careful and systematic gathering of information, and its summary and analysis according to the framework can assist professionals in making sound evidence based judgements. The practice guidance has been developed to assist this process (Department of Health, 2000a).

4.17    Sometimes, where there are multi-faceted problems, assessments can become stuck and little progress made. Reder and Duncan (1999) talk about the danger of **assessment paralysis** which they describe as 'an impasse in the professional network where the issue of whether the parent has a psychiatric diagnosis becomes the context for deciding about all interventions'. Assessment paralysis can apply in other situations, where the focus of attention becomes stuck on a particular diagnostic issue and decision making is driven by this consideration rather than the child's needs. It requires vigilance and careful management by those staff who hold responsibility for the child's welfare to ensure that progress continues to be made to help the child.

## Use of Consultation

4.18 Social services departments have lead responsibility for undertaking assessments of children in need. In order to arrive at well balanced judgements about the needs of children, practitioners and their managers may benefit from the expertise and experience of professionals in other disciplines. These professionals can act as consultants or advisers to assist and contribute to the assessment processes, which includes analysis of information gathered. This type of input may be as useful to the assessment as the commissioning of specialist assessments.

4.19 In some situations, where the available evidence requires careful analysis by those with particular expertise, sufficient information about a child and the family may already be available. Therefore, the specialist task is to assist in the analysis of available material, drawing on knowledge in particular areas about likely outcomes of certain courses of action. This expert knowledge can assist the practitioner and his or her manager when constructing a plan and deciding how to implement it.

## Decision Making

4.20 In drawing up a plan of intervention, careful distinction should to be made between **judgements** about the child's developmental needs and parenting capacity and **decisions** about how best to address these at different points in time. These decisions will have to take account of a number of factors including:

- how existing good relationships and experiences can be nurtured and enhanced;

- what type of interventions are known to have the best outcomes for the particular circumstances of the child who has been assessed as in need;

- what the child and family can cope with at each stage. Complicated arrangements regarding the provision of services and interventions might well overwhelm the child or individual family members;

- how the necessary resources can be mobilised within the family's network and within professional agencies, including social services;

- what alternative interventions are available if the resources of choice cannot be secured;

- ensuring interventions achieve early success and have a beneficial impact. The self-esteem of children and parents is critical to the outcome of longer term intervention. Good experiences are important when many other aspects of family life may be in chaos or problems feel insurmountable;

- there may be an optimal hierarchy of interventions which will require distin-guishing between what is achievable in the short term, what will have maximum impact on the child and family's wellbeing and what are the long term goals;

- identifying what the child regards as highest priority, for example, learning to ride a bicycle may be far higher on a child's list of wants than therapy, and such practical wishes should be taken account of because they may result in changes which will enable the child to make use of therapeutic help.

- It will be essential to achieve some parts of a proposed intervention within a predetermined timescale, in order to meet the child's needs. Other components of a plan will be less pressing and although desirable to achieve, not considered necessary for the prevention of future significant harm.

4.21   Underlying these critical considerations is the importance of keeping the child at the centre of the planning processes. Three key aspects of a child's health and development must inform the content and timing of the plan:

- ensuring the child's safety;

- remembering that a child cannot wait indefinitely;

- maintaining a child's learning.

4.22   The development of secure parent-child attachments is critical to a child's healthy development. The quality and nature of the attachment will be a key issue to be considered in decision making, especially if decisions are being made about moving a child from one setting to another, or re-uniting a child with his or her birth family. (For further discussion of attachment see Crittenden and Ainsworth, 1989; Schofield, 1998; Howe, 2000).

4.23   In complex situations, it may be helpful for those involved in the assessment process to meet to discuss the findings and formulate the plan. This should involve the parents and, as appropriate, the child. Family Group Conferences or multi-disciplinary meetings may provide for the construction of plans for children in need. *Working Together to Safeguard Children* (1999) sets out the processes to be followed for children about whom there are concerns that they are suffering or likely to suffer significant harm. The role of the key worker appointed when a child's name has been placed on a child protection register, the role of the group of professionals responsible for developing and implementing the child protection plan and the aims, content and processes for constructing such a plan are set out in paragraphs 5.75 to 5.84 of *Working Together to Safeguard Children* (1999).

4.24   For some families, the findings from the core assessment will indicate that the parents are responding appropriately to their child's needs, but in order to maximise the child's health and developmental outcomes, specific services are required to assist the parents and/or the child. In the absence of particular stress factors, such as those resulting from having a chronically ill child, the parents would be able to bring up their children without external help. However, the presence of these stressors require parents and families to develop new ways of functioning, as well as to accept support from outside their family and friendship networks. In these families, siblings may be affected significantly and services should address their needs.

4.25   It has to be recognised that in families where a child has been maltreated there are some parents who will not be able to change sufficiently within the child's timescales in order to ensure their children do not continue to suffer significant harm (Jones, 1998). In these situations, decisions may need to be made to separate permanently the child and parent or parents. In these circumstances decisions about the nature and form of any contact will also need to be made, in the light of all that is known about the child and the family, and reviewed throughout childhood. Key in these considerations is what is in the child's best interests, informed by the child's views (Cleaver, 2000).

4.26   The following criteria have been identified as suggesting a poor outcome for reuniting children who have been maltreated with their parents (Bentovim *et al*, 1987; Silvester *et al*, 1995):

- the abusing parent completely or significantly denies any responsibility for the child's developmental state or abuse;

- the child is rejected or blamed outright;

- the child's needs are not recognised by their parents who put their own needs first;

- parents have frequently failed to show concern, or acknowledge, long-standing difficulties such as alcoholism or psychiatric problems;

- during therapeutic interventions, the relationships within the family and with professionals remain at breaking point.

4.27   However, most parents are capable of change, and following appropriate interventions, able to provide a safe family context for their child. At times, children may need to be separated temporarily from their parent or parents. This enables change to take place while the child is living away from home in a safe environment. During this time, it will be important to address the changes required in the parent(s) as well as meeting any therapeutic needs of the child and other family members by active programmes of intervention, appropriate deployment of resources and careful review of progress. If a child is separated from their parent(s), it is essential that parents are able to sustain any improvements made whilst the child is living away from home, when the child returns to live with them. Careful thought should be given to the nature of services required by the parents and child during this transition phase, to ensure that earlier achievements are able to be maintained and continue to be improved upon. For some families continued intervention may be necessary for a considerable length of time until the child is no longer vulnerable.

4.28   Jones (1998, p.108) summarising relevant child maltreatment research findings reports the following features as having been identified in those cases where there are better prospects of achieving good outcomes for children:

- Those infants and children who despite abuse do not have residual disability, developmental delay or special educational needs;

- Those children subjected to less severe abuse or neglect;

- Children who have had the benefit of non-abusive or corrective relationships with peers, siblings and/or a supportive adult;

- Children who have developed more healthy and appropriate attributions about the maltreatment which they had suffered;

- Children and families who are able and willing to co-operate with helping agencies;

- Children and families who have been able to engage in therapeutic work;

- Situations where successful partnerships between professionals and family members have occurred;

- Children and families where the psychological abuse component of the maltreatment experience has been amenable to change.

4.29 When an analysis of a child's needs and parenting capacity within their family context is completed, there is then a baseline from which further assessment and re-assessment, using the Assessment Framework, can be undertaken to review progress as services are provided.

4.30 In a number of family situations where there is concern about a child's safety and future wellbeing whilst living in his or her family, the findings from a core assessment may provide an uncertain picture of the family's capacity to change. These families are characterised by one or more of the following (Bentovim *et al*, 1987; Silvester *et al*, 1995):

- uncertainty as to whether the parents are taking full responsibility for either the abuse or the child's developmental state;

- whereas the child's needs may sometimes be viewed as primary, the parents put their own needs as dominant;

- the child may be scape-goated and parent-child attachments are ambivalent or anxious;

- family patterns are rigid rather than healthily flexible;

- relationships with professionals are ambivalent.

4.31 These families often cause professionals considerable concern. It is important that services are provided to give the family the best chance of achieving the required changes. It is equally important that in circumstances where the family situation is not improving or changing fast enough to respond to the child's needs, decisions are made about the longterm future of the child. Delay or drift can result in the child not receiving the help she or he requires and having their health and development impaired.

## Plans for Children in Need

4.32 The details of the plan are bench marks against which the progress of the family and the commitment of workers are measured, and therefore it is important that they should be realistic and not vague statements of good intent (Department of Health, 1995).

4.33 The analysis, judgement and decisions made will form the basis of a plan of work with a child in need and his or her family. The complexity or severity of the child's needs will determine the scope and detail of the plan. The different circumstances under which the assessment has been carried out will also determine the form in which it is recorded and the status of the plan:

- **Children in Need Plan** at the conclusion of a core assessment, which will involve the child and family members as appropriate and the contributions of all agencies.

A format for the plan is contained in assessment records (Department of Health and Cleaver, 2000).

- **Child Protection Plan** as a decision of an inter-agency child protection conference, following enquiries and assessment under s47. The expectations of a child protection plan are outlined in paragraphs 5.81 to 5.84 of *Working Together to Safeguard Children* (1999).

- **Care Plan for a Child Looked After** as a result of an assessment that a child will need to be looked after by the local authority either in the short term or long term and placed in foster or residential care. The requirements for a care plan in these circumstances are laid out in Volume 3 of the Children Act 1989, Guidance and Regulations (paragraphs 2.59 to 2.62). A format for the care plan is an integral part of the Department of Health's Looking After Children materials (Department of Health, 1995b).

- **Care Plans** for a child who is the subject of a care or supervision order or for whom the plan is adoption (see paragraphs 3.22 to 3.24).

- **Pathway Plan for a young person who is in care or leaving care** as outlined in the Government's intentions for young people living in and leaving care (Department of Health, 1999f; Children (Leaving Care) Bill, 1999).

4.34 There are some general principles about plans for working with children and families, whatever the circumstances in which they have been drawn up. First that, wherever possible, they should be drawn up in agreement with the child/young person and key family members and their commitment to the plan should have been secured. There are two caveats which the professionals responsible for the plan need to bear in mind:

- objectives should be reasonable and timescales not too short or unachievable;

- plans should not be dependent on resources which are known to be scarce or unavailable.

Failure to address these issues can be damaging to families and jeopardise the overall aim of securing the child's wellbeing. Second, the plan must maintain a focus on the child, even though help may be provided to a number of family members as part of the plan. As Jones *et al* (1987) write 'It is never acceptable to sacrifice the interests of the child for the therapeutic benefit of the parents'.

4.35 Department of Health practice guidance (1995a) recommended that professional workers and relevant family members should be clear about the following aspects of the plan which have general application (an abridged list is in Figure 7). With clarity about these matters, it is possible for both professionals and the family to take issue with the other when their expectations are not met or when perceptions and objectives begin to differ.

4.36 Fundamental to the plan, from the beginning, is the commitment of all the parties involved and the signatures to the plan of those who have lead responsibility for ensuring it is carried forward (in social services, this should include the team manager/supervisor as well as the practitioners). There should also be a clear recorded statement on the plan about when and how it will be reviewed. Reviewing the child's progress and the effectiveness of services and other interventions is a continuous part

**Figure 7   AREAS IN WHICH CLARITY IS REQUIRED IN CHILD CARE PLANNING**

- the objective of the plan, for example to provide and evaluate the efficacy of therapeutic interventions
- what services will be provided by which professional group or designated agency
- the timing and nature of contact between the professional workers and the family
- the purpose of services and professional contact
- specific commitments to be met by the family, for example attendance at a family centre
- specific commitments to be met by the professional workers, for example the provision of culturally sensitive services or special assistance for those with disabilities
- which components of the plan are negotiable in the light of experience and which are not
- what needs to change and the goals to be achieved, for example the child's weight to increase by a specific amount in a particular period, regular and appropriate stimulation for the child in keeping with her or his development and age
- what is unacceptable care of the child
- what sanctions will be used if the child is placed in danger or in renewed danger
- what preparation and support the child and adults will receive if she or he appears in court as a witness in criminal proceedings.

of the process of work with children and families. The timescales and procedures for reviewing plans for children in need which are also part of other guidance, regulations and legislation (child protection plans, care plans for children looked after and pathway plans) are already prescribed. For children in need plans, where work is being undertaken to support children and families in the community, it is good practice to review the plan with family members **at least every six months**, and to formally record it. Key professionals should also be involved in the review process and in constructing the revised plan.

4.37   The purpose of an assessment is to identify the child's needs within their family context and to use this understanding to decide how best to address these needs. It is essential that the plan is constructed on the basis of the findings from the assessment and that this plan is reviewed and refined over time to ensure the agreed case objectives are achieved. Specific outcomes for the child, expressed in terms of their health and development can be measured. These provide objective evidence against which to evaluate whether the child and family have been provided with appropriate services and ultimately whether the child's wellbeing is optimal.

# Local Authority Circular LAC(2003)13[2]

## GUIDANCE ON ACCOMMODATING CHILDREN IN NEED AND THEIR FAMILIES

### 1. SUMMARY

This Local Authority Circular covers guidance to councils with social services responsibilities on providing assistance to families of children in need, and to lone children, in the light of the amendments to Sections 17 and 22 of the Children Act 1989 which came into effect when the Adoption and Children Act 2002 received Royal Assent on 7 November 2002.

### 2. ACTION

Authorities and copy recipients are asked to note the contents of this circular, and pass this document to those staff who may be engaged in applying the new legislation.

### 3. CANCELLATION OF CIRCULARS

This Circular will remain in effect until further notice.

### 4. ENQUIRIES

Enquiries about this Circular and its enclosures should be made to:

Children's Services
Room 118
Wellington House
133–155 Waterloo Road
London SE1 8UG

## PROVIDING ASSISTANCE UNDER SECTION 17 OF THE CHILDREN ACT

### Introduction

A series of Court of Appeal judgements (*A v London Borough of Lambeth*, followed by *W v London Borough of Lambeth*) cast doubt on Local Authorities' powers under section 17 of the Children Act 1989 to help families and children with accommodation. For the avoidance of future doubt about the use of section 17 of the Children Act 1989 in relation to accommodation, and to help with accommodation, amendments to the section were made by the Adoption and Children Act 2002. Those amendments have the effect of confirming the position, which was generally understood to have applied before the judgement in *A v London Borough of Lambeth*. That is, that section 17 of the Children Act 1989 includes the power for local authorities to provide accommodation for families and children; and that the provision of accommodation in this way does not make a child looked after. The amendments came into force on 7 November 2002.

## Amendment to section 17

Section 17 (provision of services for children in need, their families and others) to the Children Act 1989 now reads

> "17(6) The services provided by a local authority in the exercise of functions conferred upon them by this section may include providing accommodation, giving assistance in kind or, in exceptional circumstances, in cash."

Because section 22 of the Children Act defines a child as a looked after child if they are accommodated by a local authority in the pursuit of its duties, and the power in section 17 is not and was not previously intended to provide a route by which a child should enter the looked after system, section 22 has been amended so as to exclude children provided with accommodation under section 17. Section 22 (general duty of local authority in relation to children looked after by them) now reads

> "22(1) In this Act, any reference to a child who is looked after by a local authority is a reference to a child who is –
> (a)  in their care; or
> (b)  provided with accommodation by the authority in the exercise of any functions (in particular those under this Act) which are social services functions within the meaning of the Local Authority Social Services Act 1970, apart from functions under sections 17, 23B and 24B."

## Framework for the Assessment of Children in Need and their Families

The amendment to section 17 did not affect the duties and powers of local authorities to provide accommodation for lone children under section 20 of the Children Act 1989, or under a care order. Accordingly, the power to provide accommodation under section 17 will almost always concern children needing to be accommodated with their families. However, there may be cases where a lone child who needs help with accommodation, but does not need to be looked after, might appropriately be assisted under section 17.

Before deciding which section of the Children Act 1989 provides the appropriate legal basis for provision of help or support to a child in need, a local authority should undertake an assessment in accordance with the statutory guidance set out in the *Framework for the Assessment of Children in Need and their Families*, published by the Government in April 2000. It should then use the findings of that assessment, which will include taking account of the wishes and feelings of the child (as required by section 20(6) of the Children Act), as the basis for any decision about whether he should be provided with accommodation under section 20 (and therefore become looked after) or whether other types of services provided under section 17 of the Act are better suited to his circumstances.

The assessment should first determine whether the child meets the criteria set out in section 20(1). Those criteria are:

(a)  there being no person who has parental responsibility for him;
(b)  his being lost or abandoned
(c)  the person who has been caring for him being prevented (whether or not permanently, and for whatever reason) from providing him with suitable accommodation and or care.

For example, where a child has no parent or guardian in this country, perhaps because he has arrived alone seeking asylum, the presumption should be that he would fall within the scope of section 20 and become looked after, unless the needs assessment reveals particular factors which would suggest that an alternative response would be more appropriate. While the needs assessment is being carried out, he should be cared for under section 20.

Local authorities have reported cases where older asylum seeking children have refused to become looked after, but where because of their immigration status the Children Act provides their only lawful means of support in this country. In such cases the child's being without a family or responsible adult in this country would appear to trigger a duty under section 20(1), However, after taking account of the child's wishes as required by section 20(6), the local authority might judge that the child is competent to look after himself. In such circumstances it would not need to assume the whole responsibility for accommodating him under section 20 (and thereby taking him into the looked after system). In such cases section 17 may be used for support, including help with accommodation, without making the child a looked after child.

Similarly, there has been some uncertainty about the legal basis for the jointly funded placements with LEAs of children in residential schools. Children should not normally be maintained in schools by social services departments unless they are looked after, whether under section 20 or section 31. This will ensure that their progress is regularly reviewed and their welfare safeguarded. However, it will not be necessary or desirable for all children known to/funded by social services and placed in residential schools to be looked after. This judgement should be made following a thorough assessment of the needs of the child and family. It will consider whether the child needs the local authority to take responsibility for the provision of accommodation, with attendant looked after status. In particular, it will need to take into account the length of time spent away from the child's family, the degree of contact between the child and his parents, the quality of the child's primary attachments and any particular vulnerabilities of the child. Where this assessment concludes that section 20 criteria are not met, the local authority may then consider providing financial support for the placement under section 17.

### Suitability of accommodation

Where Social Services Departments provide accommodation, or money towards the cost of accommodation, under section 17, they should ensure that the accommodation is suitable for the families and children for whom it is intended. Councils will be aware of the Homelessness Code of Guidance for Local Authorities issued jointly by the Department of Health and the Office of the Deputy Prime Minister in July 2002. This provides guidance, specifically to housing authorities, about the suitability of accommodation provided by them in meeting their duties under the Homelessness Act 2002. Social Services Departments might find it helpful to refer in particular to Chapter 12 of the Code, which deals with suitability of accommodation, and to work closely with Housing Departments in putting it into practice.

**Placements out of area**

Where a Social Services Department provides help under section 17 which involves providing or funding accommodation out of their own area, the placing Department does not relinquish responsibility for the case unless it is specifically and formally transferred to another local authority. In addition, the placing authority should consider whether it is the child's best interests to advise the second authority of the placement, and should do so unless there are strong reasons not to.

**Conclusion**

This guidance draws the attention of councils with social services responsibilities to amendments to section 17 and section 22 of the Children Act 1989, which came into force on 7 November 2002.

# Provision of Accommodation for 16- and 17-year-old young people who may be homeless and/or require accommodation[1]

*Guidance to children's services authorities and local housing authorities about their duties under Part 3 of the Children Act 1989 and Part 7 of the Housing Act 1996 to secure or provide accommodation for homeless 16- and 17-year-old young people.*

For the purposes of this guidance the term 'homeless' should be taken to mean 'homeless and/or requiring accommodation' The term 'young people' should be taken to mean 16- and 17-year-old children.

## 1. Introduction

1.1 In recent years a number of judgments have been handed down by the House of Lords in cases concerning the interrelationship between the duty under section 20 of the *Children Act 1989* ('the 1989 Act') and duties under Part 7 of the *Housing Act 1996* ('the 1996 Act') in the case of young people aged 16 or 17 who require accommodation. The most recent of these has been *R (G) v Southwark [2009] UKHL 26*, but these have also included *R (M) v Hammersmith and Fulham [2008] UKHL 14*. These judgments have restated and clarified the established legal position that the duty under section 20 of the 1989 Act takes precedence over the duties in the 1996 Act in providing for children in need who require accommodation, and that the specific duty owed under section 20 of the 1989 Act takes precedence over the general duty owed to children in need and their families under section 17 of the 1989 Act.

1.2 This guidance does not address the wider responsibilities of local authority children's services and their partners to identify and support families where children and young people may be at risk of negative outcomes, including homelessness in the future, by delivering integrated and targeted services in their area. This guidance is solely concerned with the functions of children's services and housing services when young people seek help from, or are referred to, local authorities because of homelessness.

1.3 This guidance is issued jointly by the Secretary of State for Children, Schools and Families and the Secretary of State for Communities and Local Government under section 7 of the *Local Authority Social Services 1970* and section 182 of the *Housing Act 1996*. Section 7 of the 1970 Act requires local authorities in exercising their social services functions to act under the general guidance of the Secretary of State; unless there are exceptional reasons in individual cases authorities are expected to comply with this guidance. Section 182 of the 1996 Act requires housing authorities and social services authorities, in the exercise of their functions relating to homelessness and the prevention of homelessness, to have regard to such guidance as may from time to time be given by the Secretary of State.

---

1   © Crown Copyright. Published by Department for Schools and Families and the Department for Communities and Local Government, April 2010. Available from www.education.gov.uk.

1.4  This guidance replaces the paragraphs in Circular LAC (2003) 13 Guidance *on Accommodating Children in Need and the Families,* issued by the Department of Health, which refer to how lone 16- and 17-year-olds should be accommodated under the Children Act 1989 Act.

*Structure of the guidance*

1.5  **Part 2** of this guidance addresses children's services' and housing services' initial responses to 16- and 17-year-olds seeking help because of homelessness. **Part 3** gives guidance on the provision of suitable accommodation for 16 and 17 year olds. In many cases, both children's services and housing services will need to have contact with, and provide services for, homeless 16 and 17 year olds. **Part 4** gives guidance on the provision of suitable accommodation for 16- and 17-year-olds who are not owed a duty under section 20 or who refuse section 20 accommodation. **Part 5** provides guidance on joint working between children's and housing services at strategic and operational level.

2.   **Responding to 16- and 17-year-old young people seeking help because of homelessness.**

*Supporting families to stay together and re-unification*

2.1.  It is in the best interests of most young people aged 16 or 17 to live in the family home, or, where this is not safe or appropriate, with responsible adults in their wider family and friends network. Local authority responses to 16- and 17-year-olds seeking help because of homelessness should explicitly recognise this and work pro-actively with young people and their families to identify and resolve the issues which have led to the homelessness crisis. This could involve family support such as family mediation or family group conferences.

2.2.  It may be possible for children's services to prevent a young person from having to leave home at all, or it may take much longer to work through significant family tensions and problems while the young person is accommodated by the local authority. It is therefore important that services are designed to enable this family focus to begin on day one and continue throughout the processes of assessment and, where necessary, the provision of accommodation.

2.3.  This preventative work should be undertaken alongside the statutory assessment processes outlined in this guidance and should not delay assessment or the delivery of statutory services to 16- and 17-year-olds who may be homeless or at risk of homelessness.

2.4.  If key issues affecting the young person's welfare and/or the sustainability of their living at home remain unresolved, post-reunification support should be provided to the family after the young person returns home.

*16- and 17-year-olds who may require accommodation with children and/ or partners*

2.5  By the age of 16 or 17 most young people are forming relationships and a few may themselves have children. Assessment, support and accommodation services should take into account young peoples' relationships as well as any dependent children and, where appropriate, support them to build a positive family life.

2.6 The needs of 16 and 17 year olds' for accommodation should be assessed in the context of their relationship with any 'partner'. In some cases it may be appropriate for a 16 or 17 year old to be accommodated in a situation where where they can live with their partner. This should not prevent local authorities from accommodating a 16 or 17 year old under section 20 where the young person is owed a duty under this section. Specific consideration should be given to placement options for young people accommodated under section 20 whilst living with a partner. For example, placement in an alternative arrangement such as a self contained property with visiting support may be appropriate. It will also be important to have contingency plans in place in case relationships break down.

2.7 Where young parents are provided with accommodation by children's services and become looked after, it does not follow that their child will also be looked after. This is an issue for an entirely separate assessment based on the needs of the infant.

*Accessing services*

2.8 16- and 17-year-olds who seek assistance from a local authority because they are homeless or at risk of homelessness may either seek help initially from the local housing authority or from the children's services authority. Within unitary authorities, the initial approach for help may be made to either housing services or children's services. 16- and 17-year-olds may also seek help from multi-disciplinary teams including co-located children's and housing services staff where local authorities have established such arrangements (these arrangements may be made in both unitary and two tier areas and will be referred to as **integrated services** for the purposes of this guidance).

*Initial approaches to housing services*

2.9 Where the initial approach or referral for housing assistance is made to housing services, the authority should treat the approach/referral as an application for assistance under Part 7 of the 1996 Act. The authority will therefore need to decide whether there is reason to believe the young person may be homeless or likely to become homeless within 28 days (section 184 of the1996 Act) and, if so, the authority will need to make inquiries to determine whether any duty is owed under Part 7 of the 1996 Act.

2.10 If there is reason to believe the young person may be eligible for assistance, may be homeless and may be 16 or 17 years of age, the authority will have an immediate duty to secure interim accommodation (section 188(1) of the 1996 Act) pending a decision whether any substantive duty is owed under Part 7. Such accommodation must be suitable for a 16 & 17 year old and, in considering suitability, authorities should bear in mind that 16- and 17-year-olds who are homeless and estranged from their family will be particularly vulnerable and in need of support. The Secretary of State considers that Bed and Breakfast accommodation is unsuitable for 16 and 17 year olds.

2.11  If the young person may be homeless or may be likely to become homeless within 28 days, housing services should make an immediate referral to
children's services for an assessment. This applies to all 16- and 17-year-old
applicants without exception, for example including those who are pregnant
and/or a parent. The question whether any substantive duty is owed under
Part 7 of the 1996 Act will depend in part on the outcome of the assessment
by children's services, and whether any duty is owed under section 20 of
the 1989 Act. Housing services should continue to secure accommodation
under section 188 (1) until they have notified the young person whether any
substantive duty is owed under Part 7 of the 1996 Act. Children's services
should undertake and complete an initial assessment as soon as possible
and no later than the ten days set out in the Framework for the Assessment
of Children in Need and their Families. (See paragraphs 2.36- 2.40). Where
children's services have accepted that they have a duty under section 20 duty
to provide accommodation and the 16 or 17 year old has accepted the accommodation, the young person will not be homeless and no further duty will be
owed under Part 7 of the 1996 Act.

*Young people from one district who seek assistance from housing services in
another district*

2.12  Housing services are reminded that they must consider all applications for
accommodation or assistance in obtaining accommodation. Authorities cannot refuse to assist an applicant on the basis that the applicant may not (or
does not) have a local connection with the district. Authorities can refer an
applicant to another authority only if they have accepted that the applicant
is eligible for assistance, unintentionally homeless and in priority need but
consider that the applicant does not have a local connection with their district
and does have one elsewhere in Great Britain. For further guidance about
local connection and referrals, authorities should refer to Chapter 18 of the
*Homelessness Code of Guidance for Local Authorities.*[2]

*Initial approaches and referrals to integrated services*

2.13  Integrated services can assist in the delivery of a seamless, child-centred
response to the needs of 16- and 17-year-olds who are homeless or threatened with homelessness. Given that the 1989 Act takes precedence over the
1996 Act, and given their responsibilities for children in need in their areas,
children's services should be the lead agency with regard to assessing and
meeting the needs of 16- and 17-year-olds who seek help because of homelessness. The Secretary of State for Children, Schools and Families and the
Secretary of State for Communities and Local Government consider that an
initial approach or referral to integrated services should be treated in the
same way as an initial approach or referral to children's services (see below).

2.14  The involvement of housing staff in this process can have a number of benefits, for example:

–   improvement of joint working through better understanding and communication between children's services and housing services;

2   www.communities.gov.uk/publications/housing/homelessnesscode.

– giving 16 and 17 year olds, and their families, access to information directly from both services regarding the support and, if necessary, accommodation options that may be available both now and in the future;
– removal of the need for a referral to housing services for a fresh assessment
under the homelessness legislation if the young person is not accommodated under section 20, e.g., following the initial assessment and consideration of their wishes and feelings in the context of their needs.

*Approaches and referrals to children's services.*

2.15 Where a 16 or 17 year old seeks help from local authority children's services
or is referred to children's services by some other person or agency (including housing services) as appearing to be homeless or at risk of homelessness, or they are an unaccompanied asylum seeker without a parent or guardian with responsibility for their care, then children's services must assess
whether the young person is a child in need, and determine whether any duty
is owed under section 20 of the 1989 Act to provide the young person with
accommodation.

2.16 Where a 16 or 17 year old seeks help or is referred, and it appears he or she
has nowhere safe to stay that night, then children's services must secure suitable emergency accommodation for them. This will mean that the young
person will become looked after (under section 20 (1)) whilst their needs,
including their need for continuing accommodation and support, are further
assessed. Bed and breakfast accommodation is not considered suitable for
16- and 17-year-olds even on an emergency accommodation basis. Where the
young person is accommodated under section 20 they will not be eligible for
welfare benefits, including housing benefit[3] and children's services will have
a duty to maintain them (including meeting the cost of accommodation).

2.17 Section 17 of the 1989 Act sets out the responsibilities of local authorities to
provide services for children in need and their families. It is the general duty
of every local authority _
(a)-to safeguard and promote the welfare of children within their area who are
in need; and
(b)-so far as is consistent with that duty, to promote the upbringing of such
children by their families
by providing a range and level of services appropriate to those children's
needs.

2.18 Section 17(10) of the 1989 Act defines a child as being in need if –
(a) he is unlikely to achieve or maintain, or to have the opportunity of achieving or maintaining, a reasonable standard of health or development without the provision for him of services by a local authority under this Part;
(b) his health or development is likely to be significantly impaired, or further
impaired, without the provision for him of such services; or
(c) he is disabled,

The duties described in section 17 apply to all children in need in the area of
the local authority.

3 There are exceptions for lone parents and for disabled young people who may have
established entitlement to non-means tested benefits.

A child is any person under the age of 18. (see section 105(1) of the 1989 Act.)

2.19   Section 20(1) requires that:

Every local authority shall provide accommodation for any child in need within their area who appears to them to require accommodation as a result of –
(a) there being no person who has parental responsibility for him;
(b) his being lost or having been abandoned; or
(c) the person who has been caring for him being prevented (whether or not permanently, and for whatever reason) from providing him with suitable accommodation or care.

2.20   In addition, even if the criteria in section 20(1) do not apply, section 20(3) requires that:

Every local authority shall provide accommodation for any child in need within their area who has reached the age of sixteen and whose welfare the authority consider is likely to be seriously prejudiced if they do not provide him with accommodation.

2.21   In addition, section 20 (4), provides that:

a local authority may provide accommodation for any child within their area (even though a person who has parental responsibility for him is able to provide him with accommodation) if they consider that to do so would safeguard or promote the child's welfare.

2.22   Local authority duties for accommodating young people under this section are not simply a matter for local policy. The duty is engaged whenever any authority has determined that the young person is in fact in need and requires accommodation as a result of one of the factors set out in section 20(1)(a) to (c) or in section 20(3).

2.23   There can be no doubt that where a young person requires accommodation as a result of one of the factors set out in section 20(1)(a) to (c) or section 20(3) then that young person will be in need and must be provided with accommodation. As a result of being accommodated the young person will become looked after and the local authority will owe them the duties that are owed to all looked after children, set out in sections 22 and 23 and once they cease to be looked after, the duties that are owed to care leavers under that Act.

2.24   Identifying the needs of the young person and the best response to these needs will be the function of each assessment. The critical factors to be taken into account in assessing whether a young person is in need under the 1989 Act are what will happen to the young person's health and development without services being provided or secured by children's services and the likely effect of the provision of services will have on the young person's health and development. Where a young person is excluded from home, is sofa surfing among friends, or is sleeping in a car, it is extremely likely that they will be a child in need. Similarly, where a 16- and 17-year-old teenage parent is homeless they are also likely to have significant needs and require accommodation and support as a child in need. Determining who is in need and the extent of any needs requires professional judgment by children's services staff, informed by consultation with other professionals familiar with the circumstances of the individual young person and their family. The young person's and their family's wishes and feelings must be taken into account (see paragraphs 2.44 – 2.53 below).

2.25   At the point when the need for a children's services assessment is identified, it will be necessary for the professional undertaking the assessment to agree an assessment plan with the young person and with their family. (For a 16 or 17 year old who may be homeless, this will be the point at which they first seek help from, or are referred to, children's services). This assessment plan will make clear from the outset who is doing what, within what timescales, and what the possible outcomes of the assessment might be. These could range from the young person becoming, or continuing to be (if children's services has provided or secured emergency accommodation) accommodated by children's services to no services being provided.

2.26   Young people seeking help because of actual or threatened homelessness are likely to have a range of concurrent needs [4] and these should be assessed fully in accordance with the assessment process set out in the Framework for the Assessment of Children in Need and their Families. The most crucial issue to be determined through the assessment process will be whether the young person is actually homeless and therefore requires accommodation. However, assessment will need to take into account every dimension of the young person's needs and, as well as the need for accommodation, it will be necessary to assess what further support the young person needs. A homeless young person not participating in education or training would in the first place need suitable accommodation but this should be arranged in conjunction with plans to re-engage them with education or training.

2.27   The majority of young people seeking help because of homelessness cite the breakdown of relationships with parents or other carers as the reason for their homelessness. The assessment will need to determine whether or not the young person can return home, with support for them and their family if necessary, or whether this is not a possible or safe option.

*Undertaking assessments*

2.28   An initial assessment should be carried out involving interviewing the young person and family members and making enquiries with other agencies. Where a young person seeks help because of homelessness it is good practice for an assessment of the young person's needs to be conducted jointly by both children's and housing services. Alternatively, assessment and referral processes should be underpinned by appropriate information-sharing so that young people do not have to repeat their stories each time and navigate between offices which may be some way apart. The lead agency will be children's services, given their responsibilities for children in need in their areas.

---

4   Statutory Homelessness in England: The Experiences of Homeless Families and 16 and 17 year olds' – CLG 2008, www.communities.gov.uk/publications/housing/experienceoffamilies.

2.29   It will be essential to establish very close contact and rapport with the young person throughout the assessment process, in order to make sure their wishes and feelings are properly understood and to take their views into account (see paragraphs under 2.44 below). Similarly, it will also be important to maintain contact with the adults who retain parental responsibility for the young person and with any other family members in the young person's network. It will generally be necessary to visit the family home or other accommodation where the young person has been living as part of the assessment process.

2.30   The assessment will need to establish whether the factors set out in sections 20(1), 20(3) or 20(4) of the 1989 Act are applicable to the young person's circumstances.

2.31   Careful account will need to be taken of the factors which will promote the welfare of the young person , including the significance of the young person's relationship with their parents, or other adults in their life responsible for their care up until the point that they seek help, or are referred, as homeless. The assessment should identify the young person's and their family's, strengths as well as any difficulties and should build on strengths to attempt to develop sustainable solutions so that the young person's needs, including the need for suitable accommodation, are met for the future.

2.32   At the conclusion of the initial assessment, staff should have reached a provisional assessment of the young person's needs and the services that they are likely to require to support them in making a positive transition into adulthood. The Annex to this guidance sets out the issues that should generally be considered during the assessment process. The Framework for the Assessment of Children in Need and their Families (2000) [5] provides comprehensive information about the factors that the assessment must take into account.

2.33   Where a young person seeks help because of homelessness, the assessment must necessarily reach a decision as to whether or not the young person is a child in need and requires accommodation as a result of one the scenarios set out in section 20(1)(a) to (c) or section 20(3).

2.34   In some cases, it may not be necessary for the young person to be accommodated by children's services because the young person's needs can be met by providing other services – for example, support to enable the young person to return to the care of their family or other responsible adults in the young person's network. If children's services conclude that the young person does not require accommodation for this reason, they should consider whether they should provide services under section 17 of the 1989 Act, which could include financial support under section 17(6)) to sustain any plan for the young person to live with members of their family. Children's services will also need to put in place a strategy to try to avoid the young person being threatened with homelessness in the future. Where the young person is a child in need, children's services should use their powers under section 17 of the 1989 Act to provide these services.

2.35   However, if the young person requires accommodation, then this must be provided by children's services and the young person concerned will become

5   www.archive.official-documents.co.uk/document/doh/facn/fw-00.htm.

or continue to be (if children's services has provided or secured emergency accommodation) looked after under section 20 of the 1989 Act, with the authority having the responsibilities towards them set out in sections 22 and 23 and once they cease to be looked after, the duties that are owed to care leavers under that Act.[6]. The child becomes looked after at the point that the local authority determines the young person needs accommodation (including emergency accommodation) under section 20.

## Timescales

2.36 *The Framework for Assessment of Children in Need and their Families* sets out the timescales that should, except in exceptional circumstances involving difficulty in obtaining relevant information or children with very complex needs, be followed when assessing whether a not a child is in need and whether, as a result, services should be provided.

2.37 Within <u>one working day</u> a decision must be taken about whether to carry out an initial assessment . Where a young person refers themselves, or is referred by housing services or another agency as appearing to be homeless, children's services should proceed with an assessment unless they are able to determine very quickly that the young person is not homeless and does not require support.

2.38 A decision to gather more information constitutes an initial assessment. This should be completed within ten working days.

2.39 Where housing services have been providing interim accommodation pending assessment of the young person, once the initial assessment by children services is complete and it has been determined whether the young person will be accommodated by children's services under section 20, children's services should notify housing services immediately. Where accommodation is to be provided under section 20 arrangements for the move to a new placement should be made as quickly as possible.

2.40 An assessment is not complete until children's services have decided what action is necessary to respond to the young person's needs and this has been communicated to the young person, the adults responsible for their care, housing services and any other relevant agencies.

## 16- and 17-year-olds from one local authority area who seek assistance from children's services in another local authority area

2.41 Where a 16 or 17 year old who was living in one local authority area and moves to another local authority area and seeks assistance from children's services in that local authority, the duty to assess falls on the authority from which they seek assistance. The authority cannot refuse to consider the young person's immediate needs and expect them to return to the authority in the area presumed to be their 'home' district.

---

6 A looked after child who is aged 16 or 17 and has been looked after for a total of at least 13 weeks (which began after they reached the age of 14 and ends after they reach the age of 16) is an 'eligible child', and will be entitled to care leaving support under the 1989 Act. A 16 or 17 year old who was an eligible child but has ceased to be looked after, is a 'relevant child', and will also be entitled to support as a care leaver.

2.42   An initial interview, perhaps combined with enquiries in the area where the young person came from, should be sufficient to establish their connection with the area where they have sought help and their reasons for seeking help there rather than in their 'home' district. These enquiries may be able to establish whether it may be possible it for the young person to return to the area where they may be presumed to have a stronger local connection. For example, it might be possible for the authority where the young person seeks help to negotiate with their 'home' authority to take over the assessment of the young person's needs, so that the young person is assessed in a familiar setting close to their family and friends.

2.43   It is essential that disputes about responsibility for the young person in the medium term should not get in the way of the authority that received the young person's request for assistance responding to the young person's immediate needs. The young person concerned must not be passed from pillar to post while the authorities determine where he or she comes from.

*Young person's wishes and feelings*

2.44   Section 20(6) of the Children Act requires that:

Before providing accommodation under this section, a local authority shall, so far as is reasonably practicable and consistent with the child's welfare;

(a) ascertain the child's wishes and feelings regarding the provision of accommodation; and

(b) give due consideration (having regard to his age and understanding) to such wishes and feelings of the child as they have been able to ascertain.

2.45   This will include assessing their emotional and behavioral development and their capacity to make use of wider resources to manage independent living.

2.46   However, where a young person says they do not wish to be accommodated, a local authority should reach the conclusion that the young person's wishes are decisive only as part of an overall judgment of their assessed welfare needs and the type and location of accommodation that will meet those needs.

2.47   The approach to assessment must be child-centred. It will be very important that children's services staff responsible for the assessment are able to communicate the assessment plan to the young person so that he or she is provided with information about the enquiries that need to be made and the timescales involved. A key aspect of the assessment will involve reaching an understanding about how the young person views their needs.

2.48   It will be essential that the young person is fully consulted about and understands the implications of being accommodated by children's services and becoming looked after. The staff conducting the assessment must provide realistic and full information about the support that the young person can expect as a looked after child and, subsequently, as a care leaver. Children's services should also ensure that the young person receives accurate information about what assistance may be available to them, including from housing services under Part 7 of the 1996 Act, if they do not become looked after, and how any entitlement for assistance under Part 7 will be determined. In particular, the possible risk of becoming homeless intentionally in future, and the implications of this for further assistance with accommodation, should be made clear to the young person. This information should be provided in a 'child friendly' format at the start of the assessment process and be available for the young person to take away for full consideration and to help them seek advice.

2.49   Where there is any doubt about a 16 or 17 year old's capacity to judge what may be in his or her best interests, e.g. whether they should become looked after or seek alternative assistance, there will need to be further discussion involving children's services, housing services, the young person concerned and their family, to reach agreement on the way forward.

2.50   Young people should have access to independent advocacy and support to assist them in weighing up the advantages and disadvantages and coming to a balanced decision.[7]

2.51   Some 16- and 17-year-olds may decide that they do not wish to be provided with accommodation by children's services, for example, because they do not wish to be supported as a looked after child. However, in these circumstances, it is important that children's services are clear that the young person's decision is properly informed, and has been reached after careful consideration of all the relevant information.

2.52   The fact that a young person may be reluctant to engage with the assessment process outlined above is not in itself a basis for assuming that the young person has rejected any children's services' intervention to provide them with accommodation. Lack of co-operation is no reason for the local authority not to attempt to carry out its duties under the 1989 Act. In these circumstances, the assessment will need to involve careful recording of how the authority has attempted to engage with the young person to assess their needs in order to determine and provide appropriate services. Ultimately, however, it is not possible to force services on young people who persistently continue to refuse them.

2.53   Where a 16 or 17 year old child in need wishes to refuse accommodation offered under section 20 of the 1989 Act, children's services must be satisfied that the young person :
   –   has been provided with all relevant information
   –   is competent to make such a decision

### Provision of accommodation under section 17 of the 1989 Act

2.54   Children's services authorities have powers to accommodate children under section 17(6) of the 1989 Act. A young person provided with accommodation under this section would not be looked after and the local authority would not have the corresponding duties set out at in sections 22, 23 and 24 of the 1989 Act. However, the provision of accommodation under section 17 will almost always concern children needing to be accommodated with their families.

---

7   Children and young people who have received services under the 1989 Act are able to be supported to make complaints and representation with the help of an independent advocate. Children's services should provide information about access to advocacy services when they explain the assessment process to 16 and 17 year olds seeking help because of homelessness.

2.55 The powers of local authorities to provide accommodation under section 17 cannot be used to substitute for their duty to provide accommodation under section 20(1) of the 1989 Act to homeless 16- and 17-year-olds who are assessed as being children in need following the process described in Part 2, above. Children's services do not have the option of choosing under which provision they should provide accommodation for homeless 16 and 17 year olds. Section 20 involves an evaluative judgment on some matters but not a discretion.[8]

## 3. Provision of suitable supported accommodation under section 20 of the 1989 Act by children's services

3.1. Children's services must only provide children with supported accommodation which is suitable and of high quality. A range of different types of accommodation may provide suitable accommodation for 16- and 17-year-olds who cannot live with their families, carers or guardians. These include foster care, children's homes, supported lodgings, foyers, properties with visiting support tailored to the young person's needs and other types of supported accommodation. In order for services to work well it is important that children's services work closely with housing services to ensure that a range of suitable supported accommodation placements are available for young people in their area, whether or not they are looked after children. Bed and breakfast accommodation is not suitable for 16 and 17 year olds. For teenage parents it is particularly important that they are provided with accommodation which gives them the holistic support they require to meet their individual needs and improve their outcomes. This should include support around parenting and independent living skills; their health and well-being; access to education and training; and their readiness for future independent living.

3.2. The choice of placement for any individual young person will be informed by the assessment of their needs.

3.3 Section 23(2) of the 1989 Act sets out the range of placement options in which a young person who is looked after by the local authority may be accommodated. These will include placements in foster care or in children's homes.

3.4 Some 16- and 17-year-olds who require accommodation may be reluctant to take up these kinds of accommodation options and the assessment of their emotional and behavioural development will indicate that they do not require the level or kind of supervision and support that foster or children's home care provides.

3.5 Section 23(2)(f)(i) of the 1989 Act permits local authorities to make *such other arrangements* as seem appropriate when they place a looked after child. This provision offers scope for children's services to ensure that they are able to make appropriate provision with support tailored to the needs of the young person for those homeless 16- and 17-year-olds who they accommodate, and are looked after, but for whom fostering or a children's home placement would not be the most suitable option.

---

8   *R (G) v Southwark LBC* [2009] UKHL 26, para 31 at www.publications.parliament. uk/pa/ld200809/ldjudgmt/jd090520/appg-2.htm.

3.6 From the point at which children's services accommodate a 16 or 17 year old child, they should look forward to the support that the young person will need to make a positive transition to greater independence. This might include, for example, the provision of supported accommodation (perhaps jointly funded) where young people can remain beyond the age of 18 and develop the skills they will need to manage the transition to adulthood. This kind of accommodation might be jointly commissioned by children's services and housing services and will enable children's services to meet their forthcoming duties to secure sufficient accommodation for looked after children and care leavers in their area. [9]For example, a formerly homeless young person may be placed in 'supported lodgings' to offer them opportunities to take on more responsibility for their own care in order to prepare them for the tranition to adulthood.

3.7 The primary issue to be addressed in making each and every placement in 'other arrangements', just as in any other placement setting, will be: how will making this placement meet the assessed needs of the individual young person?

3.8 Where a young person is placed in *other arrangements* then the local authority must prepare a placement plan which is agreed between the young person and the person responsible for supporting the young person in the accommodation. This should be the person who will have the most day to day contact with the young person, for example their 'key worker' or supported lodgings host/carer. Any support plan setting out how the supported accommodation service will support the young person should be integral to the placement plan and avoid duplication.

3.9 The placement planning process should involve an exchange of appropriate information included as part of the core assessment process which informed the development of the looked after young person's care plan, so that the accommodation provider has a full understanding of the young person's needs and their role in meeting these needs. It will be essential that the provider appreciates the arrangements that the local authority proposes to put in place to make sure that the young person is adequately supported. The placement plan must be explicit about the respective roles and responsibilities of the placement provider and the young person's social worker, their Independent Reviewing Officer and of other staff employed or commissioned by the authority to contribute to the plan for the young person's care.

3.10 The plan must set out:
   – the respective safeguarding responsibilities of the provider and local authority
   – the frequency of visits the young person can expect from their responsible authority
   – communication arrangements between the provider and the local authority
   – the provider's responsibilities for notifying the young person's social worker and accountable staff of the authority of any significant change in the young person's circumstances
   – arrangements for giving notice of intention to terminate the placement

9   Section 22G of the 1989 Act inserted by section 9 of the Children and Young Persons Act 2008 s9.

(along with the authority's responsibilities for convening a review of the young person's care plan where there is a risk of the placement being terminated).

## 4   Provision of accommodation for 16- and 17-year-olds to whom a section 20 duty is not owed or who refuse section 20 accommodation

4.1   If children's services decide that they do not have a duty to provide accommodation for a homeless 16 or 17 year old or the young person has refused provision of accommodation, children's services must consider what other support and services should be provided for the young person to meet their needs in conjunction with housing services.

*Securing accommodation under Part 7 of the 1996 Act (housing services)*

4.2   Under Part 7 of the 1996 Act, and the *Homelessness (Priority Need for Accommodation) (England) Order 2002*[10], applicants aged 16 or 17 have a priority need for accommodation if they are not owed a duty under section 20 of the 1989 Act. Where such applicants are also eligible for assistance and unintentionally homeless, the local housing authority will owe them a duty under section 193 (2) of the 1996 Act to secure that accommodation is available for their occupation. Authorities should refer to the *Homelessness Code of Guidance for Local Authorities* for general guidance on discharging their homelessness functions under Part 7 of the 1996 Act.

4.3   Where children's services have decided that a section 20 duty is not owed for one of the reasons above, and the young person applies to housing services for accommodation or assistance in obtaining accommodation, housing services will need to consider whether any duty is owed under Part 7 of the 1996 Act (section 184).

4.4   In any case where housing services provide accommodation for a child in need, children's services will need to consider the provision of services under section 17 of the 1989 Act to meet the young person's other needs.

4.5   Where an application for housing assistance is already under consideration (for example, because the young person's initial approach for help was made to housing services and the young person had been referred to children's services for an assessment of need), the notification by children's services that a section 20 duty is not owed will enable housing services to complete their inquiries under section 184 of the 1996 Act and decide whether any duty is owed under Part 7.

4.6   In considering whether a duty under Part 7 is owed to a 16 or 17 year old who has refused section 20 accommodation, it is for the housing authority to satisfy themselves in each individual case whether the applicant is homeless or threatened with homelessness. Authorities should not adopt general policies which seek to pre-define circumstances that do or do not amount to intentional homelessness or threat of homelessness.

4.7   Where a 16 or 17 year old is secured accommodation under Part 7 of the 1996 Act, children's services should work closely with housing services to ensure that the young person is provided with sufficient support to ensure he or she

10 www.opsi.gov.uk/SI/si2002/20022051.htm.

does not become homeless intentionally in the future, for example, as a result of accruing rent arrears or being evicted due to bad behaviour.

4.8   Where children's services hold open the offer of accommodation on a temporary basis to ensure that a 16 or 17 year old has accommodation available to meet his or her immediate needs, housing services should not necessarily consider that the young person is not homeless. Housing services will need to consider whether, in the circumstances, it would be reasonable for the applicant to continue to occupy the accommodation indefinitely, if they did not intervene and secure alternative accommodation.

4.9   In order to help facilitate the provision of accommodation by housing services to meet the young person's accommodation needs in the longer term, children's and housing services will need to agree a procedure for children's services to inform housing services that their provision of temporary accommodation will come to an end. This process should aim to minimise anxiety for the young person associated with concerns that they may again find themselves without anywhere to live. Children's services and housing services will need to work together closely to ensure that the young person's ongoing housing needs can be met in the most practical and timely way possible.

4.10   Housing services are reminded that applicants cannot be considered to have become homeless intentionally because of failing to take up an offer of accommodation; homelessness is only capable of being 'intentional' where the applicant has ceased to occupy accommodation that it would have been reasonable for him or her to continue to occupy.

4.11   Case law has established that in some circumstances a person does not do, or fail to do, something 'deliberately' for the purpose of Part 7 of the 1996 Act if he makes a considered choice between two courses of action or inaction, either of which he or she is able to take. Thus, the Secretary of State considers that where a 16 or 17 year old is required to leave accommodation as a result of his or her decision to refuse section 20 accommodation (for example, where children's services bring to an end interim accommodation provided pending assessment of the young person's needs), that decision should not be treated as deliberate action or inaction that contributed to intentional homelessness, subject to it being an informed and considered decision.

4.12   If, for whatever reason, a 16 or 17 year old is found to have become homeless intentionally, housing services should inform children's services immediately (see section on joint protocols below). For further guidance about intentional homelessness, authorities should refer to Chapter 11 of the *Homelessness Code of Guidance for Local Authorities*.[11]

## 5.   Joint working to tackle youth homelessness

5.1   There is a clear legal framework for co-operation between children's services and housing services to meet the needs of children and young people. Section 27 of the 1989 Act empowers a children's services authority to ask other authorities, including any local housing authority, for 'help in the exercise of any of their functions' under Part 3; the requested authority must provide

---

11 www.communities.gov.uk/publications/housing/homelessnesscode.

that help if it is compatible with their own statutory or other duties and does not unduly prejudice the discharge of any of their own functions. The Children Act 2004 broadened and strengthened the statutory framework requiring co-operation between relevant statutory services to improve outcomes for children and young people as part of developing an area's Children's Trust's arrangements. [12]

*Operational joint working – joint protocols*

5.2 It follows from the guidance above that the particular services a 16 or 17 year old should be provided with by children's services and housing services will depend on a range of factors in each case, including which service they initially seek help from; the outcomes of assessments and enquiries; and the wishes and feelings of the young person and the young person's family. It is therefore essential that services for homeless 16- and 17-year-olds are underpinned by written joint protocols which set out clear, practical arrangements for providing services that are centred on young people and their families and prevent young people from being passed from pillar to post.

5.3 An effective joint protocol will set out a mutually agreed vision, objectives, systems and processes to ensure effective action to prevent youth homelessness and the provision of sufficient accommodation to meet the range of needs of homeless young people. In formulating a joint protocol, due regard should be had to the fact that the 1989 Act takes precedence over the 1996 Act in providing for children in need.

5.4 A joint protocol might cover the following:
1. Inter-agency arrangements to prevent youth homelessness and provide support to young people to remain living with their families.
2. Information for agencies, for example Connexions services and Youth Offending Teams who may refer young people about where they should refer young people for help with homelessness.
3. Arrangements for integrated or joint assessment processes where 16- and 17-year-olds seek help because they are homeless, including information-sharing procedures.
4. Agreed timescales (in line with the *Framework for the Assessment of Children in Need and their Families*) for assessing whether or not a homeless young person is a child in need and will be provided with accommodation by children's services.
5. Arrangements for timely assessment and placement provision for young people who require accommodation on release from custody
6. Arrangements for access to suitable emergency accommodation when needed.
7. Arrangements for access to longer term accommodation with support for young people (including looked after children and care leavers) who need this service.

8. Agreed standards as to how the suitability of accommodation that is not

12 See Statutory guidance on co-operation arrangements, including the Children's Trust Board and the Children and Young People's Plan (March 2010): www.dcsf.gov.uk/everychildmatters/about/aims/childrenstrusts/childrenstrusts/.

formally regulated or inspected will be assured. These might make reference to the Quality Assessment Framework (QAF) or to the Foyer Federation's Accreditation Scheme[13]

9.  Arrangements for the provision of accommodation and other services to any 16- and 17-year-olds who are neither being accommodated by children's services under section 20 nor have found to be owed the main homelessness duty by housing services (for example, because they do not wish to be accommodated under section 20 and are considered by housing services to have become homeless intentionally).[14]

10. Integrated monitoring arrangements to provide management information regarding outcomes for young people including through reconciliation with parents or carers.

11. Processes for resolving any disputes arising between staff from children's services and staff from housing services (for example, where expectations for completing assessments within specified timescales have not been met).

5.5 The effectiveness and continuing relevance of joint protocols should be reviewed at least annually. Local authorities may find it helpful to establish multi-agency arrangements to monitor the effectiveness of protocols and the performance of local services in responding to homeless young people. Local authorities will need to consider at the outset, what data will be required for monitoring purposes and how the agencies involved in providing services to homeless young people will collect and analyse this. These monitoring arrangements will contribute to wider monitoring of the overall effectiveness of the children's trust in safeguarding children and young people and promoting their welfare.

5.6 It would be good practice for young people who have been provided with services to be consulted about the quality of services and contribute to service reviews.

*Strategic joint working*

5.7 Children's services will need to work with housing services (which will be within district councils in two-tier areas), registered social landlords; housing related support services and with other partners to secure a range of suitable housing and support options for young people and their families. This will include options for the provision of accommodation with support for 16- and 17-year-olds who seek help because they are homeless, and for care leavers.

5.8 Children's services should be linked to housing authorities' strategic housing function, and housing authorities should be represented on the Children's Trust Board.

5.9 The anticipated accommodation and support needs of vulnerable young

---

13 See www.sitra.org.uk/index.php?id=1019 and www.foyer.net/level3.asp?level3id=184.

14 In this situation, where a young person remains homeless housing services should make a fresh referral to children's services – and children's services should undertake a further assessment of the young person's needs in the light of the change of circumstances. This will give the young person the opportunity to reconsider the option of being assisted under section 20.

people, including homeless 16- and 17-year-olds and care leavers, should be represented in the following strategies and plans:
- The Children and Young People's Plan
- Housing and Homelessness Strategies
- Supporting People or Housing Related Support Strategies

5.10  Consideration should be given to developing collaboration between children's services and commissioners of housing and support services to meet the housing needs of young people in the area including providing suitable accommodation placements for looked after children aged 16 and 17. Services jointly planned and secured might include supported accommodation projects, floating support services, foyers, supported lodgings, and more specialist housing provision for particularly vulnerable young people.

### Annex

**Factors to be considered by children's services when assessing 16/17 year olds who may be homeless children in need**

|   | Dimensions of Need | Issues to consider in assessing child's future needs. |
|---|---|---|
| 1. | Accommodation | Does the child have access to stable accommodation? How far is this suitable to the full range of the child's needs? |
| 2. | Family and Social Relationships | Assessment of the child's relationship with their parents and wider family. What is the capacity of the child's family and social network to provide stable and secure accommodation and meet the child's practical, emotional and social needs |
| 3. | Emotional and Behavioural Development | Does the child show self esteem, resilience and confidence? Assessment of their attachments and the quality of their relationships. Does the child show self control and appropriate self awareness? |
| 4. | Education, Training and Employment | Information about the child's education experience and background Assessment as to whether support may be required to enable the child to access education, training or employment. |
| 5. | Financial Capability and independent living skills | Assessment of the child's financial competence and how they will secure financial support in future Information about the support the child might need to develop self-management and independent living skills, |
| 6. | Health and Development | Assessment of child's physical, emotional and mental health needs. |
| 7. | Identity | Assessment of the child's needs as a result of their ethnicity, preferred langrage, cultural background, religion or sexual identity. |

# Practice guidelines for age assessment of young unaccompanied asylum seekers[1]

Assessment of age is a complex task, which is a process and not an exact science. This is further complicated by many of the young people attempting to portray a different age from their true age.

In completing the assessment, please be mindful that clients have the right to legally challenge the conclusion. UNICEF publishes the figure of 50 million children who are currently not registered at birth, depriving them of nationality, a legal name and proof of when they were born. Many societies calculate age in a different way from the method used in the UK; internationally millions of young people do not know their age. The Royal College of Paediatricians (1999) states that 'in practice, age determination is extremely difficult to do with certainty. More over, for young people aged 15 to 18 it is even less possible to be certain about age'.

Young unaccompanied asylum seekers both at the ports of entry, and as in country applicants, sometimes give a stated age that is disputed by the immigration authorities. The Home Office will often, based purely on appearance, judge the young person to be an adult and refer directly to NASS. A proportion of young people are referred to the local social services department for an assessment of age. Additionally young asylum seekers self refer to social services and an assessment of their age becomes necessary.

A young person's age is a key part of the information needed when making an assessment of need and subsequently for the appropriate provision of service. The Local Authority has a responsibility under the Children Act 1989 to assess whether a young person is in need and to provide services to safeguard and promote welfare.

It is important to explain to the young person that an assessment must be undertaken in order to identify what services may be provided. An assessment of age concluding that the asylum seeker is a minor will become an important component of the initial assessment.

The task of the assessing worker is to assess from a holistic perspective, and in the light of the available information, to be able to make an informed judgement that the person is probably within a certain age parameter. It is a process of professional judgment.

Age assessments are sometimes undertaken at the port of entry and the asylum screening unit where a decision is required in a short period of time, or sometimes at a later stage. In circumstances of age uncertainty, the benefit of doubt should always be the standard practice. When practical, two assessing workers is beneficial. Age assessments are also undertaken following the acceptance of a referral to social services to ascertain if the person is entitled to a service as a child. However, in some Local Authorities age assessments are undertaken on presentation when the stated age is disputed. Here the assessment can sometimes be undertaken over a period of time, and involve

1   Developed by London Boroughs of Croydon and Hillingdon in 2003.

other professionals, for example residential social work staff, foster carers, doctors, panel advisors, teachers and other young people.

It is very important to ensure that the young person understands the role of the assessing worker, and comprehends the interpreter. Attention should also be paid to the level of tiredness, trauma, bewilderment and anxiety that may be present for the young person. The ethnicity, culture, and customs of the person being assessed must be a key **focus** throughout the assessment.

It is also important to be mindful of the 'coaching' that the asylum seeker may have had prior to arrival, in how to behave and what to say. Having clarified the role of the social services, it is important to engage with the person and establish as much rapport as the circumstances will allow. This process is sometimes known as 'joining'. The assessing worker needs to acknowledge with the young person that they will have had to already answer many questions, and that it may be difficult and distressing to answer some of the questions.

In utilising the assessment framework, the practitioner should ask open-ended, non-leading questions. It is not expected that the form should be completed by systematically going through each component, but rather by formulating the interview in a semi structured discussion gathering information at different stages. The use of circular questioning is a useful method, as it is less obvious to the person being assessed that the questions relate directly to age, and hence may reveal a clear picture of age-related issues. It is essential to feed back to the young person the conclusion of this assessment and a written form is included for this purpose.

# AGE ASSESSMENT OF UNACCOMPANIED ASYLUM SEEKING CHILD

**Name of UASC:**
**DOB UASC is claiming:**

**Name of Assessing Worker:**
**Date of Assessment:**

## 1) Physical Appearance, Demeanour

**All assessments begin with initial impressions, made from visual presentation.**

An initial hypothesis of age range is formed based on height, facial features (facial hair, skin lines/folds, etc), voice tone, and general impression.

It is important to consider racial differences here e.g. It is normal in some cultures for boys to have facial hair at an early age and for girls to develop at different ages.

*Life experiences and trauma may impact on the ageing process, bear this in mind.*

*Demeanour, it is essential to take account of how the person presents, style, attitude and authority and relate this to the culture of the country of origin and events preceeding the interview, journey experiences etc.*

*It is useful to establish the length of time that the person has taken to arrive in the UK from the time they left their country of origin and include this into the age calculation.*

## 2) Interaction of Person During Assessment

**The manner in which the person interacts with the assessing worker conducting the assessment will provide an indication of whether or not the person is responding in an age appropriate manner.**

*It is important to note both the verbal and non-verbal (body language) behaviour of the person. The practitioner conducting the assessment should be observing factors such as the manner in which the person copes with the assessment, does he or she appear confident or overwhelmed, does the person appear to take a "one down" position or not.*

*Take account of differing cultural terms, e.g. some people may believe it impolite to make direct eye contact.*

*But remember to be aware of cultural variations in attitudes to elders.*

*Does the person appear to be uncomfortable with speaking to an adult?*

*Keep in mind that your position will be seen as one of power, which may influence the way the person interacts with you;, your role needs to be clarified and the differences in the roles of social services and the Home Office.*

### 3) Social History and Family Composition

Establishing as detailed as possible, a family tree will help the assessing worker to identify the likely age of the person compared with the stated age. Ages of parents, siblings and extended family should be established. In the case of deceased family members, the year and age at the time of death should be recorded. Drawing a graphic family tree is useful where names of family members and ages can be included, which may help the person to be more accurate whilst also allowing the person to feel involved. The information gained may indicate discrepancies or impossibilities, which need to be clarified.

*Do indicate to the young person that you are aware that talking about their family may be very painful and difficult for them; for some, it may be too painful to open up at this time. This must be understood and respected.*

It is important to clarify the nature of their parent and sibling relationships as some cultures for example, call a half-brother their brother, or stepmother their mother.

Additionally ask if either parent had more than one wife/husband.

**Please insert Genogram:**

**Client's view of how they know their stated age:**

## 4) Developmental Considerations

**Questions about the types of activities and roles that the person was involved in prior to arriving in the UK can often give an indication of age.** *Remember to use open-ended questions, as this will allow for the person to disclose information without prompting.*

Cultural considerations need to be taken into account as in some cultures it could be normal for a young teenager to be working full-time. A person may appear to answer a question about alcohol in a shy manner because their religion does not allow for this.

"Tell me what you did in your spare time" is the sort of question that can give an idea of the age appropriate interests and activities. Remember to relate answers to what would be appropriate in the young persons country of origin and culture.

 Ask about peer relationships at school/work/neighbourhood

Questions about age related *rituals* should be asked; including forced marriage, and any sexual relationships.

*Does what the person is describing seem age appropriate?*

Remember that some young people may possible have been involved in armed conflict, have been child soldiers, involved in sexual exploitation and may have experienced a number of traumatic situations.

*Answering questions related to many of the above may be too difficult and painful until a relationship of trust has been established.*

*Arranging for a person to be involved in social situations with other young people of the age Arranging for a person to be involved in social situations with other young people of the age stated, and observing how this person interacts and is accepted, can be useful.*

## 5) Education

Obtaining a detailed account of the person's educational history is a valuable source in the age assessment process.

Listed below are important facts that need to be gained:

### Age at which school was started

*Number of completed years spent in any school.*

*Establish if there were any gaps in education and if so, how long was the gap/s and why.*

*Adding the number of years of school attendance to the age school was started at, including possible disruptions in schooling should equate to the stated age.*

*Names and addresses of schools attended.*

*Subjects studied.*

*Gaining knowledge or consulting with experts educated in different countries, is useful to validate the authenticity of the information provided.*

*It may be possible to contact schools in some countries of origin.*

e.g., it may be of use to know that it is the norm to have six years of junior and six years of senior school in some countries.

## 6) Independent/Self-Care Skills

**Understanding the level of ability, experience and confidence that a person has in being able to care for themselves can be an indicator of age.**

*The assessing worker may wish to ask the person directly how they feel about living in an independent setting and observe their reaction.*

Has the person lived at home or have they lived on their own/in an independent setting?

Is there a clear impression that the person has never lived away from home and has been cared for by adults?

Does the person have experience in managing money, paying bills, arranging appointments, buying food and other supplies etc?

Is the person able to cook more than just a basic meal?

It is essential to take account of the local situation from which the person has come from – e.g. war, famine etc; and of cultural norms, for example it may not be expected that men should have any domestic skills in some countries.

Has the person stated a preference during the assessment of how they wish to live in the UK?

Would this person be at risk living independently? Give reasons for this.

*The assessing worker, may wish to pose a scenario to the person at this point or at the end of the assessment; that if the person is believed to be under 16 he or she will be placed in foster care where certain house rules will have to be followed, and be expected to be home at a certain times etc. The reaction to this may provide valuable information.*

### 7) Health and Medical Assessment

**A medical opinion and view on age will always be helpful .**

Questions about the person's health history can be informative in assessing age, both from the information given and the reactions to specific questions.

The Royal College of Paediatricians advised in November 1999 that there can be a five-year error in age assessment, invasive methods and medically unnecessary examinations of course should never be used. However, opinions and views on age from a paediatrician, GP, dentist and optician can be very helpful in assisting in the process.

## 8) Information from documentation and Other Sources

Documentation when available should always be carefully checked; authenticating documents however, is a specialist task.

If the assessment is an ongoing process, it is important to obtain the views of other significant figures involved with the young person.

Other sources may include foster carers, residential workers, school teachers, panel advisors, doctors, solicitors, interpreters and other young people.

Observations of how the person interacts in different social situations can provide useful age indicators.

### 9) Analysis of information gained

**Conclusion of the assessment.**

*Key indicators of the conclusion.*

*The assessing worker should draw together the information obtained, and present his/her views and judgement on the age of the person being assessed, giving clear reasons for the conclusion. If this differs from the stated age, clear reasons for this disagreement should be given.*

*Please remember this process is not an exact science and that conclusions should always give the benefit of doubt.*

### Conclusion

BASED ON THE ASSESSMENT, THE CLIENT'S AGE IS: ...................

DOB IS ESTIMATED TO BE: ...................

**Form to be handed to the person assessed**

**AGE ASSESSMENT FORM**

Name:

Nationality:                          Port Ref No:

Claimed Age/DOB:                      Home Office Ref No:

Name & Address of Local Authority Undertaking Assessment:

Name of Assessing Workers:

Date of Assessment:

You have been assessed to be over 18: ☐
You have been assessed to be a child, age: ☐ Years; DOB: ☐
Your assessment is inconclusive and further work is necessary: ☐

Conclusions and Reasons for this:

*It was explained to you at the end of your interview that you have the
right to disagree with the outcome of the assessment, and to challenge
our decision; you may do so by contacting a manager at the
at            on            , or by requesting the 'Complaints Procedure
for Children and Young People' on the same number.*

# Index